To Nick,
From one beer lover to another.
Cheers, Dan Rabin

COLORADO BREWERIES

DAN RABIN

D1308053

STACKPOLE
BOOKS

0 11557 01068 8

To my wife, Karen
The yin of my yang and my best beer-drinking buddy.

Also,

To my daughter, Melissa
Whose charm and good nature give me a reason to smile every day.

Copyright © 2014 by Stackpole Books

Published by
STACKPOLE BOOKS
5067 Ritter Road
Mechanicsburg, PA 17055
www.stackpolebooks.com

All rights reserved, including the right to reproduce this book or portions thereof in any form or by any means, electronic or mechanical, including photocopying, recording, or by any information storage and retrieval system, without permission in writing from the publisher. All inquiries should be addressed to Stackpole Books.

The author and the publisher encourage readers to visit the breweries and sample their beers and recommend that those who consume alcoholic beverages travel with a designated nondrinking driver.

Printed in the United States of America

10 9 8 7 6 5 4 3 2 1

FIRST EDITION

Cover design by Tessa J. Sweigert
Labels and logos used with permission of the breweries

Library of Congress Cataloging-in-Publication Data

Rabin, Dan, author.
    Colorado breweries / Dan Rabin. — First edition.
        pages   cm
    ISBN 978-0-8117-1068-8
    1. Brewing industry—Colorado. 2. Brewing. I. Title.
TP573.U5R33   2014
338.7'6634209788—dc23

                                                                2013049851

Contents

The Northern Front Range

The Southern Front Range

Central Rockies

Southwest Colorado

The Western Slope

Foreword

I spend more time and energy learning about where my beer comes from than I spend on any other aspect of my life. Beyond it being trendy to "buy local," I want to know anything and everything about the beer and the people who made it. Fortunately for me and many other beer lovers, craft brewers tend to be pretty transparent. I don't know any other industry, craft, or product, that makes itself more accessible to the public than the American craft-brewing industry does.

The backgrounds of Colorado's brewers are diverse. Find me another industry whose leadership comprises craftsmen, chefs, IT experts, engineers, lawyers, educators, microbiologists, CEOs, and even rocket scientists. What they all have in common is their passion for craft beer. They have given up secure careers to follow a dream of brewing and serving handcrafted beers for a living. Sounds pretty easy, right? Well, think again. Opening, owning, and operating a brewery is a tireless task that has pitfalls around every corner. Producing and selling alcohol is highly regulated at the local, state, and federal levels. Good thing Colorado has some of the country's most favorable laws, which can allow these small, independent businesses to grow, create jobs, and contribute to their local economies—just one reason Colorado has more than 160 breweries in operation and dozens more on the way.

The story doesn't end with the brewers; every beer has its story too. What ingredients were used? Where did those ingredients come from? How long was the beer aged? What is its ABV? Brewers are aging their beers in used whiskey, rum, and wine barrels to create complexity and depth. Brewers are experimenting with infusing their beers with fruits, vegetables, and herbs to create flavors not found in any traditional beer style. The best part about all this experimentation is that each and every brewer is more than willing to share his or her knowledge with fellow brewers far and wide. Homebrewers can find recipes for just about any of their favorite craft brews so they can replicate those beers at home.

Brewers across Colorado are playing key roles in building local communities. In 2011, it's estimated Colorado craft brewers contributed more than $1.2 million in cash and donations to local charities and events. Colorado brewers are also putting people to work. Colorado craft brewers are responsible for about $446 million per year in revenue and support more than forty-two hundred people in jobs directly related to craft beer. Breweries are undergoing constant expansion, creating space for new and larger brewhouses, tanks, and packaging lines.

I encourage you to learn where your beer comes from, how it's made, what it was made with, where it's made, and who created it for us to enjoy. Go ahead, talk to a brewer; it's probably the guy at the brewery who has the biggest beard. If you're not the talkative type, follow the pages of this book—Dan has done much of the work for you. He has visited each and every brewery in these pages. New or old, the largest to the smallest, he's been there. He's spent hours researching and traveling around the Centennial State sipping beers, interviewing brewers, and attending beer festivals. It's hard work, but someone had to do it.

Steve Kurowski
Marketing and Communications Director
Colorado Brewers Guild

Acknowledgments

The Colorado brewery landscape covers a vast geographic area. The brewery closest to my Boulder home is a ten-minute walk away. The farthest is four hundred miles away. The complexities of coordinating visits to more than 150 breweries across the state presented a daunting challenge. I want to thank the following agencies for their invaluable logistical assistance in my travel planning: Chaffee County Visitors Bureau, Durango Area Tourism Office, Fort Collins Convention & Visitors Bureau, Glenwood Springs Chamber Resort Association, Grand Junction Visitors and Convention Bureau, Gunnison-Crested Butte Tourism Association, Ore Communications, Pagosa Springs Town Tourism Committee, Snowmass Tourism, and Telluride Ski Resort. Thanks also to the Denver Convention & Visitors Bureau for its input and suggestions related to Denver destinations.

A heartfelt thanks to the various brewery personnel—brewers, founders, owners, and others—across the state who took time out of their busy schedules to tell me their stories and proudly share samples of their beers. To the brewers especially, I have profound respect for the many hours of tedious labor you devote to your craft, which goes mostly unseen by your thirsty audience.

I owe several Colorado beers to my beer-writing colleague John Holl, who introduced me to my awesome publisher, Stackpole Books. John has authored several of the Stackpole brewery guides and his sound advice saved me from taking some wrong turns early on.

I appreciate the efforts of Steve Kurowski, Marketing and Communications Director for the Colorado Brewers Guild, for contributing the foreword to this book.

Thanks to "Chipper" Dave Butler, whose comprehensive Colorado beer blog, *Fermentedly Challenged*, was a trusted resource for staying up-to-date on the rapidly evolving Colorado beer scene.

The contributions of my wife, Karen, a top-notch technical writer, cannot be overstated. She read every entry in this book, offered spot-on suggestions, made sure every t was crossed and every i dotted, and led back me to the trail during those times when I became disoriented and went astray.

Although they weren't directly involved with this project, I want to offer my gratitude to the roundtable of Denver travel writers, coordinated by selfless veteran writer Doris Kennedy, whose monthly baptism-by-fire critique sessions early in my career helped launch my travel-writing exploits and learned me to write pretty good.

Introduction

"Our happiest moments as tourists always seem to come when we stumble upon one thing while in pursuit of something else."

—Lawrence Block

"Travel brings power and love back into your life."

—Rumi, thirteenth-century Persian poet and theologian

"What's your favorite Colorado brewery?" It's a question I was asked time and time again during many months of brewery visits across the state. Despite the frequency with which the question arose, I never had a proper answer. The truth is I had so many memorable visits to breweries of vastly different character in the course of my travels that it was impossible to limit the answer to a single location.

Colorado is a fantastic state to explore if you like beer. The best state in the country, in my opinion. Breweries of all flavors abound in the cities, in the suburbs, in small towns, and in the mountains. And there are endless activities you can combine with your brewery visits. Denver has great cultural resources. The vibrant communities along the Front Range have their own personalities and attractions. Colorado's vast mountain landscape is a world-class playground for sightseers and outdoor enthusiasts. I've come to believe that beer tastes better after a day in the mountain air. But don't trust me on this. Find out for yourself.

In the past few decades, beer has become an integral part of Colorado's active yet laid-back lifestyle. When it comes to beer, Coloradans are knowledgeable, opinionated, and insatiably thirsty. They love to drink beer, talk beer, and meet people who share their interest. In many places across the state, brewery taprooms serve an important social function as neighborhood gathering spots.

One thing I've tried to do in this book is provide information that will lead you to breweries you'll enjoy. There's more to it than that, however. Breweries are not just about stainless steel vessels and taprooms and beer styles. They're about people. People created these breweries because at some point in their lives they decided that making beer for other people to enjoy was so important to them that they wanted to devote their careers to it. These people all have stories, some of which are quite compelling. I've shared many of them with you. I hope that knowing the brewers' backgrounds will enhance your appreciation of their labor of love.

Breweries exist within a geographic context, be it a small town, an urban neighborhood, or a mountain resort. Quite often, the context helps define the character of a brewery and its patrons. For most of the entries in this book, I've included some information about the brewery's surroundings, past or present. I hope you find this information enlightening, interesting, and sometimes amusing.

This book is a travel guide, not a rating guide. If you want to know whether a particular beer is rated an eighty-four or a ninety-one, go to one of the online rating sites. To me, an enjoyable brewery visit is not just about the beer, although beer quality is certainly important to the experience. While I appreciate exceptional beers, and seek them out, I also believe that a rewarding brewery visit involves factors beyond the relative quality of the beers the brewery dispenses.

At the end of the day, you're as likely to remember the person at the bar who directed you to a great campsite, the fellow homebrewer you talked beer with at the tiny neighborhood taproom, or the friends you made on a brewery's outdoor patio as the day's last rays of sunshine disappeared behind the ridge, as you are the great oatmeal stout or bracing barleywine you consumed.

Colorado has a wealth of these experiences waiting for you. Come drink it in.

Regions

Colorado is a large state. For purposes of this book, I've divided it into six regions: Denver and the Burbs, the Northern Front Range, the Southern Front Range, the Central Rockies, Southwest Colorado, and the Western Slope. Each region is geographically distinct, and each has its own character. This regional breakdown is intended to make your trip planning easier.

Brewery Types

While all of the entries in this book feature breweries, the businesses fall into different categories within the industry. With the exception of Colorado's two huge corporate breweries—Anheuser-Busch and MillerCoors—the businesses described in this guide are called *craft breweries*. The Brewers Association defines a craft brewery as being small, independent, and traditional, with an annual production of less than 6 million barrels. A *brewpub* is a restaurant with an in-house brewery. A *production brewery* is a brewery that produces and packages beer primarily for sale and consumption outside the brewery. A *nanobrewery* is a very small-scale brewery. Although there's no one agreed-upon definition, I consider a brewery that makes beer on a 3.5-barrel (about 108 gallons) system or smaller a nanobrewery.

Area Beer Sites

In the chapter introductions and within individual entries, I've listed other nearby beer sites that are not breweries. While there were far too many of these for me to visit, those I haven't visited were recommended by brewers, brewery personnel, or other reputable sources. I've listed beer bars, pubs, restaurants, and other types of businesses of interest to beer enthusiasts.

New Openings

Breweries were opening at a fast clip while I was traveling around Colorado researching this book. When I began my travels, there were approximately 120 brewing businesses operating in the state. To meet my publishing deadline, I wasn't able to visit new breweries that opened after April 1, 2013. At that time, there were more than 150 breweries in Colorado. That number continues to grow.

The Picks

I visited every brewery covered in this book. There was one brewery I chose not to include because of its obvious lack of concern for producing even a marginally palatable beverage. Nearly every entry includes an author's beer pick. In a very few instances, I chose not to include a Pick because the beers I sampled were problematic and couldn't be recommended. Hopefully, the breweries in question have taken steps to rectify this situation since my visit.

Drink up—Water, That Is

Colorado's dry climate and high elevation exacerbate alcohol's negative effects. You can temper these effects by drinking plenty of water. I highly recommend that you sip water whenever you're drinking beer. You'll be better off for it.

A Mini-Glossary

Throughout the book I've included some terms that may not be familiar to all readers. Some of these are technical jargon, some are not. See the next page for an abbreviated list of terms that appear with some frequency. If there are other terms in this book that are new to you, ask a brewery employee or the person at the bar next to you for an explanation. Chances are, they'll be more than happy to share their knowledge with you.

- *AHA* is the abbreviation for the American Homebrewers Association, a branch of the Boulder-based Brewers Association.

- A *beer engine* or *hand pump* is a manually operated pump used to dispense cask-conditioned beers.

- The *Front Range* refers to the part of Colorado along the base of the Rocky Mountain foothills. More than 80 percent of Colorado's population and about two-thirds of the state's breweries reside on the Front Range.

- *IPA* is short for India pale ale, a beer style that emphasizes hop aroma, flavor, and bitterness.

- *High-gravity* is synonymous with high-alcohol.

- A *nitro tap* is a special type of beer dispenser used to pour beers carbonated with mostly nitrogen gas. This produces beers with a creamier texture than the more prickly texture of standard beers carbonated with 100 percent carbon dioxide.

- A *session beer*, or a sessionable beer, is a low-alcohol beer that can be consumed throughout a beer-drinking session, causing less impairment than stronger beers would. Session beers generally contain less than 5 percent alcohol by volume (ABV). Low-alcohol session beers can still cause impairment, just not as quickly. Know your limits and make good judgments.

Who Is This Guy? My Journey

I arrived in Colorado in 1986 fresh out of grad school with a job in the software industry and an interest in beer, but little beer knowledge. After living south of Denver for a few years, my wife and I moved to Boulder, which we still call home. In 1990, I took up homebrewing, and like many of the brewers featured in this book, my life was forever changed. That same year, I joined the local homebrew club, Hop Barley & the Alers, and remain a member to this day.

In 1993, when my daughter was an infant, our babysitter, a college student, asked me to teach her to homebrew. It was late in the year, so I devised a recipe for a spiced holiday beer. The following spring, the beer won a gold medal in the National Homebrew Competition.

Around that time, I began writing articles for several beer magazines including *Zymurgy*, the homebrew magazine published by the

BREWERY LOCATIONS

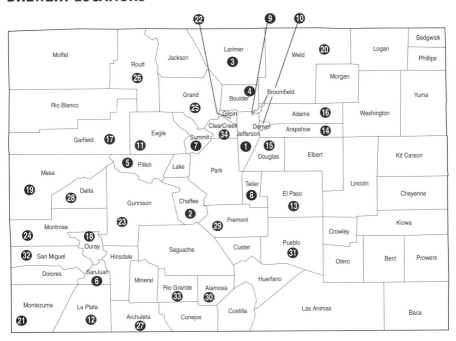

- ❶ AC Golden Brewing Company
- ❷ Amícas Pizza & Microbrewery
- ❸ Anheuser-Busch Fort Collins Brewery
- ❶ Arvada Beer Company
- ❹ Asher Brewing Company
- ❺ Aspen Brewing Company
- ❻ Avalanche Brewing Company
- ❹ Avery Brewing Company

- ❼ Backcountry Brewery
- ❽ BierWerks
- ❸ Big Beaver Brewing Company
- ❾ Big Choice Brewing
- ❹ BJ's Restaurant & Brewhouse
- ❸ Black Bottle Brewery
- ❿ Black Shirt Brewing Company
- ❿ Blue Moon Brewing Company at the Sandlot
- ⓫ Bonfire Brewing Company
- ❹ Bootstrap Brewing Company

- ❹ Boulder Beer Company
- ❼ Breckenridge Brewery & Pub
- ❿ Breckenridge Brewery—Denver
- ⓬ Brew Pub & Kitchen
- ❶ Brewery Rickoli
- ⓭ Bristol Brewing Company
- ❹ BRU Handbuilt Ales & Eats
- ❿ Bull & Bush Brewery

- ⓮ C.B. & Potts Restaurant and Brewery Denver Tech
- ❾ C.B. & Potts Restaurant and Brewery Flatirons
- ⓯ C.B. & Potts Restaurant and Brewery Highlands Ranch
- ⓰ C.B. & Potts Restaurant and Brewery Westminster
- ❸ C.B. & Potts Restaurant and Brewery Fort Collins
- ❶ Cannonball Creek Brewing Company

17 Carbondale Beer Works
12 Carver Brewing Company
10 Caution: Brewing Company
3 City Star Brewing
18 Colorado Boy Pub & Brewery
13 Colorado Mountain Brewery at InterQuest Marketplace
13 Colorado Mountain Brewery at the Roundhouse
3 Coopersmith's Pub & Brewing
19 Copper Club Brewing Company
14 Copper Kettle Brewing Company
20 Crabtree Brewing Company
11 Crazy Mountain Brewing Company
10 Crooked Stave Artisan Beer Project
4 Crystal Springs Brewing Company

14 Dad & Dude's Breweria
10 De Steeg Brewing
10 Denver Beer Company
10 Denver Chophouse
7 Dillon Dam Brewery
21 Dolores River Brewery
22 Dostal Alley Brewpub and Casino
14 Dry Dock Brewing Company
12 Durango Brewing Company

20 Echo Brewing Company
2 Eddyline Brewery & Taproom
2 Elevation Beer Company
15 Elk Mountain Brewing
3 Equinox Brewing Company
3 Estes Park Brewery

4 Fate Brewing Company
16 Floodstage Ale Works
3 Fort Collins Brewery and Gravity 1020 Modern Tavern
3 Funkwerks

17 Glenwood Canyon Brewing Company
1 Golden City Brewery
9 Gordon Biersch Brewery Restaurant
11 Gore Range Brewery
4 Gravity Brewing

10 Great Divide Brewing Company
13 Great Storm Brewing
3 Grimm Brothers Brewhouse
23 Gunnison Brewery

20 High Hops Brewery
10 Hogshead Brewery
24 Horsefly Brewing Company

1 Ironworks Brewery & Pub

4 J Wells Brewery

19 Kannah Creek Brewing Company

4 Left Hand Brewing Company
25 Library Sports Grille and Brewery
15 Lone Tree Brewing Company
3 Loveland Aleworks

26 Mahogany Ridge Brewery & Grill
21 Main Street Brewery and Restaurant
1 MillerCoors
2 Moonlight Pizza & Brewpub
4 Mountain Sun Pub & Brewery

3 New Belgium Brewing Company

3 Odell Brewing Company
14 Old Mill Brewery & Grill
4 Oskar Blues Brewery and Tasty Weasel Taproom
4 Oskar Blues Grill & Brew
10 Our Mutual Friend Malt & Brew
18 Ouray Brewery
18 Ourayle House Brewery

27 Pagosa Brewing & Grill
19 Palisade Brewing Company
8 Paradox Beer Company
3 Pateros Creek Brewing Company
13 Phantom Canyon Brewing Company
13 Pikes Peak Brewing Company
10 Pints Pub Brewery and Freehouse
10 Prost Brewing Company

Brewers Association. In the late 1990s, my high-tech career and I parted ways by mutual agreement, and I turned my attention to a writing career. I continued writing about beer and became the Rocky Mountain correspondent for *Celebrator Beer News*, a position that put me in frequent contact with breweries around Colorado. At the same time, I began writing travel articles—often featuring Colorado destinations—that were published by newspapers across the country. When the opportunity arose to produce a guidebook of Colorado breweries, it seemed a natural fit.

For updates and other information on Colorado's breweries, visit http://coloradobreweriesbook.com.

Denver
and the Burbs

There are two things you need to know about Denver. First, Denver is among the country's great beer cities, but you probably know that already. Second, the Colorado capital is not located in the mountains. The majestic Rockies rise abruptly from the Great Plains about ten miles west of downtown. The snow-blanketed mountain peaks can be seen in the distance from many locations throughout the city.

Denver's designation as the "Mile High City" is no misconception, however. There's a marker placed on the thirteenth step on the west side of the state capitol at exactly 5,280 feet above sea level. Even more conspicuous is the row of purple seats in the upper deck of Coors Field, home of the Colorado Rockies baseball team. The seats are one mile above sea level. The custom paint job is intended to intimidate visiting ballplayers unused to Denver's thin, oxygen-starved air. Talk about home-field advantage.

There is a vibrant brewing scene in Denver and the surrounding communities. For our purposes, this includes the area within Highway 470, which encircles the city on three sides and makes a convenient geographic boundary for us to work with. The Rocky Mountain foothills define the western boundary. I've also included the mountain town of Central City in this chapter because it's a close-in gambling retreat that's an easy day trip from Denver, and because it has a different character than the central Rockies communities covered in a separate section of this book.

Many Denver residents were lured here from other parts of the country by the active, outdoor-oriented lifestyle and an average of three hundred days of sunshine a year. Winters in the city are surprisingly mild and lack the harsh extremes of the nearby mountains. Claims that Denver residents can ski and play golf on the same day are often true, if a bit logistically challenging. Since I arrived in Colorado in 1986, I've watched Denver evolve into an energetic, dynamic, forwarding-looking metropolis with an appealing combination of urban sophistication and a laid-back demeanor. Good beer is deeply ingrained in the Denver lifestyle.

The city has much to offer visitors of diverse interests. The majority of Denver's most-touristed sites are locals' favorites as well. *The Denver Art Museum* and *The Clyfford Still Museum* are highly regarded among art enthusiasts. For a more intimate look at the local art scene, spend a day gallery-hopping in the city's various art districts. The *Art District on Santa Fe* has more than sixty galleries.

For a laid-back outdoor outing, visit one of the city's leafy parks. Denver's largest is *City Park*, which is also the home of the *Museum of Nature & Science* and the *Denver Zoo*. The nearby *Botanic Gardens* offer a peaceful urban getaway. The *16th Street Pedestrian Mall* in downtown Denver, with more than two dozen sidewalk cafés, is prime people-watching territory. A free shuttle runs the length of the mile-long mall. You can gear up for outdoor adventure at the 100,000-square-foot *REI Flagship Store*. For thrill seekers, the *Elitch Gardens Theme & Water Park* is close to downtown.

Denverites love to go out on the town. The *Denver Center for Performing Arts* offers a rich mix of theater, dance, classical music, and opera. Denver supports a lively music scene. Jazz fans head to the venerable *El Chapultepec*, near Coors Field. Rock venues abound and include the *Fillmore*, the *Ogden*, the *Paramount*, and the intimate *Hi-Dive*. If country-western is more your style, don your best cowboy or cowgirl gear and dance up a storm at the *Grizzly Rose*, one of the country's top country music clubs.

With the emergence of numerous high-profile chefs, Denver's reputation as a foodie mecca continues to grow. An ongoing trend features creative preparations of top-quality, locally sourced meats and produce. Many of the city's highest-rated restaurants have climbed aboard the craft beer bandwagon and offer a well-chosen selection of bottled and draught beers. *Euclid Hall* and *Freshcraft* are among the favorites of local beer fans, but there are many more eateries that "get it" when it comes to beer and food pairing.

Many Denver destinations are easily accessible by bicycle. You'll get a different appreciation for the outdoor-loving city by exploring the 850-mile network of bike paths. The city's B-cycle bike sharing program allows you to check out a bike from more than fifty different stations and return it to any B-cycle station.

The Beer Scene

The Mile High City has seen an explosion of new breweries in recent years. That trend shows no signs of abating. Many of city's breweries are small, neighborhood-focused gathering spots and are great places to talk beer with the friendly, knowledgeable, opinionated locals.

For three days each fall, Denver becomes the center of the craft beer universe when it hosts the Great American Beer Festival. With more than three thousand beers available from more than six hundred breweries, the GABF is said to have more beers available for tasting than at any other single spot in history. The festival's commercial beer competition is the largest and most prestigious beer competition in the country. Denver Beer Fest, a nine-day celebration of all things beer, is coordinated by Visit Denver and coincides with GABF.

A Classic Walking Tour

It wasn't too long ago that you could visit most of Denver's top beer spots on a self-guided walking tour through Lower Downtown, or LoDo. While the city's beer offerings have greatly expanded, the tour is still a great way to spend a few beer-intensive hours in the city. Start on the 16th Street Mall at Rock Bottom, the original location of the nationwide brewpub chain. A ten-minute walk northwest will bring you to the Wynkoop Brewing Company, Colorado's first brewpub. It was founded in 1988 by the state's current governor, John Hickenlooper.

A few blocks east is the Falling Rock Tap House, one of the country's premier beer bars featuring hard-to-find beers from local, national, and international breweries. On the next block is Coors Field, home of the Sandlot Brewery inside the ballpark. Across the street is Breckenridge Colorado Craft, the original location of Denver's Breckenridge Brewery and now a taphouse featuring Colorado beers. A short walk up 22nd Street brings you to Great Divide Brewing Company, a required stop on your Denver beer itinerary and the end of this classic beer-themed walking tour.

Other Area Beer Sites

Along with Denver's large and growing list of breweries is a constantly evolving collection of other places of interest to beer fans. These range from atmospheric neighborhood pubs to historic watering holes to sports bars to pizza joints to full-service restaurants. I've listed many of them here and arranged them by neighborhood so you can plan visits to several stops in close proximity and minimize your travel time in the city.

Arts District on Santa Fe

Buckhorn Exchange (1000 Osage St., 303-534-9505)

Interstate Kitchen & Bar (1001 Santa Fe Dr., 720-479-8829)

Rackhouse Pub (208 S. Kalamath St., 720-570-7824)

Baker

Historians Ale House (24 Broadway, 720-479-8505)

Hornet (76 Broadway, 303-777-7676)

Irish Rover (54 Broadway, 303-282-4643)

Punchbowl Social (65 Broadway, 303-765-2695)

Berkeley

Ernie's Bar & Pizza (2915 W. 44th Ave., 303-955-5580)

Hops & Pie (3920 Tennyson St., 303-477-7000)

West End Tap House (3945 Tennyson St., 303-433-4759)

Capitol Hill

City, O' City (206 E. 13th Ave., 303-831-6443)

Stoney's Bar & Grill (1111 Lincoln St., 303-830-6839)

Central Business District

Appaloosa Grill (535 16th St., 720-932-1700)

Yard House (1555 Court Pl., 303-572-9273)

Cherry Creek

Cherry Cricket (2641 E. 2nd Ave., 303-322-7666)

Chopper's Sports Grill (80 S. Madison St., 303-399-4448)

World of Beer (660 S. Colorado Blvd., 303-757-0506)

City Park West

Denver Bicycle Café (1308 E. 17th Ave., 720-446-8029)

Thin Man (2015 E. 17th Ave. Pkwy., 303-320-7814)

Five Points

Matchbox (2625 Larimer St., 720-437-9100)

Populist (3163 Larimer St., 720-432-3163)

Star Bar (2137 Larimer St., 720-328-2420)

Highlands

Ale House at Amato's (2501 16th St., 303-433-9734)

Colt & Gray (1553 Platte St., 303-477-1447)

Highland Tap and Burger (2219 West 32nd Ave., 720-287-4493)

Mead Street Station (3625 W. 32nd Ave., 303-433-2138)

LoDo

Breckenridge Colorado Craft (2220 Blake St., 303-297-3644)

Euclid Hall (1317 14th St., 303-595-4255)

Falling Rock Tap House (1919 Blake St., 303-293-8338)

Freshcraft (1530 Blake St., 303-758-9608)

Lucky Pie (1610 16th St., 303-825-1021)

Mellow Mushroom (1201 16th St., Ste. 108, 720-328-9114)

Wazee Supper Club (1600 15th St., 303-623-9519)

Southeast

Lowry Beer Garden (7577 E. Academy Blvd., 303-366-0114)

Stapleton

Stapleton Tap House (8286 Northfield Blvd., Unit 1525, 720-449-2337)

University

Boone's Tavern (1135 E. Evans Ave., 720-961-0320)

Renegade Publik House (2043 S. University Blvd., 303-282-6243)

Uptown

Cheeky Monk (543 E. Colfax Ave., 303-861-0347)

Jonesy's EatBar (400 E. 20th Ave., 303-863-7473)

Steuben's (523 E. 17th Ave., 303-830-1001)

The Suburbs

It's not just Denver that has seen an unprecedented number of new breweries open recently. Scores of new brewing businesses have popped up in the communities surrounding the city. Pick a town near Denver and chances are there will be a hometown brewery worthy of a visit.

Perhaps the best known of these is the oft-decorated Dry Dock Brewing Company in Aurora, just east of Denver. West of the city, Golden is best known as the home of the massive MillerCoors brewery, but a growing number of small breweries have put Golden on the radar of craft beer enthusiasts.

Not far from Golden is the Red Rocks Amphitheatre, the country's most beautiful outdoor music venue. If your timing isn't right to catch a show, you can still stop by the visitor's center and take a tour of the legendary concert facility that has hosted performers from the Beatles to Springsteen.

AC Golden Brewing Company

Located in the MillerCoors Golden Brewery,
13th and Ford Streets, Golden, CO 80401
(303) 277-2337 • www.acgolden.com

The AC Golden Brewing Company is a specialty brewing arm and beer brand incubator for MillerCoors. The brewery resides deep within the belly of the monolithic Golden brewery. You can't visit AC Golden, as the operation has no tasting room and doesn't offer tours. Most of the beers produced by AC Golden have very limited distribution.

The mission of AC Golden, according to company president Glen "Knip" Knippenberg, "is to discover, introduce, and develop brands of beer, above premium brands of beer, which have the potential to fit into the larger organization's portfolio." In essence, this translates to creating brands that can be marketed to the growing number of American beer drinkers seeking more flavorful alternatives to mass-produced American light lagers.

AC Golden produces three full-time beers and a wide selection of specialty creations. The brewery's first release was Herman Joseph's Private Reserve, a resurrected and reformulated Coors brand first released in the 1980s. The name comes from the two middle names of Coors founder Adolph Coors. It's available on draught in about forty Colorado restaurants.

Another regularly produced offering is Barman, a traditional German-style pilsner. The beer is named for the town in Prussia (now Germany) where Adolph Coors was born. It's served in its own distinctive glassware, and is ideally dispensed with a traditional seven-minute pour. (Not all bartenders pour it to spec, however.) It's available on draught in about a dozen bars.

Year-round beers: Colorado Native Lager, Herman Joseph's Private Reserve, Barman Pilsner.

The brewery's most recognizable brand is Colorado Native Lager. The amber lager is produced with 100 percent Colorado-sourced ingredients. In order to procure the necessary quantity of Colorado-grown hops, AC Golden offered to pay Colorado farmers four times the going rate for Cascade, Centennial, and Chinook hops in exchange for their commitment to become hop growers.

The Pick: Though hard to find, Barman Pilsner is worth seeking out. The golden-hued brew has a creamy texture and a firm malt base nicely balanced with spicy noble hops.

The inflated prices were intended to cover start-up costs associated with installing the necessary infrastructure needed for hop production. Colorado Native is on tap at more than two hundred locations in Colorado, and is widely distributed in bottles throughout the state. You can sample it fresh in the MillerCoors tasting room following a tour of the brewery (see page 70).

The annual production of Winterfest, a long-running Coors seasonal, was handed over to AC Golden. "It was the original seasonal, before seasonals were cool," said Knippenberg. Prior to its commercial release more than twenty-five years ago, the beer was brewed "for friends and family and after work." The Winterfest recipe is modified every year.

An ever-changing variety of styles are produced at AC Golden, from traditional European beers to barrel-aged sour beers to experimental creations. Many appear only at beer festivals and at a very small network of taphouses. The sour beer program is nicknamed "the Hidden Barrel Collection." When it originated, these microbe-inoculated beers were secretly aged in an unused room on the top floor of the MillerCoors brewery, unbeknownst to the plant manager. The cover was blown when someone requested an interview with the plant manager about the in-house sour beer program.

AC Golden is keenly aware that its ownership by a multinational corporation presents credibility issues among craft beer enthusiasts. "In order to be considered legitimate, we've got to be able to demonstrate that we can make lagers and all different styles of beer as good or better than anybody," stated Knippenberg. "We do a lot of these beers just to win medals, just to get acclaim for our brewers." That strategy is working: since 2009, AC Golden has been awarded eight medals at the Great American Beer Festival.

AC Golden Brewing Company

Opened: July 2007.
Owner: MillerCoors Brewing Company.
AC Golden President: Glen "Knip" Knippenberg.
Head brewer: Jeff Nickle.
Potential annual capacity: 7,500 barrels.
Hours: Not open to public.
Tours: Not offered. You can sample Colorado Native Lager after touring the MillerCoors brewery.

Arvada Beer Company

ARVADA BEER COMPANY

5600 Olde Wadsworth Boulevard, Arvada, CO 80002
(303) 467-BEER (2337) • www.arvadabeer.com

I was acquainted with Cary and Kelly Floyd, proprietors of Arvada Beer Company, long before their brewery opened in 2011. In fact, anyone who was involved in homebrew competitions in the Denver area a decade ago knows of the Floyds. For years, they were the most prolific medal-winning homebrewers in the area, amassing more than four hundred medals over their amateur brewing careers. When I heard in 2010 that they were planning to open a commercial brewery, my only question was, "What took you so long?"

The Floyds located their brewery in Arvada, a suburban community about ten miles northwest of downtown Denver. Unlike many of the newer suburbs that have sprung up in recent decades to house Denver commuters, Arvada's history goes back to the mid-1800s. The town was originally settled by gold prospectors who eventually acquired land and turned their attention to farming. They grew a variety of crops including fruits, vegetables, wheat, oats, and corn. Arvada once had the unique title of "celery capital of the world."

Olde Town Arvada, the historic downtown district that is home to the brewery, has undergone a major revitalization in recent years. "Five years ago, you could walk down the streets on Friday night, roll a bowling ball, and not hit anybody," said Cary. Century-old brick buildings now house small businesses and restaurants. The pedestrian-friendly National Historic District has a small-town feel even though the community is home to more than 100,000 residents. When locals want to gather for some casual socializing, they head to Arvada Beer Company.

The brewery resides in an interesting wedge-shaped brick building on a corner lot in Olde Town. The building was constructed in 1916 to house a drug store and a car dealership. It more recently housed a stationary shop. "We would drive by this place all the time and I would say, 'Man, if this place ever opened up, it would be the perfect place for a brewery,'" Cary recalled. "It just so happened that it did right around the same time we were ready to open up the brewery."

Year-round beers: Olde Town Brown, Poolhall Porter, Ralston's Golden Ale, Goldline IPA, Water Tower Wheat, Arvada Red.

The Pick: Olde Town Brown is low in alcohol and high in drinkability, with a clean maltiness that'll keep your interest through several pints.

Converting the old structure to a functioning brewery was no simple task. "When we came in, we had to completely gut the building. All the electrical. All the plumbing. All the walls. It's all brand new," said the cofounder and brewer.

The taproom is spacious and casual. High ceilings and tall windows create a bright, open atmosphere. A collection of historic photos is on display in the minimally embellished space. Board games donated by local patrons provide entertainment for the many families who visit the taproom. Local restaurants make frequent deliveries to the community gathering spot. Manneken Frites, a business in the adjoining space, specializes in authentic Belgian fries and can be accessed without stepping outside.

Arvada Beer Company keeps up to a dozen beers on tap including a half-dozen year-round offerings. The company takes pride in being a hometown brewery and taproom. All the beer names—Olde Town Brown, Poolhall Porter, Ralston's Golden Ale, Goldline IPA, Water Tower Wheat, Arvada Red—have references to the town's history from 1850 to 1950.

Not surprisingly, the emphasis is on familiar European and American-style ales and lagers. "We're not trying to be the wild and crazy brewery," Cary explained. "We're trying to specialize in traditional-style beers. What Kelly and I did was make beer to style. That's how we won so many awards."

Arvada Beer Company

Opened: October 2011.

Owners: Cary and Kelly Floyd.

Head brewer: Cary Floyd.

Potential annual capacity: 1,300 barrels.

Hours: Monday through Thursday, noon to 10 p.m.; Friday and Saturday, 11 a.m. to 11 p.m.; Sunday, 11 a.m. to 9 p.m.

Tours: Saturday at 2 p.m. or by appointment.

Take-out beer: Growlers and kegs.

Food: Nearby restaurants with delivery. Belgian frites restaurant located in same building.

Extras: AHA member deals program participant.

Parking: Free nearby lots and on-street parking.

Area attractions: The Johnny Roberts Memorial Disc Golf Park (8001 W. 59th Ave.). Arvada Flour Mill Museum (5590 Wadsworth Blvd., 303-431-1261).

Other area beer sites: Archive Room (5601 Olde Wadsworth Blvd., 303-432-0400). Udi's (7600 Grandview Ave., 303-421-8000). D Note (7519 Grandview Ave., 303-463-6683). Manneken Frites (5616 Olde Wadsworth Blvd., 303-847-4357).

Big Choice Brewing

BIG CHOICE

CHOOSE   WISELY

BREWING
BROOMFIELD, CO

7270 West 118th Place, Unit A, Broomfield, CO 80020
(303) 469-2616 • www.bigchoicebrewing.com

Unbeknownst to many brewery visitors, a lot of thought and even anguish can go into naming a new business venture. "It's one of the top five most difficult things when you're starting a business, regardless of the industry," according to Nathaniel Miller, who with his partner, Tyler Ruse, opened Big Choice Brewing in May 2012. "We were looking for something that said something about us," the former University of Colorado economics major explained. They settled on the name Big Choice because of its dual meaning. On one level, it reflects their belief that everyone should have a choice of drinking whatever beer suits their fancy, be it locally produced craft beer or something else.

The second meaning is derived from their younger years when they were skateboarders and fans of punk and ska music. *Big Choice* was the name of an album by Face to Face, a raucous Southern California band. In fact, the brewery's flagship beer, Disconnected Red, is named after the band's most popular song, "Disconnected."

Big Choice is located in Broomfield, about fifteen miles from either downtown Denver or downtown Boulder along "The Turnpike" (aka Highway 36). The brewery is in a mixed-use area of offices, small businesses, and some light industrial operations. There's a residential neighborhood within walking distance.

When Miller and Ruse, who are both from the Boulder area, first considered opening their own brewery, they targeted Boulder for the location. But when Upslope Brewing opened in Boulder in 2008, adding yet another brewing entity to an already crowded beer scene, they decided to look at communities in their "home turf" that had a less-congested brewing landscape. The search process took several years. When it finally opened, Big Choice became Broomfield's first brewing business since a short-lived brewery came and went in the mid-1990s. Locals were quick to embrace Big Choice as their hometown beer hub.

Year-round beers: Type III IPA, Hemlock Double IPA, Disconnected Red Ale, #42 Poblano Stout, 10,000 Summers Saison.

The Pick: Go big at Big Choice with a Hemlock Double IPA. Gobs of chewy malt are kept in check with ample hopping. Be careful. The alcohol in this burly 9.5 percent ABV brew is well hidden.

The vibe at Big Choice is friendly and welcoming. The small, ground-floor tasting room attracts a mostly local clientele, with repeat customers being the norm. The tasting room contains a few high-top tables and a counter along the front windows. The bar, constructed of wood salvaged from a former bowling alley, sits atop a base of corrugated metal. A popcorn machine sits in a corner. It's a simple space, conducive to conversation, without a lot of embellishment.

There's a second room upstairs with a couch, a few tables, a foosball game, and two TVs. The upstairs is a popular spot for board games and families. A wall of windows looks west to the distant mountains. On the opposite wall, a window looks down into the brewhouse.

Miller, who heads the brewing operations at Big Choice, acquired some valuable brewhouse skills while working in the family's thirty-year-old sheet metal business. He built the 7-barrel boil kettle himself. It looks like something from a science-fiction movie. "My wife calls it 'the Tin Man' because it reminds her of the original *Wizard of Oz*," he explained. "Maybe someday we'll actually paint the face on it." Flights of tasters arrive on stainless steel stands fabricated at the sheet metal shop.

The five house beers encompass a range of styles from a saison to a double IPA to a stout brewed with poblano peppers. Three rotating tap handles further increase the diversity of offerings. After all, it's all about choice.

Big Choice Brewing

Opened: May 2012.

Owners: Nathaniel and Andrea Miller and Tyler Ruse.

Head brewer: Nathaniel Miller.

Potential annual capacity: 2,000 barrels.

Hours: Monday through Thursday, 3 p.m. to 9 p.m.; Friday and Saturday, 2 p.m. to 10 p.m.; Sunday, 2 p.m. to 8 p.m.

Tours: On request.

Take-out beer: Growlers and kegs.

Food: Food trucks on Thursday, Friday, and Saturday. Bavarian pretzels available for purchase. Restaurant delivery menus available. Free popcorn.

Extras: Trivia and Family Movie Nights every other Sunday. AHA member deals program participant.

Parking: On-site lot.

Area attractions: 1st Bank Event Center (11450 Broomfield Lane, Broomfield, 303-410-0700).

Other area beer sites: Old Chicago (1280 East 1st Ave, Broomfield, 303-466-5834). BJ's Restaurant & Brewery (10446 Town Center Dr., Westminster, 303-389-6444).

Black Shirt Brewing Company

3719 Walnut Street, Denver, CO 80205
(303) 993-2799 • www.blackshirtbrewingco.com

"If you want to be successful, do one thing and try to do it better than anyone else," was the advice given to brothers Chad and Branden Miller by their father. Years later, that advice had the brothers, along with Chad's wife, Carissa, seeing red. The trio founded Black Shirt Brewing in 2012 with the singular focus of brewing only red ales. The company name was derived from the brothers' younger years, when they were outcasts of sorts in the small town of Westcliffe. As a social statement, they wore black shirts.

The trend among upstart Front Range breweries is to carve out a unique identity in order to stand out from the increasingly crowded pack. Breweries specializing in German-style beers, Belgian-style beers, session beers, and sour beers have all sprung up in recent years. The idea of producing only red beers was not only a way for Black Shirt to create a distinctive niche, but also a way for its sibling cofounders to embrace the place of their upbringing. "We grew up in the Sangre de Cristo Valley. That means 'blood of Christ,'" explained Chad Miller, who attends to Black Shirt's business matters while brother Branden runs the brewing operation. The area gets its name from the dramatic red sunrises that often occur.

That idyllic image is a far cry from the scruffy environs where the brewery resides. The gentrification that has permeated much of Denver's RiNo neighborhood has yet to reach the northern end of Walnut Street. That's not a concern for Black Shirt's proprietors, who revel in taking a less-traveled path.

"After crawling through different neighborhoods in Denver we knew that RiNo, as rough as it was when we were looking here, had the grit, the soul, the authenticity, the artistic potential, that we knew we wanted," said Chad. "We wanted this to be a place that people had to seek out." People certainly do seek out the brewery during its abbreviated four-day schedule. The brewery quickly built a core of devoted followers, largely from the

Year-round beers: BSB Red Ale, Red Saison, Red Rye, Red IPA.

The Pick: The BSB Red Ale weaves a tapestry of sweet caramel and bright hoppy flavors in a complex and satisfying multilayered brew.

neighborhood. There's a bit of a social club aspect to the brewery. Black Shirt hosts a variety of events that are by invitation only for people within the brewery's inner circle.

Black Shirt sits between a vacant lot and a liquor store. You can't miss the bright red door that contrasts with the building's dark, unrevealing façade. The interior has a stylish urban feel with gray walls and a few pieces of modern black-and-white artwork. The tables and the U-shaped bar are constructed of repurposed flooring from railroad cars. A large garage door opens to a sidewalk patio with picnic table seating. Food trucks, parked steps from the taproom, are on-site regularly.

Producing red ales exclusively is not as limiting as it may first sound. While Black Shirt beers have a narrow spectrum of color, the styles are actually quite broad. There are four regular beers—a red ale, a red saison, a red rye, and a red IPA—along with several rotating brews.

All Black Shirt beers are aged at least two months, far longer than is typical for most ale-producing craft breweries. It seems to make a difference. The beers appear bright and clear, with distinct layers of flavor that evolve as the beers warm. I sampled six beers and enjoyed them all. Beers are served in odd-shaped custom glassware with uniquely slanted rims. I was instructed to sip from the low end. The effect is twofold: First, it directs aromas to your nose, intensifying the flavors. Second, it forces you to pay attention to the drinking experience, lest you risk wearing your beer rather than drinking it.

Black Shirt Brewing Company

Opened: October 2012.
Owners: Chad Miller, Carissa Miller, and Branden Miller.
Head brewer: Branden Miller.
Potential annual capacity: 1,200 barrels.
Hours: Wednesday through Friday, 5 p.m. to 9 p.m.; Saturday, 2 p.m. to 9 p.m.
Tours: By appointment only.
Take-out beer: Growlers and kegs.
Food: Food trucks on-site regularly.
Extras: Live band recording sessions taped and broadcast on YouTube.
Parking: On-street.

Blue Moon Brewing Company at the Sandlot

2145 Blake Street, Denver, CO 80205
(303) 298-1587 • www.bluemoonbrewingcompany.com

When you visit a baseball stadium, you don't typically see a grain silo sitting alongside the ballpark. Coors Field, the home of the Colorado Rockies baseball team, is not a typical baseball stadium. Within the depths of the lovely venue resides the country's first ballpark-based brewery, the Sandlot.

When Coors Field was under construction in Denver's Lower Downtown district in the early 1990s, someone at the Coors brewery proposed the idea of putting a brewery in the ballpark. The idea had legs, and a 10-barrel system was installed under the right-field stands. It was named the Sandlot. When the stadium opened for the 1995 season, the brewery was producing beers for the pub located in the right-field corner. The beers were given baseball-themed names such as Right Field Red Ale, Wild Pitch Hefeweizen, and Pinch Hit Pilsner.

From the start, Coors used the brewery to test experimental beers, with immediate feedback provided by baseball fans on game days. That first summer, a Coors brewer named Keith Villa asked the Sandlot crew to make a test batch of an experimental Belgian white ale, an almost unknown style at the time. "We brewed it. Put it on tap. It was called Bellyslide Belgian White to keep with the baseball-themed beer-naming scheme," recalled brewmaster John Legnard who, along with Tom Hail, has been brewing at the Sandlot from the start. The beer sold well in the ballpark. Coors thought it was on to something and decided to market the beer outside the stadium. Someone came up with the slogan, "a beer this good only comes along once in a blue moon." The brew was renamed Blue Moon.

While the hugely successful beer is now brewed and packaged off-site, it's also still brewed at the Sandlot for sale in the ballpark and to a few nearby accounts. Some people swear that the Blue Moon brewed at Coors Field is a superior beer to that brewed elsewhere.

Beginning in 2013, the Blue Moon Brewing Company at the Sandlot, which is operated by Coors

Year-round beers: Right Field Red, Blue Moon Belgian White Ale.

The Pick: You've no doubt had Blue Moon Belgian White Ale before, but probably never fresh from the source. Many swear there's a difference. Find out for yourself.

Field concessionaire Aramark, began opening its doors to the public on non-game days, Tuesday through Saturday. Food is only available during Rockies games. The Sandlot Brewery doesn't offer tours.

The pub is a large space with copious use of beetle kill pine throughout. Copper-clad brewing vessels sit behind glass panels opposite the long bar. There's plentiful table seating and a patio populated with picnic tables and high-tops. Up to ten beers are available on tap. The Blue Moon Belgian White and Right Field Red are brewed on-site. Other beers either originate at the Sandlot or are brought in from another Blue Moon brewing facility.

MillerCoors, owner of the Sandlot, gives the ballpark brewers a wide berth to create beers of their choosing. Lagers are their specialty, and the brewery is among the most decorated in the history of the Great American Beer Festival, the only competition the brewery enters. Through 2013, the Sandlot has amassed an impressive forty-three GABF medals, with at least one medal every year since 1999. The brewery was named the 2013 Large Brewing Company of the Year.

Surprisingly, the brewery is as busy in the winter as it is during baseball season. For years, the Sandlot has been brewing Mary Jane Ale for the Winter Park Ski Resort. "They actually sell more beer at the ski area than we do at the ballpark," said Legnard.

While they make seriously good beers, the Coors Field crew doesn't take themselves too seriously, as evidenced by some of the names they've bestowed on their beers. Among the Sandlot's award-winning creations are Second Hand Smoke, Clueless Beer Writer, Most Beer Judges Are Boneheads, and Yep, Still Boneheads.

Blue Moon Brewing Company at the Sandlot

Opened: April 1995.

Owner: MillerCoors.

Brewmasters: John Legnard and Tom Hail.

Potential annual capacity: 2,500 barrels.

Hours: Tuesday through Saturday, 2 p.m. to 8 p.m. Hours change on days when the Colorado Rockies play home games.

Tours: Not offered.

Take-out beer: None.

Food: Only available on game days. Brisket and pulled-pork sandwiches, sausages, burgers, nachos, and baked potatoes.

Extras: Live Major League Baseball.

Parking: Numerous nearby lots and two-hour metered street parking.

Breckenridge Brewery—Denver

471 Kalamath Street, Denver, CO 80204
(303) 623-BREW (2739), (800) 328-6723
www.breckbrew.com

Beer and barbecue is a match made in hog heaven. A visit to Breckenridge Brewery offers both in copious quantities, as Denver's largest craft brewery is also a house of 'cue.

Breckenridge Brewery has its origins in the mountain town of Breckenridge, a trek of eighty miles and 4,300 vertical feet from the Mile High City. In 1990, the mountain brewpub became one of Colorado's first craft breweries when it opened in the historic ski town (see the Breckenridge Brewery & Pub entry on page 237). It wasn't long before expansion plans turned the brewery's attention to Denver.

In 1992, Breckenridge opened a brewpub north of downtown on Blake Street. It proved to be a fortuitous location, as three years later, Coors Field opened across the street. As brewing and packaging operations expanded, a larger facility was needed to house the growing company. In 1996, Breckenridge Brewery & Bar-B-Que opened in its current Kalamath Street location. Brewing at the Blake Street location was gradually phased out, although the facility still operates as a craft beer bar named Breckenridge Colorado Craft. That taphouse features beers from around the state and is a bustling gathering spot when the Rockies play home games.

The current brewery and restaurant resides a few miles south of downtown Denver within the Santa Fe Arts District, a neighborhood that boasts the highest concentration of art galleries in Colorado. The brick façade of the single-story structure is recognizable by the green awnings over the door and windows and several stainless steel kegs mounted on either side of the entryway. Inside, the restaurant-taproom is a modest-sized casual space. On one end is a counter where you order food. The adjacent bar features a selection of sixteen house beers. There's counter seating along the front wall, and a dining area with simple booth and table seating. A row of tall windows

Year-round beers: Avalanche Amber, Lucky U India Pale Ale, Agave Wheat Ale, Oatmeal Stout, Vanilla Porter.

The Pick: The Well Built ESB builds flavors of oak and whiskey atop a malty base with patient aging in a Stranahan's Colorado Whiskey barrel procured from the distillery just down the road.

provides views of the brewing operation, which occupies most of the building.

The heady aroma of smoked meat permeates the room. The kitchen has no fryer and no grill, as the food is all about barbecue. The menu hits all the basics with beef brisket, pulled pork, chicken, turkey, sausage, ribs, and salmon. The meats are smoked over hickory wood that's been soaked in oatmeal stout. Daily specials are offered, including Tuesday's popular all-you-can-eat ribs.

Longtime employee Todd Usry holds the dual titles of Breckenridge head brewer and director of brewing operations. He started with Breckenridge in the early 1990s. His first job with the company was to drive to the mountain brewpub, pick up beer, and deliver it to liquor stores along the Colorado Front Range.

Usry's beers cover a broad spectrum of styles, from the light, quaffable Agave Wheat to the heady whiskey barrel-aged Well Built ESB. Two of the beers produced in the original mountain brewery—Avalanche Ale and Oatmeal Stout—are still brewed today. The extensive something-for-everyone beer portfolio includes ales and lagers in light, dark, hoppy, malty, seasonal, small-batch, and barrel-aged selections. From its humble mountain origins, the brewery now distributes to thirty-two states and is among the country's fifty largest craft breweries.

Having maxed out the brewing capacity at its Kalamath Street location, Breckenridge is constructing a new $20 million brewery complex on a twelve-acre site along the South Platte River in Littleton, south of Denver. The ambitious project, designed to mimic a large farm, will include a 100-barrel brewhouse, a visitors center, a special event loft, a retail center, a growler station, a barbecue restaurant, and a hop farm. The estimated opening date is March 2015.

Breckenridge Brewery—Denver

Opened: December 1992. In current location since April 1996.

Owners: Breckenridge/Wynkoop LLC.

Head brewer: Todd Usry.

Potential annual capacity: 70,000 barrels.

Hours: Monday through Saturday, 11 a.m. to at least 9 p.m.

Tours: Saturdays and by appointment.

Take-out beer: Growlers, bottles, and kegs.

Food: House-smoked barbecue.

Extras: AHA member discount program participant.

Parking: On-site lot and free street parking.

Brewery Rickoli

4335 Wadsworth Boulevard, Wheat Ridge, CO 80033
(303) 344-8988 • www.breweryrickoli.com

Reality sometimes has a way of interfering with grand schemes. It certainly did for brewer Rick Abitbol and his business partners including wife, Jaqua, and Deb Zanker. "We started with a grand idea of doing a full brewpub/restaurant/bar in a purchased location," explained Abitbol. "That was going to cost about a million-and-a-half dollars. When we came to our senses and realized what we could actually borrow, we came up with this." "This" turned out to be Colorado's smallest-capacity commercial brewery.

Brewery Rickoli is in Wheat Ridge, a Denver suburb about nine miles west of downtown. The brewery sits along Wadsworth Boulevard, a high-traffic roadway lined with mixed retail. Residential neighborhoods with a growing number of young homeowners lie on either side of the busy thoroughfare. The location attracts both repeat local customers and curious passersby who notice the tall business sign along the street. "We get over fifty thousand cars in front of us every day," said Abitbol of his high-visibility storefront.

Abitbol's brewing career started in 2000 at the Shamrock Brewery in Pueblo, with stops at several other Front Range breweries including Golden City, the Denver Chophouse, Renegade Brewing, and Rock Bottom's South Denver restaurant, where he brewed for seven years. After working for others for more than a decade, the desire to call his own shots became Abitbol's focus. "I think I have fairly strong beers and a good lineup, so I thought, 'Why should I do this for anybody but me?'"

Brewery Rickoli, the first craft brewery in Wheat Ridge, opened in late 2012. "Rickoli" is a nickname Abitbol acquired years ago while working at a police station doing data processing. It's a play on the Spicoli character, a stoned surfer played by Sean Penn, in the 1982 movie *Fast Times at Ridgemont High*. "I wasn't the type you normally see working in a police station," said Abitbol.

Year-round beers: M.E.H. Cream Ale, Aldo Red, Old Elke Brown Ale, Totally EYE-P.A., Social Lubricant Scotch Ale, Disturbed Reflection Double IPA, The Black Pline Imperial Black IPA, VannFaw Hefeweizen.

The Pick: Social Lubricant is a copper-colored Scotch ale with a British character derived from Golden Promise malt and English hops. Tummy-warming but not too sweet, this tasty brew would be equally at home in an Edinburgh watering hole as it is in a Wheat Ridge nanobrewery.

The brewery is wedged between a video game store on one side and a used book and movie store on the other. The interior could be mistaken for a friendly neighborhood breakfast café if not for the impressive row of sixteen tap handles protruding from a stainless steel wall at the far end of the attractive wooden bar. A half-dozen matching wood tables fill the room, and additional counter seating resides along the glass front wall, looking out toward Wadsworth. Co-owner Deb Zanker, a former chef, runs the front of the house and welcomes visitors as if they were dinner guests at her home.

The brewhouse is located in the back of the building. The slogan of Brewery Rickoli is "brew small. DRINK BIG." It's a fitting one. Abitbol brews on a .5-barrel brewing system, the same size used by many homebrewers. The hardworking brewer makes six fifteen-gallon batches of a single beer in order to fill a three-barrel fermenter.

Despite his limited capacity, Abitbol keeps a remarkable selection of clean-tasting, flavorful beers on tap. Most are British and American styles ranging from 4 percent session beers to a variety of hoppy IPAs, to high-gravity brews including a smooth and delicious Scotch ale. All Rickoli beers, except for its wheat beers, are gluten-reduced.

The brewer's long-range goals include a larger brewing system, keg accounts in "snobby beer bars," and a kitchen to produce beer-centric cuisine. These plans got a huge boost when, in the fall of 2013, the brewery was named a recipient of the Samuel Adams Brewing the American Dream Experienceship. With that honor comes financial assistance and business mentoring to help grow the company.

Brewery Rickoli

Opened: November 2012.

Owners: Rick and Jaqua Abitbol and Deb Zanker.

Head brewer: Rick Abitbol.

Potential annual capacity: 500 barrels.

Hours: Monday and Tuesday, 3 p.m. to 11 p.m.; Wednesday and Thursday, 7 a.m. to 9 a.m. and 3 p.m. to 11 p.m.; Friday and Saturday: 2 p.m. to midnight; Sunday, 2 p.m. to 9 p.m.

Tours: On request.

Take-out beer: Growlers.

Food: Popcorn, pretzels, and cookies or bring your own food. Lots of nearby restaurants.

Extras: AHA member deals program participant.

Parking: On-site lot.

Other area beer sites: Right Coast Pizza (7100 W. 38th Ave, 303-431-6077). Colorado Plus Brewpub (6995 W. 38th Ave., 720-353-4853).

Bull & Bush Brewery

4700 Cherry Creek Drive South, Denver, CO 80246
(303) 759-0333 • www.bullandbush.com

The venerable Bull & Bush is the granddaddy of Denver watering holes. And if you arrive on a Sunday evening for live Dixieland jazz, you'll see plenty of granddaddies in attendance. Grandmothers as well. Some have been regulars for decades and now bring their grown kids and grandkids along for the weekly jazz performances. It's a great tradition, and quite unique for a brewpub.

Uniqueness has been a trademark of the Bull & Bush since it opened in 1971. The English-style pub was built by Dean and Dale Peterson, twin brothers who gave up their careers as stockbrokers to become restaurateurs. The Tudor-style building was modeled and named after a seventeenth-century pub near London. The Bull & Bush is technically in Glendale, a small enclave within the city of Denver, about six miles southeast of downtown. At one time, Glendale was Denver's party central, while LoDo, Denver's current nightlife hotspot, was still an urban wasteland. Early on, satellite dishes were installed on the bar's roof to bring in broadcasts of sporting events from around the world. The Bull & Bush claims to be the country's first sports bar.

The Bull & Bush has been run by Dale's sons, Erik and David Peterson, since the mid-1990s. The second-generation owners have maintained the pub's distinctive character while keeping things fresh and lively. Their most significant upgrade was the addition of a brewery. The first Bull & Bush house beer was brewed on New Year's Day 1997.

The pub's main dining area, which is also where the bar is located, is dripping with character. Dark wood abounds in the low-lit room. "Look at these chairs," said co-owner Erik Peterson, whose job title is Minister of Progress. "They have forty-one years of being rubbed on. You can't build that in. Our copper bar—it's kind of warped in spots," he continues, referring to the well-worn bar that was imported from England. A pair of

Year-round beers: Happy Hop Pilsner, Hail Brau Hefeweizen, Allgood Amber Ale, The Tower ESB, Man Beer English-style IPA, Big Ben Brown Ale, Stonehenge Stout.

The Pick: Man Beer is an assertive yet well-balanced English IPA that greets you with an outgoing malty premiere that soon succumbs to a palate-cleansing hoppy finale.

plush leather sofas sits in front of a fireplace in the back of the room. There is also a second smaller dining area. A bright airy, indoor and outdoor patio is a more recent addition to the brewpub.

The menu features good-quality pub-style comfort food with a few southwestern dishes. Mashed potatoes topped with green chili has been a signature dish for more than forty years.

Bull & Bush beers have been among Colorado's most awarded in prestigious competitions in recent years. Brewmaster Gabe Moline began working in the kitchen in 1997, and took over the brewing tasks a year and a half later. His well-crafted fermentations have garnered eleven Great American Beer Festival awards and an equal number from the World Beer Cup, including an impressive four medals at the 2012 WBC. Man Beer, an English-style IPA, was a gold medal winner as was Turnip the Beets, a Belgian-style tripel brewed with organic turnips, organic beets, organic beet juice, and beet sugar. The unique brew was aged in a chardonnay barrel.

Hop lovers can experiment with tableside hop infusions. A 20-ounce beer of your choice is served in a French press along with your choice of several hop varieties from a Colorado hop farm. The length of time the hops marinate in the beer—a minimum of three minutes is recommended—determines the level of hop intensity in the brew.

The brewpub has been cellaring beers long before it became fashionable. The vintage beer list contains an impressive selection of aged bottled beers. The oldest on the menu is a Belgian ale dating from 1985. "They don't really get better, they just change. That's what's fun about it," said Peterson. The brewpub also has one of Denver's most extensive whiskey menus.

Bull & Bush Brewery

Opened: Opened in 1971. Brewery added in 1997.

Owners: David Peterson, Erik Peterson, Uncle Dean Peterson.

Head brewer: Gabe Moline.

Potential annual capacity: 4,000 barrels.

Hours: Monday through Friday, 11 a.m. to 2 a.m.; Weekends, 10 a.m. to 2 a.m.

Tours: On request.

Take-out beer: Growlers.

Food: Well-prepared pub-style comfort food including burgers, sandwiches, steaks, and southwestern entrées. Brunch on weekends.

Extras: Dixieland and traditional jazz and movies on Sunday.

Parking: On-site lot.

C.B. & Potts Restaurant and Brewery

Four locations

C.B. & Potts is a brewpub chain with multiple outlets in Colorado. The parent company, Ram International, is based near Seattle. Ram has been around since 1971 and has restaurants in a half-dozen states. There are six C.B. & Potts restaurants in Colorado. All but one has an in-house brewery. The brewing operations go by the name Big Horn Brewing Company.

The food menu is of the American pub fare genre, designed to appeal to a broad audience. Burgers, sandwiches, steaks, seafood, and pasta are among the familiar offerings. Consistency and affordability attract repeat customers.

Each C.B. & Potts location keeps an inventory of seven core beers including an IPA, a hefeweizen, a blond ale, a pale ale, an amber ale, a porter, and a rotating lager. Three or four additional handles are assigned to seasonal and specialty beers of the individual brewer's choice and formulation. The Colorado-based C.B. & Potts outlets have garnered eleven Great American Beer Festival medals since 2005.

Four C.B. & Potts restaurants are located in the suburbs of Denver and are described below. The other brewing location is in Fort Collins (see page 125). The lineup of full-time brews is the same across each of the franchise's locations.

Year-round beers: Big Red IPA, Big Horn Hefeweizen, Colorado Blonde, 71 Pale Ale, Buttface Amber Ale, Total Disorder Porter, and a rotating lager.

The Pick: Big Red IPA is an aromatic American IPA with a big, yet not overbearing, hop presence supported by an underlying malty base.

Denver Tech

6575 South Greenwood Plaza Boulevard, Englewood, CO 80111
(303) 770-1982 • www.cbpotts.com/colorado/denvertech.html

They say if it ain't broke, don't fix it. C.B. & Potts found a few successful footprints for its brewpub designs and replicated them, with minor variations, in different locations. If you get déjà vu in the Denver Tech

Center location of C.B. & Potts, you've probably been to the Westminster restaurant, or vice versa.

The Denver Tech Center, or DTC as it's commonly called, sits along Interstate 25, about fifteen miles south of downtown Denver. The C.B. & Potts restaurant is located amid a sea of large corporate office buildings that were built in a mix of modern architectural styles in the 1970s. The office-intensive location brings a thirsty happy-hour crowd into the restaurant on weekdays.

The layout is typical of the C.B. & Potts model. The dining area is plush yet casual. TVs broadcasting nonstop sports abound in the expansive bar area. Banners of local teams hang from oars suspended from the ceiling. There's a patio out front. A pool table is tucked into a dining area beyond the bar. As with some of the other C.B. & Potts locations I visited, the service in the Denver Tech location doesn't come off as rehearsed, which is a refreshing and unexpected feature for a chain restaurant.

Jake Robinson has been running the brewhouse at this location since mid-2013. Robinson had been working as a server, and expressed an interest in the brewing operation. He helped out where needed: hauling grain bags, cleaning fermenters, and performing other not-so-glamorous tasks required to run a brewery. He gradually transitioned from server to brewer. When the head brewer departed to launch a new brewing endeavor, Robinson stepped into the job. He has a fondness for IPAs and black lagers, which are likely to appear on the specialty beer list with increasing frequency.

C.B. & Potts Restaurant and Brewery—Denver Tech location

Opened: 1995.

Owners: Ram International Restaurants.

Head brewer: Jake Robinson.

Hours: Sunday through Thursday, 11 a.m. to midnight; Friday and Saturday, 11 a.m. to 2 a.m.

Tours: On request.

Take-out beer: Growlers, six-packs, and kegs.

Food: Extensive menu of American pub favorites including sandwiches, burgers, steaks, and other entrées. Gluten-free menu available.

Extras: Trivia on Tuesday.

Parking: On-site lot.

Area attractions: Fiddler's Green Amphitheatre, also known as Comfort Dental Amphitheatre (6350 Greenwood Plaza Blvd., 303-220-7000).

Other area beer sites: Mellow Mushroom (9271 Park Meadows Dr., Lone Tree, 303-792-3700). Bar Louie 6911 S Vine St., Centennial, 720-214-3400). Parry's Pizza (12624 Washington Ln., Englewood, 303-790-8686). Root25 Taphouse & Kitchen (Hyatt Regency Denver Tech Center, 7800 E. Tufts Ave., 303-221-ROOT).

Flatirons

555 Zang Street, Broomfield, CO 80020

(720) 887-3383 • www.cbpotts.com/colorado/flatironsNew.html

The Flatirons location of C.B. & Potts is close by Flatirons Crossing, a large regional shopping mall in Broomfield, about twenty miles from downtown Denver and ten miles from Boulder. Although in close proximity to the shopping complex, the brewpub draws much of its customer base from the nearby business park, apartment complexes, and several large hotels.

The brewpub resides in a modern stand-alone red-and-black brick structure. Like other restaurants in the chain, the interior is expansive, with a polished, upscale-casual ambience. The interior is divided into separate bar and dining areas. As in its sibling restaurants, there's a boat suspended from the ceiling. In this location, it's a vintage eight-person scull.

The sports bar theme permeates the bar area, with a huge flatscreen over the U-shaped bar and other TVs scattered around the room. An adjacent function room contains two pool tables and a Skee-Ball game. There's a walled-in outdoor patio with a space heater.

The ten-barrel brewhouse, visible from the parking lot through a tall wall of windows, is under the direction of Bernie Tonning, who assumed the head brewer position in the summer of 2012. Tonning has an extensive brewing background, which is evident in the quality of his beers.

His brewing career started in Boulder at the now-defunct Oasis production brewery. He worked for five years at Denver's Great Divide, followed by a four-year stint making mead at Boulder's Redstone Meadery. From the start, Tonning had wanted to brew in a pub environment, rather than in a large production facility. After many years, he finally got that opportunity at C.B. & Potts. "It just feels better because you have immediate response to your beers," said Tonning.

C.B. & Potts Restaurant and Brewery—Flatirons location

Opened: 2000.

Owners: Ram International Restaurants.

Head brewer: Bernie Tonning.

Hours: Daily, 11 a.m. to close; Breakfast served Saturday and Sunday, 10 a.m. to 1 p.m.

Tours: On request.

Take-out beer: Growlers and limited variety of six-packs.

Food: Extensive menu of American pub favorites including sandwiches, burgers, steaks, and other entrées. Gluten-free menu available.

Extras: Live music on some Wednesdays. AHA member deals participant.

Parking: On-site lot.

Area attractions: Flatirons Crossing shopping mall. 1st Bank Event Center (11450 Broomfield Lane, Broomfield, 303-410-0700).

Other area beer sites: Old Chicago (1280 East 1st Ave, Broomfield, 303-466-5834). BJ's Restaurant & Brewery (10446 Town Center Dr., Westminster, 303-389-6444).

Highlands Ranch

43 West Centennial Boulevard, Highlands Ranch, CO 80126
(720) 344-1200 • www.cbpotts.com/colorado/highlandsranch.html

C.B. & Potts' Highlands Ranch restaurant is the southernmost of the chain's Colorado outlets. Highlands Ranch is a family-centric, leafy suburban community that sprang to life in the 1980s. Downtown Denver is about seventeen miles away. The planned community of 100,000 is one of the fastest-growing cities in the country, and has been named among the best places to live by several prominent publications in recent years. As of this writing, C.B. & Potts is the only place to get fresh-brewed beer in the community, although several breweries are in the planning stages.

The restaurant is a near mirror image of the C.B. & Potts Broomfield location. It has the typical expansive interior divided into separate dining and sports bar areas. There's a vintage scull hanging from the rafters with banners of local schools suspended from the oars. There are a few arcade-type games and a semicircular kitchen bar. TVs abound in the bar area, and the dining room offers lots of booth seating and a casual atmosphere with some upscale embellishments.

Head brewer Ty Nash feels right at home in the brewpub, having grown up about five miles away. While many professional brewers started out as homebrewers, he did it backward. Nash took up home-brewing after a short stint as an assistant brewer at the Rockyard brewpub in Castle Rock. After several years as a homebrew hobbyist, he joined C.B. & Potts in 2009. When I visited, Nash was preparing to brew his 100th batch at the brewpub, an India pale lager. His reason for selecting that particular style for his commemorative brew was straightforward: "Just cuz."

C.B. & Potts Restaurant and Brewery—Highlands Ranch location

Opened: 1999.

Owner: Ram International Restaurants.

Head brewer: Ty Nash.

Hours: Monday through Thursday, 11 a.m. to midnight; Friday and Saturday, 11 a.m. to 1 a.m.; Sunday, 11 a.m. to 11 p.m.

Tours: On request.

Take-out beer: Growlers, six-packs, and kegs.

Food: Extensive menu of American pub favorites including sandwiches, burgers, steaks, and other entrées. Gluten-free menu available.

Extras: Trivia on Wednesday. AHA member deals program participant.

Parking: On-site lot.

Area attractions: Chatfield State Park (11500 N. Roxborough Park Rd.).

Other area beer sites: Parry's Pizza (9567 S. University Blvd., 303-683-0600).

Westminster

1257 West 120th Avenue Westminster, CO 80234
(303) 451-5767 • www.cbpotts.com/colorado/westminster.html

You know you've arrived at the Westminster C.B. & Potts when the futuristic Avaya building, with its huge circular glass atrium, comes into view. The brewpub sits directly across busy 120th Street. A grain silo stands guard next to the entrance to the attractive brick structure.

Just inside the door is a pair of arcade-type machines; one dispenses candy and the other offers a chance to win a stuffed animal. In this mixed business and residential area, the brewpub attracts a lot of families. In typical C.B. & Potts fashion, a collection of banners of local high school sports teams hang from the oars of a scull suspended over the bar area. TVs are in plentiful supply. Large windows look into the brewhouse, which occupies a space opposite the irregular-shaped bar.

A glass half-wall separates the bar area from the smaller dining room, which features lots of booth seating. The staff has a relaxed, friendly demeanor that is sometimes lacking in chain restaurants.

Head brewer Tom Herber had only been on the job for a few months when we met. Prior to his on-the-job training, Herber was well-traveled over a thirty-year restaurant career. He had most recently been a manager at the Flatirons C.B. & Potts. When the brewing position opened up in Westminster, he was given the opportunity to learn the brewing craft.

"It's a tough job," said Herber of his new livelihood. "It's very physical. It's very time consuming. A lot of hurry up and wait. I don't think it's what everyone thinks it is when they think about the brewer sitting back swilling a beer. It's a lot of book learning. It's a lot of science and math, things I was no good at when I was young. It's been rewarding. It really makes your brain work."

C.B. & Potts Restaurant and Brewery—Westminster location

Opened: November 1977.

Owners: Ram International Restaurants.

Head brewer: Tom Herber.

Potential annual capacity: 800 barrels.

Hours: Sunday through Thursday, 11 a.m. to midnight; Friday through Saturday, 11 a.m. to 2 a.m.; opens at 10 a.m. during football season.

Tours: On request.

Take-out beer: Growlers, six-packs, and kegs.

Food: Extensive menu of American pub favorites including sandwiches, burgers, steaks, and other entrées. Gluten-free menu available.

Extras: Trivia night on Tuesday. AHA member deals participant.

Parking: On-site lot.

Other area beer sites: Old Chicago (3909 E. 120th, Thornton, 303-252-1113).

Cannonball Creek Brewing Company

393 North Washington Avenue, Golden, CO 80403
(303) 278-0111 • www.cannonballcreekbrewing.com

Golden, Colorado, is synonymous with beer, and has been since 1873, when Adolph Coors partnered with Jacob Schueler to open a brewery on the banks of Clear Creek. The original name of Clear Creek was Cannonball Creek. The name has been revived, and Golden's brewing tradition continues to diversify with the opening of Cannonball Creek Brewing Company.

Unlike many of the new wave of breweries tucked into out-of-the-way business parks, Cannonball Creek has a high-visibility location. The brewery and taproom are located north of downtown Golden in a small retail complex fronting Highway 93, the north-south route that follows the base of the Rocky Mountain foothills connecting Golden and Boulder, about nineteen miles apart. Cannonball Creek is easy to spot. The word BREWERY is mounted in big block letters on the exterior of the modern brick-and-stucco building.

The roomy taproom can accommodate big crowds, which has been the norm since the brewery opened in early 2013. The minimalist décor has a modern-industrial feel. Rust-colored walls add some warmth to the interior. Walls of windows let in lots of natural light, creating a bright, open atmosphere. The windows also provide views of the grass-covered foothills just across the highway. There's plentiful seating at tables and at the sinuous bar that faces the partially open brewhouse. Several picnic tables are set up outside. Food trucks are often on-site and do a brisk business.

While the brewery attracts a steady stream of locals from nearby residential neighborhoods, the easily accessible location also brings in commuters as well as travelers returning from mountain outings. "[We see] lots of snow pants on Sundays," said head brewer and Golden resident Brian "Hutch" Hutchinson, who cofounded Cannonball Creek with partner Jason Stengl, the brewery's general manager.

The two met while working for the Boulder-based Mountain Sun family of brewpubs, where

Year-round beers: Solid Gold Belgian Golden, Mindbender IPA, Victorville Red.

The Pick: Mindbender IPA is an IPA drinker's IPA. Gobs of citrusy hops dominate the aroma and flavor, with just enough background malt to carry the flavorful elixir to a pleasantly bitter finish.

Hutchinson was Mountain Sun's director of brewing operations. Coincidently, his first experience in a commercial brewery came as an unpaid assistant at the Golden City Brewery, a few miles from Cannonball Creek.

The brewery keeps all options open in regard to beer styles. "At the end of the day, we just really wanted to make the beers that we wanted to drink ourselves," explained Hutch. "You'll see a lot of Belgian beers, and you'll see a lot of American-style beers as well. These tend to be the beers I enjoy the most." Apparently, his tastes parallel those of his patrons. Cannonball Creek's eclectic offerings have drawn praise both for their quality and their diversity.

The locals have an insatiable thirst for IPAs, and for hop lovers, Mindbender IPA hits all the right notes. A big hit of grapefruit up front is supported by just enough malt to keep the citrusy hops in check. It finishes with a palate-cleansing bitterness without being harsh. The Solid Gold Belgian Golden Ale takes a different path, with a complex spiciness produced by the Belgian yeast strain used to ferment the 7 percent ABV ale. Other options, such as the red ale, stout, saison, and pale ale, are all distinctly flavored and skillfully produced. In fact, the pale ale and stout were both silver medal winners at the 2013 Great American Beer Festival.

As to future offerings, Hutch was noncommittal, preferring to let his evolving preferences dictate what beers will emerge from the brewhouse: "To me, that's what makes brewing fun. My tastes have changed over the years, and I want to still be passionate about it."

Cannonball Creek Brewing Company

Opened: January 2013.

Owners: Brian Hutchinson and Jason Stengl.

Head brewer: Brian Hutchinson.

Potential annual capacity: 2,000 barrels.

Hours: Wednesday, 3 p.m. to 10 p.m.; Thursday and Friday, 3 p.m. to 11 p.m.; Saturday, noon to 11 p.m.; Sunday, noon to 10 p.m. Closed Monday and Tuesday.

Tours: On request (call ahead for large groups).

Take-out beer: Growlers.

Food: Food trucks on-site daily or bring your own food.

Extras: Homebrewer discounts.

Parking: On-site lot.

Area attractions: Colorado Railroad Museum (17155 W. 44th Avenue, 303-279-4591). Golden Gate Canyon State Park.

Other area beer sites: Yard House (14500 West Colfax Ave., Lakewood, 303-278-9273).

Caution: Brewing Company

12445 East 39th Avenue, Unit 314, Denver, CO 80239
(970) 315-BREW (2739) • www.cautionbrewingco.com

It's safe to say that you won't unintentionally stumble upon Caution: Brewing Company while out and about in the Mile High City. The brewery is buried deep within a nondescript business park in northeast Denver, just south of Interstate 70. As you approach from 39th Avenue, convinced you've made a wrong turn, a seemingly out-of-place water tank will appear on the north side of the street. That's where you turn. The brewery resides on the back side of the third row of buildings. Air travelers with some time to kill should note that Caution is the closest brewery to Denver International Airport. The tasting room is currently open four days a week, Thursday through Sunday.

Caution is owned and operated by Danny and Betty Wang, a youthful, energetic, and personable couple whose upbeat demeanor permeates the brewery's modest-sized tasting room. The inspiration for the business came during a visit to New Belgium Brewing in Fort Collins. After sampling beers in New Belgium's Liquid Center, Danny and Betty were smitten with the idea of someday opening their own brewery. At the time, they'd never brewed a drop of beer. They soon immersed themselves in homebrewing and were rewarded with favorable results in competitions, as well as positive input from friends.

After homebrewing for several years, they began to search for a small commercial brewing system. Their timing couldn't have been better. The former five-barrel pilot system from Odell Brewing had just been listed for sale. The young couple jumped at their good fortune and purchased the system.

When they arrived at Odell Brewing to pick up their hardware, they were met by brewery founder Doug Odell, who forklifted the vessels onto their U-Haul. "He gave us a six-pack of beer, patted us on the heads, and said 'Good luck, kids.' At this point we had no facility. We had a five-barrel system and our dream. It sat in our backyard for a year," said Danny. Eventually they found a location that met their needs. Rather than add to the

Year-round beers: Lao Wang Lager, Honey Matrimony Brown Ale, Wild Blonde Ale, Hippity Hops Chrysanthemum IPA.

The Pick: Lao Wang Lager, Caution's flagship beer, is a light, delicate, clean-tasting lager with an interesting herbal character derived from an infusion of Asian spices.

growing list of breweries opening in and around downtown Denver, they decided to locate in northeast Denver, where several new housing developments were underserved by the city's craft beer community. Brewing commenced in early 2011, and the tasting room opened in the summer of 2012.

When I arrived for a Saturday afternoon visit, Danny was preparing for a Sunday brew day, crushing grain in a small mill set up in the parking lot in front of the brewery. Inside, a mixed crowd of residents from the nearby developments and curious beer explorers maintained an animated dialogue at the ten-seat bar, constructed of beetle kill pine from Colorado forests.

Two TVs are mounted above the bar, but don't expect to watch sporting events here. The young proprietors, fully immersed in technology and social media, use the screens to display live Twitter and Facebook feeds, as well as information about the house beers. The taproom has little embellishment, so the focus is on beer and banter.

A wide range of flavorings are used to brew Caution beers. Ingredients such as honey, wild rice, smoked malt, and roasted hops are used to produce complex and uniquely flavored beers. Several Caution beers are infused with Asian spices, which seems only natural. Danny lived in Taiwan until moving to the United States when he was eight. Danny's parents were born in China and operate the Lao Wang Noodle House, a Denver institution located on South Federal Boulevard. Lao Wang Lager, Caution's flagship beer, is flavored with an Asian spice blend concocted by Danny's father. The brewery's Hippity Hops Chrysanthemum IPA is brewed with Chinese rock candy and chrysanthemum flowers, which are more commonly used to make Chinese chrysanthemum tea.

Caution: Brewing Company

Opened: Brewery opened in early 2011. Taproom opened in May 2012.

Owners: Danny and Betty Wang.

Head brewer: Danny Wang.

Potential annual capacity: 1,500 barrels.

Hours: Thursday and Friday, 4 p.m. to 8 p.m.; Saturday 2 p.m. to 8 p.m.; Sunday, 2 p.m. to 6 p.m.

Tours: On request.

Take-out beer: Growlers.

Food: Bavarian pretzels. Delivery menus available or bring your own food.

Extras: AHA member deals program participant.

Parking: On-site lot.

Copper Kettle Brewing Company

1338 South Valentia Street, Unit 100, Denver, CO 80247
(720) 443-CKBC (2522) • www.copperkettledenver.com

Opening a neighborhood brewery in Denver was the last thing on Jeremy Gobien's mind as he was walking home one day after working on his PhD in materials engineering in North Carolina. But fate intervened. On his way home that day, Gobien encountered a neighbor brewing beer. He spent the afternoon observing.

Soon after, the neighbor departed for brewing school and returned as head brewer at a local craft brewery. Meanwhile, Gobien had become addicted to homebrewing. While completing his doctorate, Gobien would spend ten to fifteen hours a week in the brewery where his neighbor worked, learning the craft from a professional. He knew he wanted to be a brewer. "I never even did an interview for a real job after I graduated," said Gobien.

Gobien and his wife, Kristin, relocated to Colorado in 2010 for the outdoor-oriented lifestyle and the opportunity to work in the craft beer industry. "I applied in every brewery in town," Gobien recalled. "Nobody would hire me." With Jeremy unable to get his foot in the door of a commercial brewery, Jeremy and Kristin decided to open their own. Financing was difficult. Banks wouldn't work with them. Eventually, they were able to scrape together the necessary funds. "It took a lot of begging to a lot of places," Gobien recalled. Copper Kettle opened in April 2011. "The day we opened, we had no money and everything we owned was on lien."

Copper Kettle Brewing Company sits in an office park in a mixed business-residential area just off busy Parker Road in southeast Denver. The taproom has a comfortable, relaxed ambience with a bar that seats eight and a collection of tables of varying sizes. Two walls of windows let in plenty of natural light. A pair of cushy sofas sits in a corner, encouraging relaxed conversation. The beige and plum walls and some contemporary furnishings add a touch of style to the simple space. The wooden bar sits atop an attractive base of cut stone. A large window behind the bar looks into the brewhouse. During the week, the

Year-round beers: Helles, Mexican Chocolate Stout.

The Pick: The Mexican Chocolate Stout is a complex and intriguing creation. Spices emerge from a sweet chocolatey base leading to a hot finish of fruity chilis.

taproom attracts an older, mostly local crowd from nearby neighborhoods. Beer explorers show up on weekends.

A trip to Germany instilled in Gobien an appreciation for German-style beers, which appear with regularity on the tap list. "I really enjoy doing more traditional beer styles," the owner-brewer explained. Yet it was hardly a traditional style that drew attention to the upstart brewery early in its existence. At the 2011 Great American Beer Festival, Copper Kettle won a gold medal in the herb and spice beer category for its Mexican Chocolate Stout.

"I think that was the second batch I had made. People went nuts the first time I made it," Gobien explained of the beer's instant popularity. "It became its own thing. I couldn't control it anymore." Although it was originally intended to be brewed once a year, popular demand made it a full-time offering. It is Copper Kettle's best-selling beer. It's also the most difficult to brew due to the variable nature of the chili peppers used in the mole-like recipe.

The other year-round brew is a clean, easy-drinking Bavarian helles. A second German-style beer is generally available and other offerings often include a Belgian-style ale. Other styles come and go regularly. While the chocolate stout receives the most attention, the brewery keeps regulars returning with consistent, high-quality beers. The brewery gives back to the community with a weekly Pints for Purpose program. Each Tuesday, partial proceeds from beer sales go to a different charity.

Copper Kettle Brewing Company

Opened: April 2011.

Owners: Jeremy Gobien and Kristen Kozik.

Head brewer: Jeremy Gobien.

Potential annual capacity: 1,500 barrels.

Hours: Monday through Thursday, 3 p.m. to 9 p.m.; Friday and Saturday, noon to 10 p.m.; Sunday, noon to 9 p.m.

Tours: On request.

Take-out beer: Growlers.

Food: Food trucks three to five days a week. Restaurant delivery menus available or bring your own food.

Extras: Trivia on Monday. Tuesday is Pints for Purpose day, during which partial proceeds go to charity. Firkin Wednesday. AHA pub discount program participant.

Parking: On-site lot.

Area attractions: Cherry Creek State Park.

Other area beer sites: Lowry Beer Garden (7577 E. Academy Blvd., 303-366-0114).

Crooked Stave Artisan Beer Project

3350 Brighton Boulevard, Denver, CO 80216
(720) 508-3292 • www.crookedstave.com

It wasn't long ago that a brewery like Crooked Stave Artisan Beer Project would have been unthinkable in this country. Today, it's merely extraordinary. The Denver brewery has created a buzz in the beer community with its primary focus on barrel-aged "wild beers."

"The individual pieces that make up a barrel are the staves," explained company founder and head brewer Chad Yakobson. "The crooked stave would be the stave that's different. We very much see ourselves within the industry as being that crooked stave."

Yakobson's brewing background is certainly unique. He began his foray into fermentation studying winemaking in New Zealand. His next stop was in Scotland, where he began working on a master's degree in brewing and distilling. The focus of his research involved *Brettanomyces*. (For the uninitiated, brett, as it's often referred to, is a wild yeast that contributes distinct flavors to beer.) Yakobson then returned to the United States to work at Odell Brewing in Fort Collins. In early 2011, he founded Crooked Stave.

From the start, Crooked Stave was a different type of operation. For one thing, the company had no brewery of its own. Brewing and barrel-aging took place at the Funkwerks brewery in Fort Collins. The business eventually moved to Denver, but still lacked its own brewhouse. Beers were contract-brewed at a Denver brewery, then transported to the Crooked Stave facility for aging in the company's massive collection of wooden barrels and foeders (a foeder is a giant oak barrel).

In October 2013, Crooked Stave opened its own brewery and taproom at The Source, an indoor marketplace located in a former foundry building dating from the 1880s. The Source is located on Brighton Boulevard in the up-and-coming River North neighborhood northeast of downtown Denver. Among the vendors in the historic structure are a specialty grocer, a bakery, a butcher shop, several

Year-round beers: Vieille Artisanal Saison, Surette Provision Saison, Hop Savant 100% Brett IPA, St. Bretta 100% Brett Citrus, L'Brett d'Or Surreal Golden Ale, Origins Burgundy Sour, Nightmare on Brett Dark Sour.

The Pick: The dry-hopped Vieille Artisanal Saison is an intriguing and refreshing low-alcohol brew. It pours a hazy yellow with a fruity, earthy character and tangy, dry finish.

restaurants, an artisanal spirits bar, a coffee bar, and a florist, among others. Crooked Stave occupies a space at the far end of the building.

The open brewhouse, with its gleaming stainless steel vessels, occupies about half of the lofty space. The black and gray right-angle bar adds a contemporary touch and contrasts with the well-weathered and graffiti-adorned brick walls. The pitched roof rises several stories above the concrete floor.

Crooked Stave's unique and intriguing creations include saisons, sours, and other barrel-aged wild ales. While there's an underlying fruity, earthy character to the beers, each has its own unique identity and complexity that transcends commonly used style definitions. The brewery has plans to broaden its beer offerings with some non-wild beers including a pale ale, an IPA, a coffee Baltic porter, and others.

Yakobson described his beers as wild because of the use of *Brettanomyces* in their creation. People sometimes describe brett as imparting a "barnyard" or "horse blanket" character, but Yakobson considers these off-flavors and strives to minimize them in his beers. He uses descriptors such as tropical fruit, ripe fruit, citrusy, earthy, leathery, dry, or musty. He has ten strains of brett to work with, but there's one in particular that gives Crooked Stave beers their "house character." The sour beers result from the introduction of bacteria, as brett alone does not create sourness.

According to the brewer, working with wild yeast requires a disciplinarian approach. "*Brettanomyces* is like that dog that every once in a while will play fetch," said Yakobson. "Every once in a while he'll sit and shake your hand. And then other times he completely ignores you and runs off on his own and does his own thing. I have to be very firm with the yeast. It's a labor of love."

Crooked Stave Artisan Beer Project

Opened: January 2011. In current location since October 2013.
Owner and head brewer: Chad Yakobson.
Potential annual capacity: 5,000 barrels.
Hours: Daily, 11 a.m. to 11 p.m.
Tours: On request.
Take-out beer: Bottles and growlers.
Food: Several food vendors within marketplace.
Extras: AHA member discount program participant.
Parking: On-site lot.
Area attractions: See chapter intro.
Other area beer sites: See chapter intro.

Dad & Dude's Breweria

6730 South Cornerstar Way, Suite D,
Centennial, CO 80016
(303) 400-5699 • www.breweria.com

Tom Hembree and his son Mason, also known as Dad & Dude, weren't originally planning to locate their small brewery in a shopping mall. So when they found a spot they liked in a high-rent shopping complex, the concept for the brewery required some tweaking. "You could put a brewery almost anywhere and draw people to it. But if we decided to go here, we had to have food," Tom explained of the decision to create a mall-based pizza restaurant with an in-house brewery. It didn't hurt that the elder Hembree had spent twenty-five years in the restaurant industry. The business launched in late 2010 with the name Dad & Dude's Breweria, a combination brewery and pizzeria.

The family-friendly brewpub sits within the newly constructed Cornerstar shopping mall at the high-traffic intersection of Arapahoe and Parker Roads in southeast Denver. It's an unusual location for a small family-owned brewpub, as large shopping complexes are more typically the domain of the corporate brewpub chains. In fact, Dad & Dude's is the only family-owned restaurant in the area, and sits within a sea of national-brand eateries and retail shops.

The brewpub's interior is divided into two sections. The small bar faces the brewhouse, which is visible through a window. A few high-tops are opposite the bar. Table seating is on the other half of the room. There's additional seating on a pleasant outdoor patio with umbrella-shaded tables and cheery flower boxes.

One wall is adorned with a collection of masterfully drawn caricatures created by a former bartender. A collection of Prohibition-era photos is also on display. A few unobtrusive TVs are mounted on the walls if you want to catch a game over a pizza and a brew.

Year-round beers: IPA.

The brewpub has the vibe of a neighborhood pizza joint, rather than a typical shopping mall eatery. Tom's experience in the restaurant business is on display as he circulates around the room, offering warm greetings to the many regulars that amble in.

The Pick: Dad & Dude's produces an ever-changing lineup of interesting specialty beers. Find one that sounds appealing and take it for a test ride.

The food menu includes pizza, calzones, sandwiches, salads, pasta, and a few desserts. The tasty pizzas, which don't conform to any particular pie style, are the major attraction. "It looks like a thick crust and it eats like a thin crust," Tom told me. "We take the grains after brewing and incorporate them into the pizza dough and we also add agave nectar instead of sugar. It makes it a little sweeter, a little crisper, and a little darker than most pizzas."

When I visited, the brewing operation was in the midst of tripling its capacity from its homebrewer-sized .5-barrel (fifteen gallon) system to a 1.5-barrel system. On the original system, brewing took place seven days a week. In the previous year-and-a-half, Dad & Dude's had created 140 different beers!

There is only one full-time beer: an India pale ale, not surprisingly. Other house beers range from standard styles like amber ales and pale ales to more playful creations, such as a watermelon basil wheat beer and a toffee porter. In addition, the brewpub offers a rotating lineup of all-Colorado guest beers.

Dad & Dude's has expanded its beer production beyond the brewpub. Dank IPA, a canned beer produced under the Dude's Brews label, is produced off-site and distributed throughout the Denver metro area.

Dad & Dude's Breweria

Opened: November 2010.

Owners: Tom and Mason Hembree.

Head brewer: Brad Nielsen.

Potential annual capacity: 1,100 barrels.

Hours: Sunday through Thursday, 11 a.m. to 10 p.m.; Friday and Saturday, 11 a.m. to 11 p.m.

Tours: On request.

Take-out beer: Growlers and four-packs of cans.

Food: Sandwiches, pasta, pizza, and calzones. Gluten-free pizza and calzones available.

Parking: Shopping center parking lot.

Area attractions: Cornerstone Shopping Center. Cherry Creek State Park is seven miles away.

Other area beer sites: Old Chicago (6676 S. Parker Rd., Aurora, 303-400-0876).

De Steeg Brewing

4342 Tennyson Street, Denver, CO 80212
(303) 484-9698 • www.desteegbrewing.com

A cool neighborhood. A tiny taproom in a hidden alley. Beers to make your taste buds stand at attention. For residents of northwest Denver's Berkeley Park district, De Steeg Brewery is a not-so-well-kept secret. For beer explorers, it's "a find."

It you were to take the official street address literally, the brewery would sit mid-block on lively Tennyson Street, a short stroll from the vintage Oriental Theater. In reality, if you're on Tennyson Street, "you can't get there from here," as the saying goes. The brewery is instead accessed from either end of a narrow alleyway that runs parallel to Tennyson. (De Steeg is Dutch for "the alley.")

After De Steeg's founder, Craig Rothgery, arrived in Colorado from upstate New York, it wasn't long before the mechanical engineer had acquired an obsession with homebrewing. "Within a year, I had a touchscreen automated system in my garage that I built from scratch," Rothgery explained of his tricked-out garage brewery. "A little over the top for your average homebrewer."

When Rothgery got laid off from his job with Nestlé, a long-anticipated event, he had already put in motion a plan to open a commercial brewery. By the time he received his pink slip, the only thing missing was a location for the business. The search for an affordable space in a desirable area that was lacking a brewery proved challenging. Eventually, he found the site behind a workout facility in the alleyway near Tennyson. It fit the bill.

The up-and-coming Berkeley Park district is located about four miles from downtown Denver. It's a largely residential area with a growing number of young professionals and families. Tennyson Street is the area's lively center of attraction with art galleries, restaurants, boutique shops, and now, a neighborhood brewery. "The people coming in are just fantastic," said Rothgery of his mostly local clientele. "They all love beer and just want to hang out and enjoy a nice glass in a comfortable location."

Year-round beers: Het Huis Strong Ale, French Saison.

The Pick: The French Saison is an assertively flavored, golden-hued ale with a complex interplay of yeasty-spicy flavors with a hint of citrus.

The brewery's nondescript façade of painted concrete blocks provides little hint as to the nature of the business within. In fact, from the outside, De Steeg is identifiable only by a textless sign depicting a white chalice on a black background. The interior is a small, pleasantly unassuming space. The only ornamentation consists of a few photographs on the walls. A collection of eight tables fills most of the room. A popcorn machine gets heavy use. The taproom's most distinctive feature is the classy wooden bar that was fabricated from a former bowling alley. Two rows of fermentation tanks are visible in the back of the room. Sitting out of sight behind the walk-in cooler is the 1-barrel brewing system that Rothgery assembled from scratch. At first glance, the trio of stainless steel brewing vessels looks like mutant soup cans with their labels removed.

Of the eight beers on tap, only two are full-time beers, both in the 9 percent ABV range. "I really love bigger, bolder beers," Rothgery explained of the assortment of the mostly high-gravity ales on the tap list. "I really appreciate the character you can get from malts as you get up into the higher alcohol content. I like hops, but I'm not going to create an unbalanced beer."

Het Huis (Dutch for "the house"), a year-round offering, is a well-fortified deep copper ale that defies style categorization. The creamy texture carries an assertive malt character with spicy hop accents. The French Saison, the brewery's second full-time beer, is a golden-hued ale with a complex yeasty-spicy essence and hints of citrus. Rothgery is a fan of Belgian-style ales, and you're likely to find several available when you visit.

De Steeg Brewing

Opened: February 2013.

Owner and head brewer: Craig Rothgery.

Potential annual capacity: 720 barrels.

Hours: Thursday and Friday, 4 p.m. to 11 p.m.; Saturday, 2 p.m. to 11 p.m.; Sunday, 2 p.m. to 8 p.m.

Tours: On request.

Take-out beer: Growlers.

Food: Soft pretzels, free popcorn, or bring your own food.

Parking: A few spots out front and nearby on-street parking.

Denver Beer Company

1695 Platte Street, Denver, CO 80202
(303) 433-2739 • www.denverbeerco.com

If you tell a brewer he has to do things a certain way, he's likely to do it differently, just to prove that rules are meant to be broken. There's an unwritten rule that states that a brewery should maintain a core lineup of full-time beers, and supplement them with a supporting cast of seasonal and specialty offerings. Denver Beer Company has taken a contrarian approach, eschewing full-time selections in favor of an ever-changing lineup of libations.

"The fun for us, and what we really believe, is that craft beer drinkers are promiscuous beer drinkers," explained Charlie Berger, head brewer at Denver Beer. "They want to try what's interesting and new and different. I can't think of any craft beer drinkers who go to the liquor store and buy the same brand every single time. So we don't make the same brand every single time."

Berger and business partner Patrick Crawford were college buddies in upstate New York. Following graduation, their lives took different paths, or flight plans in this case. Crawford headed to Colorado and took up homebrewing while working on classified satellite programs for an aerospace and defense contractor.

Charlie went to St. Louis where he worked at the Morgan Street and O'Fallon breweries. He then headed off to brewing school, first in Chicago, then in Munich. He was working at Denver's Wynkoop Brewing in 2009 when he reunited with his former college friend and began formulating a plan for a commercial brewery. Denver Beer Company opened in the summer of 2011.

The brewery resides on Platte Street, in the Riverfront neighborhood just west of LoDo and downtown. It's a fortuitous location, with easy access to central Denver, yet far enough removed to be out of the hustle and bustle. While there's often parking available along Platte Street, the nearby Platte River Trail and the 15th Street Bridge provide easy nonmotorized access to the brewery.

Year-round beers: There are no year-round beers. Some recipes are repeated throughout the year.

The Pick: Behind the cookies-and-cream aroma, the Graham Cracker Porter is a very palatable dark ale with a touch of roastiness and some hard-to-pinpoint background flavors.

From the outside, it doesn't take much imagination to envision the brewery's original use as an auto shop. A row of garage doors on the front of the building's boxy brick exterior opens to a roomy sidewalk beer garden populated with picnic tables. "One of the major reasons that this building was enormously appealing to Patrick and I was the six large garage bay doors that we replaced with glass," said Berger. "In the summertime, we can roll them up. It's airy. It's breezy."

Inside, the founders have repurposed many of the fixtures. Several floor jacks that once hoisted cars now support the wraparound bar. Another former floor jack supports a large metal tree grate that functions as a table. The bar and backbar are faced with metal sheeting. The open brewhouse sits at the far end of the building. With the front wall of glass, the taproom feels both urban industrial and bright and cheery.

Beers range from the familiar to the unusual. On any given visit you might find a saison, a pineapple pale ale, a rauchbier, or a kaffir lime wheat. Despite the variety of styles, there's a theme to their creation. "We trend towards seasonally appropriate brews," Berger explained. "There's something to be said for drinking the perfect dopplebock on a snowy February day and a nice light wheat beer in the beer garden during the summer."

Some beers, such as the Graham Cracker Porter, make semiregular appearances. The paint had barely dried in the Denver Beer Company taproom when this inspired concoction was awarded a bronze medal in the specialty beer category of the 2011 Great American Beer Festival. The unusual elixir is brewed with real graham crackers and some "secret spices," according to Berger. "It's a crowd-pleaser. It's reminiscent of eating s'mores around a campfire in the summertime."

Denver Beer Company

Opened: August 2011.

Owners: Patrick Crawford and Charlie Berger.

Head brewer: Charlie Berger.

Potential annual capacity: 1,750 barrels.

Hours: Monday through Thursday, 3 p.m. to 11 p.m.; Friday and Saturday, noon to midnight; Sunday, noon to 9 p.m.

Tours: Daily at 4 p.m. or on request.

Take-out beer: Growlers and kegs.

Food: Big pretzels, daily food trucks, or bring your own food.

Extras: Live music on Sunday. Running club on Tuesday. AHA pub discount program participant.

Parking: On-street metered parking.

Denver Chophouse

CHOPHOUSE & BREWERY™

1735 19th Street, Suite 100, Denver, CO 80202
(303) 296-0800 • www.denverchophouse.com

In April 1995, Coors Field, the home of the wildly popular Colorado Rockies baseball team, opened with great fanfare in a former warehouse district north of downtown Denver. That same year, a new brewpub opened a block away in a handsome 1920s brick building that had once been a warehouse for the Union Pacific Railroad.

The Denver Chophouse was a different type of endeavor for the Colorado-based Rock Bottom restaurant chain, which was in the midst of a major expansion with new brewpubs opening at a rapid pace across the country. The Chophouse was no wings-and-a-brew type of place. It was a sophisticated urban steakhouse with the added amenity of an in-house brewery.

From the corner of 19th and Wynkoop Streets, the Chophouse presents a classy image with a pair of tall Greek columns framing the entrance, and red-and-white-striped awnings above the ground floor windows. Two white grain silos sit alongside the building on the pedestrian-only block of Wynkoop that leads to the ballpark. A block away, the brick and steel façade of Coors Field dominates the streetscape.

The Chophouse interior's dark wood, brick walls, dim lighting, plush upholstered booths, and white tablecloths create a feeling of old-school elegance. It's a large space, but it is divided into separate dining areas to maintain a feeling of intimacy. Railroad-themed photographs of decades past adorn the walls. There's a long granite bar facing a row of windows, behind which sit a row of shiny stainless steel serving tanks. Old-style jazz emanates from the sound system. The bartender's white shirt and black vest are reminders that this isn't a shopping mall brewpub.

The Chophouse doesn't stray far from classic steakhouse fare. The lunch menu features salads, sandwiches, and a selection of meat and pasta dishes. The dinner menu builds on this with an

Year-round beers: Pilsner Lager, Dortmunder Lager, Wheat Ale (Wit), Dark Munich Lager, Red Ale, Pale Ale, Dry Stout, Bourbon Barrel Conditioned Stout.

The Pick: A Dortmunder lager is a rare find in an American brewery. The Chophouse version has a clean malt foundation and crisp, dry finish, producing an approachable quencher of some substance.

expanded selection of meat and seafood entrées, including five different cuts of beef and prime rib. The restaurant also serves a weekend brunch.

The nine house beers are produced by veteran brewmaster Kevin Marley. Marley's two-decade brewing career started at Boulder's Walnut Brewery, the original brewpub of the Rock Bottom family. After a stint in a now-defunct Rock Bottom property in Houston, Marley arrived in Denver to flex his brewing chops at the Chophouse. "I'm the last-standing original Rock Bottom brewer," said Marley of his senior status with the company, which is now operated by Craftworks Restaurants & Breweries.

The Chophouse generally keeps eight full-time beers and two specialty beers on tap. These regular offerings include three European-style lagers and two stouts. The Dry Stout recipe stems from Marley's younger years. "I learned to drink stout in Ireland when I was an adolescent. I've modeled it on my remembrances," he explained. The second stout is aged in a bourbon barrel. Half the batch sits in bourbon barrels for four months, then is blended with a fresh batch of the same beer. "We don't sell the most of it, but if I happen to be out of it, it's the one I hear the most about," said Marley. The rotating selections often include high-gravity or hoppy beers.

The brewery has more than enough capacity to meet the needs of the restaurant, which also pours a lot of wine and mixed drinks. The excess capacity is used to produce beer for non-brewing Chophouse restaurants in Boulder and at Denver International Airport. There are times that excess beer is needed downtown: Crowds descend on the Chophouse in droves each year on opening day of baseball season at Coors Field. On opening day of the 2013 season, thirsty fans consumed thirty-two kegs (about one thousand gallons) of Chophouse beer.

Denver Chophouse

Opened: 1995.

Owners: Craftworks Restaurants & Breweries.

Head brewer: Kevin Marley.

Potential annual capacity: 2,500 barrels.

Hours: Monday through Thursday, 11 a.m. to 11 p.m.; Friday and Saturday, 11 a.m. to midnight; Sunday, 11 a.m. to 10 p.m.

Tours: On request (before 3 p.m., if brewer is available).

Take-out beer: Growlers and kegs.

Food: Classic steakhouse selection of sandwiches, steaks, prime rib, chops, and seafood.

Parking: Valet parking, metered on-street parking, or nearby lots.

Dostal Alley Brewpub and Casino

1 Dostal Alley, Central City, CO 80427
(303) 582-1610 • www.dostalalley.net

One of the joys of researching this book was finding little gems in unlikely places. Dostal Alley Brewpub and Casino is a prime example. The small, uniquely situated casino-brewery was among the most unexpectedly pleasant stops on my brew-themed explorations.

Dostal Alley is located in Central City, a former mining outpost in the mountains thirty-five miles west of Denver. The town came into existence when gold was discovered in a nearby gulch in 1859. Numerous gold deposits were discovered shortly thereafter, and the area acquired the title of "The Richest Square Mile on Earth." Within two years, there were more people in Central City than in Denver. When the territorial government voted on a capital for Colorado in 1867, Denver beat out Central City by one vote.

In 1991, Colorado voted to allow gambling in Central City and neighboring Black Hawk. Dostal Alley opened that same year. The casino resides in a building dating from 1874, constructed after a fire wiped out most of Central City's business district. If your only experience with casinos is with the massive, opulent resorts of Las Vegas or Atlantic City, Dostal Alley will take you by surprise. The business is a small, family-run operation. The atmosphere is relaxed, friendly, and personal.

The first indication that Dostal Alley is not a typical casino appears on the window outside the entrance, where, under the business name, it reads, "Children Welcome. Homemade Pizza. Beer To Go." You enter the stately old brick building into the bar area, which contains a few high-tops and a bar inlaid with a dozen video poker machines. The adjacent space is the gaming room. Beyond the bar is a small enclosure containing the 7-barrel brewhouse. A staircase leads to the lower level where there is a second bar, some booth and table seating, and a walk-up window for ordering food.

Year-round beers: Shaft House Stout, Jacob Mack Mild, Gilpin Gold IPA, American City Pale Ale.

The Pick: The smooth and creamy Irish-style Shaft House Stout has just the right balance of sweetness and roastiness. At 5 percent ABV, it remains drinkable for more than one pint.

In the summer months, Dostal Alley is a favorite haunt of performers from the Central City Opera, one of the country's oldest opera companies. Visiting vocalists have been known to break into song over beers at the bar. Workers from other casinos are regular guests. "A lot of employees from the casinos will come here because this is more like a pub than a casino," explained Buddy Schmalz, a member of Dostal Alley's ownership family and the head brewer. Schmalz is a former mayor of Central City and is now a Gilpin County commissioner.

When Dostal Alley added a brewery in the late 1990s, customers were slow to come on board, preferring familiar bottled light lagers to the house beers. Over time, their preferences changed. "The day that our draught sales exceeded our bottle sales we were pretty excited," Schmalz remembered. Today, it's a challenge for the business to keep up with demand for its beers.

On brew days, Schmalz is joined in the brewhouse by Dave Thomas. Thomas has lived in Gilpin County for more than thirty years and, before retiring in 2007, worked as a brewmaster for Coors. Dostal Alley is the only brewery operating in the county, but it wasn't always that way. Thomas has authored a book, *Of Mines and Beer*, documenting 150 years of brewing and mining in Gilpin County.

The brew team outputs a collection of English and American-style session beers including a mild, a pale ale, an IPA, a dry Irish stout, and several seasonal brews. The Irish stout is a two-time Great American Beer Festival medal winner, and like the entire Dostal Alley lineup, is flavorful, well crafted, and easy drinking. Best of all, the beers are free while you're gambling.

Dostal Alley Brewpub and Casino

Opened: October 1991. Brewery added in 1998.

Owners: The Schmalz family.

Head brewer: Buddy Schmalz. Brewer Emeritus: Dave Thomas.

Potential annual capacity: 500 barrels.

Hours: Weekdays, 10 a.m. to 2 a.m.; open twenty-four hours Friday through Sunday.

Tours: On request.

Take-out beer: Growlers and bombers.

Food: Pizza, calzones, and sandwiches.

Extras: Occasional karaoke. Casino. Free beer while gambling.

Parking: On-site lot and free street parking.

Area attractions: Casinos in Central City and neighboring Black Hawk. Central City Opera in summer (303-292-6700).

Dry Dock Brewing Company

15120 East Hampden Avenue,
   Aurora, CO 80014
(303) 400-5606
www.drydockbrewing.com

Many new breweries surface with barely a splash. Dry Dock Brewing Company surfaced with a flood of attention that, years later, shows little sign of receding.

In 2002, Kevin DeLange purchased an existing homebrew shop, The Brew Hut, which was located in a nondescript strip mall in Aurora, Colorado's third-largest city and just east of Denver. The business did well, and in October 2005, when an eight-hundred-square-foot space next to the store became available, DeLange pieced together a brewing system and opened Dry Dock Brewing Company.

Local beer fans steered a course to the fledgling brewery when, six months later, Dry Dock won a gold medal at the 2006 World Beer Cup. Fittingly, the award-winning ESB was named HMS Victory. "That gave us tons of publicity," DeLange recalled. "It put us on the map, especially in Colorado where people follow that sort of thing. [Then] all of a sudden, people started seeking us out." There would be many decorations to follow.

In 2008, the brewery won another WBC medal as well as its first Great American Beer Festival award. The following year was a big one for Dry Dock. The brewery expanded into the neighboring space in a former auto parts store. The brewing system was upgraded, including much-needed temperature-controlled fermenters. Previously, beer was fermented in a cold room. "I would have to come open the doors in the middle of the night to keep it the right temperature," DeLange recalled. The brewing capacity increased substantially, as did seating for visitors to the taproom. Later in the year, Dry Dock received a tidal wave of attention when it was awarded the prestigious Small Brewing Company of the Year award at the 2009 Great American Beer Festival.

Riding a swell of popularity, Dry Dock began packaging its beers for distribution in stores, bars,

Year-round beers: Dry Dock Amber Ale, Dry Dock Hefeweizen, Breakwater Pale Ale, Dry Dock Vanilla Porter, USS Enterprise IPA, Dry Dock Double IPA, Dry Dock Apricot Blonde, Hop Abomination IPA.

The Pick: Dry Dock Hefeweizen is a wonderful example of this Bavarian staple. It's cloudy, light, effervescent, and refreshing with the wheaty flavor and the banana-clove character that typifies the style.

and restaurants. In early 2013, the brewery opened a large production facility in Aurora.

The original brewery is still going strong. The spacious taproom has an understated nautical theme. A row of tables is lined up along the front wall of windows. Outside, picnic tables sit under a protective overhang. Behind the bar, a chalkboard above a long row of tap handles lists the extensive beer offerings. Above it is a model of a clipper ship. An adjacent room shares space with wine and whiskey barrels used to age sour and specialty beers.

Dry Dock seems to offer a great beer in whatever style floats your boat. At the 2013 GABF, Dry Dock wowed the judges, earning five medals and bringing its combined GABF and WBC medal count to twenty-two. In the warm-weather months, the Dry Dock Hefewiezen is a personal favorite. The Apricot Blonde is a great fruit beer with a bounty of tangy apricot flavor, but without cloying sweetness. In winter, heartier beers, such as the Old Ale and Wee Heavy, cut through the brisk mile-high air. Hopheads will find properly pungent examples of the standard and double IPA. Belgian styles appear from time to time. "We love making Belgian and German and American style beers, and also some weird, eclectic stuff. We also like to make traditional styles from any region of the world. It keeps it exciting for us," explained DeLange. When it comes to brewing up excellent beers, Dry Dock has done it by the boatload.

Dry Dock Brewing Company

Opened: October 2005.

Owners: Kevin and Michelle DeLange.

Head brewers: John Schneider and Brett Williams. Director of Brewing Operations: Doug Hyndman.

Potential annual capacity: 3,000 barrels at original facility. 12,000 barrels at production facility.

Hours: Monday and Tuesday, noon to 9 p.m.; Wednesday, noon to 9:30 p.m.; Thursday, noon to 10 p.m.; Friday, noon to 11 p.m.; Saturday, 11 a.m. to 11 p.m.; Sunday: 11 a.m. to 9 p.m.

Tours: On request or by appointment.

Take-out beer: Growlers, cans, bombers, and kegs.

Food: Lots of nearby takeout and restaurant delivery available.

Extras: Live music on Tuesday. Trivia on Wednesday. Firkin Friday. AHA member discount program participant.

Parking: On-site lot.

Area attractions: Cherry Creek State Park.

Other area beer sites: Royal Hilltop (18581 E. Hampden Ave., 303-690-7738).

Elk Mountain Brewing

18921 Plaza Drive, Unit 104, Parker, CO 80134
303-805-BREW (2739) • www.elkmountainbrewing.com

It wasn't long ago that Parker and the surrounding area southeast of Denver was a wasteland for beer enthusiasts. With the opening of Elk Mountain Brewing and a few other upstart breweries in recent years, the area is showing signs of becoming productive turf for area beer hunters.

Elk Mountain Brewing is named for a favorite elk-hunting destination of brewer and co-owner Tom Bell. Bell was a longtime homebrewer with aspirations to become a professional brewer. Years ago, he did an internship at the now-defunct Tabernash brewery, an early and well-respected Denver brewery specializing in German-style beers. Bell purchased a commercial brewing setup in the mid-1990s, but had to sell it when his hopes of opening a brewery were dashed by the realities of raising a family and working a full-time job.

The brewery concept continued to simmer, however. Once Bell's kids had grown up, the business idea was reborn. The town of Parker, a bedroom community about twenty-five miles from downtown Denver, was a logical choice for the brewery's location, as Bell had been a Parker resident for almost two decades. The site where the brewery now resides was a hayfield when Bell first arrived in town. Along with his wife, Marcia, Bell opened Elk Mountain Brewing Company in the summer of 2010.

The brewery resides in a modern business and light industrial complex a block west of Parker Road, the town's primary north-south artery. The Bells have infused a rustic mountain theme into the taproom. Charcoal-colored walls are adorned with wildlife photos, a hunting trophy, and a pair of vintage snowshoes. An elkhorn chandelier hangs from the corrugated metal ceiling. A wood stove sits on a brick platform in front of an old wagon wheel. The long bar is handsomely constructed of laminated beetle kill pine, as are the tables that fill the spacious gathering spot. There's

Year-round beers: Rock Slide Amber Ale, Mine Shaft Kolsch, Wild Wapiti Wheat, Ghost Town Brown, Elk Horn Stout, Ute Bill Pale Ale, Puma IPA.

The Pick: Wild Wapiti Wheat, a German-style hefeweizen, is based on Tom Bell's award-winning homebrew recipe. The hazy yellow beer has a touch of sweetness up front, and the requisite banana-clove character that defines the style.

additional seating on an outdoor patio. A pool table resides in front of a wall of windows. A pair of flatscreens is mounted over the bar, and two more are placed in opposite corners of the room.

A half-wall behind the bar separates the taproom from the 7-barrel brewhouse. German influences are present in several of the house beers including the Mine Shaft Kolsch, a pale German-style ale and satisfying summer quencher. Other beers in the full-time lineup include an amber ale, a pale ale, a wheat beer, a brown ale, an oatmeal stout, and an IPA. The IPA is the top seller. "You have to have an IPA when you open a place like this," said Bell, referring to the insatiable appetite for hops among the local beerfolk. Firkin tapping is a Wednesday tradition at Elk Mountain. Food trucks regularly set up shop at the brewery. Root beer is also on tap in the family-friendly pub.

Elk Mountain Brewing

Opened: July 2010.
Owners: Tom and Marcia Bell.
Head brewers: Tom Bell and Duane Taylor.
Potential annual capacity: 700 barrels.
Hours: Monday through Thursday, 3 p.m. to 9 p.m.; Friday and Saturday, noon to 11 p.m.; Sunday, noon to 9 p.m.
Tours: On request.
Take-out beer: Growlers.
Food: Local restaurant delivery menus available, food trucks, or bring your own food.
Extras: Firkins on Wednesday.
Parking: On-site lot.

Golden City Brewery

920 12th Street, Golden, CO 80401
(303) 279-8092 • www.gcbrewery.com

Golden City is a neighborhood brewery in the most literal sense. The brewery is in a residential area, adjacent to the large brick Victorian home of founders Charlie and Janine Sturdavant. The beer garden is in their backyard. With well-crafted beers and an ultra-laid-back outdoor space, the twenty-year-old brewery is a rewarding warm-weather destination.

Golden City is located in Golden, a few blocks from Washington Avenue, the town's main drag. As you turn off Washington into a residential neighborhood, you'll probably think you made a wrong turn. You haven't. Despite the 12th Street address, the brewery is actually located on Cheyenne Street, which intersects 12th. The location is so inconspicuous, some longtime locals are unaware of the business. The humongous MillerCoors brewery is just four blocks away. For years, Golden City has billed itself as Golden's second-largest brewery.

The brewery was founded by the Sturdavants in 1993. Charlie was a homebrewer and geologist who worked at a mine about forty miles from Golden. Nervous about his job security, he started the brewery as an alternative income source. By the time he got laid off from his day job, the brewery was up and running.

A visit to Golden City is really about the beer garden, as relaxed a beer-drinking spot as Colorado has to offer. It's like hanging out in your neighbor's backyard, assuming your neighbor has a lot of beer-loving friends. Picnic and patio tables are scattered about. You can order beer through a window on the side of the tasting room or inside. To keep peace with the neighbors, the brewery closes at six-thirty each day.

The tiny taproom sits adjacent to the beer garden. The nondescript brick structure would hardly be noticeable from the street if not for the original 7-barrel electric brew kettle sitting out front as ornamentation. The tasting room is a petite, no-frills space. There are a few tables, a refrigerator

Year-round beers: Mad Molly's Brown Ale, Evolution IPA, Lookout Stout, Clear Creek Gold Kolsch, Legendary Red Ale Altbier.

The Pick: Subtle and satisfying, Legendary Red Ale, a German-style altbier, is a lovely beer for multi-pint quaffing. Clean malt flavors step forward without being overly sweet. A delicate hop finish works in perfect harmony.

containing bombers and soft drinks, an ATM machine, a rack of T-shirts, and a counter where you order beer.

Brewing operations take place in a cinder block structure behind the taproom. The original brewing system was pieced together from used dairy equipment but has been upgraded to a modern system. Sturdavant was the original brewer. When the brewery first opened, he produced only one beer, an altbier called Legendary Red Ale. It's still made today. When people requested more variety, he brewed a Kolsch. Requests for a dark beer led to an oatmeal stout.

Over the years, the full-time beer lineup expanded to include a brown ale and an IPA, Golden City's biggest seller. Specialty beers appear with regularity. A barleywine was brewed early on and continues to be a seasonal crowd pleaser. Sturdavant retired from brewing long ago. As an accomplished home winemaker, he's planning to start offering homemade wines at the brewery.

Sarah Henderson became Golden City's head brewer in fall 2012. Henderson is one of two female head brewers in Colorado as of this writing. She received an engineering degree from the well-respected Colorado School of Mines, located in Golden. After completing the American Brewers Guild certification program and an internship at Avery Brewing, she was hired as Golden City's assistant brewer in 2011. When the head brewer departed to take the reins at a new Boulder brewpub, Henderson stepped into the head brewing position. Under her direction, the under-the-radar refuge continues to offer clean, flavorful beers brewed true to style.

Golden City Brewery

Opened: October 1993.
Owners: Janine Sturdavant and a team of minority owners.
Head brewer: Sarah Henderson.
Potential annual capacity: 2,000 barrels.
Hours: Daily, 11:30 a.m. to 6:30 p.m.
Tours: On request.
Take-out beer: Growlers and bombers.
Food: Pizza delivery available or bring your own food.
Extras: Beer garden with fire pit.
Parking: On-street.

Gordon Biersch Brewery Restaurant

1 West Flatiron Circle, Broomfield, CO 80021
(720) 887-2991
www.gordonbiersch.com/locations/broomfield

Like Betty Crocker and Aunt Jemima, Gordon Biersch is not an actual person. Rather, Gordon Biersch is the name of a national brewpub chain formed of a partnership between entrepreneurs Dave Gordon and Dean Biersch.

Gordon was attending the prestigious Weihenstephan brewing school near Munich when he purchased a used brewing system and shipped it back to the United States. After returning to his native California, he teamed up with longtime restaurateur Dean Biersch in a brewpub endeavor. The first Gordon Biersch Brewery Restaurant opened in Palo Alto in 1988. The Gordon Biersch brand has expanded considerably since its inception. There are now thirty-three Gordon Biersch brewpubs throughout the United States, and three in Taiwan. The original Palo Alto facility is still in operation, as is the original brewing system.

In 2010, the private equity firm Centerbridge acquired the company along with the Colorado-based Rock Bottom brewpub chain, which also includes Boulder's Walnut Brewery, several Chophouse restaurants, and Old Chicago taphouses. This arranged marriage of the two national brewpub chains operates under the name Craftworks.

The single Gordon Biersch facility in Colorado is located at Flatiron Crossing, a large regional shopping mall in Broomfield, about twenty miles from downtown Denver and ten miles from Boulder. The restaurant is located in an attractive modern building a few steps from a large movie theater complex. A tall metal grain silo is prominently visible from the parking lot. There's plenty of outdoor seating on a large patio that wraps around three sides of the building. The interior is expansive with separate bar and dining areas. Dark wood and upholstered booths contribute to an upscale but comfortable atmosphere. Four big-screen TVs are mounted above the large island-style bar. The twenty-barrel brewhouse resides within a glass enclosure in a corner of the building.

The food menu is extensive and eclectic, designed to appeal to a broad range of palates.

Year-round beers: Golden Export, Hefeweizen, Czech Pilsner, Märzen, Schwarzbier.

The Pick: The golden-colored Czech Pilsner begins with a slightly sweet introduction that leads to a crisp, palate-cleansing finish of distinctive Saaz hops.

Pub standards, such as burgers and sandwiches, share the menu with pizza, flatbreads, and a wide range of entrées including steaks, pasta, and seafood. Southwestern, southern, and Asian influences appear in various incarnations.

One thing that sets Gordon Biersch apart from most other brew-pubs, and the majority of American craft breweries, is its singular focus on German-style beers. "We stick to making very traditional German recipes adhering to the Reinheitsgebot [the German Beer Purity Law], so there are no fruits, nuts, or berries in any of our beers," explained Tom Dargen, the director of brewing operations for Gordon Biersch restaurants nationwide. Dargen's brewing career began at Denver's Wynkoop Brewing Company soon after it opened in the late 1980s. He ran the brewhouse at Broomfield's Gordon Biersch for several years before assuming his current position.

Ryan Grady is now in charge of the brewhouse in Broomfield. Grady started out as a bartender before moving into a brewing job in 2010 to work as Dargen's assistant. Grady keeps at least six beers on tap and sometimes up to eight. These always include the standard five Gordon Biersch beers and a rotating seasonal beer. The five standards include a golden export, a hefeweizen, a Czech pilsner, a Märzen, and a schwarz-bier (black lager). The beers are consistently clean-tasting, approachable, and excellent representations of their styles.

For those new to the world of craft beer, these traditional German-style beers provide a nonthreatening entryway for exploration. For more experienced palates, they can be a refreshing change of pace from the heartier, more complex ales produced by most craft breweries.

Gordon Biersch Brewery Restaurant

Opened: August 2000.

Owners: CraftWorks Restaurants & Breweries

Head brewer: Ryan Brady. Director of Brewing Operations: Tom Dargen.

Potential annual capacity: 2,000 barrels.

Hours: Monday through Thursday, 11 a.m. to midnight; Friday and Saturday, 11 a.m. to 1 a.m.; Sunday, 11 a.m. to 11 p.m.

Tours: By reservation or on request.

Take-out beer: Growlers and kegs.

Food: Extensive selection of flatbreads, burgers, sandwiches, steaks, seafood, chicken, pasta, and other entrées with international influences. Gluten-free selections available.

Extras: Live music on Thursday (summer only). AHA member discount program participant.

Parking: On-site lots in shopping mall.

Area attractions: Flatiron Crossing Shopping Mall is ten miles from Boulder.

Great Divide Brewing Company

2201 Arapahoe Street, Denver, CO 80205
(303) 296-9460 • www.greatdivide.com

The Great Divide, another name for the Continental Divide, is one of Colorado's most prominent geographic features. It seems appropriate that Denver's Great Divide Brewing Company holds a place of prominence in Colorado's craft beer scene.

Great Divide's founder and president, Brian Dunn, grew up in an environment where good food and good drink were an integral part of family life. While attending graduate school in the early 1990s, he acquired an obsession with homebrewing "that went totally off the deep end," as he described it. Colorado's craft beer scene was gaining momentum at that time. The entrepreneurial-minded Dunn decided to climb aboard the craft beer bandwagon.

When Great Divide opened in 1994 in a former dairy processing plant at the corner of Arapahoe Street and 22nd Avenue, the neighborhood of aging brick warehouses was a sketchy place. When Coors Field opened four blocks away the following year, there began a slow revitalization that has accelerated in recent years. Old buildings are being transformed into condos and lofts. Neighborhood-focused restaurants and small business are popping up. The once-forgotten Ballpark Neighborhood, as it's now called, is on the upswing.

The Great Divide Brewery is an integral part of the neighborhood. The taproom is among Denver's busiest. The eclectic crowd that keeps the taproom hopping includes a solid core of locals, but also lots of out-of-town visitors. Daily brewery tours are very popular, especially on weekends. The taproom plays a dual role of social gathering spot and destination for discerning beer drinkers who come to drink beer, talk beer, and repeat.

The brewery has retained its industrial brick façade. What was once a parking lot alongside the building is now populated with an army of towering stainless steel vessels. A collection of tables is lined up on the sidewalk by the entrance, providing a relaxed spot for warm-weather sipping, away

Year-round beers: Hercules Double IPA, Yeti Imperial Stout, Titan IPA, Hoss Rye Lager, Claymore Scotch Ale, Colette Farmhouse Ale, Nomad Bohemian Pilsner, Hades Belgian-Style Strong Golden Ale, Lasso IPA.

The Pick: Hops play the lead part in Titan IPA, but malt provides a strong supporting role. The bold brew is packed with personality without being palate-fatiguing.

from the boisterous crowds that typically fill the taproom. Food trucks are regularly parked out front.

You enter into a modest-sized space that is dominated by a twelve-seat bar. Servers are in constant motion, filling glasses from a row of sixteen taps. An impressive collection of seventeen medals from the Great American Beer Festival hangs without fanfare on the far wall. A second room behind the bar offers additional seating with a view of the brewhouse activities through a large window.

Great Divide maintains a diverse portfolio of nine year-round beers and a dozen seasonals, all of high quality. While there are numerous selections above 7 percent alcohol, you won't be lacking for a less assertive, more approachable ale or lager. Styles vary widely, from the crisp and tangy Hoss Rye Lager to the hop-laced yet balanced Titan IPA to the humongously flavored Yeti Imperial Stout. A chocolate oak-aged version of Yeti was a 2013 Great American Beer Festival gold medal winner. Belgians, barrel-aged, and specialty beers round out the lineup. I always enjoy my much-too-infrequent visits to Great Divide because there's always an excellent beer available that fits my mood.

The brewery is continually tweaking its lineup and adding new styles based on input from a variety of sources. "It's a collaborative effort between Brian Dunn, the sales staff, the brewers, and anyone who's got input," explained head brewer Taylor Rees, who started on Great Divide's bottling line a decade ago and worked his way up. "Occasionally, we'll brew a beer on the pilot system that goes over so well that we decide to do it on a full scale." Orabelle, a Belgian tripel, is a prime example. Great Divide beers are currently distributed to twenty-five states and to Sweden.

Great Divide Brewing Company

Opened: May 1994.

Owner: Brian Dunn.

Head brewer: Taylor Rees.

Potential annual capacity: 65,000 barrels.

Hours: Sunday through Tuesday, noon to 8 p.m.; Wednesday through Saturday, noon to 10 p.m.

Tours: Monday through Friday, 3 p.m. and 4 p.m. Saturday and Sunday, every 30 to 45 minutes between 2:30 p.m. and 5 p.m.

Take-out beer: Growlers, six-packs, twelve-packs, bombers, and kegs.

Food: Food trucks daily around 5 p.m.

Extras: AHA member discount program participant.

Parking: Free two-hour on-street parking.

Hogshead Brewery

4460 West 29th Avenue, Denver, CO 80202
(303) 495-3105 • www.hogsheadbrewery.com

When you arrive at Hogshead Brewery, ask the bartender what is drinking well. You'll likely get an answer along the lines of, "Everything is, however, you should definitely try the . . ." Whatever cask ale is recommended, go for it. Hogshead specializes in traditional English-style cask-conditioned session ales. These short-shelf-life beers, when served at their peak, are a joy. If you haven't experienced well-crafted cask ales served from a traditional hand pump, or even if you have, Hogshead is an excellent place to enjoy a "proper pint." Regular kegged beers are also available.

Hogshead was the cumulative effort of four entrepreneurial-minded beer lovers. One of them, Stephen Kirby, is a transplanted Brit whose prowess for brewing traditional English cask ales provided much of the inspiration for launching the brewery. Kirby had done some professional brewing in the United Kingdom and had a singular motivation for recreating English "real ales" in Denver. "I missed them," he said matter-of-factly.

The brewery resides in Denver's West Highland neighborhood. It's a largely residential area of older homes northwest of downtown. Sloan's Lake is three blocks away. From the outside, the brewery presents a surprisingly handsome image for a remodeled 1950s-era car repair shop. The exterior is surfaced with repurposed wood and lots of glass. There's a patio in front with a half-dozen picnic tables. Food trucks make regular appearances.

The former car bay doors open to the highly automated brewhouse. Setting up the brewing system to Kirby's specifications was largely the work of engineer and brewery cofounder Jeff Kipp. With his extensive experience in the soft drink industry, Kipp described himself as a "Pepsiologist."

The taproom sits adjacent to the brewery. It's a small space, but not so small as to feel cramped. The bar seats eight, and there's table seating of varying configurations. It's a bright, uncluttered, inviting space conducive to conversation.

Year-round beers: Chin Wag ESB, Lake Lightening English Pale Ale, Gilpin Black Gold London Porter.

The Pick: Go with whatever cask ale the bartender said is drinking well. A proper pint of real ale served at its prime is a rare treat on this side of the pond.

The circular brewery logo—a stylized pig face above the brewery name and the number 54—appears over the parking lot, above the entrance, and behind the bar. The name Hogshead refers to a cask of a particular size. A hogshead has a capacity of 54 imperial gallons. "The 54 (on the logo) is just to prompt conversation," explained brewery cofounder Mike Manczer. "The curious ask about it, which leads to a good story."

Though Kirby's personal passion is for traditional cask-conditioned English ales, he's not dogmatic about it. Hogshead has four hand pumps dispensing the cellar-temperature, lightly carbonated cask ales. The brewery also serves regular kegged versions of its beers, catering to American palates more attuned to cooler, spritzier brews. "I'm not here to tell you what temperature to drink your beer at," said Kirby.

Hogshead is not adverse to a bit of playful experimentation, either. "One of the features of cask beer is that it allows you to take a base beer and dry-hop it differently," said Manczer. For a bit of variety, Hogshead will often dry-hop a house ale with an American hop variety. The brewery has also served a cask-conditioned version of a German-style black lager. A popular offering has been the house porter flavored with cocoa nibs.

The heartiest of the three full-time beers is Chin Wag ESB, which weighs in at a bit over 5 percent ABV. "Four of those, your chin wags. You start talking a lot of shit," said Kirby. So what's the brewer's favorite Hogshead beer? "They're like children. You love them all," said the brewer. "We create new ones. Sometimes they come out good and sometimes they're just bastard children," he said chuckling. "But you still love 'em."

Hogshead Brewery

Opened: June 2012.

Owners: Jeff Kipp, Michael Manczer, Stephen Kirby, and John Cianci.

Head brewer: Stephen Kirby.

Potential annual capacity: 1,000 barrels.

Hours: Monday through Wednesday, 4 p.m. to 9 p.m.; Thursday and Friday, 2 p.m. to 10 p.m.; Saturday, noon to 10 p.m.; Sunday, noon to 8 p.m.

Tours: On request.

Take-out beer: Growlers and kegs.

Food: Bavarian pretzels. Food trucks four or five days a week.

Extras: Firkin tapping on Wednesday. Homebrewer discounts.

Parking: On-site lot.

Ironworks Brewery & Pub

12354 West Alameda Parkway, Lakewood, CO 80228
(303) 985-5818 • www.ironworkspub.com

Ironworks Brewery & Pub is a bit of an odd duck in the Colorado beer scene, with a split personality that's part neighborhood dive bar and part brewpub. When I located the Lakewood watering hole, tucked away in a declining strip mall along West Alameda Parkway, I thought I was in the wrong place.

A banner on the building façade next to the business name advertised happy hour specials on Miller Lite. Neon signs, mounted on the front windows, displayed Budweiser and Bud Light logos. A shade umbrella on a smokers' patio near the entrance was printed with the Coors Light logo.

Ironworks goes way back in the Colorado beer scene. It opened in 1989 as a production brewery. It eventually floundered and was sold. The new owners broadened the scope of the business with the addition of a bar, kitchen, and seating area. It was sold again in 1997 to the current owner.

You enter into a large, dimly lit interior with a dated feel. The center of the space is populated with wooden tables. In the back of the room are three pool tables, two dartboards, and a few pinball machines. The bar is off to one side. The kitchen and brewery are out of sight behind the bar. There's a patio in the back that, like the front patio, is smoker-friendly. A few items scattered about include an Internet jukebox and a very cool floor lamp radiating multicolored light from a collection of lava lamps in place of light bulbs. A vending machine dispenses snacks, candy, and cigarettes. The walls are adorned with beer and sports paraphernalia.

In the afternoons, Ironworks is frequented by an after-work crowd of light beer–sipping employees from nearby federal office buildings. In the evenings, Ironworks attracts a steady crowd of regulars with a variety of weekly events. There's live music on Saturdays, karaoke on Sundays and

Year-round beers: Hop Killa IPA, Agave Wheat, Green Mountain Pale Ale, Alameda Amber, Doc Henry's Irish Stout.

The Pick: Doc Henry's Irish Stout is proof that stouts are not necessarily the sweet, heavy, viscous beers that many people believe them to be. This dark ale is light-bodied with a dry, roasty, coffee-like character.

Thursdays, trivia on Mondays, and an open stage on Wednesdays. In addition, there are weekly pool and dart leagues.

An abbreviated menu lists bar snacks, sandwiches, and pizza. Ten beer taps dispense seven house beers with three taps dedicated to Bud, Bud Light, and Coors Light. The house beers include an IPA, an agave wheat beer, a pale ale, an amber ale, a dry Irish stout, and two rotating taps. The stout was the best of the beers I sampled.

Ironworks Brewery & Pub

Opened: Brewery opened in 1989. In 1996 it became a brewpub.

Owner: Mike Mader.

Head brewer: Mike George.

Potential annual capacity: 1,750 barrels.

Hours: Daily, 11 a.m. to 2 a.m.

Tours: On request.

Take-out beer: Growlers.

Food: Small menu of snacks and sandwiches.

Extras: Live music on Saturday, open stage on Wednesday, karaoke on Thursday and Sunday, trivia on Monday, pool and dart leagues.

Parking: On-site lot.

Area attractions: Bandimere Speedway (3051 S. Rooney Rd., Morrison). Red Rocks Amphitheatre (18300 W. Alameda Pkwy., Golden).

Other area beer sites: Old Chicago (145 Union Blvd., 303-988-5990).

Lone Tree Brewing Company

8200 Park Meadows Drive, Suite 8222, Lone Tree, CO 80124

(303) 792-LTBC (5822) • www.lonetreebrewingco.com

With a few exceptions, fresh beer in Denver's southern suburbs is largely the domain of the chain store brewpubs. One of the notable exceptions is Lone Tree Brewing, which is gracing the burbs with a welcoming vibe and exceptional beers.

The town of Lone Tree, where the brewery resides, is a small bedroom community about twenty miles south of Denver. It's an area of busy thoroughfares, modern housing developments, and a sea of retail. The brewery sits just off Highway 470, in the thick of the suburban landscape.

Lone Tree opened in late 2011 through the combined efforts of German scholar and high school teacher Jason Wiedmaier and his partner John Winter, a retired airline pilot. Wiedmaier was a longtime homebrewer who was working at Aurora's Brew Hut homebrew supply as the owners were gearing up to open the Dry Dock brewery. That's where he met Winter. The idea of opening a brewery had been fermenting with Wiedmaier for several years. He discussed it with Winter, and the two become partners.

Their search for a suitable location eventually led to Lone Tree. "Honestly, I didn't even know Lone Tree existed except for a sign on I-25," Wiedmaier recalled. "We looked at the demographics. They were right." Lone Tree had one more invaluable asset. "It just had a nice feel to it," said the cofounder and head brewer.

After getting the blessing of the Lone Tree city council to open the brewery, Wiedmaier and Winter had one additional hurdle to overcome: they had to get permission from the HOA of the neighboring Acres Green housing development. "They welcomed us with open arms with the stipulation that we name a beer after them," Wiedmaier explained. "That's why we have Acres O'Green Irish Red."

Year-round beers: Acres O'Green Irish Red, Ariadne's Belgian Blonde, Hoptree IPA, Mountain Mama Helles, Outta Range Pale Ale, Toots' Oatmeal Stout.

The Pick: The Outta Range Pale Ale greets you with the enticing aroma of freshly grated grapefruit zest. A hint of sweetness creates a smooth finish to the flavorful, hoppy brew.

The taproom is expansive and attractive, with a contemporary look and an amiable ambience. Any vestige of its office park environs is left in the parking lot. There's a patio in the front enclosed by a metal fence. Within it grows, fittingly, one lone tree. The interior is well-populated with tables and a long wraparound bar of light laminated wood. A few TVs are scattered about but are not particularly distracting. A short transparent wall is all that separates the taproom from the brewhouse.

The taproom is largely a local's place. Families frequent the neighborhood brewery, which welcomes them with board games and homemade sodas. Shoppers stop by to rest their credit cards, as do commuters waiting out the rush hour traffic snarls.

For those who appreciate well-made beers brewed to style, visits are amply rewarded. Of the six full-time beers, a Bavarian helles holds down the light end of the flavor spectrum. A double IPA, the taproom favorite, packs a pungent punch of hops with a finish that's not overly aggressive. A Belgian blonde, a pale ale, an oatmeal stout, and the Irish red complete the well-rounded lineup, with seasonals and specialties filling in the gaps. The Lone Tree brews provide well-tuned palates a reason to venture to the southern suburbs. That suits the brewer just fine.

"In education, rarely do you get to see the fruits of your labor," related Wiedmaier. "Whereas with beer, I can look out any night and see people enjoying what I did. That's the coolest thing for me, seeing people enjoy what I make."

Lone Tree Brewing Company

Opened: December 2011.

Owners: John Winter and Jason Wiedmaier.

Head brewer: Jason Wiedmaier.

Potential annual capacity: 1,100 barrels.

Hours: Sunday, 11 a.m. to 8 p.m.; Monday through Wednesday, noon to 8 p.m.; Thursday, noon to 9 p.m.; Friday, noon to 10 p.m.; Saturday, 11 a.m. to 10 p.m.

Tours: On request.

Take-out beer: Bombers and growlers.

Food: Restaurant delivery menus on hand. Food trucks Wednesday through Sunday, or bring your own food.

Extras: Live music on Friday. Trivia Night on Thursday. AHA member discount program participant.

Parking: On-site lot.

Other area beer sites: Yard House (8437 Park Meadows Center Dr., 303-790-7453). Parry's Pizza (12624 Washington Ln., Englewood, 303-790-8686).

MillerCoors

 **MillerCoors™**

13th & Ford Streets, Golden, CO 80401
(800) 642-6116 or (303) 277-BEER (2337)
www.millercoors.com

Decades before Colorado's emergence as a craft beer mecca, the state was synonymous with beer in the minds of many Americans. This was due to Golden's iconic Coors brewery, the world's largest single-site brewery and one of Colorado's most visited tourist sites, attracting 300,000 visitors a year. The massive brewery is near downtown Golden, and a twenty-minute drive from downtown Denver.

The company came into existence in 1873 when a twenty-six-year-old German immigrant Adolph Herman Joseph Coors partnered with Jacob Schueler to start a brewing business. With Coors's $2,000 investment, and Schueler's $18,000, they converted an abandoned tannery on the banks of Clear Creek into a brewery they named "The Golden Brewery." The business was so successful that in 1880, Coors bought out his partner and became sole owner. The brewery survived Prohibition by marketing a variety of non-alcoholic products including malted milk balls and near beer. In 2005, Coors merged with Canada's Molson brewing company to create Molson Coors, and in 2008, the company entered into a joint venture with SABMiller, creating MillerCoors. Today MillerCoors is the world's second-largest brewing company behind Anheuser-Busch InBev.

A visit to the Golden brewery begins with a mini-bus ride from the visitor's parking lot to the brewery's reception area. You enter the imposing complex into a large lobby where you queue up to get photographed against a blank background. At first, I thought it was some type of security measure. As it turned out, at the completion of the tour, you have an opportunity to purchase your photo with a choice of beer-themed backgrounds superimposed on the image.

You're then issued an audio device, as the tours are self-paced and self-guided. The lobby contains a few displays, dioramas, and informational signs containing historical information about the company.

Year-round beers: Batch 19, George Killian's Irish Red, Miller High Life, Blue Moon Belgian White, Miller Lite, Blue Moon Vintage Series, Henry Weinhard's Private Reserve, Milwaukee's Best, Colorado Native, Icehouse, Milwaukee's Best Ice, Coors Banquet, Keystone, Milwaukee's Best Light, Coors Light, Keystone Ice, Steel Reserve, Extra Gold, Miller Genuine Draft.

The Pick: Batch 19 is a firm-bodied pre-Prohibition lager with a hoppy punch.

One display that hit a particularly nostalgic note for me was a re-creation of an old Ford Mustang with New Jersey license plates. Its open trunk is packed with cases of Coors beer. I spent part of my college days in New Jersey and first tasted Coors when some friends returned from a western road trip with a trunkload of the legendary golden elixir. Of course, when the company expanded distribution to the eastern United States in the 1980s, any cachet Coors had soon faded.

The tour proceeds to a series of numbered stations. Some stations offer views of different sections of the brewery. Other stations are merely informational displays. The stops are accompanied by a some-what hokey narration on the audio device. One stop overlooks the world's largest brewhouse, containing eighteen copper-topped kettles, each with a capacity greater than 600 barrels, or more than 19,000 gal-lons each. You're unlikely to see any brewers in the brewhouse. The brewing operations are monitored in an adjacent high-tech control room. I was disappointed that the tour didn't include a visit to the malting area, as an in-house malting operation is rare in breweries of any size.

After a visit to the packaging area, the tour ends in the lounge, where you're offered three generous pours of beers of your choice. During my visit, choices included three of the Coors brand light lagers, two Blue Moon beers, and several more flavorful lagers produced by AC Golden, a semi-autonomous brewing entity residing within the MillerCoors facility (see page 14). Among them was a beer that was being test-marketed; Batch 19 was an interesting amber-hued pre-Prohibition lager with a hoppy punch.

MillerCoors

Opened: 1873.

Owners: MillerCoors.

Head brewer: Warren Quilliam.

Potential annual capacity: 22 million barrels.

Hours: Monday through Saturday, 10 a.m. to 4 p.m.; Sunday, noon to 4 p.m. Closed Monday and Tuesday from Labor Day to May 30.

Tours: See above.

Take-out beer: N/A.

Food: N/A.

Parking: Visitors lot at 13th & Ford Streets.

Area attractions: See Cannonball Creek Brewing Company on page 36.

Other area beer sites: See Cannonball Creek Brewing Company on page 36.

Old Mill Brewery & Grill

5798 South Rapp Street, Littleton, CO 80120
(303) 797-2433 (CHEF)
www.oldmillbrewery.com

If you live in a part of the country where grain is grown, you've probably noticed that you rarely see an old grain elevator. There's a good reason for this. Grain dust is quite flammable. Grain elevators, especially old ones, have a habit of burning down.

In the late 1800s and early 1900s, the Denver suburb of Littleton was a thriving agricultural community. In 1901 the town's founder, Richard Little, built a grain elevator on a parcel of land he had homesteaded as a storage and distribution facility for his prosperous Rough and Ready Flour Mill. The mill, which was capable of producing one hundred barrels of flour per day, marketed its flour in Denver and the mountain communities under the quaint brand names Snow Drift, White Cloud, Blue Goose, Legal Tender, and Standard Patent.

The Columbine Mill, as it was commonly called, is unique in that it survives to this day and is one of the few old grain elevators still standing on the Colorado Front Range. Beginning in the late 1970s, a succession of restaurants operated in the historic structure. Among them were two brewpubs. When the businesses departed, the brewhouse stayed behind. After sitting vacant for several years, the building was acquired by Vasilios and Kathy Frangiskakis, who revived the Littleton landmark as the Old Mill Brewery & Grill.

Littleton is located about ten miles south of downtown Denver. The brewpub sits close to Littleton's amiable downtown, which features turn-of-the-century buildings housing shops, galleries, and restaurants. The Old Mill is hard to miss, with its tall white tower looming over the surroundings. The interior has the dual personality of a nostalgic family eatery and a sports bar. Historic photos are on display along one of the rust-colored walls of the large dining room. The bar sits along the opposite wall. A neon Bud Light sign with the figure of a bronco (Vasilios is a big Denver Broncos fan) is mounted next to a flatscreen, one of several TVs distributed throughout the room. Off the dining room is a large outdoor deck facing the street. A series of chutes, once used to transport

Year-round beers: Old Mill Pilsner, Rapp Street Vienna Lager, Riverside Red, Colossus IPA, Downtown Littleton Brown, Devout Stout, Western Welcome Wheat.

grain, are still in place in a room used for private functions in the back of the building.

The brewpub is a popular lunch stop for faculty members of Arapahoe Community College, located one block away. Families arrive for early dinners. A younger crowd shows up in the evening for late-night happy hour.

The menu is long and includes familiar pub fare such as burgers, sandwiches, pasta, and some Mexican dishes. The brewpub serves breakfast on weekends. Frangiskakis, who operates the Old Mill along with his wife and son, is both head chef and brewer. The Greek-born Frangiskakis, who came to the United States in 1974 and has been in the restaurant business since he was twelve, had no brewing experience when the Old Mill opened. "I didn't know anything about beer," he said. He learned the brewing process from two brewers who worked at Old Mill early on. Eventually, he took over the beer-making operation. Though he's not a beer drinker himself, Frangiskakis has a simple philosophy of brewing. "It's like making a good soup," said the chef-brewer. "With the right ingredients, you will make good beer." He keeps seven full-time beers on tap including a pilsner, a Vienna lager, a red ale, an IPA, a brown ale, a stout, and a wheat beer.

Old Mill Brewery & Grill

Opened: April 2007.

Owners: Vasilios and Kathy Frangiskakis.

Head brewer: Vasilios Frangiskakis.

Potential annual capacity: 600 barrels.

Hours: Monday through Friday, 11 a.m. to 11 p.m.; Saturday and Sunday, 8 a.m. to midnight.

Tours: On request.

Take-out beer: Growlers.

Food: Extensive selection of American pub standards and assorted entrées.

Extras: Late-night happy hour bargains on beer and food.

Parking: On-site lot and street parking.

Area attractions: Littleton Historical Museum (6028 S. Gallup St., 303-795-3950).

Other area beer sites: Glass Half Full Taproom (7301 S. Santa Fe Drive). Jake's Brew Bar (2540 W. Main St. Littleton, 303-996-1006).

Our Mutual Friend Malt & Brew

2810 Larimer Street, Denver, CO 80205
(720) 722-2810 • www.omfmb.com

Sometimes you just want a place to hang out. A no-frills place where you can show up in a grubby T-shirt and nobody cares. A place where you can play a board game with a friend without distraction. A place where you can show up alone and make new friends. That's the type of scene you'll find at Our Mutual Friend, a low-key neighborhood brewery located in RiNo, a neighborhood northeast of downtown Denver.

Our Mutual Friend was the inspiration of Brandon Proff, Andrew Strasburg, and Bryan Leavelle—three homebrewers who met, not surprisingly, through mutual friends. The idea of opening a brewery took root during group homebrewing sessions. The idea gained momentum after the trio found an available space on Larimer Street in a former gelato shop. "We all live in this neighborhood. It was so perfect. It already had a patio, a garage door, everything. We barely had to do anything," said Proff, whose responsibilities include "everything but the accounting and the brewing." They pieced together a tiny one-barrel brew system and opened their doors in late 2012. The name Our Mutual Friend refers to beer, and its power to bring people together.

When I approached on Larimer Street, I saw no signage, but noticed the business logo—a handshake within a circle—painted on one end of the building's white-brick false façade. The interior has a sparse industrial look with concrete flooring, three gray-painted walls, and the fourth wall partially covered with attractive wooden boards painted different shades of gray. The same boards are used as facing on the rollaway six-seater bar. There's a long communal high-top in the middle of the room with other communal tables, and a few smaller ones along the perimeter. The garage door on a side wall opens to a patio containing a pair of long picnic tables. A ten-tap beer tower emerges from a kitchen-style counter along the far wall.

As I toured the brewhouse, I noticed a drum set in one corner and a guitar in another. Proff

Year-round beers: Proletariat Session Ale, Saison, Pale Ale, India Pale Ale, Brown Ale, Dry Coffee Stout.

The Pick: The Dry Coffee Stout is for coffee lovers only. The aroma is of a fresh cup of joe that carries through in the flavor. It finishes dry and roasty.

informed me that he and Leavelle, the lead brewer, were former touring musicians. Screen-printed concert posters hang on the walls of the taproom. A functioning record player sits on a desk behind the bar with a collection of LPs alongside. More LPs share shelf space with glassware, travel books, and various knick-knacks on a bookshelf that functions as the backbar. The music in the taproom is loud. There's a DJ on-site each Thursday. "I find a lot of parallels between brewing and music," Proff told me.

The brewhouse resides out of sight in the back half of the building. The original one-barrel brew system has been upgraded to a larger one. The brewery's full-time beers include a session ale, a saison, a pale ale, an IPA, a brown ale, and a coffee stout. Of these, only one has a name. Proletariat Session Ale honors "the working class of our capitalist society, the common men and women who are always welcome at OMF," according to the beer menu. A rotating seasonal beer is also available.

The brewery was built and continues to operate with a hands-on, do-it-yourself approach. In an effort to control as many variables as possible, Our Mutual Friend doesn't purchase roasted specialty grains. Rather, it purchases commercial pale malts and does its own roasting and toasting. There are future plans to launch an in-house malting operation, an ambitious and seldom-seen practice in breweries of any size. "We find that we really like our beers when they're brewed using grain that is freshly malted and freshly roasted," Proff explained. "In our wildest dreams, we'd love to have land and grow hops and all the things we need to make our beer."

Our Mutual Friend Malt & Brew

Opened: December 2012.
Owners: Brandon Proff, Andrew Strasburg, and Bryan Leavelle.
Head brewer: Bryan Leavelle.
Potential annual capacity: 700 barrels.
Hours: Sunday through Thursday, 2 p.m. to 10 p.m.; Friday and Saturday, 2 p.m. to midnight.
Tours: On request.
Take-out beer: Growlers and occasionally bombers.
Food: Food trucks regularly or bring your own food.
Extras: Monday Beer & Yoga. Wednesday Running Club. DJ on Thursday.
Parking: On-street, free.

Pints Pub Brewery and Freehouse

221 West 13th Avenue, Denver, CO 80204
(303) 534-7543 • www.pintspub.com

From Denver's Civic Center Park, walk a block south on Bannock. Turn right on 13th Avenue and enter the unusual brick building with the red phone booth in front. You'll find yourself somewhere in England. At least, you'll think you're in England. You'll actually be in Pints Pub, a brewpub with a decidedly English flavor.

Pints Pub was the creation of Scott Diamond, a self-confessed Anglophile. He opened Pints two decades ago because he felt Denver lacked a proper gathering spot like those commonly found across the pond. He saw the city's watering holes as either too fancy or too sketchy. He created Pints to give Denverites a taste of British pub culture. Pints opened in 1993 and the British-themed brewpub has been a fixture in Denver's Golden Triangle neighborhood ever since.

In addition to the red phone booth out front, Pints is easily recognizable by the pair of Union Jacks fluttering above the sidewalk. Outdoor dining is available on the front porch. The two-story interior is divided into a series of dining areas, creating a cozy atmosphere. Dark wood and wainscoting contribute to the British pub feel. The small brewhouse is visible through a tall window in the bar area.

There's a dartboard as well as bar billiards, an obscure pool-like game. The *London Times* is available for perusal. Music comes from an iPod containing four thousand hand-selected recordings that are of British origin or are British-themed. They range from medieval chants to Led Zeppelin to Monty Python to speeches by Winston Churchill.

The kitchen creates mostly traditional pub fare with some deviations. You can get bangers and mash, a ploughman's platter, and a sheepherder's stew. You can also get a pile of chicken wings. Burgers are called Wimpys. The Pints version of fish-and-chips replaces the standard batter-fried

Year-round beers: Czechmate Pilsner, Bitchcraft Blonde Ale, Phonebox Red Ale, Gael Force Scottish Ale, Alchemy ESB, Idyllweiss Wheat, Lancer IPA, Dark Star Olde Ale, Airedale Pale Ale, John Bull Brown Ale, Black Ajax Stout.

The Pick: Dark Star, a Yorkshire-style olde ale, is cask-conditioned and served at cellar temperature from a hand pump. The dark ale derives its unique character from English hops, roasted grains, and treacle sugar.

cod or halibut with a piece of broiled salmon. "Britannia waives the rules," according to the menu.

Two years after opening, Diamond added a small brewing system pieced together from used dairy equipment. From the start, Pints set itself apart from other small breweries that were popping up at the time by creating British-style cask-conditioned ales.

"At that time, no one knew what cask ale was. I don't think there were twenty places in the U.S. at that time making cask ale," said Diamond. Part of the challenge early on was to educate his patrons about the virtues of traditional cask-conditioned ale.

"We try not to say 'warm, flat beer.' We say 'less carbonated.' 'Cellar temperature.' 'Live yeast.' 'Bolder, deeper, more profound flavor,'" Diamond explained. There are always two cask ales available: an English IPA and a Yorkshire-style olde ale. The remainder of the eleven house beers are mostly British styles, with two exceptions. The Czechmate Pilsner is a Bohemian-style pilsner. The Idyllweiss Wheat is a German-style hefeweizen. In addition to the house beers, imported cider is also available.

Pints' most impressive claim to fame is its extraordinary collection of single-malt Scotch, which Diamond purports to be the largest outside of Britain. Inverted bottles are mounted row after row above and behind the bar. Some are quite rare, and will set you back close to $900 a pour.

Painted on a ceiling beam is the quote that reads, "Malt does more than Milton can to justify God's ways to man." "If I was naming this place today, I'd probably just call it Malt," said Diamond.

Pints Pub Brewery and Freehouse

Opened: October 1993.

Owner: Scott Diamond.

Head brewers: Scott Diamond and Tom Barker.

Potential annual capacity: 600 barrels.

Hours: Open daily at 11 a.m.

Tours: Not offered.

Take-out beer: Growlers.

Food: Traditional British pub fare, burgers, and sandwiches.

Parking: Small lot across the street. Also on-street metered parking and nearby lots.

Prost Brewing Company

2540 19th Street, Denver, CO 80211
(303) 729-1175 • www.prostbrewing.com

Of the scores of new brewing businesses that have opened in Colorado in recent years, the majority are modest-sized operations producing American, English, and Belgian-inspired ales. When Prost Brewing Company opened in the summer of 2012, it broke the mold with a huge 50-barrel brewhouse and a singular focus on authentic German-style beers.

Prost is a dream fulfilled for Bill Eye, a Colorado craft beer veteran and instigator of the ambitious venture. Eye began his professional brewing exploits with an apprenticeship at Denver's now-defunct Tabernash Brewing Company. When it opened in the early 1990s, the brewery distinguished itself by producing high-quality, German-style beers when nearly all American craft breweries were producing English-style ales. After the closure of Tabernash, Eye moved on to the C.B. & Potts brewpub chain, where he worked for thirteen years. This was followed by a two-year stint as head brewer at Dry Dock Brewing Company. During his tenure at Dry Dock, the brewery received the prestigious Small Brewery of the Year award at the 2009 Great American Beer Festival.

Ashleigh Carter was also working at Dry Dock at the time. The Colorado native had been a collegiate soccer coach in the Midwest before deciding to switch to a career in brewing and return to her home state. Carter, who shares the brewing duties at Prost with Eye, is among a growing number of females working in brewhouses across the state.

Procuring a brewing system for the upstart brewery was no easy task. Eye got wind of a fifty-year-old, all-copper system for sale in a small German town near Bamberg. After traveling to Germany and finding the system to be both operational and "stunningly beautiful," he purchased it. Getting it to Denver was a long, laborious endeavor. "The Germans don't build anything like Americans," Eye related. "They make everything out of concrete and cinder blocks." Extensive jackhammering was required to disassemble the brewing vessels. "It took a couple of months to get it out of the building in Germany and on a boat across the ocean. It got here about two months after that and it took us about six

Year-round beers: Altfränkisches Dunkel Bier, Weißbier, Prost Pils.

The Pick: Altfränkisches Dunkel Bier, a dark lager, hits all the notes that a German lager should. It has a clean-tasting malt character and can be consumed in some quantity without palate fatigue or severe impairment.

months to get it back together," Eye recalled. The effort was worthwhile. "I enjoy making beer on this thing. It's very manual, it's very beautiful, and they don't make them like that anymore."

Prost produces three full-time beers and rotating seasonals. The regulars include a crisp pilsner, a refreshing Hefeweizen, and a smooth, malty dunkel. These are augmented with traditional seasonals such as a bock or dopplebock, a Kolsch, an altbier, and a Märzen.

Prost beers are notable for their approachability, clean flavors, and restrained alcohol content, all of which reflect Eye's Germanic attitude toward beer consumption. "I think beer is something to be drunk in quantity," said Eye. "For me, a perfectly made pilsner or a really well-made weissbier is the kind of beer I can sit down and drink four of with a friend and not get up from the table legless."

The brewery's large tasting room is modeled after a German beer hall. Long communal tables invite socializing. Banners, flags, and posters were purchased from a collector who had a sizeable collection of German beer paraphernalia from the fifties, sixties, and seventies. Crowds gather in the outdoor beer garden during Denver's copious mild sunny days.

There are no plans to expand beyond the confines of the current space, which is located just off Interstate 25 across the 20th Street Bridge from Coors Field and Lower Downtown. "The German brewmaster says you should be able to see all of your customers from the roof of your brewery," Eye explained. "That's what we're going to try to do."

Note: Shortly before publication, Eye and Carter relinquished their brewing positions at Prost. The new head brewer is Larry Leinhart, who arrived at Prost after twenty-six years at Anheuser-Busch.

Prost Brewing Company

Opened: August 2012.

Owners: Bill Eye, Kevin Sheesley, Troy Johnston, Barry Van Everen, Steve DeLine, Ken DeLine.

Brewer: Larry Leinhart.

Potential annual capacity: 10,000 barrels.

Hours: Monday through Thursday, noon to 10-ish; Friday and Saturday, noon to midnight; Sunday, noon to 8-ish.

Tours: On request.

Take-out beer: Growlers and kegs.

Food: Bavarian pretzels. Food trucks every day except Monday or bring your own food.

Extras: Live music on Wednesday. German-themed events throughout the year. AHA member deals program participant.

Parking: On-site lot.

Renegade Brewing Company

925 West 9th Avenue, Denver, CO 80204
(720) 401-4089 • www.renegadebrewing.com

Renegade Brewing Company may have been born of a rebellious outlaw spirit, but the only time you'll see malcontents at this lively neighborhood gathering spot today is when a tap runs dry.

The brewery sprang to life in 2011 through the efforts of Brian O'Connell and his wife, Khara. Brian was a homebrewer working as a researcher and statistician at the University of Colorado in Denver when he decided he'd rather be crushing grain than crunching numbers. "I just decided that beer was my passion and numbers were not," said O'Connell.

Renegade resides in Denver's Arts District on Santa Fe, a short jaunt south of downtown. The area is notable as the home of Colorado's largest concentration of art galleries. Beer is not the first beverage integral to Renegade's West 9th Avenue abode. The building was constructed in 1910 as a bottling plant for Dr Pepper and Orange Crush, a purpose it served for three decades. By the time it was acquired to be the home of Renegade, it had been vacant for five or six years.

"The reason that I chose this building was because of its character," O'Connell explained. "It has a barrel roof, original wood, exposed brick walls, and bare concrete floors. All of those elements I wanted to keep and really accentuate."

From the outside, Renegede presents an inviting image, with a sandstone-colored stucco exterior and plenty of glass. The taproom is equally appealing. Older elements, such as the weathered brick walls and the original wood ceiling, provide a pleasing contrast to more modern accoutrements that include a gorgeous multicolored wooden bar atop a base of silver corrugated metal.

People from all walks of life congregate at the community meeting place. "It's a very diverse neighborhood," O'Connell said of his largely local customer base. "It brings people [in] who are very open-minded and looking to try new things and to mingle with all different types of people. We're

Year-round beers: Elevation Triple IPA, Redacted Rye IPA, 5:00 Afternoon Ale, Hammer and Sickle Russian Imperial Stout.

The Pick: "Offensively delicious" is the Renegade slogan, and a just description of the intensely flavored Elevation Triple IPA. At over 11 percent ABV, it coats your palate with layers of malt while simultaneously delivering a big blast of hops.

here for people to engage in conversation." A pint or two of fresh Renegade beer provides a proper stimulus for elevated discourse.

Production of the house beers falls under the jurisdiction of Ali Benetka, Renegade's head brewer. The twenty-something Benetka had thoughts of going to med school, but when she discovered homebrewing and microbiology, her career goals quickly shifted. The native Denverite attended Loyola University in Illinois, worked a stint at a Chicago brewery, and studied brewing at Chicago's Siebel Institute. After returning to Colorado, she landed a job as Renegade's assistant brewer. When the head brewer departed, Benetka took over the position she refers to as "Chairlady of the Brew." Benetka joins Golden City's Sarah Henderson as the only two female head brewers in the state.

With a few exceptions, Renegade beers have little to do with subtlety. The brewery labels its beers as "offensively delicious," and delivers on that slogan with the majority of the lineup being assertively flavored, high-gravity creations.

A popular offering is the flagship Redacted IPA, a tangy, hoppy ale with a substantial infusion of rye malt. "That was a beer that I developed in my backyard as a homebrewer and spent I don't know how much time tweaking the recipe trying to come up with an IPA that was unique and different," O'Connell recalled. A few notches up the intensity ladder is the Elevation IPA. Labeled a triple IPA, this 11 percent ABV sipper is surprisingly smooth for a devilishly potent elixir. Hammer and Sickle, a 9 percent ABV Russian Imperial Stout, was a bronze medal winner at the 2013 GABF.

On the opposite end of the intensity scale is 5:00 Afternoon Ale. Compared to the type A personalities of its renegade brethren, this easy-drinking golden ale is the family's well-behaved mild child.

Renegade Brewing Company

Opened: June 2011.

Owners: Brian and Khara O'Connell.

Head brewer: Ali Benetka.

Potential annual capacity: 3,000 barrels.

Hours: Monday through Thursday, 3 p.m. to 10 p.m.; Friday and Saturday, 2 p.m. to 10 p.m.; Sunday, 1 p.m. to 8 p.m.

Tours: On request.

Take-out beer: Growlers and cans.

Food: Food trucks most days.

Extras: AHA member deals program participant. Social deals member participant.

Parking: Free on-street parking.

River North Brewery

2401 Blake Street, No. 1, Denver, CO 80205
(303) 296-2617 • www.rivernorthbrewery.com

In case you weren't aware, the Heisenberg Uncertainty Principle states that the better you know the position of a particle, the less you know the momentum, and vice versa. If pondering this makes your head hurt, you should position yourself in front of a glass of Hoppenberg Uncertainty Principle Belgian-Style Double IPA, one of the unique formulations created by ex-aerospace engineer Matt Hess of Denver's River North Brewery.

Hess was a homebrew hobbyist and space scientist working on the Orion manned spacecraft project. The ups and downs of the aerospace industry left him craving a less turbulent existence. "I decided to take a leap and do something a little crazier," he said of his decision to leave his engineering job in early 2011 and focus on a high-flying new endeavor, a craft brewery. He and his wife, Jessica, opened River North in early 2012.

The River North Brewery, named for the River North Art District, or RiNo, is located on Blake Street, north of downtown Denver and a few blocks from Coors Field. The former warehouse district is in the midst of a major redevelopment. Former industrial structures are being converted into studios, galleries, and offices for artists, architects, designers, photographers, and other creative professionals. Several new breweries have sprung up in the neighborhood in recent years, including River North.

The brewery location is a familiar one to local veteran beer enthusiasts, as it was the former home of the Flying Dog Brewery before that business relocated to the East Coast. The space had been vacant for several years, and the brewing equipment removed, but the remaining infrastructure, including floor drains and gas lines, simplified the process of setting up a new brewery.

The taproom is of modest proportions. Dark gray surfaces contrast with the blond wood construction of the U-shaped bar, tables, and seating

Year-round beers: River North White, BPR Belgian-Style Pale Red Ale, J. Marie Saison, Hello Darkness Black IPA, Hoppenberg Uncertainty Principle Belgian-Style Double IPA.

The Pick: J. Marie Saison is surprisingly drinkable for a 7.5 percent ABV ale. It begins with a subtle sweetness before its complex fruity, spicy character emerges.

to create a smart modern-industrial look that seems in harmony with the neighborhood's ongoing revitalization. A garage-style door opens to Blake Street. Along the back wall of the taproom, a series of tall windows looks into the expansive brewery that occupies most of the building's interior.

Neighbors and local craft beer fans have taken to River North's vibrant taproom and to the lineup of robust-flavored Belgian and hybrid beers. "My goal was just to brew beer that I wanted to brew," Hess explained. "If you come in here, you won't find a traditional lineup. You're not going to find a pale ale and a porter and a brown ale. We almost exclusively do Belgian-style beers, Belgian-American hybrid beers, and whatever else we feel like brewing. We like to brew interesting beers. Hopefully, everybody else thinks they're interesting as well."

The atypical list of full-time offerings includes several familiar Belgian styles including a white ale and a saison. Hopheads can indulge in a black IPA, a well-hopped Belgian pale ale, and a Belgian-style double IPA. Rotating specialty beers tend toward high-gravity offerings that have included a Belgian quadruple, an oaked imperial wit, and a Belgian-style imperial stout.

The brewery has amassed a collection of wine and whiskey barrels used to age some of the full-time beers as well as specialty beers, resulting in brews of unique character and multi-layered complexity. Some appear on draught in the taproom, while others are only available in bottles.

River North Brewery

Opened: February 2012.

Owners: Matt and Jessica Hess.

Head brewer: Matt Hess.

Potential annual capacity: 800 barrels.

Hours: Monday through Thursday, 3 p.m. to 9 p.m.; Friday, 3 p.m. to 10 p.m.; Saturday, 1 p.m. to 10 p.m.; Sunday, 1 p.m. to 7 p.m.; and one hour before all Rockies home games.

Tours: On request.

Take-out beer: Growlers and bombers.

Food: Food trucks on weekends or bring your own food. Local restaurant menus available.

Extras: Wayward Wednesdays experimental beer releases. AHA member deals participant.

Parking: Free two-hour parking in front of the brewery. Also metered street parking and nearby lots.

Rock Bottom

Four locations

Rock Bottom is now a nationwide chain, but it has its roots in Boulder. In the spring of 1990, a local restaurateur named Frank Day teamed up with brewer Mark Youngquist (see Dolores River Brewery on page 276) to open the Walnut Brewery, one of the first brewpubs in Colorado. Day was no stranger to the beer world, having founded the Old Chicago chain of taphouses in Boulder in 1976.

When the brewpub concept appeared to have legs, a second brewpub was opened in Denver in the fall of 1991. It was located in the bottom of what at the time was called the Prudential Plaza. Prudential's marketing scheme at the time included the catchy slogan "own a piece of the rock," so the name Rock Bottom was given to the new restaurant-brewery. In the mid- to late 1990s, the independent Colorado-based company opened Rock Bottom restaurants from coast to coast at a rate of four or five per year.

In 2010, Rock Bottom merged with national brewpub chain Gordon Biersch. The two companies, along with Old Chicago, the Walnut Brewery, and several Chophouse restaurants, now operate under a parent company called Craftworks.

The food menu is standardized throughout the various locations. The extensive menu, designed to appeal to diverse preferences, includes a wide range of pub standards including snacks, sandwiches, burgers, fish-and-chips, pizza, and steaks. Numerous southwestern dishes are available.

Originally, the Rock Bottom brewpubs had a similar spectrum of beer styles; however, individual brewers were free to interpret the styles with their own homegrown recipes. Each location would also have several rotating specialty beers to supplement the core offerings. After the merger, it was decided to standardize the recipes for the core beers produced at the different locations. The standard beers became a Kolsch, a white ale, a red ale, an IPA, and a rotating black beer that can vary from place to place. In addition to the standard beers, each location

Year-round beers: Kolsch, White Ale, Red Ale, India Pale Ale, and a specialty dark beer.

The Pick: To get a taste of the brewer's individuality and creativity, select a specialty beer that sounds appealing.

also offers a collection of seasonal and specialty beers that can equal or exceed the number of core beers on tap. Many of these seasonals are the inspiration and creation of the local brewers, giving the brewers a chance to show off their skills and express their individual style preferences. These beers have covered a near-limitless range of styles from lagers to Belgian-style ales to barrel-aged fermentations.

"We're not interested in becoming complacent in any way within the beer market," said Kevin Reed, who joined the Rock Bottom family in 1993 as a brewer at the Walnut Brewery. Reed now holds the title of Director of Brewing Operations for the thirty-three Rock Bottom and Chophouse locations across the country. "If we want to continue to grow better beer drinkers, we need to offer them their next step at all times. Otherwise, they might leave us," he explained.

Rock Bottom beers have been awarded numerous medals from prestigious competitions over the years. Brewers from some of the most respected breweries in the U.S. honed their craft in Rock Bottom brewhouses. Many former drinkers of mass-produced American light lagers were introduced to more flavorful and interesting craft beers in Rock Bottom brewpubs.

Rock Bottom operates six restaurants in Colorado, all on the Front Range. Four are in the Denver metro area and are profiled below. There's a location in Loveland (see page 177), and another in Colorado Springs (see page 215).

Denver

1001 16th Street, Suite 100, Denver, CO 80265
(303) 534-7616 • www.rockbottom.com/locations/denver-downtown

Rock Bottom's downtown Denver location is the oldest Rock Bottom Restaurant in the country and is unique among the half-dozen outlets in Colorado. While its siblings are situated in suburban shopping and entertainment complexes, the Denver facility is in the heart of the city, on the high-traffic 16th Street walking mall.

Given its urban environs, the brewpub attracts a broad cross section of patrons, and emanates a more upbeat, vibrant atmosphere than you'll encounter in the suburban mall locations. Beer explorers will also discover a larger selection of beers, especially specialty beers, than is available in the 'burbs. The brewpub also bottles some of its beer in bombers, which can be purchased to go.

The restaurant is huge, with a half-dozen separate eating and drinking spaces, including a sprawling outdoor patio affording great people-watching along the 16th Street Mall. The brewhouse resides within a glassed-in island near the front of the building, across from the main bar. A large chalkboard mounted on the wall lists the names and detailed specifications of the many house beers. A second bar in the back of the building contains several pool tables and a photo booth.

Longtime head brewer John McClure began his brewing career at Boulder's Walnut Brewery in 1997. When he moved to the Denver brewpub two years later, he discovered that the volume of beer being quaffed in downtown Denver in a week equaled what was consumed at the Walnut in a month. He also discovered that the logistics of brewing in the city presented certain unfamiliar challenges: in order to access the downstairs grain mill, he has to leave the restaurant and go through a parking garage.

It's not unusual to find fifteen beers on tap, many of which are specialty beers brewed only at this facility. McClure has a collection of oak barrels that numbered sixteen when I visited. He makes a raspberry porter specifically intended for aging in a whiskey barrel. Among the interesting specialty beers I sampled was the Gnome Baltic Porter, a 2012 World Beer Cup gold medal winner.

McClure takes a practical approach to brewing specialty and experimental beers. "I want to sell the beer," he explained. "I don't want to get stuck with it. I think some of my experimentations are a little conservative. I want to sell something that people are going to enjoy several pints of versus just one."

Rock Bottom—Denver location

Opened: November 1991

Owners: CraftWorks Restaurants and Breweries.

Head brewer: John McClure.

Potential annual capacity: 5,000 barrels.

Hours: Daily, 11 a.m. to 2 a.m.

Tours: On request.

Take-out beer: Growlers, bombers, and kegs.

Food: Broad selection of pub favorites and diverse entrées.

Extras: Live music on the patio on Fridays in the summer. AHA member discount program participant.

Parking: Validated parking in lot below restaurant. Nearby metered street parking and lots.

Orchard Parkway

14694 Orchard Parkway, Suite 400, Westminster, CO 80023
(303) 255-1625
www.rockbottom.com/locations/westminster-orchard-town-center

The Rock Bottom Brewery in the Orchard Town Center is typical of the newer Rock Bottom restaurants along the Colorado Front Range: The location is in a sprawling suburban shopping mall. The interior has a polished, upscale appearance with a large, centrally placed island-style bar dividing the dining area from the livelier, sports bar–themed bar area. The Orchard Town Center, the modern pedestrian shopping mall where the brewpub resides, is located just west of Interstate 25, about seventeen miles from downtown Denver.

Greg Matthews runs the brewhouse at the Orchard facility. Matthews discovered good beer while completing his college studies with a semester in Berlin. After returning to his home state of Texas, and unable to find beers of the quality to which he had become accustomed, he began homebrewing. He was working as the general manager of a California hotel when he decided to pursue a professional brewing career.

He attended the American Brewers Guild and apprenticed at San Diego's Alesmith brewery. His first paying brewery job was at the Rock Bottom brewery in La Jolla. "That's really where I learned how to put together an IPA," he explained of his West Coast brewing experience. "There are a lot of tricks to it."

His next stop was at a Rock Bottom location in the Chicago area, where he learned the ins and outs of barrel-aging, a skill he puts to use in his current position. When the new Orchard Parkway brewpub opened in 2008, Matthews, an avid skier, happily moved to Colorado to assume the head brewing job. He's especially fond of the brewhouse that was installed in the new brewery. "This is a Ferrari. If you don't know what you're doing in here, you're going to end up off the road," he said of the finicky yet versatile brewing system.

Matthews generally keeps a half-dozen specialty beers on tap. His West Coast-style IPAs are especially well-received, although his personal preference is for flavorful low-gravity beers. "I like the styles that people overlook," said Matthews. "I love a good British mild."

Rock Bottom—Orchard Parkway location

Opened: March 2008.
Owners: Craftworks Restaurants & Breweries.

Head brewer: Greg Matthews.

Potential annual capacity: 2,000 barrels.

Hours: Sunday through Thursday, 11 a.m. to 11 p.m.; Friday and Saturday, 11 a.m. to midnight.

Tours: On request.

Take-out beer: Growlers and kegs.

Food: Broad selection of pub favorites and diverse entrées.

Extras: AHA member deals program participant.

Parking: On-site lots.

Other area beer sites: Cheeky Monk Belgian Beer Café is in the same building as Rock Bottom.

South Denver

9627 East County Line Road, Centennial, CO 80112
(303) 792-9090
www.rockbottom.com/locations/south-denver-park-meadows-mall

The South Denver Rock Bottom resides in a shopping complex in Centennial, eighteen miles south of downtown Denver alongside Interstate 25. Across the parking lot is Denver's IKEA store. As one of the older members of the brewpub chain—it opened in 1997—this Rock Bottom has a somewhat different look and feel than some of its younger siblings on the Front Range.

The standalone building has an attractive, partially covered beer garden along two sides. The main room is divided down the middle with the bar area on one side and the elevated dining area on the other. The long wooden bar runs along one side of the room facing a row of serving tanks partially visible through windows behind the bar. The brewhouse is on the second level. There's a large function room in the back with a second bar and a pool table. The overall feel is more casual than at the newer Rock Bottom restaurants.

Brewer Jason Leeman has come full circle at the South Denver brewpub. He started his Rock Bottom career here as a server in 2002, and then worked as an assistant brewer for a few years. When the chain opened a Colorado Springs restaurant in 2005, he transferred to that location and was head brewer for seven years. When the head brewer position opened up in South Denver, he returned to the brewpub where he had launched his career.

Leeman keeps beer flowing from a dozen taps and two casks. These include the four standard Rock Bottom house beers and a variety of seasonal and specialties including the "Zombeer Apocalypse" series, which Leeman described as "old recipes that I bring back from the dead." These were beers that were discontinued when Rock Bottom went to a standard lineup of core beers. Leeman's preference for seasonally appropriate beers results in lighter offerings in the warm-weather months and heartier beers when it's cool. He's also responsive to input from a solid core of regulars, some of whom have been visiting the brewpub for a decade or more.

Rock Bottom—South Denver location

Opened: 1997.

Owners: Craftworks Restaurants & Breweries.

Head brewer: Jason Leeman.

Potential annual capacity: 1,000 barrels.

Hours: Sunday through Thursday, 11 a.m. to 11 p.m.; Friday and Saturday, 11 a.m. to midnight.

Tours: By reservation.

Take-out beer: Growlers and kegs.

Food: Broad selection of pub favorites and diverse entrées.

Extras: AHA member deals program participant.

Parking: On-site lot.

Area attractions: Park Meadows Mall.

Other area beer sites: Yard House (8437 Park Meadows Center Dr., 303-790-7453). Parry's Pizza (12624 Washington Ln., Englewood, 303-790-8686).

Westminster Promenade

10633 Westminster Boulevard, Suite 900, Westminster, CO 80020
(720) 566-0198 • www.rockbottom.com/locations/westminster-promenade

The older of two Westminster Rock Bottoms resides within the Westminster Promenade, an entertainment and dining complex containing a movie theater, comedy club, bowling alley, and ice rink. Across the street is the Butterfly Pavilion, a fascinating insect zoo. The brewpub is located along the Denver-Boulder Turnpike, roughly midway between downtown Denver and downtown Boulder, each about fifteen miles away.

The facility dates from 2000, and has a somewhat different layout then the newer, more standardized Rock Bottom locations elsewhere along the Front Range. The facility lacks the large, centralized island bar found in most of the locations. A long bar faces the glass-enclosed brewhouse along one wall. There's a second bar in an elevated lounge-like section in the back. Two rows of tables sit in an airy sunroom that looks out onto an outdoor patio.

The head brewer is Ryan Piec, a transplanted Chicagoan and Siebel Institute graduate. His first brewery job was a packaging position at Longmont's Left Hand Brewing. He became the assistant brewer at Westminster Promenade in early 2012. When the head brewer departed in June 2013 to start an independent brewing venture, Piec stepped into the position.

A unique feature of this particular Rock Bottom facility is its over-sized brewing capacity. The extra capacity is used to supply beer to nonbrewing Rock Bottom outlets at Denver International Airport, Minneapolis—St. Paul International Airport, and a restaurant in Omaha, Nebraska.

Piec has a fondness for brewing what he calls Old World styles. "I like traditional, classic beer styles," he explained. "I like to try to hit them in a very balanced way." Belgian-style ales make frequent appearances in the brewpub. In addition to the regular Rock Bottom IPA, Piec keeps a second, rotating IPA on tap. It's generally the best-selling beer in the house.

Rock Bottom—Westminster Promenade location

Opened: November 2000.

Owners: Craftworks Restaurants and Breweries.

Head brewer: Ryan Piec.

Potential annual capacity: 2,500 barrels.

Hours: Sunday through Thursday, 11 a.m. to midnight; Friday and Saturday, 11 a.m. to 1 a.m.

Tours: Wednesday, 5 p.m. to 7 p.m. or by reservation.

Take-out beer: Growlers and kegs.

Food: Broad selection of pub favorites and diverse entrées.

Extras: AHA member deals participant.

Parking: Large on-site lot in shopping and entertainment complex.

Area attractions: Butterfly Pavilion (6252 W. 104th Ave., 303-469-5441). 1st Bank Event Center (11450 Broomfield Lane, Broomfield, 303-410-0700).

Other area beer sites: Bar Louie (Westminster Promenade, 720-214-3300). BJ's Restaurant & Brewery (10446 Town Center Dr., Westminster, 303-389-6444).

Strange Craft Beer Company

1330 Zuni Street, Unit M, Denver, CO 80204
(720) 985-2337 • www.strangebrewingco.com

There's an old saying that goes, "when life gives you lemons, make beer," or something like that. Workmates and homebrewing partners John Fletcher and Tim Myers were certainly soured by their seventy-hour workweeks at their IT jobs at the *Rocky Mountain News*. When the newspaper folded in 2009, they put their bitterness aside and seized the opportunity to make a fresh start producing fresh beer.

The idea of opening a commercial brewery had been simmering for several years, beginning when the homebrewing duo acquired a 20-gallon brewing system they found on Craigslist. With the possibility of someday going pro, they used it to tweak their homespun recipes. In 2010, after a combined twenty-six years with their former employer, they abandoned the high-paying world of high-tech, cashed in their retirement savings, and opened a brewery under the name Strange Brewing Company.

According to Myers, there are two versions as to the origin of the name Strange Brewing. In one version, the name is borrowed from *Strange Brew*, the movie featuring the amiable beer-swilling Canadians Bob and Doug McKenzie. In the second version, the name comes from being fans of guitarist Eric Clapton, who performed the song "Strange Brew" with the group Cream in 1967.

"We always jokingly say whoever sues us first, it was the other story," said Myers. In a strange twist of fate, the brewery was forced to change its name to Strange Craft Beer Company after legal action over naming rights was brought on by an East Coast homebrew supply shop.

The brewery resides in a nondescript, one-story structure of mixed businesses that sits alongside Interstate 25 in an industrial area just south of Sports Authority Field at Mile High, home of the Denver Broncos. The interior is divided into adjacent rooms with table seating of varying configurations. At the far end, a wooden bar that

Year-round beers: Strange Pale Ale, IPAphany IPA, 1000 Barrels Imperial IPA, ZORA Rosemary Pale, Le Bruit Du Diable Farmhouse Ale, Juliette Belgian Pale Ale, Cherry Bomb Belgian Stout, Cherry Kriek, Powerhouse Porter, Gluten Free Pale.

The Pick: The Cherry Kriek has a massive presence of pie cherries and a slight tartness that'll keep you coming back for more.

seats a half-dozen is adorned with real hop vines encased in see-through laminate. The brewhouse resides beyond the bar. Outdoor seating is available at communal picnic tables behind the building, with the tracks of a recently completed light rail expansion close by behind a chain link fence.

As the nearest brewery to the football stadium, Strange has had a unique opportunity to expose devotees of light American lager to the pleasures of craft beer. It's not unusual for football fans to stop by thinking they are visiting a bar, only to discover they're in a microbrewery. "Their first instinct is to run away," said Myers. "I force them to sit down and taste our Belgian wit or our Belgian farmhouse. They usually end up leaving with a growler. We've got quite a few now that are regulars that we've converted to craft beer."

At any given time you'll likely find American pale ales, IPAs, and double IPAs on tap alongside Belgian farmhouse ales, English ales, and an occasional German lager. An intensely fruity cherry kriek has a devout following. Dr. Strangelove Barleywine was a medal winner at the 2012 Great American Beer Festival. Strange also brews a gluten-free beer.

"Three months after we opened, my wife found out she was gluten-intolerant," Myers explained. "Free beer for life just went out the window. I started working on a gluten-free recipe. All the ones I was making were horrible." Help arrived when homebrewer Mike Plungis showed up in the taproom one day with a tasty homebrewed gluten-free beer. He shared the recipe, and after some tweaking, Strange began to offer it in the taproom. The lemony gluten-free pale ale was awarded a gold medal at the 2011 GABF.

Strange Craft Beer Company

Opened: May 2010.

Owners: Tim Myers and John Fletcher.

Head brewer: Tim Myers.

Potential annual capacity: 700 barrels.

Hours: Monday through Thursday, 3 p.m. to 8 p.m.; Friday and Saturday, noon to 9 p.m.; Sunday, 1 p.m. to 6 p.m.

Tours: On request.

Take-out beer: Growlers.

Food: Food trucks daily, pizza delivery available, or bring your own food.

Extras: One-Barrel Wednesday experimental brews. Occasional live music. AHA member deals program participant.

Parking: On-site lot.

Trve Brewing Company

TRVE
BREWING COMPANY

227 Broadway, No. 101, Denver, CO 80203
(303) 351-1021 • www.trvebrewing.com

If you were to be blindfolded and led through the entrance of Trve Brewing Company, you'd know immediately which brewery you were in. The giveaway? The pounding drum beat and pulsating bass line of the heavy metal music permeating the taproom of this unique and atmospheric Denver brewery.

If Slayer, Red Fang, Nazareth, and Yob are not on your top-ten list of favorite bands, put your preferences aside for a while and enjoy a taste of counterculture, along with a highly respectable pint or two, in Colorado's first heavy metal-themed craft brewery.

Trve is the creation of Nick Nunns, who was inspired to open a brewery to fill a creative void he experienced while working as an engineer. The idea of a metal-themed brewery came naturally. "I've been listening to metal since I was fifteen," Nunns explained. "Pretty much half of my entire life at this point."

His search for a location that would fit his concept led him to Denver's Baker neighborhood. "It's got the weirdos. It's got more of a punk rock, hipster, metalhead thing going on here," he said. He found a spot on busy Broadway, amid the neighborhood's independent shops, nightspots, galleries, and bars.

The brewery occupies a long, narrow space. By the entrance, a garage-style door opens to the sidewalk. An extraordinary communal picnic table, constructed of contiguous thirty-foot-long boards, occupies the front of the room. A lengthy wooden bar sits beyond. Past that is the open brewhouse.

The color scheme is gray and black, or as Nunns described it, "black, lighter black, and even lighter black." Along one wall is a collection of striking black-and-white photographs of abandoned rural homes in a state of decay. If it sounds a bit gloomy, or even foreboding, relax. Although the metal theme is done without irony, Nunns keeps a sense of humor about it.

Year-round beers: Wanderlust Belgo-American Pale Ale, Hellion Table Beer, Tunnel of Trees IPA, Death Ripper Session Ale, Stout O))).

The Pick: Ignore the style geeks who say that IPAs have to be bracingly bitter, and enjoy a Tunnel of Trees IPA. The aroma is a pine forest of hops leading to juicy hop flavors intermingled with a sweet malt base. The finish is gently bitter and balanced.

The name Trve (pronounced "True") "is an inside joke with the heavy metal crowd," Nunns explained. "The short story is it's making fun of people who take it [metal] a little too seriously. There's an overlap of people within metal and people within beer who both take themselves a little too seriously."

And besides, the beers are really good. "Most of our beers are taking a standard style and then maybe tweaking one thing about it so that it doesn't fit within that style anymore," said the owner-brewer. A good example is Hellion, described as an American table beer. It's suggestive of an English bitter, but is brewed with oats and American hops. At under 5 percent ABV, it won't end your evening too early. Another low-alcohol offering is Prehistoric Dog, based loosely on the obscure German gose style. The American wheat ale is flavored with Hawaiian black lava salt and coriander. "It wasn't my intention from the outset to do a lot of session beers, but now we're earning a reputation for being a good session brewery," said Nunns.

Most of the other beers are interpretations of Belgian and hoppy American styles. One exception is Death Ripper, a dark session ale of no definable style, brewed with corn and rye. All Trve beers have names derived from metal music. Death Ripper is the name of a song by a local band named Speedwolf. "They actually came out and brewed it with us," said Nunns.

One surprise aspect of Trve is the entirely average-looking crowd that frequents the taproom. When I visited on a Friday night, the majority of the tattoos, piercings, leather clothing, and chains were those adorning the staff. "We get all types. Just because we're a metal brewery doesn't mean you're not going to have a good time here if you don't like metal," said Nunns. I can vouch for that.

Trve Brewing Company

Opened: June 2012.

Owner and head brewer: Nick Nunns.

Potential annual capacity: 500 barrels.

Hours: Tuesday through Thursday, 4 p.m. to 11 p.m.; Friday and Saturday, 2 p.m. to midnight; Sunday, 2 p.m. to 10 p.m. Closed Monday.

Tours: No formal tours. Feel free to look around.

Take-out beer: 32-ounce growlers (must be a Cvlt member).

Food: Bring your own.

Parking: Metered street parking (free after 6 p.m.).

Vine Street Pub & Brewery

1700 Vine Street, Denver, CO 80206
(303) 288-BEER (2337) • www.mountainsunpub.com

Denver's Vine Street Pub & Brewery is the youngest of the Mountain Sun trio of brewpubs. Its two older siblings—Mountain Sun and Southern Sun—are located in Boulder. If you've visited either of these locations, Vine Street will feel like an old acquaintance. There's been little tinkering with the time-tested formula that keeps people returning to the popular casual pubs.

The brewpub sits on a corner lot on 17th Avenue and Vine Street, in Denver's vibrant Uptown neighborhood. City Park, home to the Denver Museum of Nature and Science and the Denver Zoo, is a few blocks away. The location is along Restaurant Row, a stretch of 17th Avenue populated with dining choices ranging from funky to fine.

Vine Street opened without an in-house brewery in the spring of 2008. Beer was brought in from the two Boulder breweries for the first four years of Vine Street's existence. Construction of the in-house brewery was completed in 2012.

Like its Boulder counterparts, Vine Street projects a laid-back demeanor. The tables, booths, bar, and backbar are constructed of blond wood. Ceiling-mounted ventilation pipes are painted with hop vines. A collection of potted plants adds a homey touch. The walls display a collection of decorative fabrics and a variety of framed posters and artwork. The otherworldly chalk art of Boulder artist Bryce Widom changes seasonally. Denverites love to dine al fresco, and Vine Street accommodates with a sidewalk patio. Free live music is a Sunday night tradition.

The company's "no credit cards" policy extends to Vine Street. If you have no means to get cash, and you don't have a check, you'll be given an addressed envelope to use to send in your payment. The pubs claim a 97 percent return rate on their "karma envelopes."

The menu features pub-fare favorites such as nachos, wings, sandwiches, and burgers. It's not an extensive menu, but the food is well prepared

Year-round beers: Annapurna Amber, Colorado Kind Ale, Illusion Dweller IPA, Isadore Java Porter, FYIPA, XXX Pale Ale, Big Krane Kolsch, Blackberry Wheat (or specialty fruit), and a specialty stout.

The Pick: The FYIPA is the hophead's go-to brew with a big blast of hoppy goodness up front and a palate-cleansing bitterness to finish.

and high quality. There's a good selection of vegetarian options. If you're a chicken wing fan, the Vine Street version is a must. They're meaty, perfectly spiced, and irresistible. The service is efficient and beyond friendly. The waitstaff uses a team approach to keeping customers fed and watered. Tips are pooled among servers and kitchen staff, who periodically swap positions.

John Fiorilli is Vine Street's head brewer, and also the director of brewing operations for the three Mountain Sun brewpubs. The 12-barrel brewhouse is the largest of the group's brewing facilities. When it went online, the production of the family's eight full-time beers shifted to Denver. The smaller-capacity breweries in the Boulder pubs are now used to brew specialty and seasonal beers. Each pub gets each other's beers, so the beer selections at all three pubs are nearly identical. This arrangement also allows the group to produce sixty to seventy different beers each year. There are generally several Belgian-style ales among the eleven seasonal and specialty beers. The aggressively hopped FYIPA is Vine Street's most popular quencher.

Like its two Boulder counterparts, Vine Street hosts Stout Month each February. For the entire month, ten beer taps dispense only stouts. The dark ales rotate throughout the month and include both house-brewed beers and guest stouts from breweries across the country.

You can read more about the Mountain Sun family of brewpubs in the Northern Front Range section of this book.

Vine Street Pub & Brewery

Opened: April 2008. Brewery began operating in April 2012.
Owners: Kevin and Tom Daly.
Head brewer: John Fiorilli (also director of brewing operations for Mountain Sun pubs).
Potential annual capacity: 5,000 barrels.
Hours: Monday, 4 p.m. to 1 a.m.; Tuesday through Sunday, 11 a.m. to 1 a.m.
Tours: On request.
Take-out beer: Growlers.
Food: Above-average sandwiches, burgers, and burritos. Excellent buffalo wings. Good vegetarian options.
Extras: Live music on Sunday (no cover).
Parking: On-street.

Wit's End Brewing Company

2505 West 2nd Avenue, Unit 13,
Denver, CO 80219
(303) 359-4739
www.witsendbrewing.com

"If you brew it, they will come," could easily be the mantra of Wit's End Brewing Company, one of a growing number of very small-capacity breweries, or nanobreweries, that have sprung to life in the Denver area in recent years. Like many of these overgrown homebreweries, Wit's End is situated in an obscure setting away from the high-rent districts. Despite its off-the-beaten-path location and minimal aesthetics, beer enthusiasts seek out the brewery for its unique creations and ultra-laid-back ambience.

Wit's End is located in a nondescript business park in a mixed industrial-residential area on Denver's west side, about three miles from downtown. The brewery resides in a one-story, sand-colored structure it shares with an eclectic assortment of other businesses. While it's not an area you're likely to stumble upon by accident, it's not exactly in the boonies either. Interstate 25 is just a few blocks away.

There's nothing fancy about the large, open space that houses the brewery and tasting area. The floors are concrete and the high ceiling is of corrugated metal, sitting above a network of exposed piping. The small bar is conducive to conversation. A row of high-top tables provides additional seating. Embellishment consists of makeshift wallpaper made of empty grain bags and mounted on a few wall sections and on the garage door that opens to the parking lot. The simple, no-frills space has a certain appeal in its minimalism. "I've tried to create an atmosphere here where it's not pretentious. It's about beer. It's about conversation," said owner-brewer-bartender Scott Witsoe.

Witsoe was exposed to good beer at an early age during summer trips to Bavaria, where his mother is from. His beer palate continued to evolve while he lived in Seattle and explored the city's vibrant craft beer scene. However, it wasn't until he moved to Denver that he was bitten by the homebrew bug, and bitten hard. He took

Year-round beers: Jean-Claude Van Blond, Wilford Belgian Oatmeal IPA, Green Man Ale, Super FL Black IPA, Kitchen Sink Porter.

The Pick: Jean-Claude Van Blond is a bit hard to classify, but who cares. The light-colored 6.5 percent ABV ale has a lovely fruity-spicy Belgian character and is surprisingly refreshing and drinkable.

possession of his father-in-law's homebrew kit that was collecting dust and put it to use. "It was truly like falling in love for the first time," Witsoe recalled of popping the cap on his first bottle of homebrew. "It was just so amazing. I knew this would always be a part of my life."

He toyed with the idea of opening a nanobrewery as a side project while working full-time for an online university. When he was unexpectedly laid off in early 2011, he decided to get serious about launching a commercial brewing business. Wit's End opened later that year. The brewery's slogan is, quite fittingly, "at every end lies a new beginning."

Those who seek out Wit's End will be amply rewarded with a warm greeting from the outgoing, bearded publican, and an intriguing assortment of creatively inspired, unconventional fermentations. While incorporating a wide range of influences, there's little regard for either stylistic parameters or brewing traditions. "I've never been big on following a particular style guideline," Witsoe explained. "That's never really excited me." He uses the term "New American brewing" to describe his approach to beer making. This attitude is typified in beers such as Wilford, a Belgian oatmeal IPA, and Super FL, a black IPA aged on cedar chips. The Kitchen Sink Porter puts an unusual twist on the dark ale with a complex grain bill that includes rye and a touch of smoked malt.

While the majority of visitors are local craft beer fanatics, the brewery also attracts a growing number of beer travelers seeking an under-the-radar gem. They've found it at Wit's End.

Wit's End Brewing Company

Opened: September 2011.

Owners: Scott and Heather Witsoe.

Head brewer: Scott Witsoe.

Potential annual capacity: 200 barrels.

Hours: Thursday, 4 p.m. to 8 p.m.; Friday and Saturday, 2 p.m. to 8 p.m.; Sunday, 2 p.m. to 6 p.m.

Tours: On request.

Take-out beer: 40-ounce stainless steel canteens.

Food: German-style pretzels sometimes available. Food trucks on-site on occasion or bring your own food.

Extras: AHA member deals participant.

Parking: On-site lot.

Wynkoop Brewing Company

1634 18th Street, Denver, CO 80202
(303) 297-2700 • www.wynkoop.com

In the late 1980s, Denver's Lower Downtown district, or LoDo, was a much different place than it is today. "There were literally tumbleweeds blowing down the street," recalled John Hickenlooper, who gathered a team of investors to open Wynkoop Brewing Company in 1988. Denver's first craft brewery and Colorado's first brewpub is now an institution in the Mile High City, and wears its patriarchal crown with dignity and a sense of humor.

The brewpub resides on the corner of 18th and Wynkoop Streets, across from historic Union Station. Coors Field is two blocks away. Hickenlooper was a laid-off geologist who had visited a brewpub in California and thought the concept might take off in Denver. At the time, the city was in dire financial straits. No one had opened a restaurant in the downtown area in five years. "Everybody thought I was crazy. It took me two years to raise the money. I couldn't get my own mother to invest," said Hickenlooper.

Funds eventually materialized and a location was procured. The Wynkoop Brewing Company opened in the fall of 1988 in the vintage J. S. Brown Mercantile Building, which dates from 1899. The brewpub was a hit. Not only did the Wynkoop attract scores of curious and thirsty urbanites, it helped trigger a neighborhood revival that has transformed LoDo into a vibrant entertainment district. Hickenlooper went on to become a two-term mayor of Denver—during which time his financial interests in the Wynkoop were divested—and he currently serves as the governor of Colorado.

Although the brewpub's interior is expansive, it manages to maintain a publike ambience with lots of wood, thick pillars, and pressed-tin ceilings. The large island-style bar is abuzz during after-work hours. There's outdoor seating on a covered patio overlooking Wynkoop Street. On the second floor is an elegant bar and Denver's largest pool hall with twenty-two regulation-sized billiards tables.

Year-round beers: Patty's Chile Beer, Rail Yard Amber Ale, St. Charles ESB, London Calling IPA, Mile HIPA, B3K Black Lager, Cowtown Milk Stout, Silverback Pale Ale, Uber Lager, Colorojo Double Red, Belgorado, Rocky Mtn. Oyster Stout.

The Pick: B3K Black Lager, a German-style schwarzbier, has a touch of sweet, a hint of smoke, a bit of roast, and the clean smoothness of a lager.

More than any other Denver brewery, the Wynkoop attracts a true cross section of the urban population. On any day you'll encounter professionals, couples, families, beer geeks, and out-of-town visitors.

The kitchen creates good-quality pub-style comfort food with English and American influences. Burgers and fried chicken share the menu with bangers and mash and shepherd's pie. A few southwestern dishes round out the selections.

The Wynkoop's original brewer, the late Russell Schehrer, favored English-style ales. They were served at cellar temperature and dispensed from a hand pump. "Warm and flat is where it's at," became the brewer's mantra. The beer portfolio has expanded considerably under head brewer Andy Brown. Under his guidance, the brewery has supplemented its standard and specialty lineup of mostly English- and American-style beers with adventurous Belgian-American hybrids, high-gravity beers, and barrel-aged offerings.

The most attention-grabbing creation to emerge from the Wynkoop brewhouse began as an April Fools' Day prank. In an online video, the brewery claimed to have released Rocky Mountain Oyster Stout, a beer brewed with bull testicles. When people showed up to try it, and requests for samples arrived from brewers and beer writers nationwide, Wynkoop had only one choice: brew it.

For the inaugural batch, twenty-five pounds of the locally sourced cowboy delicacy were roasted, hand-sliced, and added to the mash during the brewing process. The beer was released during the 2012 Great American Beer Festival. It was a huge hit, and is now produced regularly. The foreign-style stout is described as 7.5 percent ABV and 3 BPBs, or balls per barrel.

Wynkoop Brewing Company

Opened: October 1988.

Owners: Breckenridge/Wynkoop LLC.

Head brewer: Andy Brown.

Potential annual capacity: 5,000 barrels.

Hours: Daily, 11 a.m. to 2 a.m.

Tours: Tuesday through Saturday, 3 p.m. and 4 p.m., or private tours by appointment.

Take-out beer: Growlers, cans, and kegs.

Food: English and American pub fare.

Extras: Numerous monthly and annual events including sustainability and science seminars, festivals, and the Beerdrinker of the Year awards. Billiards and darts. AHA member deals program participant.

Parking: Metered on-street parking and nearby lots.

Yak & Yeti Restaurant & Brewpub

7803 Ralston Road, Arvada, CO 80002
(303) 431-9000 • www.theyakandyeti.com

It's always rewarding to find a brewery or brewpub that has a truly unique feature. Yak & Yeti has three. First, the brewpub is unusual in that it features Indian, Nepalese, and Tibetan cuisine. Second, the brewpub resides in a gorgeous Victorian mansion. Third, the building is haunted.

Yak & Yeti is located on busy Ralston Road in Arvada, a short stroll from the city's Olde Town district. The stately brick mansion in which the restaurant resides was built in 1864, the year before the Civil War ended and a dozen years before Colorado officially became a state. It was a private home for many years before being converted into apartments. It became run-down and sat vacant for a decade before it was renovated and turned into an English-style brewpub. In 2008, it was sold to restaurateur Dol Bhattarai as a second location for his successful Yak & Yeti restaurant. Thankfully, he decided to retain the brewery.

The mansion is said to be haunted by a former resident who died from a fall on the staircase in the 1940s. Following a series of unusual occurrences, Yak & Yeti's owner brought in a team of paranormal investigators for an overnight stay. Among several unexplained events that night was the spontaneous movement of a chair, which was caught on tape.

The building's two-story interior includes a handsome bar area and a variety of dining rooms, each with its own distinctive ambience. My favorite is a main-floor space lavishly decked out with green walls, a granite-framed fireplace, Himalayan mountain photos, and Indian artwork. Other rooms are less ornate, but all are atmospheric in their own way. Outdoor seating is available on a small porch. The brewery is in the basement.

The kitchen creates an enticing medley of curries, tandoori meats and breads, spicy vindaloo, and many other exotically flavored dishes. There are numerous vegetarian options. With its pronounced spicing, Indian cuisine is a wonderful

Year-round beers: Himalayan IPA, Namaste Pilsner, Chai Milk Stout, West Coast Glutton Double IPA, Jalapeno Lena, GF Apple Ale (gluten-free).

The Pick: The Chai Milk Stout is brewed with the same spice blend used to make the house chai. The spices merge seamlessly with the rich flavors of the smooth, sweet dark ale.

match for the full-flavored beers that Yak & Yeti's head brewer, Adam Draegar, produces prodigiously.

Draeger was previously working as an engineer while spending weekends homebrewing. His wife used logic to convince him to turn his hobby into his profession. "You realize that if you would brew during the week, you'd have your weekends free, as opposed to working all week long and having no weekends free," Draeger recalled her saying. She was right, of course. After completing studies with the World Brewing Academy, Draegar moved from the Midwest to Colorado, seeking a brewing job. He soon discovered that, in most production breweries, the path to the brewhouse required starting on the bottling line and working your way up. This didn't sit well with Draeger. "I really wanted to brew," he said. He finally got his chance at Yak & Yeti.

The brewpub's full-time offerings include several well-tested styles—an IPA, a pilsner, a double IPA—and a few more unique creations including a chai milk stout, a chili pepper beer, and a gluten-free apple ale. In the summer, Wheat Wednesdays feature the release of a wheat beer flavored with fruit. In the winter, there's a weekly release of a porter infused with spices, coconut, or other flavorings. There's a rotating tap assigned exclusively to Belgian-style beers, and one to amber ales. Another is reserved for small-batch experimental brews. Draeger calls these the Haunted Series. "If a beer is produced in a haunted kettle and fermented in a haunted vessel and put into haunted kegs and served from a haunted tap into a haunted glass, we should call it the Haunted Beer Series," the brewer explains on his blog.

Yak & Yeti Restaurant & Brewpub

Opened: July 2008.
Owner: Dol Bhattarai.
Head brewer: Adam Draeger.
Potential annual capacity: 700 barrels.
Hours: Monday through Saturday, 11 a.m. to 9:30 p.m.; Sunday, 11 a.m. to 9 p.m.
Tours: On request.
Take-out beer: Growlers.
Food: Indian, Nepalese, and Tibetan cuisine with house-made bread, cheese, and yogurt. Gluten-free and vegan menus.
Parking: On-site lot.
Extras: Game Nights on the second Wednesday and fourth Sunday of each month. Poses and Pints (yoga and beer) on the first Sunday of each month.
Area attractions: See Arvada Beer Company on page 16.
Other area beer sites: See Arvada Beer Company on page 16.

The Northern Front Range

With its high concentration of breweries, easy access from Denver, and lively towns such as Boulder and Fort Collins, the Northern Front Range offers beer fans a bounty of rewarding destinations. This region begins where the suburbs end north of the Mile High City. For our purposes, a convenient dividing line is Highway 470 and the Northwest Parkway, located about twenty miles from downtown Denver. The region includes all communities east of the Rocky Mountain foothills. I've expanded the boundaries a bit to include the mountain towns of Nederland and Estes Park, which are closely connected to the Front Range. Many of Colorado's most recognizable brewing companies are located in this part of the state, including Avery Brewing, Boulder Beer, Left Hand Brewing, Oskar Blues Brewery, New Belgium Brewing, and Odell Brewing.

Nearly all of the brewery towns in this region are located west of Interstate 25, the major north-south thoroughfare along the Front Range. The few exceptions are Brighton, Frederick, Windsor, and Greeley, which sit farther east on the plains.

Boulder

Boulder, my home since 1988, is a great place to start a Northern Front Range beer tour. The progressive community offers a plethora of breweries and other beer stops in and around the city, great restaurants, a lively downtown scene, excellent music and entertainment options, and a wealth of thirst-inducing outdoor activities.

Boulder has made numerous "best of" lists in categories such as Fittest, Smartest, and Foodiest. Many world-class athletes, especially runners and cyclists, live and train in Boulder. It seems that everyone in town either jogs or bikes regularly. The Bolder Boulder 10K Road Race, held on Memorial Day, is one of the largest in the country, attracting fifty thousand runners in recent years.

The engaging *Pearl Street Mall*, a four-block-long pedestrian mall in downtown Boulder, is frequented by locals and visitors for its dining, shopping, people-watching, and street entertainment. A patio table at West Flanders Brewing Company is one of the top people-watching spots on Pearl Street. The locals-favorite Mountain Sun Pub & Brewery is just east of the walking mall. The Shine brewpub and neighboring Bohemian Biergarten are a half-block from the mall. The Walnut Brewery and several good beer bars, such as Reuben's, the Kitchen (Upstairs and Next Door), and The West End are also nearby.

Boulder is home to the *University of Colorado* (locals call it CU). College football fans are familiar with the school's buffalo mascot, Ralphie, who does a spirited lap around the field prior to games and after halftime. There have been five Ralphies over the years, all female.

Boulder is also the home of Boulder Beer, Colorado's first microbrewery and one of the oldest craft breweries in the country. Avery Brewing Company, in east Boulder, is considered one of the state's most cutting-edge breweries. The Brewers Association, the trade group promoting craft brewing in the United States, has its offices in downtown Boulder.

Other Area Beer Sites

In addition to visiting the city's numerous breweries, you may be interested in exploring some of the places listed below.

Backcountry Pizza & Tap House (2319 Arapahoe Ave., 303-449-4285)

Bohemian Biergarten (2017 13th St., 720-328-8328)

The Kitchen Next Door (1035 Pearl St., 720-542-8159)

The Kitchen Upstairs (1039 Pearl St., 303-544-5973)

Old Chicago (1102 Pearl St., 303-443-5031)

Redstone Meadery (4700 Pearl St., No. 2A, 720-406-1215)

Reuben's Burger Bistro (1800 Broadway, 303-443-5000)

The Sink (1165 13th St., 303-444-7465)

Under the Sun (627 S. Broadway, 303-927-6921)

The West End Tavern (926 Pearl St., 303-444-3535)

You'll also find good beer stops in the neighboring towns of Niwot and Louisville, and the nearby mountain town of Nederland.

Points North

Longmont is an easy twenty-minute drive northeast from Boulder. Two prominent Colorado breweries, Oskar Blues Brewery and Left Hand Brewing Company, are located in Longmont as is the Pumphouse brewpub. You can get a meal and a good brew at these Longmont restaurants.

CHUBurger (1225 Ken Pratt Blvd., 303-485-2482)

CyclHOPS (600 S. Airport Rd., 303-776-2453)

Oskar Blues Home Made Liquids and Solids (1555 S. Hover Rd., 303-485-9400)

Old Chicago (1805 Industrial Cir., 303-651-7000)

West of Longmont, the small community of Lyons was hit hard by the 2013 floods. Downtown businesses, including the original Oskar Blues brewpub, were forced to close while the town's infrastructure could be rebuilt. A popular stop for travelers on the way to Rocky Mountain National Park, the town is also home to Planet Bluegrass, an outdoor concert venue and site of the popular RockyGrass and Folks Fest summer music festivals.

The town of Berthoud, just north of Longmont, is home to City Star, an enjoyable small-town brewery. A bit farther north is the city of Loveland. Colorado's "Sweetheart City" sponsors a popular Valentine's Day re-mailing program in which valentines received in large envelopes are hand-stamped with a valentine's verse, then forwarded to their recipients bearing a "Loveland" postmark. The city has a thriving arts scene, especially sculpture. The *Benson Sculpture Garden* and the downtown district are well-populated with public art pieces.

Loveland has exploded on the craft beer scene in recent years with the opening of a host of small breweries. Other Loveland beer destinations include the following:

Henry's Pub (234 E. 4th St., 970-613-1896)

Next Door Food & Drink (222 E. 4th St., 970-541-3020)

Old Chicago (1436 Hahns Peak Dr., 970-593-1003)

Pourhouse Bar & Grill (124 E. 4th St., 970-669-1699)

Estes Park sits west of Loveland at the entrance to *Rocky Mountain National Park*. In the summer months, visitors from around the world descend upon the town. The park itself is well worth a visit. There are many miles of hiking trails of varying length and difficulty and abundant wildlife. *Trail Ridge Road*, which crosses the park, tops out at 12,183 feet and is the highest continuous road in the country. More than eight miles of roadway sit above 11,000 feet.

Fort Collins

Fort Collins is the northernmost brewery town along the Northern Front Range and one of the best beer towns anywhere. If you're seeking the highest concentration of great breweries requiring the least amount of travel, Fort Collins is an excellent destination.

The home of Colorado State University, this town is a young, active, beer-obsessed community located sixty-five miles north of Denver. Each June, Fort Collins hosts the Colorado Brewers' Festival, one of the largest beer festivals in the state. Some of the town's numerous breweries—including Coopersmith's, Equinox, and Pateros Creek—are located in or near the historic Old Town district, the downtown center of activity. A short distance away is a cluster of other notable brewing businesses including Odell, Fort Collins, Funkwerks, and New Belgium Brewing Company. New Belgium, the country's third-largest craft brewery, offers an awesome tour. Be sure to make a reservation online well in advance. Closer to the University are Black Bottle Brewery and C.B. & Potts.

In addition to its many breweries, Fort Collins has an expanding list of tap houses and beer-centric restaurants. Here are some of the best:

Café Vino (1200 S. College Ave., 970-212-3399)

Choice City Butcher and Deli (104 W. Olive St., 970-490-2489)

Crankenstein (215 N. College Ave., 970-818-7008)

The Crown Pub (134 S. College Ave., 970-484-5929)

The Forge Publick House (232 Walnut St., 831-332-8060)

The Mayor of Old Town (632 S. Mason St., 970-682-2410)

Moot House (2626 S. College Ave., 970-226-2121)

Tap N Handle (307 S. College Ave., 970-484-1116)

TAPS Sports Bar & Grill (165 E. Boardwalk Dr., 970-449-4462)

Just outside Fort Collins, the Cache La Poudre River flows through the sinuous Poudre Canyon. The scenic canyon is a popular recreation destination for hiking, biking, camping, white water rafting, kayaking, fishing, and crosscountry skiing.

Anheuser-Busch Fort Collins Brewery

2351 Busch Drive, Fort Collins, CO 80524
(970) 490-4691
www.budweisertours.com/z01/index
.php/fort-collins/overview

If you ever set foot in one of the country's large corporate breweries, you will find it as different from microbreweries as American light lager is from imperial stout. The Fort Collins–based Anheuser-Busch InBev facility offers a glimpse as to how beer is produced on an industrial scale.

The roots of Anheuser-Busch date back to the mid-1800s when Adolphus Busch, the second-youngest of twenty-two children and a partner in a brewing supply business, married the daughter of German-born Eberhard Anheuser, owner of a St. Louis brewery. In 1876, the brewery created an American-style lager that would become the company's flagship brand. The beer was given the German-sounding name "Budweiser" to appeal to German immigrants.

In 2008, Anheuser-Busch was acquired by the Belgian beer giant InBev in one of the largest-ever purchases of an American company by a foreign entity. The brewing conglomerate now goes by the name Anheuser-Busch InBev and produces dozens of well-known brands including Budweiser, Michelob, Shock Top, Stella Artois, Hoegaarden, Leffe, Beck's, Bass, Goose Island, Rolling Rock, and many others.

The company's Fort Collins brewery was built in 1988. It's the second-youngest and third-largest of the company's twelve U.S. breweries. The brewery produces 10.5 million barrels annually. The packaging operation has the capacity to output 7.8 million cans, 5.1 million bottles, and 7,680 draught kegs every day!

Tours convene in a building that houses the hospitality room, gift shop, and expansive beer garden. The brewery is a short stroll away. According to the personable retiree who guided my group of springtime visitors, the biggest crowds arrive on summer weekends and when the famous Clydesdale horses are on the premises.

The first stop on our tour was the horse quarters, a few steps from the large, leafy beer garden. Unfortunately, the horse team had an out-of-town gig in Los Angeles for the beginning of the baseball

Year-round beers: More than two dozen brands available in tasting room.

The Pick: Of the many beers produced in the Fort Collins facility, the clean, hoppy, Goose Island IPA will have the greatest appeal to craft beer drinkers.

season—like rock stars and politicians, the Clydesdales spend a lot of time on the road. The large European-bred horses were brought to the U.S. in the 1840s and were used to deliver beer and other products before trucks took over the task in the early 1900s. Several of the ornate red Budweiser delivery wagons are also on display at the Fort Collins facility.

A short walk brought us to the huge brewery, where we were escorted to a second-story observation area overlooking the brew-house. It immediately struck me that there were no people present in the brewing area. All of the brewing operations are monitored from a high-tech control room adjacent to the brewhouse.

A short video presentation followed, providing a rather elementary explanation of the beer-making process, clearly geared to beer novices and tourists. The tour continued to other observation areas overlook-ing the fermentation room and packaging area. Along the way, there were short lectures on a variety of topics including canning, beech-wood aging, and philanthropic initiatives. A series of displays, photos, and information signs provided details on beer ingredients, advertising history, the company's product portfolio, and other subjects.

Following the tour, we made our way to the hospitality center for a product sampling that I found surprisingly enjoyable. Visitors of legal age are permitted two free 11-ounce pours. There is a wide variety of beers available for sampling, ranging from the expected American light lagers to more interesting German- and Belgian-brewed beers and the Goose Island IPA, originally created by the Chicago brewery that was acquired by A-B InBev in 2011. The bartenders were friendly and knowledgeable and enthusiastic about sharing impressions of beers, including non–A-B InBev beers.

Anheuser-Busch Fort Collins Brewery

Opened: 1988.

Owner: Anheuser-Busch InBev.

Head brewer: Katie Ripple.

Potential annual capacity: 10.5 million barrels.

Hours: June through September: daily, 10 a.m. to 4 p.m.; October through May: Thursday through Monday, 10 a.m. to 4 p.m.

Tours: Same as above.

Take-out beer: N/A.

Food: N/A.

Parking: On-site lot.

Area attractions: See chapter intro.

Other area beer sites: See chapter intro.

Asher Brewing Company

4699 Nautilus Court, Suite 104, Boulder, CO 80301
(303) 530-1381 • www.asherbrewing.com

Until I visited Asher Brewing Company, my only experience with "green beer" was in my younger years when St. Patrick's Day celebrations would feature light American lagers artificially colored in a shade of green that doesn't occur in nature. Asher Brewing Company has, thankfully, given green beer a new meaning. The Boulder brewery is Colorado's first all-organic brewing company.

Asher's founder, Chris Asher, began homebrewing while attending college in Connecticut. By his senior year, he was teaching a homebrewing class. He moved to Colorado and landed his first professional brewing job at Golden City in 1996. Four years later, he returned to school and earned an MBA. During his graduate studies, he became interested in sustainable and environmentally friendly business practices. After a stint at the now-defunct Redfish Brewhouse in Boulder, he focused his efforts on implementing a long-simmering business idea. Asher Brewing Company opened in late 2009 as Colorado's only organic brewery.

Asher Brewing is tucked discreetly into a quiet business park in a mixed business and residential area on the northeast fringe of Boulder. The well-known Celestial Seasonings tea company is in the neighborhood (on Sleepytime Drive) and offers free tours. Avery Brewing Company has plans to construct a large brewing complex in the area.

From the outside, the Asher brewery would be indistinguishable from its neighboring businesses if not for the tables encroaching into the parking lot. The taproom is a small and simple space. A ten-seat bar and a half-dozen tables fill the narrow room. There's additional seating in a small adjacent room along with a TV and a collection of board games. Beyond the bar, a large garage space is available for cornhole games and darts. The brewhouse is in the back of the building, out of sight of the taproom.

Year-round beers: Greenade Organic Double IPA, Green Bullet Organic IPA, Green Lantern Organic Kolsch, Tree Hugger Organic Amber.

The Pick: Tree Hugger Organic Amber Ale is a good anytime beer that's neither too aggressive nor too mundane. It greets you with a toasty nose followed by a mildly sweet maltiness and dry finish.

Operating an all-organic brewery presents challenges that few breweries have to deal with. A limited availability of organic ingredients, especially hops, was a limiting factor in the brewery's early days. "We had to look at what ingredients we could get and then say, 'What can we make with this?'" Asher recalled. Procuring hops still requires additional effort, though the situation is improving. "You just can't go through the normal distribution routes when you're looking for organic hops," explained Asher. The owner-brewer has called every organic hop farm in the country seeking the pungent flowers for his brews: "It's getting better. We definitely have to improvise with the hops once in a while." The organic theme goes beyond brewing ingredients. Biodegradable, environmentally friendly cleaning products are used both in the brewery and the tasting room.

The organic brewery attracts a diverse crowd. "We get people who come here just because we're organic. We get people who come here because they live across the street. We have people who care that we're organic, and then we have people who just care about good beer," said Asher.

Visitors to Asher will generally find seven beers on tap. The brewery's flagship brew is Tree Hugger Organic Amber, an approachable everyday ale. Green Lantern Organic Kolsch is a summertime favorite. Hopheads gravitate to Green Bullet Organic IPA and Greenade Organic Double IPA. Additional offerings include several seasonal brews. There's often a barrel-aged beer available. The wine barrels used for these distinctly flavored creations come from the nearby award-winning Boulder Creek Winery, whose proprietors are frequent visitors to the Asher taproom.

Asher Brewing Company

Opened: November 2009.

Owner and head brewer: Chris Asher.

Potential annual capacity: 1,500 barrels.

Hours: Saturday through Wednesday, 2 p.m. to 10 p.m.; Thursday and Friday, 2 p.m. to midnight.

Tours: By appointment or on request.

Take-out beer: Growlers, cans, and kegs.

Food: Food trucks are often on-site on Wednesday, Thursday, and Friday, or you may bring your own food.

Extras: AHA member discount program participant.

Parking: On-site lot.

Avery Brewing Company

5763 Arapahoe Avenue, Unit E, Boulder, CO 80303
(303) 440-4324 • www.averybrewing.com

Avery Brewing Company has a well-earned reputation as a cutting-edge innovator, constantly challenging our perception of what beer can be. Not surprisingly, the Boulder brewery is a hugely popular stop on the northern Colorado ale trail.

Brewery cofounder Adam Avery was a homebrewer and manager of a Boulder outdoor store in the early 1990s. He applied to law school and got accepted, but was having second thoughts. As an alternative, he put together a business plan for a brewery and began shopping for investors. Meanwhile, his father, Larry, was planning to open a running store in Boulder but couldn't find a location. After reading the brewery's business plan, he decided to back his son's business. Avery Brewing Company's first beers hit the shelves in early 1994.

The brewery trudged along for several years producing a lineup of English and American-style ales. Sales were sluggish and the brewery's future was uncertain. "We weren't making a living or building anything. Just kind of spinning our wheels," Adam Avery recalled. With little to lose, he threw caution to the wind and brewed an intensely flavored, high-gravity barleywine called Hog Heaven. It caught the attention of the craft beer world. "That kind of sent us down a road toward more aggressive, flavorful beers," said Avery.

Soon afterward, Avery released The Reverend, a burly, high-alcohol, Belgian quadruple ale brewed as a tribute to an Avery brewer's late grandfather, who was an Episcopal reverend. It sold well. A strong Belgian golden ale called Salvation came next, completing what became known as The Holy Trinity of Ales. Sales turned around and Avery developed a devout, almost cultish, fan base of beer enthusiasts seeking the most palate-challenging, cutting-edge beers they could find.

The brewery itself is well hidden in an East Boulder business complex that it shares with an eclectic hodgepodge of companies. As Avery

Year-round beers: India Pale Ale, White Rascal Belgian-Style Wheat Ale, Ellie's Brown Ale, Out of Bounds Stout, Joe's Premium American Pilsner, Hog Heaven Barleywine Style Ale.

The Pick: If any one beer defines Avery's approach to beer and brewing, it's Hog Heaven Barleywine Style Ale. Massive amounts of chewy malt and zesty hops produce a bold-flavored 9 percent ABV ale that demands your taste buds stand at attention.

Brewing has grown over the years and maxed out its interior space, an expanding collection of towering fermentation vessels has taken over a chunk of the parking lot. It's an imperfect situation, but a solution is in the works. Avery is constructing a new multimillion dollar brewery complex in northeast Boulder. The ambitious project will include a state-of-the-art brewery, a taproom, an outdoor beer garden, and a full-service restaurant.

The current taproom is a simple, convivial gathering spot with table and bar seating. Outside the taproom, a row of picnic tables and benches is set up within the parking lot for fair-weather imbibing.

While bold-flavored, high-gravity beers put Avery on the radar of beer enthusiasts across the country, the brewery has been exploring numerous other brewing frontiers. Most notable is its barrel-aging program. Avery's collection of wine, whiskey, rum, and neutral barrels numbers around 250.

Avery's sour beer program has ramped up in recent years. While these creations are occasionally bottled and released in small quantities, more typically they are available for sampling only in the tasting room. Though each blend is different, they go by the generic name Emerita—Latin for "hermit"—because they never leave the house.

Avery continues to produce boundary-bending high-gravity beers such as Uncle Jacob's Stout, a bourbon barrel-aged dark ale in the 17 percent alcohol range. The beer was named for Avery's sixth great-grand uncle, a distiller from Kentucky who apparently was the first to label his spirits "bourbon" more than two centuries ago. Not all Avery beers are over-the-top creations: among the brewery's best sellers is White Rascal, an easy-drinking Belgian white ale that is a wonderful summer quencher.

Avery Brewing Company

Opened: September 1993.

Owners: Adam and Larry Avery.

Head brewer: Matt Thrall.

Potential annual capacity: Currently 65,000 barrels. Will increase to 350,000 barrels in new facility.

Hours: Daily, 11 a.m. to 11 p.m.

Tours: Offered daily. Check website for times.

Take-out beer: Six-packs of bottles and cans, 12-ounce specialty beers, kegs.

Food: Full lunch and dinner menu from neighboring caterer.

Extras: Fun runs, bike rides, homebrew support meetings, Sign Language Night, and numerous other events. Check website for dates and details.

Parking: On-site lot.

Big Beaver Brewing Company

2707 West Eisenhower Boulevard, Loveland, CO 80538
(970) 818-6064 • www.bigbeaverbrew.com

Breweries are sometimes built around a theme, be it dogs, fairy tales, musical styles, or what have you. For better or worse, Loveland's Big Beaver Brewing Company is the only brewing business I've encountered with a theme based on genitalia. The company logo is a cartoonish figure suggestive of the company name. The company's slogan is "'bout got 'er licked," and the beers carry names such as Potent Pecker Pilsner and Black Curly's IPA. You get the idea.

The brewery sits along Highway 34 a few miles from downtown Loveland. The entrance is a bit hidden around the back of a large industrial-looking shed, which itself is situated behind a nondescript brick building next to a bank. The One Love head shop is across the street.

Big Beaver is the creation of Peter Villeneuve, who began homebrewing while working on a PhD in industrial microbiology. His doctorate work involved growing beer yeast for a manned mission to Mars. The idea was to use yeast as a recyclable food product, one that was also capable of producing a variety of other useful stuff too bulky to carry on long space missions. The sedentary desk work and endless meetings of the biotech world were not to Villeneuve's liking. "When you're working on high-tech stuff, there's a reward but it's often a fifteen-year process to get your product in the market," said the Big Beaver owner-brewer. He left his career in the sciences for the rewards of physical labor and immediate feedback from brewing and selling beer.

Originally, Villeneuve had planned to package beer in six-packs for retail sales. The unconventional marketing scheme was devised as an attention-grabber. "The names were designed to be catchy on the shelf," he explained. "When you're marketing in such a hyper-competitive arena, you have to have brand recognition. You have to have something that's crazy. You have to have something that's going to catch your eye. Something that's appealing."

Year-round beers: Shaved Tail Belgian Ale, Wonder Wiener Wheat, Bust-A-Nut Brown Ale, Stroke a Strip Saison, Beaver Stubble Stout, Whiskey Dick Stout, Screw the Pooch Pale Ale, Potent Peter IPA, Doppelbock, Breezy Bean Bag Scottish, Black Curly's IPA, Big Woody IPA 3.0, Beaver Patch Ale, Sweet-n-Sour Booty, Burning Beaver Ale, Potent Pecker Pilsner.

When he concluded that the funds needed to launch a production brewery were too extravagant, and the packaging process too environmentally impactful, he decided to keep it simple and sell beer directly to consumers by the glass or growler. The marketing concept, however, was retained.

The taproom at Big Beaver consists of a small bar with seating for eight. There's an adjoining room that had been the meeting space of a nondenominational church. Weekly organ and vocal rehearsals would shake the brewery walls. When the church relocated, the brewery expanded into the space. There's a garage-style door on one end and a large TV on the wall. A dozen or so high-top tables fill the room. It's a simple space, without much embellishment.

Villeneuve has rigged an unconventional brewing system of his own design. Once a batch of beer has completed fermentation, it's moved into plastic containers to age. As needed, beer is transferred into kegs and force-carbonated. This system allows Big Beaver to keep a large variety of beers on tap while maintaining a small inventory of kegs.

When I stopped by, many of the customers, predominantly older males, were on a first-name basis with the owner and staff. A card-stamping program rewards customers with a free beer after ten purchases. The brewery regularly hosts live music. Fresh-cooked brats are available and there are occasional weekend barbecues in the warm-weather months.

Big Beaver Brewing Company

Opened: October 2010.

Owner and head brewer: Peter Villeneuve.

Potential annual capacity: 800 barrels.

Hours: Monday through Thursday, 2 p.m. to 9 p.m.; Friday and Saturday, 2 p.m. to 10 p.m.; Sunday, 2 p.m. to 8 p.m.

Tours: On request.

Take-out beer: Growlers.

Food: Beer brats.

Extras: Biweekly Saturday barbecue and beer pairings. Local acoustic musicians perform on Sunday. On Free Beer Friday, $1/6$ of a barrel of the featured beer is given away (1 pint per customer) every half hour and hour; the event starts at 2 p.m. and ends when the keg is kicked.

Parking: On-site lot.

BJ's Restaurant & Brewhouse

RESTAURANT BREWHOUSE

1690 28th Street, Boulder, CO 80301
(303) 440-5200 • www.bjsrestaurants.com/locations/co/boulder

From a beer drinker's perspective, Boulder's new BJ's Restaurant & Brewhouse is not the BJ's you think you know. Innovative and experimental are not descriptors you normally associate with large, corporate brewpub chains. That's what makes Boulder's BJ's an unexpected and pleasant surprise.

Many people know BJ's as a chain of casual-dining restaurants with roots in California and locations in fifteen states. Most locations receive their house beers from a few centralized brewing facilities. In the mid-1990s, BJ's opened a brewpub in an enviable location along Boulder's Pearl Street walking mall. Over the years, as the company expanded to 134 restaurants, the modest-sized, two-level space in downtown Boulder no longer fit the company's well-defined model. With its lease scheduled to expire in 2012, BJ's vacated downtown Boulder and built a new restaurant from the ground up at the Twenty-Ninth Street shopping mall. For beer enthusiasts, the story became more interesting.

When the new, larger, more upscale facility opened, there was a big change in the direction of the Boulder brewing operation. While the former facility was producing the standard lineup of BJ's core beers, the new facility is used exclusively for research and development. This is much to the delight of brewer Aaron Stueck, who has embraced his new mad scientist role with a passion. The Boulder brewery produces a constantly changing selection of small-batch experimental beers that most BJ's visitors around the country will never get to sample.

To my knowledge, no one has ever investigated the possible existence of a hereditary brewing gene. Given Stueck's background, there might be something to it. When he was growing up in Wisconsin, his grandmother told stories of how her father would make beer on the farm during Prohibition. When Stueck came by his great-grandfather's bottle filler and capper from the 1920s, "It just sparked something in my brain," he remembered.

Year-round beers: Light-Switch Lager, Brewhouse Blonde Kolsch, Harvest Hefeweizen, Piranha Pale Ale, Hopstorm IPA, Jeremiah Red, Nutty Brewnette, P.M. Porter, Tatonka Stout, Oasis Amber. All are brewed out of state and shipped to Colorado.

The Pick: This BJ's location has produced a variety of barrel-aged beers. The whiskey barrel-aged creations are especially notable for their complexity and balance.

At age nineteen, he attended school in Scotland where he was able to drink legally. "I was blown away by the malty beers and the nitro beers," he recalled of his first experiences with beers other than mass-produced American light lagers.

He began homebrewing when he returned to the States. "The first batch of beer turned out pretty good. The next one was better. Soon I was on the fast track to becoming a beer snob," Stueck said of his early homebrewing exploits. "Since my great-grandfather was brewing beer on the farm, it's almost like I've got beer in my blood." After college, a job in graphic arts brought him to Boulder, but six months later, he was laid off. Soon after, he landed the assistant brewing position at BJ's. When the head brewer moved on, Stueck stepped into the job.

The R&D brewer operates with several goals: to create interesting beers for local beer fans, to develop new beers that may someday be implemented on a company-wide level, and to explore new territories in brewing. Among the esoteric creations that have emerged from the new brewhouse are a Berliner weisse, a gratzer (smoked wheat beer), a wine barrel-aged sour beer, and a whiskey barrel-aged Dortmunder double alt.

While few recipes are brewed more than once, an exception is the Got Beer, an unusual Swedish farmhouse ale that won a gold medal at the 2012 Great American Beer Festival in the Indigenous Beer category. The beer is brewed without hops, with juniper instead used as a bittering agent. According to Stueck, "It's got a very nice piney, almost woody flavor followed by some very nice honey residual sweetness and a little bit of smokiness at the end. It tastes like Christmas smells."

BJ's Restaurant & Brewhouse

Opened: Original Boulder location opened in 1997. Current location opened in August 2012.

Owners: BJ's is a publicly traded company.

Head brewer: Aaron Stueck.

Potential annual capacity: 200 barrels.

Hours: Sunday through Thursday, 11 a.m. to midnight; Friday and Saturday, 11 a.m. to 1 a.m.

Tours: On request.

Take-out beer: None.

Food: Extensive and diverse menu of burgers, pizza, sandwiches, pasta, steaks, Mexican and Asian dishes, and other entrées. Gluten-free menu available.

Extras: AHA member deals program participant.

Parking: On-site lot.

Black Bottle Brewery

1605 South College Avenue, Fort Collins, CO 80525
(970) 493-BEER (2337) • www.blackbottlebrewery.com

Some businesses, such as Black Bottle Brewery, have found success going against the grain. The Fort Collins brewpub is one of a small number of businesses in the state that combines the restaurant and in-house brewery of a standard brewpub with a beer bar featuring a broad selection of guest beers.

This hybrid business model was not the original intent of Black Bottle founder Sean Nook. The Fort Collins native made his first batch of homebrew around 2005. It evolved into an obsession. "I was brewing two to three times a week," he recalled. "I had thirteen beers on tap at my house. I was quite popular with the neighbors."

Tiring of his job as a master auto technician, Nook applied for work at Fort Collins's numerous breweries, but no job offers were forthcoming. He abandoned his job search and decided to create his own brewery. His original plan was to start small, relying on taproom sales to generate income while gradually building a network of outside keg accounts in order to grow. A meeting with a business consultant convinced him that adding a restaurant to the business plan made financial sense, if added complexity. "All the great breweries out there, I liked their model better," said Nook. "Oskar Blues started as a brewpub. [So did] Dogfish Head. Three Floyds."

Though he had no restaurant experience, Nook opened Black Bottle in late 2012 with an 8-barrel brewery, a full kitchen, and twenty-three employees. Among the things that set Black Bottle apart from other brewpubs was that, in addition to the ten to twelve house beers, the brewery offered around thirty guest taps and an extensive collection of bottled beers from outside breweries. Customers wondered why Nook would compete against his own beers. "It's not about just my beer," Nook explained. "My fridge at home is not just full of my beers. It's full of beer from all over the world, just like the concept we have here."

Black Bottle is located in a strip mall on College Avenue, Fort Collins's major north-south artery.

Year-round beers: Hipster IPA, Social Insecurity Belgian Session Ale, Ginger American Red, Aviation Black IPA.

The Pick: Social Insecurity is an easy-drinking, golden-hued Belgian ale with a refreshing pilsner-like malt base and complex spicy aromas and flavors.

Old Town is about two miles away, and Colorado State University is within a short walk. The interior has a contemporary look and stylish flair with a black, gray, and orange color scheme and eye-catching artwork scattered about. There's a long bar facing the forty beer taps and shelves populated with spirits bottles. There's plentiful table seating and a patio out front. The brewery is out of sight in the basement.

While Nook expected a mostly younger crowd to frequent Black Bottle, the brewpub's diverse offerings have attracted an unexpectedly mixed clientele. "It's like a melting pot of different people here," he observed. "I was really surprised by that. It really shows the need for something different."

The menu is a spin on traditional pub fare. Fries can be ordered in several varieties including green chili, garlic, and malt vinegar. Rather than offer standard burgers, Black Bottle creates a variety of sliders. Instead of chicken wings, the menu lists pork wings, which look like riblets but are actually pork shank. Other items include flatbread pizzas, cheese plates, and oysters.

The brewery's non-standard beer selection is interesting, diverse, and well-executed. Social Insecurity is a complex yet refreshing Belgian session ale. Ginger—which isn't brewed with ginger, but pokes fun at redheads—is a caramelly American red ale well laced with citrusy hops. It pairs beautifully with the pork wings with Thai chili sauce, as I discovered. A collection of almost thirty wine and spirits barrels is used to create sour beers, both blended and unblended. Black Bottle's approach to brewing is straightforward. "We're all over the place," said Nook.

Black Bottle Brewery

Opened: December 2012.

Owners: Sean and Erin Nook.

Head brewer: Sean Nook.

Potential annual capacity: 3,000 barrels.

Hours: Daily, 11 a.m. to midnight.

Tours: Weekends only. Check website for times.

Take-out beer: Growlers, bombers, 750 ml bottles, and kegs.

Food: Flatbread pizzas, sliders, crab cakes, oysters, and pub-style food with a twist.

Extras: Trivia on Tuesday. AHA member discount program participant.

Parking: On-site lot.

Area attractions: See chapter intro.

Other area beer sites: See chapter intro.

Bootstrap Brewing Company

6778 North 79th Street, Niwot, CO 80503
(303) 652-4186 • www.bootstrapbrewing.com

There's no one particular feature that qualifies Niwot's Bootstrap Brewing as a great neighborhood brewery. In a classic example of the whole exceeding the sum of its parts, Bootstrap's laid-back demeanor and well-crafted beers create a welcoming refuge that attracts many return visitors, including me.

Leslie and Steve Kaczeus, Bootstrap's gregarious proprietors, grew up in Longmont and worked together at a disk drive company. He was a mechanical engineer and she worked in marketing, both areas of expertise that would serve them well down the road. When the high-tech company went under, they moved to California's Bay Area to find work. There they discovered craft beers such as Sierra Nevada Pale Ale and Pete's Wicked Ale. Steve also discovered homebrewing, and was soon hooked on the hobby.

Eventually, they returned to Colorado and settled in Niwot, a pleasant bedroom community with a lively arts scene sitting halfway between Boulder and Longmont. After years in the turbulent tech industry, the couple began talking about starting a business of their own. These conversations often took place in small breweries, so it's not surprising that the idea of a brewery began to take hold. They proceeded cautiously at first. After Steve returned from a week of hands-on learning at a Toronto-based craft brewery, the handwriting was on the wall. "I just fell in love," Steve recalled. "It was so much fun. I just had a blast."

Once they had committed to the new endeavor, things began to fall into place. They purchased a used 3.5-barrel brewing system and put it in storage while they searched for a location for the business. "We wanted to do something here in Niwot because we live here," Steve explained. "Our kids went to school here. We love the community and we thought it would be really cool to have a small neighborhood brewery." Three months after purchasing their brewing hardware,

Year-round beers: 1956 Golden Ale, Flagstaff Amber, Red Beerd, Boomer Brown, Insane Rush IPA, Backfire Chili, Worthog Stout.

The Pick: Insane Rush IPA has a devout local following, and for good reason. The amber elixir is laced with luscious hop goodness from start to finish, while an undercurrent of malt adds nuance and complexity to this satisfying brew.

they found a space in a retail and office complex a few blocks from downtown Niwot.

The couple agonized about what to name their fledgling business. With scores of new breweries coming on the scene, each time they came up with a new business name, they discovered it was already in use. One day, while crunching numbers on their business plan, Leslie said to her husband, "This is going to be such a bootstrap operation." The name clicked. Bootstrap Brewing opened in June 2012.

Bootstrap quickly established itself as a community gathering spot. The vibe is relaxed and friendly, reflecting the attitude of the owners. The couple are natural publicans, constantly circulating around the taproom, chatting with regulars, meeting newcomers, and making sure everyone feels like a welcome guest. There's a second, smaller room where bands perform on Saturdays. Guests gather on the outdoor patio throughout the warm-weather months.

The seven full-time beers include Insane Rush IPA, an excellent hoppy ale with a growing presence in area taphouses and restaurants. There's a chili beer that some people enjoy mixed with tomato juice. "It tastes like an enchilada," according to Leslie. 1956 Golden Ale is named in tribute to Steve's Hungarian-born father and his compatriots. In 1956, the elder Kaczeus joined scores of students in Budapest protesting communist rule. It led to the revolution in which many Hungarians were killed. Today, Steve's parents are frequent visitors to Bootstrap. They're the older couple shaking it on the dance floor during the weekly live music sessions.

Bootstrap Brewing Company

Opened: June 2012.

Owners: Steve and Leslie Kaczeus.

Head brewer: Steve Kaczeus.

Potential annual capacity: 750 barrels.

Hours: Daily, 3 p.m. to 9 p.m.

Tours: On request.

Take-out beer: Growlers and bombers.

Food: Delivery menus available. Food trucks on Friday. Tapas on Saturday.

Extras: Open Mic on Monday. Trivia on Tuesday. Euchre on Wednesday. Live music on Saturday. AHA member deals program participant.

Parking: On-site lot.

Area attractions: Nearby art galleries in downtown Niwot. Boulder is nearby.

Other area beer sites: See Boulder and Longmont in chapter intro.

Boulder Beer Company

2880 Wilderness Place, Boulder, CO 80301
(303) 444-8448 • www.boulderbeer.com

The story of Colorado's pioneering role in America's craft beer movement begins with Boulder Beer Company, Colorado's first microbrewery and one of the oldest craft breweries in the country. The original protagonists were David Hummer and Randolph "Stick" Ware, two University of Colorado professors and homebrewers who had acquired a taste for flavorful beers while traveling in Europe. In September 1979 they launched Boulder Brewing Company, the forty-third operating brewery in the United States. The business was later renamed Rockies Brewing, and eventually Boulder Beer Company.

The original brewery was located on a small farm northeast of Boulder. A 1-barrel brewing system was set up in a shed that also housed several goats. An industrial soup pot was used as a brewkettle. The brewery quickly developed a loyal local following. With sights set on becoming a national brand, the founders raised funds to build a dedicated brewery. They moved into an East Boulder facility in 1984 in an area that has evolved into a leafy business park. A 50-barrel brewing system was installed and a bottling line was acquired from Coors Brewing Company (now MillerCoors) in nearby Golden.

The brewery hit rough times in the late 1980s and, with its future in doubt, the original founders relinquished their ownership. Under new owners, the business regained its financial footing. By the mid-1990s, the upstart brewery had earned a spot on *Inc. Magazine*'s list of five hundred fastest-growing companies. Today, Boulder Beer is distributed in thirty-eight states.

Boulder Beer is one of a small but growing number of packaging breweries in the state with an on-site restaurant. The Pub, as the eatery is called, is a popular lunch destination for professionals from neighboring businesses. Later in the day, it fills with a more diverse crowd that includes lots of regulars.

Year-round beers: Flashback India Brown Ale, Planet Porter, Buffalo Gold Golden Ale, Singletrack Copper Ale, Mojo IPA, Hazed & Infused Dry-Hopped Ale, Sweaty Betty Blonde, Shake Chocolate Porter.

The Pick: Hazed & Infused has a dominant hop character from generous additions of flavor and aroma hops but lacks the intense bitterness of an IPA. At less than 5 percent ABV, you'll be able to keep your wits about you if you decide to indulge in a second pint.

True to its namesake, The Pub has a relaxed, pubby ambience, due to its modest dimensions and an ongoing buzz of lively conversations. You enter through a small dining room where a row of windows along one wall provides a view into the brewhouse with its copper-clad kettle and mash tun. The adjacent room contains the Z-shaped bar and a small collection of booths and tables. Opposite the bar, a chalkboard lists information about the dozen or more beers on tap.

In the warm-weather months, which in Colorado can extend from April through October, the spacious patio is the place to be, especially on mild summer nights. Enclosed by fencing draped in a tangle of hop vines, the outdoor space is an inviting place to enjoy a sandwich and a few tasty pints from the extensive portfolio of ales.

The trend in recent years is to create beers with palate-blasting levels of hops and alcohol, but Boulder Beer has avoided the temptation to climb aboard the "extreme beer" bandwagon. "We're not accepting the challenge of making the most bitter beer or the highest-alcohol beer," explained head brewer David Zuckerman, an elder statesman of the craft beer industry who arrived at the brewery in 1990. "We're not trying to drive a spike through anyone's taste buds. We think we're making beers that are balanced and drinkable."

In addition to the brewery's regular and seasonal offerings, the "Brewers Choice" program gives the brew crew free reign to create anything they desire on a fifty-gallon system. The results are an eclectic, and often eccentric, collection of fruited, spiced, barrel-aged, and Belgian-style creations.

Boulder Beer Company

Opened: September 1979.

Owners: Jeff Brown, David Zuckerman, Dianne Greenlee.

Head brewer: David Zuckerman.

Potential annual capacity: 36,000 barrels.

Hours: Monday through Friday, 11 a.m. to 10 p.m.; Saturday, noon to 10 p.m.

Tours: Monday through Friday at 2 p.m. Saturday at 2 p.m. and 4 p.m.

Take-out beer: Growlers, bottles, cans, and kegs.

Food: American pub fare with some Mexican dishes.

Extras: Trivia on Wednesday (October through March). Live music on the patio on Thursday (summer only). AHA pub discount program participant.

Parking: On-site lot and free street parking.

Area attractions: See chapter intro.

Other area beer sites: See chapter intro.

BRU Handbuilt Ales & Eats

5290 Arapahoe Avenue, Boulder, CO 80303
(720) 638-5193 • www.bruboulder.com

The first time I visited BRU, the tiny brewery was located in the garage of founder Ian Clark's house in the middle of a North Boulder residential neighborhood. Technically, breweries are not permitted to operate in residential areas of Boulder, but through a zoning anomaly, Clark's neighborhood sat on an island of unincorporated space within the city. After a prolonged process, Clark was able to acquire the necessary licensing, and the brewery came to life in early 2012.

Clark's first experience with fermentation came in high school in Maine when he would get fresh-pressed apple cider from nearby orchards and let it ferment. Years later, he got the homebrew bug. As might be expected of a professional chef, he began experimenting with different spices, sugars, and yeasts. "I couldn't drink as much as I was producing. It was all about the process for me," Clark explained of his prolific homebrewing exploits.

At the urging of his wife, he decided to go commercial. Like many would-be professional brewers, Clark spent considerable time trying to come up with a name for the fledgling business. While planning a trip to Belgium, he came upon the name BRU. It stuck. BRU, of course, is the airport code for Brussels.

In the brewery's early days, Clark brewed six to eight times a week on a homebrew-sized 10-gallon system while simultaneously working full-time as a chef. His beer was kegged and served in several Boulder restaurants. He soon upgraded to a 3-barrel system, began bottling, and still had trouble keeping up with demand.

While we sipped beers in his garage-brewery during our first meeting, Clark informed me that he would be leaving his job as executive chef of a downtown Boulder restaurant and moving the brewery to an East Boulder location that would also house a restaurant. BRU Handbuilt Ales & Eats opened in June 2013. The brewpub sits in an

Year-round beers: Citrum IPA, Obitus Brown Ale, Beezel Belgian Golden Strong Ale, Belux Belgian Pale Ale, Rigley Red Rye IPA.

The Pick: Beezel is a dangerously drinkable 9 percent ABV Belgian golden ale with a sweet character up front, a touch of citrus, and a palate-cleansing kiss of bitterness in the finish.

end unit of a small strip mall on the south side of Arapahoe Avenue, just east of Foothills Parkway. Downtown Boulder is two miles away.

A half-dozen small tables line the walkway outside the new brewpub's entrance. The interior has an uncluttered, stylish appearance. The mustard, rust, and charcoal walls have minimal adornment. A smattering of repurposed materials adds a touch of rusticity. The host stand is an antique oven. The bar, which sits in the back of room, is faced with reclaimed wooden pallets. The folksy taphandles are made from antique cooking utensils. The brewpub's silverware is antique and non-matching. True to its moniker, BRU's interior is largely handbuilt. The woodwork, welding, and concrete work were completed by the BRU crew.

The handbuilt theme also permeates the kitchen. "We bake all the bread, make a good amount of the cheeses, do all the charcuterie and sausage," said Clark. The non-standard pub menu features wood-fired pizzas, bahn mi sandwiches, roasted meatballs, and other snacks, sandwiches, and entrées.

The house beers are multilayered and nuanced, often based on classic styles but infused with chef-inspired deviations. "Being a chef, I like to build on flavors," Clark explained of his incorporating spices, sugars, and flavorings into his beers. To bump up the citrusy, piney flavors of an IPA, he adds lemon zest and juniper berries. To build on the dried-fruit flavors of a brown ale, he adds roasted dates and dark caramelized sugar. To accentuate the spicy character of Belgian yeast used to ferment the Belgian golden strong ale, Clark flavors the brew with bitter orange peel and black pepper. If you didn't know these ingredients were in the beer, you probably wouldn't be able to pick them out. If you look for them, however, you might perceive them lurking in the background.

BRU Handbuilt Ales & Eats

Opened: February 2012. In current location since June 2013.
Owner and head brewer: Ian Clark.
Potential annual capacity: 550 barrels.
Hours: Monday through Saturday, 11:30 a.m. to close; Sunday, 9:30 a.m. to close.
Tours: On request.
Take-out beer: Growlers and bombers.
Food: Non-standard brewpub menu featuring wood-fired pizza (gluten-free available), sandwiches, and dinner entrées. Exotic ice cream flavors. Weekend brunch.
Parking: On-site lot.

C.B. & Potts Restaurant and Brewery
—Fort Collins

C.B.&POTTS™
RESTAURANT & BREWERY

1415 West Elizabeth Street, Fort Collins, CO 80521
(970) 221-1139 • www.cbpotts.com/colorado/fortcollins.html

C.B. & Potts, the Seattle-based brewpub chain with multiple outlets in Colorado, has one location in the Northern Front Range. The company's Fort Collins location was the first C.B. & Potts to open in the state. The restaurant opened in 1973, and was well established by the time the brewery was added in 1997.

The Fort Collins brewpub is located a short distance west of the Colorado State University campus, about two miles from Old Town Fort Collins. Given its location, and its generous beer and food specials, the Fort Collins facility attracts more college students than the other facilities.

While all C.B. & Potts locations have a sports bar theme, the Fort Collins location has a somewhat different look and layout than its younger siblings. The most obvious difference is the location of the brewing operation, which is housed in a separate building just across the parking lot from the restaurant. The brewery has its own taproom, but it's not open every day and gets light use.

The restaurant's bar area is populated with televisions. There's lots of dark wood throughout the room, creating a more publike feel than found in the chain's newer, more upscale locations. Suspended from the high ceiling is a realistic-looking model of a huge shark flashing menacing teeth and wearing an oversized Colorado State athletic shirt.

A few steps down is one of two dining areas. Dark-green vinyl booths and wooden wainscoting have an old-school look, in contrast to the slick, polished appearance typical of most brewpub chains. A second dining area on an upper level is

Year-round beers: Big Red IPA, Big Horn Hefeweizen, Colorado Blonde, 71 Pale Ale, Buttface Amber Ale, Total Disorder Porter, and a rotating lager.

The Pick: The brewpub's specialty is German-style lagers, of which several are usually available. They're approachable, clean-tasting, and fine representations of their styles.

an attractive space with high ceilings and a fireplace. There's a patio area for outdoor dining partially shaded by several large trees.

The food menu covers all the bases of what is commonly referred to as American pub fare. The menu is designed to appeal to a broad audience and brings people back with consistency and affordability.

Each C.B. & Potts location keeps an inventory of seven core beers including an IPA, a hefeweizen, a blonde ale, a pale ale, an amber ale, a porter, and a rotating lager. At each location, three or four additional handles are assigned to seasonal and specialty beers of the brewer's choice and formulation. The Colorado-based C.B. & Potts locations have garnered ten Great American Beer Festival medals since 2005.

The Fort Collins brewery specializes in lagers, which many craft breweries shy away from because they're time-consuming to produce and unforgiving of imperfect brewing techniques. In 2011, the brewery's German-style pilsener was awarded a gold medal at the Great American Beer Festival. In 2012, it captured another GABF gold for its Munich-style helles. The winning streak continued in 2013 with the Big Horn Hefeweizen capturing a gold medal.

C.B. & Potts Restaurant and Brewery—Fort Collins

Opened: Restaurant opened in 1973. Brewery added in 1997.

Owners: Ram International Restaurants.

Head brewer: Joe Bowden.

Potential annual capacity: 2,350 barrels.

Hours: Restaurant: Daily, 11 a.m. to close. Taproom: Thursday and Friday, 3 p.m. to 10 p.m.; Saturday, noon to 10 p.m.

Tours: By appointment through restaurant or on request.

Take-out beer: Growlers, six-packs, and kegs.

Food: Extensive menu of American pub favorites including sandwiches, burgers, steaks, and other entrées. Gluten-free menu available.

Extras: Monday-night bingo. AHA member deals program participant.

Parking: On-site lot.

Area attractions: See chapter intro.

Other area beer sites: See chapter intro.

City Star Brewing

321 Mountain Avenue, Berthoud, CO 80513
(970) 532-7827 • www.citystarbrewing.com

A sign on the wall at City Star Brewing reads, "Beer will change the world. I don't know how, but it will." If I could add some words of wisdom in the same general spirit, they would be, "If every town had a brewery like City Star, it would change the world." There's a lot to like about this friendly small-town gathering spot. If it was in my town, I'd visit frequently.

The brewery is in Berthoud, a town of around five thousand located between Denver and Fort Collins. It has a slow-paced, small-town feel and a mix of old Victorian homes and new developments. City Star occupies a historic brick building in Berthoud's downtown district, which retains the feel of an earlier era. The business gets its name from the City Star Barn livery stable, which had been located on the site of the brewery. When I asked brewery cofounder Whitney Taylor what a livery stable was, she informed me it's "a parking lot for horses."

The building that houses the brewery and a few other small businesses has undergone a loving restoration. While part of the old brick façade remains, tall windows and a handsome wooden entryway are more recent additions. Old-style lamp fixtures are mounted on the building exterior over a small sidewalk patio.

City Star is a dream fulfilled for the husband-and-wife team of John Way and Whitney Taylor. John was an avid homebrewer with a job in packaging at the Oskar Blues Brewery in Longmont. He had aspirations of becoming a professional brewer. The couple had visions of opening a small brewery with a community focus. The idea sprouted roots when Taylor's parents purchased the historic building and offered the couple part of the space for the brewery. It took a year to renovate the one-hundred-year-old structure. The business opened in May 2012.

The taproom is a comfortable size: large enough for you to have a private conversation but small enough that you still feel connected to other

Year-round beers: Cowboy's Golden, 6 Shooter Pale Ale, Red Necktar, Bandit Brown, Night Watchman Stout.

The Pick: Red Necktar, an American red ale, is a beer I could sip all night without getting bored or fatigued. A big malt presence vies for dominance with an equally assertive hop character in this tasting-room favorite.

visitors. There is a long communal table in the center of the room. Smaller tables are arranged along the red-and-green walls. The small bar, with seating for six, is at the far end of the room.

Many of the fixtures in the room were made from wood salvaged during the renovation, creating a weathered quality that can't be replicated with new materials. The big table was made from wood collected from what had been a night watchman's quarters. The bar base is made from old hardwood flooring. The chalkboards listing beers and upcoming events are set in old window frames that were uncovered behind drywall during the renovation. A chandelier that John built using staves from a wooden barrel is an inspired piece of craftsmanship and complements the space perfectly.

A collection of historical photos is displayed along with a series of photos taken during a brewing session. There's not a television in sight. The relaxed and welcoming ambience is made more so by City Star's genuinely friendly servers.

When I visited on a Saturday afternoon, the room contained an even mix of locals playing board games and sipping pints, and beer travelers like me working their way through sampler trays. The beers were well-crafted and good representations of their styles, from an easy-drinking golden ale to several heartier specialty beers that included a strong ale and a double IPA. City Star's brown ale and strong ale captured gold and bronze medals respectively at the 2013 Great American Beer Festival. I'm hopeful that the current wave of new brewery openings in Colorado includes more places like City Star. The world will be better for it.

City Star Brewing

Opened: May 2012.

Owners: John Way and Whitney Taylor.

Head brewer: John Way.

Potential annual capacity: 700 barrels.

Hours: Monday and Tuesday, 2 p.m. to 9 p.m.; Wednesday through Friday, 2 p.m. to 10 p.m.; Saturday, noon to 10 p.m.; Sunday, noon to 9 p.m.

Tours: On request.

Take-out beer: Growlers and kegs.

Food: Restaurant delivery menus on hand or bring your own food.

Extras: Live music on Thursday, Friday, and Saturday. Old-time jam on the first Sunday of the month. Euchre on Tuesday. Trivia on Wednesday. AHA member discount program participant.

Parking: On-street and nearby lot, both free.

Area attractions: Check out the mural on the grain elevator near downtown.

Coopersmith's Pub & Brewing

5 Old Town Square, Fort Collins, CO 80524
(970) 498-0483 • www.coopersmithspub.com

Fort Collins, the home of Coopersmith's Pub & Brewing, is a beer lover's fantasyland, with ten breweries of unique character within the city limits. Fort Collins also has ties to another fantasyland: Harper Goff, the designer of Disneyland's Main Street USA, was born and raised in Fort Collins. He used several downtown buildings as models for his Disneyland design.

Coopersmith's, which opened in late 1989, is the oldest brewpub in northern Colorado and among the oldest in the state. It has a prominent location in Old Town Square, a pedestrian-only zone and center of activity in downtown Fort Collins. The business occupies two separate buildings on opposite sides of a walkway. The "Pubside" is the brewpub. The "Poolside" is home to an expansive pool hall where you can also get food and fresh beer.

In an unusual arrangement, the brewing operation is divided between the two locations. The brewhouse is located on the pub side, while fermentation and aging tanks are located on both sides. Precious liquid is transported between the two facilities by means of stainless steel piping.

The Pubside caters to a diverse clientele that includes downtown professionals, business travelers, and lots of families. In fact, some of Coopersmith's current employees first visited the brewpub when they were young children. Tourists, especially beer tourists, are frequent summer visitors. The outdoor patio seating offers some of the best people-watching in town.

The Poolside was added in 1993. With a dozen billiards tables, Ping-Pong, shuffleboard, and darts, it's the place to kill a few hours or an evening. The Poolside has additional patio seating and an attractive indoor-outdoor greenhouse dining area.

Dwight Hall, who runs the brewing operations, has been with Coopersmith's since it opened. His first job was in the kitchen before he moved to the

Year-round beers: Albert Damm Bitter, Horsetooth Stout, Mountain Avenue Wheat, Not Brown Ale, Poudre Pale Ale, Sigda's Green Chili Beer, Punjabi Pale Ale, Columbine Kolsch (Pubside only), Tippet Lager (Poolside only), Steamship Ale (Poolside only).

The Pick: Poudre Pale Ale is an English-style pale ale with a pleasant nuttiness balanced with Golding hops.

brewery to wash kegs and clean tanks. He worked his way into a brewing job, and then became head brewer in 1997.

Despite his longevity in the brewery, Hall is by no means set in his ways. While he maintains a core of time-tested beers, he enjoys creating beers outside the mainstream. "One of the really fantastic things about being a brewpub in Fort Collins is we have an extremely educated beer-drinking population," said Hall of the beer-savvy local populace. "I have yet to find any beer that's too challenging for our drinkers. When I started experimenting with Belgian sour beers I was pleasantly shocked when people loved it."

There's a streak of British pub influence in both the food and beer offerings. You can enjoy a plate of bangers and mash with a hand-drawn bitter or other cask-conditioned ale. If this doesn't fit your mood, you can go a completely different direction with a salmon and brie quesadilla and a chili beer.

While chili beers have become somewhat commonplace—at least in chili-loving Colorado—when Coopersmith's Sigda's Green Chili Beer was introduced in 1990, it was a ground-breaking beverage. It has an upfront flavor of Anaheim and Serrano chilies, a manageable spicy kick in the finish, and a legion of passionate fans. "We have to keep it on all the time," explained Hall. "There would be a mutiny if we didn't have it. We have people who come from out of state and fill growlers. They'll bring a dozen growlers." If you're looking for a break from malt beverages, there's always a homemade cider on tap, and often a mead.

Coopersmith's Pub & Brewing

Opened: November 1989.

Owners: Scott Smith, president. Sandra Longton, Dwight Hall, Chris O'Mara, managing partners.

Head brewer: Dwight Hall.

Potential annual capacity: 2,400 barrels.

Hours: Sunday through Thursday, 11 a.m. to 11 p.m.; Friday and Saturday, 11 a.m. to midnight.

Tours: By appointment. Call 970-498-0483, ext. 2.

Take-out beer: Growlers and kegs.

Food: American and English pub fare, sandwiches, burgers, and pizza. Separate gluten-free menu.

Extras: Pool tables. Extensive single-malt Scotch selection.

Parking: Parking garage across the street.

Area attractions: See chapter intro.

Other area beer sites: See chapter intro.

Crabtree Brewing Company

2961 29th Street, Greeley, CO 80631
(970) 356-0516 • www.crabtreebrewing.com

In a typical scenario for an upstart brewery, an impassioned homebrewer decides to go pro, raises the necessary capital, finds a location, and then learns on the fly the complexities of launching and operating a successful business. Jeff Crabtree, founder of Crabtree Brewing, had a somewhat different approach.

"I knew how to play the game on the business side," explained Crabtree, who had been working as a financial analyst for thirteen years prior to opening the brewery. "I actually entered my business with a thirty-eight-page business plan and an exit strategy."

While working in the corporate world, Crabtree would spend his weekends cooking as a way to unwind. Though he was eating well, the beer he was drinking was lacking. He figured if he could make great food, he should be able to make good beer, and so he took up homebrewing. He became intrigued with brewing as a business venture. When he decided to open a commercial brewery, his extensive business background was put to good use. He believes that his staff is an important investment, and offers tuition reimbursement for beer- or business-related education.

Crabtree brewing opened in Greeley in 2006. Greeley, an agricultural community and home to the University of Northern Colorado, sits on the rolling plains about twenty miles east of Loveland. Fort Collins is a forty-minute drive, and Boulder is an hour away. Compared with much of northern Colorado, Greeley has been slow to climb aboard the craft beer bandwagon. Over the years, the town has not been kind to hometown breweries. Before Crabtree set up shop, five brewpubs had come and gone. Local tastes are evolving, however. When I first met Crabtree in 2012, he told me that Greeley was ten years behind Fort Collins in matters of craft beer. A year later, he revised that number to four years.

Year-round beers: Head Turner Blonde Ale, Serenity Amber Ale, Berliner Weisse, Oatmeal Stout, Ginger Bee, Boxcar Brown, Dearfield Strawberry Blonde Ale, Rebel Rye IPA.

The Pick: The tasty and approachable Berliner Weisse combines a wheaty flavor with a refreshing and restrained tartness. At less than 5 percent ABV, it's a beer that can be quaffed in quantity.

Knowing that the local audience would not be enough to support a brewery, Crabtree created the business as a production brewery, packaging beer for distribution beyond the taproom. Crabtree beers are distributed throughout the Colorado Front Range and in Missouri and Nebraska.

The brewery is located in an area of mixed businesses just off Highway 34. The taproom is quite large, with an island-style bar located in the center of the room with plentiful table seating around the perimeter. It's a low-key, casual space with high ceilings and blue-and-yellow-painted walls. The brewhouse sits out of sight beyond the taproom. A homebrew shop resides in the same building as the brewery. There's an outdoor seating area with a few picnic tables. Expansion plans will increase the size of the brewing operation and create a pleasant beer garden.

With a few exceptions, Crabtree's full-time beers are a malt-forward collection of English and American-style ales covering the color spectrum from blonde to amber to brown to black. Those exceptions include the tangy and aggressively hopped Rebel Rye IPA, and the tart and refreshing Berliner Weisse. In 2011, Crabtree garnered two Great American Beer Festival medals: a silver for the Oatmeal Stout, and a gold for the Berliner Weisse. During my visit, taproom patrons were a mostly older, local crowd who seemed particularly enamored of the Dearfield Ale, a strawberry-flavored blonde ale.

Crabtree Brewing Company

Opened: May 2006.

Owner and head brewer: Jeff Crabtree.

Potential annual capacity: 3,120 barrels.

Hours: Sunday, noon to 6 p.m.; Monday through Thursday, 1 p.m. to 10 p.m.; Friday and Saturday, noon to midnight.

Tours: On request.

Take-out beer: Growlers, six-packs, bombers, 750 ml bottles, and kegs.

Food: Food trucks on-site Tuesdays, Wednesdays, and Fridays.

Extras: AHA member discount program participant.

Parking: On-site lot.

Area attractions: University of Northern Colorado.

Other area beer sites: Patrick's Irish Pub (901 8th Ave., 970-396-8095).

Crystal Springs Brewing Company

Crystal Springs

BREWING COMPANY

657 South Taylor Avenue, Louisville, CO 80027
(303) 665-8888 • www.crystalspringsbrewing.com

There were two significant openings in Boulder in the year 1875. One was Boulder High School. The second was a brewery called Boulder City Brewing. Around the turn of the twentieth century, the brewery was sold and renamed Crystal Springs Brewing and Ice Company. It was a sizeable operation, distributing to seven states in its heyday. In 2010, a music teacher at Boulder High School launched a home-based commercial brewery on the outskirts of Boulder. He resurrected the name of the old brewery, Crystal Springs.

Tom Horst discovered homebrewing in 1989. "Doc," as the PhD percussionist is known at Boulder High, has been making beer ever since. Over the years, Horst had contemplated ways to produce supplemental income to put his daughters through college once he retired from his position as an instrumental music teacher. With continued encouragement from his wife, Kristy, the idea of a commercial brewery gradually took shape. While looking for a location for a brewing operation, he learned that he could legally operate a brewing business out of his home in Sunshine Canyon, a short distance beyond Boulder's city limits. In the spring of 2010, the new Crystal Springs Brewing Company was born. The brewery had humble beginnings, with a 20-gallon brewing system set up in a detached two-car garage.

Things didn't go quite as expected. They went much better. "We went to the liquor stores that we frequented, and a couple restaurants, and they took us on. I really didn't think it would go much farther than that," said Horst. A new Boulder pizzeria put Crystal Springs's Kolsch on tap full-time. More area liquor stores called, wanting to carry the Crystal Springs beers. To keep up with demand, Horst upgraded to a 2-barrel brewing system. "I really didn't expect it to explode like it has, but it's pretty cool," said Doc.

Although the home-based brewery had no provisions for visitors, people called wanting to visit.

Year-round beers: Doc's American Porter, South Ridge Amber, Stagecoach 1899 Black IPA, Marilyn Belgian Golden Strong Ale, Butch Pale Ale, Bob's Your Uncle Mild, Black Saddle Imperial Stout, 13 IPA, BS2R Black Saddle Second Runnings.

The Pick: Butch Pale Ale has a nutty malt character balanced with all Simcoe hops. Its clean, dry finish keeps your palate refreshed.

Sometimes they just arrived at the house unannounced. Aside from these brief encounters, and an occasional beer festival, Tom and Kristy—who handles sales for the brewery—had little contact with their customers. "Somewhere along the line we decided we wanted to have a place where we could meet people," Horst recalled. In 2013, the couple procured a spot in a business park in nearby Louisville where brewing could take place under more optimal conditions.

Crystal Springs is located in a large modern complex of mixed businesses about two miles from downtown Louisville. The location is easily accessible from the neighboring communities of Lafayette, Broomfield, Superior, and Boulder. The four thousand people who work in the complex should provide a built-in base of thirsty patrons. When I visited the new brewery, it was a few weeks away from opening, so I can't provide a lot of details. The taproom is a modest-sized space with a cheery modern feel. A room on the second level is intended as a game room and overflow space, with a small outdoor patio adjacent.

The brewery has thirteen taps. Crystal Springs's full-time beers encompass a broad range of American and European styles including an English mild, a Belgian golden strong ale, a black IPA, and an imperial stout. Seasonal offerings and at least two barrel-aged brews will round out the offerings in the tasting room.

Horst told me of plans to create a lager inspired by the brewery's turn-of-the-century namesake. The owner-brewer came across a detailed newspaper review, dated 1905, of a beer called Wuerzburger, produced at the original Crystal Springs Brewery. The recipe for a revived version of the beer is based on that review.

Crystal Springs Brewing Company

Opened: May 2010. In current location since October 2013.
Owner and head brewer: Tom Horst.
Potential annual capacity: 600 barrels.
Hours: Check online.
Tours: On request.
Take-out beer: Growlers, pouches, bombers, and cans.
Food: Bring your own.
Parking: On-site.
Area attractions: The Louisville Street Faire features free outdoor concerts on Friday evenings in the summer. Downtown Boulder is ten miles away.
Other area beer sites: Empire Lounge & Restaurant (816 Main St., 303-665-2521). Lucky Pie (637 Front St., 303-666-5743). LuLu's BBQ (701 B Main St, 720-583-1789).

Echo Brewing Company

5969 Iris Parkway, Unit C, Frederick, CO 80503
(720) 445-5969 • www.echobrewing.com

If Echo Brewing Company had a theme song, it would be the jingle that accompanies the Doublemint chewing gum television ads featuring identical twins. The brewery is operated by partners Dennis and Daniel Richards, who happen to be identical twins. The name Echo is a clever reflection of their unique relationship. Two sisters also help out with the business and are part owners. Perhaps another appropriate brewery theme song would be "It's a Family Affair."

Echo Brewing is located in a modern-looking industrial complex in the small town of Frederick, on the open plains east of Longmont. The town derives its name from another tight-knit family. In the early 1900s, three sisters christened the town Frederick after their father, Frederick Clark, who owned the land where the community now resides. The area, including the neighboring towns of Firestone and Dacono, is known as Carbon Valley, a reference to the area's coal-mining heritage.

Dennis and Daniel had been homebrewing partners with aspirations of one day opening their own brewery. Both were working in high-tech jobs for the same company. After Daniel got laid off, plans for a brewery began to accelerate. While searching for a suitable location, the brothers settled on Frederick, a growing community lacking a hometown brewery. The process of securing a location, installing brewing equipment, and conquering the mountains of paperwork necessary to procure the required licensing took several years. Their efforts came to fruition in April 2012 to great fanfare as hundreds of well-wishers showed up for their grand opening. The crowds continue to arrive.

"The whole community has really embraced us," said Daniel (or was it Dennis?) in reference to the steady stream of regular visitors, many of whom the proprietors have come to know on a first-name basis. With easy access from communities like Boulder and Fort Collins, beer enthusiasts from throughout the Northern Front Range also seek out the affable brewery. Daniel takes care of the front of the house, while Dennis runs the brewhouse.

Year-round beers: Balefire Irish Red, Nocturnal Black Double IPA, Kirby Kolsch, Powder Daze Pale Ale.

The Pick: Nocturnal Black Double IPA is 10 percent alcohol and 100 IBUs of sweet, roasty, hoppy goodness. The tummy-warming finish is sure to warm your cockles, whatever cockles are.

The taproom is modern and simple. The walls are painted yellow and red, contributing to the cheery ambience. An attractive bar of laminated wood sits atop a base of shiny corrugated metal. Behind the bar, a row of tap handles, including a nitro tap, protrudes from the wall beneath a mirror. Several flatscreens are mounted on the walls. At one end of the bar, a pair of large windows looks into the brewhouse and the gleaming 7-barrel brewing system. A self-serve popcorn machine sits in a nook. A small room off the main taproom contains a collection of upholstered chairs providing a quiet, comfortable retreat. In front of the building, there's a wooden deck with views of the distant mountains. Food trucks frequent the brewery, and live music is scheduled once or twice a week. Tuesday trivia night is a popular draw.

Echo's beer selection has a something-for-everyone theme. You can go hoppy or malty, pale or dark, easy-drinking or hearty. At any one time, you're likely to find English, German, and American styles. The pale, approachable Kirby Kolsch provides an easy transition for those graduating from mass-produced light American lagers. Seasoned beer palates seeking more assertive offerings will find beers such as the Nocturnal Black Double IPA worthy of sampling. A taproom favorite is the Balefire Irish Red, which was awarded a bronze medal at the 2012 Great American Beer Festival, six months after the brewery opened. Echo Amber, a German-style altbier, was a 2013 GABF bronze medal winner.

After being open for just over a year, the brothers announced plans to open a second brewery in Erie, about ten miles away. Echo Brewing Cask and Barrel should be open in early 2014.

Echo Brewing Company

Opened: April 2012.

Owners: Dennis and Daniel Richards.

Head brewer: Dennis Richards.

Potential annual capacity: 2,500 barrels.

Hours: Monday, 5 p.m. to 9 p.m.; Tuesday through Thursday, 2:30 p.m. to 9 p.m.; Friday, 2:30 p.m. to 10 p.m.; Saturday, 11 a.m. to 10 p.m.; Sunday, 11 a.m. to 8 p.m.

Tours: On request.

Take-out beer: Cans, growlers, and kegs.

Food: Free popcorn. Soft pretzels. Food trucks three to five nights a week. Delivery menus on hand, or bring your own food.

Extras: Live music one or two nights a week. Trivia night on Tuesday. AHA member deals program participant.

Parking: On-site lot.

Area attractions: Colorado National Speedway is an auto-racing track in nearby Dacono.

Equinox Brewing Company

133 Remington Street, Fort Collins, CO 80524
(970) 484-1368 • www.equinoxbrewing.com

A friendly neighborhood pub can reside in many types of neighborhoods. Although Equinox Brewing Company sits in the heart of lively Old Town Fort Collins, it has all the attributes of a welcoming neighborhood gathering spot.

Colin and Shannon Westcott opened Equinox in April 2010 after a dozen years of planning. Colin started out as a homebrewer, and he landed his first brewery job at Kettlehouse Brewing in Montana. By the time he departed four years later, he had worked his way into the head brewer job. The next gig was at Midnight Sun Brewing in Alaska. Following a move to Fort Collins, he opened the Hops and Berries homebrew shop. Four years later, the Westcotts' plan of opening a brewery came to fruition when Equinox opened in the space next door to the homebrew shop.

The brewery is located in a nondescript one-story building on Remington Street a block from College Avenue, Fort Collins' major north-south artery. Catering to the local preference for two-wheeled transit, a series of stylish bike racks with space for eighty-five bicycles sits alongside the building.

In the crowded Fort Collins craft beer scene, it's important that each brewery find a niche.

"We're not a brewpub. We're not a production brewery either. We're a neighborhood brewery," Colin Westcott said of the popular yet low-key brewery and taproom. "It's a niche that wasn't being filled before."

The pub is divided into three separate rooms, creating modest-sized spaces conducive to socializing. You enter into a narrow room of dark wood tables and cream-colored walls, creating a comfy, pubby feel. Toward the back of the room, a granite-topped bar has room for a half-dozen patrons. There are no TVs to distract from the convivial atmosphere.

Year-round beers: Red Dwarf Amber Ale, MidSummer Pale Ale, Third Anniversary Ale, Haver Scottish Ale, Zenith IPA, Space Ghost IPA, Galaxy IPA, Eclipse Brown, One From The Vau-ALT, Darth Ryder, Dunkelweizen, Son of Space Ghost Pale Ale.

The Pick: O'Rion Irish Red, a 2011 GABF gold medal winner that is often available but not year-round or seasonal, greets you with a subtly sweet aroma and a clean malty flavor. A hint of bitterness in the finish keeps your palate refreshed.

The adjoining space is divided into two rooms. In the front is a small, intimate space with four tables and a fireplace. The larger room behind is populated with small tables. A collection of artwork hangs on the avocado walls. A shuffleboard game sits in a narrow hallway leading to the brewhouse and patio. The enclosed outdoor space is a major draw and provides a welcome refuge from the crowds that gather in Old Town. Equinox is also quite popular with families: games and toys are available for kids, and the beverage list includes homemade root beer and cream soda.

There are twenty taps, two of which are English-style beer engines. The brewery puts out a wide range of nicely crafted brews and isn't afraid to expand the boundaries of well-defined styles. "Styles exist for historic reasons," said Westcott. When I visited in the fall, the brewery had created eighty recipes that year alone. Beers are dispensed in 20-ounce imperial pint glasses rather than the typical 16-ounce pours.

Equinox enters one competition a year, the Great American Beer Festival, and has had great success there, garnering three medals in its first three years of operation. The brewery distributes kegs only to locations where it can deliver them via a custom-made tricycle.

The delivery cycle has two front wheels and a 36-inch rear wheel. Two 15-gallon kegs fit between the front wheels. Front disc brakes keep things under control. Previously, kegs were delivered by hand truck. After the bike was constructed, the distribution area increased by a factor of four, from two blocks to eight blocks.

Equinox Brewing Company

Opened: April 2010.

Owners: Colin and Shannon Westcott.

Head brewer: Colin Westcott.

Potential annual capacity: 1,400 barrels.

Hours: Monday through Wednesday, noon to 8 p.m.; Thursday and Friday, noon to 9 p.m.; Saturday, 11 a.m. to 9 p.m.; Sunday, noon to 7 p.m.

Tours: On request.

Take-out beer: Growlers and kegs.

Food: Cheese plates and munchies available or bring your own food. Local restaurant menus on hand.

Extras: Live music on Friday and Saturday. No cover. Board games, card games, and kids' toys available. Thursday-afternoon firkin tappings.

Parking: Free on-street parking and inexpensive lots nearby.

Area attractions: See chapter intro.

Other area beer sites: See chapter intro.

Estes Park Brewery

470 Prospect Village Drive, Estes Park, CO 80517
(970) 586-5421 • www.epbrewery.com

The tourist is a middle-aged male. He is short, plump, balding, and has thick eyebrows. He wears turquoise shorts and a matching short-sleeve shirt. He is holding a camera at chest level and pointing it at a target straight ahead. He is also an inanimate object—a sculpture carved out of a log—who stands guard outside the garish, mustard-colored exterior of the Estes Park Brewery.

The sculpture could not be more appropriate. The tourist-intensive town of Estes Park is the gateway to Rocky Mountain National Park, Colorado's most popular attraction, drawing 3 million visitors annually. After a tough day on the tourist trail, many visitors find their way to the Estes Park Brewery for a burger and a brew.

The national park, only seventy miles from downtown Denver, is spectacular and easily accessible. Movie fans also know Estes Park as the home of the Stanley Hotel, the inspiration for Stephen King's 1977 novel *The Shining* and its subsequent 1980 film adaptation starring Jack Nicholson. The brewpub's Shining Pale Ale pays tribute to the book and film, while the Redrum Ale is a reference to the movie's nail-biting "redrum" scene (read it backward). The brewpub is situated close to downtown Estes, but far enough removed to be out of direct contact with the hoards of vacationers who descend on the town's T-shirt shops, candy stores, and ice cream parlors each summer.

Year-round beers: Longs Peak Raspberry Wheat, Stinger Wild Honey Wheat, Estes Park Gold, Redrum Ale, Staggering Elk Lager, Estes Park Porter, Estes Park Renegade IPA, Samson Stout.

The brewpub, originally named High County Brewery, has its roots in Boulder. It was founded there in 1993 by the late Gordon Knight, a well-known figure in the local craft beer scene who launched several craft brewing businesses in the 1990s. In 1994, Knight partnered with the owner of the building where the brewpub now resides and moved High Country to Estes, changing the name to Estes Park Brewery. Shortly after, Knight sold his share of the business.

The brewpub has two levels. The main dining room is on the upper level. It's a large space

The Pick: The bitter finish of Estes Park Renegade IPA will bring you back to reality after taking in the surreal scenery of Rocky Mountain National Park.

conducive to casual family dining. A mountain mural covers the length of one wall. Tall windows overlook the neighboring amusement park. There are several pool tables, a pinball machine, and a collection of video games. Outside seating is available on the deck.

Downstairs has additional booth seating, a tasting bar, and a well-stocked souvenir shop. A half-wall separates diners from the open brewhouse. A refrigerated display case holds six-packs and bombers of Estes Park beer that tourists gobble up as souvenirs.

Not too long ago, before craft beer made inroads nationwide, the Estes Park Brewery was the introduction to craft beer for many travelers. The tasting bar allowed visitors to sample a variety of styles before heading upstairs to the main dining room. In general, the Estes Park beers are mild-mannered and won't challenge the palates of the many craft beer novices that frequent the brewpub.

One exception is the house IPA. By today's standards, Estes Park Renegade IPA may seem fairly conventional for an India pale ale. When it was first released at the original Boulder brewery in 1993 under the name Renegade Red, it was considered cutting-edge for its assertive hop character and bitterness. That year, it won a gold medal at the Great American Beer Festival in the India pale ale category.

Be forewarned that occasional fights have been known to break out outside the brewpub. They don't involve regular patrons, but rather elk, who find the spent grain stored outside the brewhouse irresistible.

Estes Park Brewery

Opened: May 1994.

Owner: Tyler Lemirande.

Head brewer: Kurt Meyer.

Potential annual capacity: 3,500 barrels.

Hours: Daily, 11 a.m. to 11 p.m. in-season; 11 a.m. to 9 p.m. off-season. Check the website before you visit.

Tours: Not offered.

Take-out beer: Growlers and six-packs.

Food: American pub fare.

Extras: Pool tables and video games.

Parking: On-site lot.

Area attractions: Rocky Mountain National Park. The Stanley Hotel (333 Wonderview Ave., 800-976-1377).

Fate Brewing Company

1600 38th Street, Boulder, CO 80301
(303) 449-FATE (3283)
www.fatebrewingcompany.com

While the scores of new Colorado breweries that have come on the scene in recent years are mostly of the modest mom-and-pop variety, Fate Brewing Company is notable for taking a different route. The young East Boulder brewpub has bucked the trend with an ambitious endeavor that includes a voluminous dining room and outdoor patio, a food menu that transcends predictable pub fare, excellent house-brewed beers, and a broad selection of guest beers to pique the interest of discerning beer drinkers.

Fate occupies a site along busy Arapahoe Avenue near Foothills Parkway. The location is close to both residential neighborhoods and large industrial installations in an area underserved by comfortable sit-down lunch and dinner eateries. Downtown Boulder is about two miles away. For years, Avery Brewing was the area's only option for fresh-brewed beer. Fate is one of three new breweries that have recently joined the East Boulder craft beer scene.

The brewpub was the creation of Mike Lewinski, who had previously been the general manager of the West End Tavern, a downtown watering hole known for its wide-ranging craft beer tap list. Fate opened in early 2013 to a receptive audience of business diners, residents, families, and local beer fans.

The stylish interior is a large, open space with a contemporary, upscale-casual ambience. Booth and table seating are in copious supply. A U-shaped bar sits in the middle of the space. Twin rows of tap handles, thirty to a row, are eye candy for bar patrons.

A collection of bright paintings hangs from the mocha-colored walls. The brewhouse occupies a back corner of the space, highly visible behind a wall of glass. The restaurant seats two hundred indoors and nearly that many on the sprawling, multilevel outdoor patio.

Fate's kitchen puts out well-prepared pub favorites, such as burgers and sandwiches, along

Year-round beers: Parcae Belgian Pale Ale, Laimas Kolsch, Moirai IPA, Sudice American Stout, Norns Roggenbier, Cascadian Dark Ale.

The Pick: Laimas Kolsch is the perfect summer beer. It's clean, crisp, refreshing, balanced, and flavorful, with subtleties that keep it interesting.

with non-standard fare such as paella, cheddar grits, and trout. House-smoked meats round out the menu. I'm a sucker for the smoky-sweet Asian sticky ribs, especially during half-price happy hour.

Fate's head brewer, Jeff Griffith, came to Fate after running the brewhouse at Golden City Brewing for eight years. While there, he gained a solid reputation among area beerfolk for elevating both the quality and breadth of the small brewery's beer portfolio.

When I visited Fate about four months after it opened, the beer selection included ten house brews and twenty guest taps. Griffith was planning to increase the number of house beers over time. About half of the guest beers were well-curated Belgian imports, while the remaining handles were mostly assigned to selections from other local craft breweries.

The core lineup of most breweries includes something light, something amber, something dark, and something hoppy. Griffith has adopted that formula, but has taken it in a different direction with a mix of familiar and non-mainstream beer styles. His standard light beer is a wonderfully flavorful and refreshing German-style Kolsch. The amber beer is a Belgian pale ale with a yeasty-bready character. The dark ale is a hearty and hoppy American-style stout.

As is de rigueur for most craft breweries, Fate offers a hoppy American IPA. Griffith's version is a fine example of the ubiquitous style, bringing hops to the forefront while maintaining an undercurrent of sweet malt. The wild card in the deck is a roggenbier, a spicy German-style rye ale that originated in medieval times.

Fate Brewing Company

Opened: February 2013.

Owner: Mike Lewinski.

Head brewer: Jeff Griffith.

Potential annual capacity: 2,500 barrels.

Hours: Monday through Friday, 11 a.m. to 10 p.m.; Saturday and Sunday, 10 a.m. to 10 p.m.

Tours: Sunday at 4 p.m.

Take-out beer: Growlers and kegs.

Food: Assorted small plates, burgers, sandwiches, smoked meats, and dinner entrées including paella, chili-rubbed trout, and steak. Weekend brunch.

Extras: Live music on patio (check schedule online). AHA member deals program participant.

Parking: On-site lot.

Floodstage Ale Works

170 South Main Street, Brighton, CO 80601
(303) 654-7972

Floodstage Ale Works keeps a low profile in the Colorado brewing scene and is not well-known among area beerophiles. The owner, John Thorngren, eschews festivals and other off-site events. For these reasons, I had no idea what to expect when I made the trip to Brighton on a pristine spring afternoon for my first visit. What I found was an unpretentious neighborhood watering hole with a devout local following and a well-rounded selection of Colorado craft beers augmented with a few house-brewed offerings.

Floodstage resides in Brighton, a farming and bedroom community on the eastern plains, about twenty miles northeast of downtown Denver. The community's long-established agricultural heritage is evident as you approach town through vast acres of fertile farmland. Suburban sprawl, a more recent phenomenon, is also in evidence by its characteristic housing developments and shopping plazas.

The taphouse is located in Brighton's somewhat downtrodden downtown district. Floodstage resides in a weathered brick structure set back from the street. If not for the word BREWERY painted in big white letters on the exterior, it's not a place that would grab your attention. It's hardly a stretch to envision the building's former use as a transmission shop.

Floodstage is the creation of Thorngren, who grew up in Brighton before relocating to the mountain town of Steamboat Springs. While living in Steamboat, he purchased the brewing system of a defunct local brewpub. In 2006, he returned to Brighton to help out on the family farm. Upon his return, he found his hometown in desperate need of a comfortable gathering spot. "When I grew up in this town," he recalled, "you didn't go to the bars if you didn't want to get stabbed or beat up. This town was just lacking. I wanted a bar where I could hang out. I built myself a clubhouse," he said jokingly.

While the idea of opening a hometown brewery had simmered for many years, the inspiration

Year-round beers: Class 6 Porter is usually available. There are generally one or two other house-brewed beers in addition to a rotating lineup of Colorado craft beers.

The Pick: Class 6 Porter is characterized by the dry roasty character of dark grains.

to proceed came during an extended homebrew drinking session. Thorngren made a pledge to his assembled companions that he would go professional with his brewing endeavors. Someone put the pledge in writing on a piece of lined notebook paper. It was signed by Thorngren and several witnesses. What had once been a distant vision was now a concrete challenge. Things happened fast after that. Within two months, a location was secured. Floodstage opened in early 2008. The pledge is now framed and kept at the brewery.

The entrance to Floodstage is framed in holiday lights, which extend along the low metal fence that encloses an expansive, partially covered patio in the front of the building. The interior has a look and feel more suggestive of your dad's corner bar than your local craft brewery. A hodgepodge of beer paraphernalia, including the ubiquitous "Free Beer Tomorrow" sign, shares wall space with a collection of photos of river-running expeditions.

As I perused the abbreviated food menu, several regulars informed me, in no uncertain terms, that Floodstage serves "the best burger in town." There are twenty draught beers available, including two or three house beers. The guest taps include a well-rounded selection of Colorado craft beers from breweries including New Belgium, Ska, Great Divide, Oskar Blues, Odell, Left Hand, and Breckenridge. In addition to the draught selections, Floodstage keeps at least seventy-five bottled and canned craft beers on hand. Thorngren brews infrequently. Class 6 Porter is as close as he has to a full-time beer. "I've been working on the recipe for twenty years," said the owner-brewer. "It's just fun. There's no such thing as the perfect beer."

Floodstage Ale Works

Opened: January 2008.

Owner and head brewer: John Thorngren.

Potential annual capacity: 250 barrels.

Hours: Tuesday through Sunday, 11 a.m. to midnight or beyond. Monday, 2 p.m. to midnight.

Tours: On request.

Take-out beer: Growlers.

Food: Wings, nachos, burgers, brats, and hot dogs. Said to be the best burgers in town.

Extras: Poker on Tuesday, Wednesday, and Saturday. Karaoke on Thursday.

Parking: On-site parking, street parking, and nearby lot, all free.

Fort Collins Brewery and Gravity 1020 Modern Tavern

1020 East Lincoln Avenue, Fort Collins, CO 80524
(970) 472-1499 • www.fortcollinsbrewery.com,
www.gravity1020.com

From your first sighting along Lincoln Avenue, the Fort Collins Brewery is an attention-grabber. With bright exterior walls contrasted against large sections of brick, the modern brewery and restaurant complex presents an attractive example of contemporary industrial design.

The business resides about a mile east of Old Town Fort Collins. Three other breweries—Odell, Funkwerks, and New Belgium—are within a one-mile radius. Many people take advantage of the town's free bike library to visit this close-in cluster of breweries.

Fort Collins is one of only a few Colorado production breweries—that is, breweries that produce and package beer primarily for off-site distribution—that also houses a full-service restaurant. The company came into being when the current owners, Jan and Tom Peters, purchased the defunct H. C. Berger brewery and rebranded it as Fort Collins Brewery. That original location was at 1900 Lincoln, a mile east of the current site, where Funkwerks Brewing now resides. Fort Collins's 1900 Amber Lager is named for the address of the company's original home. From the start, the brewery set its sights on distribution beyond the Colorado marketplace. Fort Collins beers can now be found in over twenty states and in Sweden.

In 2010, the company completed construction of the new brewery and restaurant, increasing its space almost tenfold, from 3,500 to 30,000 square feet. The restaurant occupies the south side of the building while the taproom is on the west side. Both have windows looking into the brewery, which takes up the majority of the interior space. The restaurant has an attractive outdoor patio facing Lincoln Avenue and the green expanse of a golf course beyond.

A few picnic tables sit on a small covered patio by the entrance to the taproom. The interior has a

Year-round beers: Major Tom's Pomegranate Wheat, 1900 Amber, Red Banshee Red Ale, Rocky Mountain IPA, Z Lager, Kidd Black Lager, Chocolate Stout.

The Pick: Kidd Black Lager, a schwarzbier, has a subtly sweet and roasty character with just a hint of smokiness.

cheery appearance, with brightly colored walls of red, green, and yellow. High ceilings and exposed metal ductwork contribute to an industrial theme. A mural painted on the corrugated metal bar base adds a playful element to the décor. During my afternoon stopover, most visitors were sipping from sampler trays, a telltale sign of out-of-town travelers.

Windows along the far wall look into the spotless brewhouse where the walls of yellow, green, and orange reflect off rows of gleaming stainless steel tanks. Adjacent to the brewhouse is the on-site restaurant, Gravity 1020. As with the entire complex, it's a visually striking space with a bright open feel and contemporary furnishings.

The restaurant menu changes seasonally. Many dishes are a modern take on classic pub fare. The kitchen focuses on locally sourced ingredients. Fresh herbs are grown in a rooftop garden.

Fort Collins' beer list has a pronounced German flavor. An amber lager, a rauchbier (smoked lager), and a schwarzbier (black lager) are among the full-time selections. Other interesting styles include a pomegranate wheat beer and a chocolate stout. An amber, a red, and an IPA round out the regular offerings. Seasonal offerings include a maibock, an Imperial pale ale, a dopplebock, a winter warmer, and a double chocolate stout. In 2012, a smoked beer from Fort Collins was a Great American Beer Festival gold medal winner.

Fort Collins Brewery and Gravity 1020 Modern Tavern

Opened: March 2004.

Owners: Jan and Tom Peters.

Head brewer: No designated head brewer. Five-person brew team.

Potential annual capacity: 32,000 barrels.

Hours: Pub hours: Monday through Thursday, 11 a.m. to 6 p.m.; Friday and Saturday, 11 a.m. to 7 p.m. Restaurant hours: Tuesday through Thursday, 11 a.m. to 9 p.m.; Friday and Saturday, 11 a.m. to 10 p.m.; Sunday, 10 a.m. to 3 p.m.

Tours: Hourly on Saturdays between 1 p.m. and 7 p.m.

Take-out beer: Growlers, bottles, and kegs.

Food: The 1020 Modern Tavern features a creative menu with little resemblance to standard pub cuisine. Offerings range from shrimp and grits to bacon-wrapped pretzels to a lobster BLT to chicken and waffles. Brunch is served on weekends.

Extras: Live music on Thursday nights. Free cherry root beer for kids and designated drivers. AHA member deals program participant.

Parking: On-site lot.

Area attractions: See chapter intro.

Other area beer sites: See chapter intro.

Funkwerks

funkwerks

1900 East Lincoln Avenue, Unit B, Fort Collins, CO 80524
(970) 482-FUNK (3865) • www.funkwerks.com

To have a successful brewery in the crowded beer scene of northern Colorado, it helps to have a well-defined niche. Once you've found it, you'd better do it well. For Brad Lincoln and Gordon Schuck, founders of Fort Collins's Funkwerks brewery, that niche is saisons and other Belgian-style ales. Simply put, they nailed it.

Lincoln and Schuck met while attending brewing school at Chicago's well-known Siebel Institute of Technology. They went their separate ways, but reunited to join forces in a brewing venture. They knew from the start that they needed a narrow focus that would set them apart from other Front Range breweries. In 2007, Schuck had won a gold medal in the National Homebrew Competition for his saison. Thus the duo decided to specialize in saisons and other Belgian ales, providing their brewery with a unique identity that left plenty of room for exploration and experimentation.

As is typical for a fledgling new enterprise, they agonized over a name for their business. "We knew we didn't want any geographic features in the name, or dogs. We really didn't even want 'brewery' in the name," Lincoln recalled of their early search for an appropriate moniker. They liked the sound of "Werks," and after more deliberation, agreed that Funkwerks had a nice ring to it.

They decided to locate in Fort Collins for several reasons. First, the presence of New Belgium Brewing in the city meant that the local brew-loving populace was already familiar with Belgian-style beers. Also, with other quality breweries nearby, they wouldn't feel the need to brew popular styles, such as IPAs, if they didn't want to, since that need was already being filled. Funkwerks joined the Fort Collins craft brewing community in late 2010.

Funkwerks raised some eyebrows in 2011 when its flagship beer, simply called Saison, was awarded a silver medal at the Great American Beer Festival. The following year, Funkwerks captured the attention of the craft beer community nationwide

Year-round beers: Saison, Tropic King Imperial Saison.

The Pick: The Saison is an interesting and complex yet highly drinkable brew with spicy and earthy notes and a pleasingly dry finish.

when the brewery was awarded two GABF gold medals and was honored with the prestigious title of Small Brewing Company of the Year.

The brewery resides east of downtown Fort Collins in a space that had previously housed two other brewing businesses. The exterior of the blocky one-story building has been livened up with an attention-grabbing yellow, purple, and green color scheme. The Funkwerks taproom is a low-key affair. It's a small and simply furnished space with a few high-tops and a bar that seats six. When the weather is nice, you can catch some rays on the laid-back outdoor patio.

There are typically eight to ten beers on tap, including the brewery's flagship gold-medal Saison. The style originated in Wallonia, Belgium's southern province, in the 1800s. The beers were typically brewed in farmhouse breweries in the winter months and stored until summer for consumption by farm workers. Since recipes and environments varied from farm to farm, there was a lot of variation in the beers' flavor profiles. There were similarities, of course, such as a spicy and dry character that was a result of the unique yeast strain used to ferment the beers. The Funkwerks Saison is a wonderful interpretation of the style, with a complex fruity-spicy character and hints of black pepper. It has a dry finish with more hop bitterness than is typical for Belgian-style ales.

The taproom offers an assortment of small-batch saisons, often including fruited, spiced, barrel-aged, or sour versions inoculated with wild yeast and bacteria. In true Belgian fashion, the beers are served in stemmed glassware that brings out their subtleties and complexities in ways the ubiquitous shaker pint glass can't.

Funkwerks

Opened: December 2010.

Owners: Brad Lincoln and Gordon Schuck.

Head brewer: Gordon Schuck.

Potential annual capacity: 1,500 barrels.

Hours: Sunday through Thursday, noon to 8 p.m.; Friday and Saturday, noon to 9 p.m.

Tours: Saturday at 2 p.m.

Take-out beer: 750 ml bottles.

Food: Cheese plates and nuts.

Extras: AHA member deals program participant.

Parking: On-site lot.

Area attractions: See chapter intro.

Other area beer sites: See chapter intro.

Gravity Brewing

GRAVITY
• BREWING •

1150 Pine Street, Unit B, Louisville, CO 80027
(303) 544-0746 • www.thegravitybrewing.com

"Take Your Beer Seriously. Take Yourself Lightly." is the tagline of Gravity Brewing Company. The image of a young lady in a gravity-defying horizontal levitation reaching for a glass of beer is on display in the taproom. Gravity is intertwined with the Louisville brewery in several ways.

In brewing circles, gravity refers to specific gravity, a measurement used by brewers to determine a beer's alcohol content. As a scientific term, gravity ties in to the science and engineering backgrounds of the three partners that founded the business. Additionally, the brewery has a focus on high-gravity (i.e. high-alcohol) beers. Lastly, the brewery is in Colorado, a state where gravity sports, such as skiing and mountain biking, are entrenched in the lifestyle.

The brewery was first conceived by John Frazee, a professional engineer and longtime homebrewer. When he mentioned the idea to his friend and co-worker Ryan Bowers, they decided to become partners in the new endeavor. While looking for consulting help to guide the business through the startup phase, they happened upon the resume of Julius Hummer, an experienced brewer who had recently relocated to nearby Boulder and was looking for an investment opportunity in a brewing business. A partnership of three was formed.

Early on, they focused on Louisville (pronounced LEW-is-ville), a vibrant town that *Money* magazine has ranked the best place to live among American small towns. The community had been without a hometown brewery for many years. It took the partners a year to complete a business plan and raise the necessary capital, and another year to find a location and complete construction. Gravity Brewing opened in the summer of 2012.

The brewery occupies a large space in a business complex a few blocks off Main Street. The space had previously been a banquet hall for the local American Legion post, which is housed in the adjoining space. A hole in the wall separating

Year-round beers: Louisville Belgian Ale, Mendacious Belgian Blonde, Newtonian ESB, Regular IPA, Acceleration Double IPA.

The Pick: The reddish-hued Newtonian ESB has a nice mildly sweet maltiness balanced with a clean, hoppy, not-too-bitter finish.

the two tenants allows Gravity visitors to order food from the kitchen of the Legion hall without leaving the taproom.

The long open space is divided roughly in half by an unusual zigzag-shaped bar of alternating blond and dark-stained boards of beetle kill pine. The room contains a pool table and a Ping-Pong table, as well as a collection of communal picnic tables and a few high-tops. The open brewhouse sits in full view of customers sitting at the bar.

Brewmaster Julius Hummer is one of only a few craft brewers in the country who can claim to have a parent who was also a craft brewer. His father, David Hummer, was a homebrewer and college professor who cofounded Boulder Beer in 1979. "I grew up with carboys bubbling in my bathroom," Hummer remembered of his younger years.

Hummer attended the British School of Malting and Brewing in England. His extensive brewing background includes work in breweries throughout the U.S. and in a half-dozen foreign countries.

The majority of Gravity beers are quite strong, with a nod toward Belgian styles and barrel-aged creations. The science theme appears in the names of several Gravity beers including Newtonian ESB and Acceleration Double IPA. The later contains 9.8 percent alcohol and 98 IBU (International Bittering Units). "Nine-point-eight meters per second squared is the acceleration of gravity on earth," Frazee reminded me, as I sampled the heady brew.

Gravity Brewing

Opened: August 2012.

Owners: John Frazee, Julius Hummer, and Ryan Bowers.

Head brewer: Julius Hummer.

Potential annual capacity: 800 barrels.

Hours: Wednesday and Thursday, 4 p.m. to 9 p.m.; Friday, 3 p.m. to 10 p.m.; Saturday, 2 p.m. to 10 p.m.; Sunday, 2 p.m. to 7 p.m.; closed Monday and Tuesday.

Tours: On request.

Take-out beer: Growlers and kegs.

Food: The American Legion next door serves bar food. Restaurant delivery menus are on hand, or you may bring your own food.

Extras: Live music on Friday and Saturday. AHA member deals program participant.

Parking: On-site lot.

Area attractions: On Friday evenings in the summer, the Louisville Street Faire features free outdoor concerts. Downtown Boulder is ten miles away.

Other area beer sites: Empire Lounge & Restaurant (816 Main St., 303-665-2521). Lucky Pie (637 Front St., 303-666-5743). LuLu's BBQ (701 B Main St, 720-583-1789).

Grimm Brothers Brewhouse

623 Denver Avenue, Loveland, CO 80537
(970) 624-6045 • www.grimmbrosbrewhouse.com

It seems only fitting that the city of Loveland, also known as "The Sweetheart City," would host one of the largest Valentine's Day celebrations in the country. Hometown brewery Grimm Brothers is helping spread the love.

In 2012, the city commissioned the brewery to produce a commemorative beer for the amorous holiday. The result was Bleeding Heart Cherry Chocolate Porter, which was available exclusively in Loveland bars and restaurants. The next year, the new tradition continued with the second edition of Bleeding Heart. This time, the recipe for the special release was modified to include coffee in place of cherries.

Since opening in the summer of 2010, Loveland's first production brewery has developed close ties with the community and is involved in frequent fundraising efforts for local nonprofits and the city's well-established arts community.

Grimm Brothers was the inspiration of co-founders Don Chapman and Aaron Heaton, who came together through the Fort Collins homebrew club, the Liquid Poets. Russell Fruits joined the partnership to help with sales and marketing.

The partners decided early on that they wanted to implement a German-inspired brewhouse. The adoption of Grimm Brothers fairy tales as a central theme for the business came at the urging of the wife of head brewer Don Chapman. A schoolteacher with an interest in literary art, she realized that the literary connection would give the brewery a unique identity and a wealth of public domain stories that could be used for beer names.

The brewery resides in a light-industrial business park east of downtown. The brewing operation and the taproom are a short stroll apart in separate locations within the complex. A large image of the brewery's eye-catching logo—a bird of prey with wings extended and beer mugs clenched

Year-round beers: Snow Drop Köttbusser, The Fearless Youth Munich Dunkel, Little Red Cap Altbier, Master Thief German Porter, The Griffin Hefeweizen.

The Pick: Little Red Cap Altbier is a copper-colored German ale that greets your palate with a clean, chewy maltiness followed by a pronounced hit of bitterness that provides balance but doesn't linger.

in its talons—is painted on the tasting room's brick storefront. Inside the small, uncluttered taproom, wooden wainscoting and tables constructed of repurposed old doors adds ambience to the environs.

The taproom is frequented by an eclectic clientele that includes a devoted core of local customers. Like any good hometown watering hole, many of the regulars are on a first-name basis with the servers. "I've got guys, at 3:30 every day, they walk in the door with their hand open. We know what beer goes in that hand," Fruits explained. There is a common element among taproom visitors. "Most of the people we get are the ones who really enjoy exploring [different] styles of beer," said Fruits.

The brewery's most acclaimed beer is the Little Red Cap Altbier, a medalist at both the 2011 and 2012 Great American Beer Festival. The Fearless Youth Munich Dunkel was a 2013 GABF bronze medalist. While Grimm Brothers bills itself as "German-inspired," the brewers don't limit themselves to what are commonly considered traditional German styles. While you'll find a dunkel, an altbier, and a hefeweizen among the regular offerings, you'll also find little-known historical styles and interesting hybrids on tap. "We do a Köttbusser, which is a historic ale out of Germany that was outlawed in 1516 by the Reinheitsgebot," Fruits explained. "It's a beer that uses honey, oats, and molasses." The brewery also produces a German porter that was adopted from England during the Industrial Revolution. According to Fruits, some believe this style was the precursor to German dark lagers such as the schwarzbier. "We're not afraid to do [something] like a Brett bock," he continued, referring to the unconventional use of wild yeast in a German lager. "That's German tradition married with American freedom."

Grimm Brothers Brewhouse

Opened: July 2010.

Owners: Don Chapman, Aaron Heaton, and Russell Fruits.

Head brewer: Don Chapman.

Potential annual capacity: 4,000 barrels.

Hours: Monday through Thursday, 1 p.m. to 7 p.m.; Friday, noon to 9 p.m.; Saturday, noon to 9 p.m.; Sunday, 1 p.m. to 5 p.m.

Tours: Friday and Saturday, on request.

Take-out beer: Growlers, bombers, and kegs.

Food: Cheese plates. Food trucks stop by nightly.

Extras: Trivia on Monday. Family night (games and free lemonade) on Monday. Live music on Thursday. AHA pub discount program participant.

Parking: On-site lot.

High Hops Brewery

6461 Highway 392, Windsor, CO 80550
(970) 674-2841 • www.highhopsbrewery.com

When I arrived at High Hops Brewery and encountered a larger-than-life rusted metal sculpture of a bearded, long-haired, sombrero-clad musician playing a stand-up bass, I knew I was in for a brewery visit of a different flavor.

High Hops is uniquely situated within a garden center that's part of a collection of family-run enterprises that also includes a homebrew shop and a hop farm. The complex sits on the fringes of Windsor, a northern Colorado community located a few miles east of Interstate 25, equidistant from Fort Collins and Loveland.

Pat and Amanda Weakland opened The Windsor Garden in 2000, about the same time they started homebrewing. Their son Zach, who now works as a brewer in the family business, remembers the beginning of his parents' homebrewing exploits: "I was in eighth grade then. I was in chemistry class doing about the same thing they were doing at home. I thought that was pretty cool." In response to the worldwide hop shortage of 2007, the entrepreneurial business owners planted hops on land adjacent to the garden center. The homebrew shop, housed within the garden center, was added in 2010. That same year, Zach graduated from college and joined the expanding family-run operation. With a surplus of hops at their disposal and rave reviews of their homebrews, the family's next logical step was to add a commercial brewery. High Hops Brewery was launched in 2012.

When I arrived for an afternoon appointment, my primary mission was to visit the taproom. I got distracted, however, first by the well-stocked homebrew shop and then by the collection of quirky folk art on display throughout the garden center. This led me on a meandering route through the building. The next time I need a leather-clad, bearded gnome statuette wearing sunglasses, I'll know exactly where to get it.

The tasting room is small and appealing, with a few seats at the wooden bar and additional seating along a counter facing a wall of windows. The

Year-round beers: The Golden One Lemon Pilsner, The Power of Zeus APA, The Noble One Belgian Ale, The Dark One Milk Stout, The Honeyed One American Red, The Witty One American Wheat.

The Pick: The Golden One, a light, crisp pilsner brewed with lemon verbena, has the aroma of grandma's lemon drop hard candy, a hint of sweetness, and a kiss of palate-cleansing hops.

windows look on to the patio, where a stage hosts frequent musical performances. Beyond the patio is the two-acre hop field, which is planted with three dozen different hop varieties. Everyone helps out with the multifaceted business, including the goats, whose contribution is weed control in the hopyard. Hop plants are for sale in the garden shop and online. "If you brew your own beer, you should grow your own hops," according to Zach. In the rear of the garden center is the greenhouse, which also functions as a beer garden.

The 10-barrel brewery is in a standalone structure behind the garden center. Spent grains from the brewery are fed to the resident chickens. The beer selection is true to High Hops' slogan of "All Types of Beer for All Types of People." The fourteen taps dispense a broad range of styles. On one extreme is a light, quaffable lemon-flavored pilsner. On the opposite end of the spectrum is a rich, tummy-warming, Belgian quadruple ale.

The beers have a unique naming scheme with monikers including The Golden One, The Honeyed One, The Weize One, The Witty One, The Dark One, and The Noble One. The nonconformist of the lot is The Power of Zeus Pale Ale, named for Zeus the Toad, who jumped out of a hole intended for a Zeus variety hop plant. Each beer has its own eye-catching artwork, which is on display in the taproom. High Hops offers free beer on occasion, but there's a catch: first you have to purchase a hanging plant basket.

High Hops Brewery

Opened: September 2012.

Owners: Pat and Amanda Weakland.

Head brewers: Pat and Zach Wheatland.

Potential annual capacity: 2,000 barrels.

Hours: Monday, noon to 5:30 p.m.; Tuesday through Thursday, 2 p.m. to 8 p.m.; Friday and Saturday, noon to 9 p.m.; Sunday, noon to 7 p.m.

Tours: Saturday at 2 p.m. and 3 p.m.

Take-out beer: Growlers, bombers, 16-ounce bottles, and kegs.

Food: Food trucks three or four days a week.

Extras: Firkin tapping on Wednesday. Open mic night every other Thursday. AHA member deals program participant.

Parking: On-site lot.

Area attractions: Swetsville Zoo (metal animal sculpture) (4801 E. Harmony Rd., Fort Collins, 970-484-9509)

Other area beer sites: See Fort Collins and Loveland in chapter intro.

J Wells Brewery

2516 49th Street, No. 5, Boulder, CO 80301
(303) 396-0384 • www.jwellsbrewery.com

If it's true that small is beautiful, then J Wells Brewery is a knockout. The diminutive beer-making business opened in early 2013 as the most micro of Boulder microbreweries.

The pint-sized brewery and taproom is named for its founder, Jamie Wells. Wells arrived in the Denver area from southern Colorado following high school and took up homebrewing soon after. He had to curtail his beer-making hobby while living in the dorms at the University of North Texas, where he studied computer science. After returning to the Denver area in 2008, Wells got back into beer-making on an oversized homebrew system that he constructed himself. While working as a contractor for IBM, he began contemplating opening a commercial brewery. "I wasn't that serious at first. As time went on, I realized I really could do this. I could make this work," Wells recalled. He cashed out his 401K, secured a location in an East Boulder business park, and opened J Wells Brewery.

The brewery sits in an industrial area just east of Foothills Parkway, Boulder's busy north-south commuter corridor. The area is populated with many auto-related businesses. J Wells occupies a garage-type space squeezed between an auto detailer and the offices of a building company. A big garage door opens to the taproom, which would fit one large car. The interior is very basic with concrete floors and cinder block walls painted white. There's a small four-seat bar atop a base of corrugated metal. Four small high-tops sit along a wall on which a few art prints are mounted. A half-wall encloses a narrow adjacent space containing a couch and a dartboard. When weather permits, a canopy is set up in a roped-off area in the parking lot for outdoor sipping.

The open brewhouse resides beyond the bar. A trio of 1.5-barrel brewing vessels (approximately 45 gallons) resembling oversized soup cans share space with a collection of kegs and plastic

Year-round beers: Hop Haze Imperial IPA, Jamie's Pale, The Best.

The Pick: Jamie's Pale intertwines sweet malt with tangerine-tinged hops and a nip of bitterness in the finish.

fermenters. Beers are dispensed from five-gallon kegs kept cool in a homebrew-style converted chest freezer fit with tap handles.

Wells keeps six beers on tap, three of which are available full-time. The Best is a 3.2 percent English-style best bitter brewed with British malt and hops. Hop Haze is a burly imperial IPA in the 9 percent ABV range. Jamie's Pale is an American pale ale. During my summer visit, other beers being dispensed included a Kolsch, an IPA, and a chocolate milk stout flavored with cocoa nibs. "I brew to style," Wells said of his approach to beermaking. "I want to make sure that whenever people see a particular style they're going to get what they're expecting." Although he favors English and American styles, he also likes Belgian beers and, when I visited, was planning to brew a tripel as a fall beer.

Nanobreweies such as J Wells, which have been springing up with increased frequency in recent years, blur the line between homebrewing and professional brewing. "We still ferment in old glass carboys for small batches," Wells told me. "This is the closest you can get to a homebrew operation that you can find anywhere."

J Wells Brewery

Opened: January 2013.
Owner and head brewer: Jamie Wells.
Potential annual capacity: 780 barrels.
Hours: Tuesday through Thursday, 3 p.m. to 9 p.m.; Friday, 3 p.m. to 10 p.m.; Saturday, noon to 10 p.m.; Sunday, noon to 8 p.m.
Tours: On request.
Take-out beer: Growlers, bombers, and kegs.
Food: Bring your own.
Extras: Discount for AHA members.
Parking: On-site lot.

Left Hand Brewing Company

1265 Boston Avenue, Longmont, CO 80025
(303) 772-0258 • www.lefthandbrewing.com

"Brewed on the banks of the mighty St. Vrain," reads the label on a bottle of Left Hand Brewing Company beer. Meant to be a tongue-in-cheek reference to the normally sleepy stream that flows behind the brewery, it became all too real in mid-September 2013 when the river roared out of its banks with a vengeance following days of torrential rains.

Water surrounded the brewery and came within inches of entering the building before receding. In a gesture typical of Left Hand's community focus, funds raised at the brewery-sponsored Oktoberfest celebration the following weekend were allocated to help Longmont's numerous flood victims.

Left Hand Brewing came into existence when college buddies Eric Wallace and Dick Doore decided to parlay their homebrewing endeavors into a commercial enterprise. In 1993, they incorporated their fledgling business under the name Indian Peaks Brewing Company. When a potential naming conflict arose early on, they decided to rename the fledgling business. At the time, the partners were living in the small town of Niwot, a few miles from Longmont, where the brewery resides. The town is named for Chief Niwot, the peaceful leader of the Southern Arapahoe tribe that inhabited the area when white people arrived in the mid-1800s. The Southern Arapahoe word "Niwot" translates to "Left Hand."

Left Hand Brewing Company opened for business in early 1994 in a former meat-packing plant in an industrial area not far from Longmont's downtown district. The brewery's busy taproom has some rustic flavor that is contributed by wood-paneled walls and a stone-topped bar. There's a small collection of high-tops, and plentiful overflow seating on two outdoor patios and in the "Malt Room," a space adjacent to the taproom originally used as a malt storage area.

For a brewery with nationwide recognition, the taproom is unquestionably a local's scene. "All the

Year-round beers: Sawtooth ESB, Milk Stout, 400 Pound Monkey IPA, Polestar Pilsner, Black Jack Porter, Stranger Pale Ale, Wake Up Dead Imperial Stout.

The Pick: The Milk Stout brings flavors of coffee and chocolate to the forefront, balanced by just a touch of roastiness in the finish. When served on nitro, the silky texture enhances the richness of this oft-decorated dark ale.

bartenders know every local's name," according to Emily Armstrong, Left Hand's marketing and PR coordinator. "It's not just a place to come after work for a beer. It's kind of a second home. It's a social club."

From the start, Left Hand has preached the gospel of approachable, well-balanced beers. "Our purpose is to brew beer that we're interested in drinking, and hopefully, that other people are interested in drinking too," explained cofounder and Left Hand president Eric Wallace.

While other breweries have steered their efforts toward aggressively hopped IPAs, double IPAs, and high-gravity, palate-challenging fermentation, Left Hand has found success along a different path. The brewery's flagship beer is its sweet and creamy Milk Stout, the antithesis of a hoppy, bitter IPA. In 2011, Left Hand released a first-of-its-kind nitrogenated version of the Milk Stout in a bottle. Today, the dark elixir constitutes almost 60 percent of the brewery's beer production. Milk Stout has been a medal winner at the Great American Beer Festival, the World Beer Cup, and several other international competitions.

Left Hand's head brewer is Ro Guenzel, a quiet perfectionist with an affinity for German-style beers and smoked beers. The brewer's attention to detail is evident in the across-the-board quality of his beers. At the 2013 GABF, three Left Hand beers were gold medal winners. While the brewery is highly automated, Guenzel and the brew crew take a hands-on approach to some creations. The malt used to brew a smoked Baltic porter was smoked in-house using hackberry wood from a fallen tree that had been planted by Guenzel's wife's great-great-grandfather at the family's Nebraska homestead.

The company has kept strong ties with the local community. Left Hand hosts a variety of events that have amassed hundreds of thousands of dollars for a variety of charitable causes.

Left Hand Brewing Company

Opened: September 1993.

Owners: Cofounders Eric Wallace and Dick Doore plus numerous shareholders.

Head brewer: Ro Guenzel.

Potential annual capacity: 50,000 barrels.

Hours: Monday through Thursday, 3 p.m. to 8 p.m.; Friday, noon to 9 p.m.; Saturday, noon to 8 p.m.; Sunday, 1 p.m. to 8 p.m.

Tours: Saturday and Sunday, 1 p.m. and 2 p.m. Monday through Friday by appointment.

Take-out beer: Growlers, bottles, and kegs.

Food: Food trucks on weekends.

Extras: Live music on Friday and Saturday. AHA member discount program participant.

Parking: On-site lot.

Loveland Aleworks

118 West 4th Street, Loveland, CO 80537
(970) 619-8726 • www.lovelandaleworks.com

Many professional craft brewers were bitten by the homebrew bug at some point in their lives. Nick Callaway was nearly devoured by it. The founder of Loveland Aleworks was attending the University of Northern Colorado in Greeley. His friendship with two professional brewers led to his indoctrination, and infatuation, with homebrewing. His studies in math and physics were not the only reasons for his demanding schedule. It was partly self-inflicted.

"I brewed three or four times a week in college. I'd mash in, go to class, come back, mash out. I'd get it up to a boil then knock out, leave the chiller on low, go to class, come back, and run it into the cellar," Callaway recalled of his multitasking routine. "I'd bring it to school, give it to friends. I brewed more than I could ever possibly drink."

Prior to his homebrewing hobby gone wild, he had aspired only to being a ski bum. The North Carolina native arrived in Colorado "for college officially, but really for the snow." After a year of school, Callaway dropped out and moved up to the mountains, but it was a temporary diversion: "It got old. My knees got worn out and my back started to hurt me a lot, so I decided to go back to college."

After graduating, he worked as an engineer for a half-dozen years, all the while scheming to put together his own commercial brewery. The cost of a new brewing system was prohibitively expensive, but Callaway persevered and eventually located a used 10-barrel system. His engineering skills have proved invaluable in maintaining the finicky twenty-five-year-old equipment.

He found a suitable brewery location in a building on the western fringe of downtown Loveland. The old brick structure is of unknown age, but the roof was last replaced in 1925. The building had once been used as a storage garage for Stanley Steamer automobiles. In the 1900s, people would arrive in Loveland by train and take a Steamer the remaining thirty miles to Estes Park, the jumping-off point for excursions into Rocky Mountain National Park.

Year-round beers: Saison, IPA, Tripel, Imperial Stout, American Sour Ale with Raspberries.

The Pick: The Imperial Stout is big and bold, but surprisingly smooth with a great balance of chocolate and dark fruit flavors.

The brewery's brick façade is fitted with handsome glass-paned garage-style doors opening to a small sidewalk patio. The interior maintains some of its vintage qualities juxtaposed with many stylish modern accoutrements. The room is not large, but the high ceilings create an open, airy feel. Most of the seating is at attractive communal wooden tables. There's counter seating adjacent to the bar with tall windows looking into the brewery. The downtown location attracts a mixed crowd, often including residents of the surrounding neighborhood. Beer tourists navigating Loveland's rapidly growing ale trail arrive on weekends.

Running the brewery is a team effort. Nick's wife, Kari, keeps the business on a steady course. "She pays all the bills, keeps the books, deals with the HR stuff, keeps me out of trouble. She keeps me from working eighteen hours a day," said Callaway.

My sampling session at Loveland Aleworks was especially rewarding, both for the quality of the beers and for the uncommon selection of interesting beer styles. "Imperial stout is my absolute favorite thing to brew," said the owner-brewer. He keeps a big, brawny version on tap year round. The three other full-time beers include a saison, an IPA, and a Belgian tripel. Other Belgian styles appear with frequency on the brewery's ten tap handles. Drinkers who favor high-gravity, complex-flavored ales will do especially well at Loveland Aleworks. Less assertive selections, which might include an English mild or an approachable farmhouse ale, round out the house offerings.

Loveland Aleworks

Opened: July 2012.

Owners: Nick Callaway and Kari Klapper.

Head brewer: Nick Callaway.

Potential annual capacity: 1,000 barrels.

Hours: Monday through Thursday, 2 p.m. to 10 p.m.; Friday and Saturday, noon to 11 p.m.; Sunday, noon to 9 p.m.

Tours: Sundays at 2 p.m. and by reservation.

Take-out beer: Growlers and kegs.

Food: Chips and salsa, cheese and meat plates, and free pretzels. Delivery menus available or bring your own food.

Extras: Live music on Tuesday and some weekends. Discounted growlers during NFL games. AHA member discount program participant.

Parking: On-street and nearby lots, all free.

Mountain Sun Family

Mountain Sun and Southern Sun

The Mountain Sun family consists of three brewpubs and one non-brewing restaurant, with a second in the works. The Boulder-based brewpubs are the Mountain Sun Pub & Brewery and the Southern Sun Pub & Brewery. The third brewpub, the Vine Street Pub & Brewery, is located in Denver (see page 95). The three brewpubs covered in this book have much in common. They've thrived by creating affordable, well-prepared pub fare and a wide selection of satisfying brews, all served in a laid-back and welcoming environment. Stellar service is provided by a genuinely friendly and efficient waitstaff.

The company was founded in 1993 by Kevin Daly and a former partner. Kevin's father, Tom, is now a co-owner, and there are several managing partners. From the start, Mountain Sun adopted several unique practices and policies that few food and beverage destinations would dare implement. The company's success speaks for itself.

Outside of the brewing operations, there are only two job positions: front of the house and back of the house. Most of the staff is cross-trained for both positions, and they rotate periodically between serving and food prep. Tips are pooled and distributed to the entire staff. "Everyone is helping each other. Everyone is working toward the common goal of great-quality customer service," explained Jessica Candaleria, the general manager of the busy downtown Boulder brewpub.

The pubs don't accept credit cards. There are cash machines on-site, and checks are accepted. If none of those options work for you, and you find yourself without a means to pay, the pub will give you a "karma envelope." You use the addressed, stamped envelope to send in your payment. The Mountain Sun family claims a 97 percent return on this nontraditional payment option.

The brewpubs share a similar décor. Bars, tables, and benches are built of blond wood. Potted plants fill shelf space. Ventilation pipes, suspended from the ceilings, are painted with hop vines. The walls are adorned with fabric and framed music posters. The colorful Mountain Sun logo is painted on a wall at each location. The most striking visual element, however, is the mind-blowing chalk art by Boulder artist Bryce Widom. His fantastical, temporary creations are updated seasonally at each pub. There are no TVs to dilute the sociable vibe of these family-friendly neighborhood gathering spots.

Each location has virtually the same food menu. Rather than trying to be all things to all people, the kitchens stay within their comfort range with an abbreviated yet well-rounded and well-executed menu. Burgers are made with naturally raised Colorado beef. There are several rich Mexican dishes. Vegetarian-friendly selections include a design-your-own grilled cheese option.

John Fiorilli oversees the brewing operations companywide. Different beers are brewed at different locations and distributed to the other sites. With few exceptions, you'll find the same lineup at each pub: eight core beers, a seasonal stout, and eleven seasonal and specialty offerings. The best-selling beer at all locations is the FYIPA, a robust American-style IPA. It features gobs of citrusy hops and a lingering bitterness. There's nothing subtle about this hophead's delight. The other full-time and specialty beers have considerable range, including English and American styles, Belgians, and fruited and spiced beers.

Every February is Stout Month at each of the pubs. Throughout the month, ten taps are dedicated to a rotating lineup of house-brewed and guest stouts from around the country with an occasional import showing up. Devoted stout drinkers can sample up to fifty different stouts throughout the month.

The two Boulder-based brewpubs in the Mountain Sun Family, Mountain Sun and Southern Sun, are profiled below. A thirty-tap, non-brewing Boulder restaurant, Under the Sun, opened in 2013 in the same shopping complex as Southern Sun. A second non-brewing restaurant is scheduled to open in Longmont in 2014.

Mountain Sun Pub & Brewery

1535 Pearl Street, Boulder, CO 80302
(303) 546-0886 • www.mountainsunpub.com

Mountain Sun, the original member of the Mountain Sun family, opened in 1993. The smallest of the company's three pubs is located on Pearl Street in downtown Boulder, a few steps from the eastern terminus of the Pearl Street walking mall. While lots of regulars frequent the pub, the downtown location attracts more out-of-town visitors and beer travelers than its cross-town sibling.

There's a small sidewalk seating area fronting Pearl Street. The long, narrow interior packs a lot of character into the small space. Large picture windows look out onto the sidewalk scene. The bar, at the far end of the room, is standing-room only, and can get crowded with customers waiting for tables. The atmosphere is loud, vibrant, and upbeat. A row of closely spaced two-tops is arranged along one wall with booth seating along the opposite wall. A row of larger tables fills in the middle of the room.

The Mountain Sun's 6-barrel brewing system is the smallest of the three brewpubs. The downtown Boulder brewhouse specializes in seasonal, high-gravity, and barrel-aged beers that it supplies for the company's three pubs.

Year-round beers: Annapurna Amber, Colorado Kind Ale, Illusion Dweller IPA, Isadore Java Porter, FYIPA, XXX Pale Ale, Big Krane Kolsch, Blackberry Wheat (or specialty fruit), and a specialty stout.

The Pick: Small-batch specialty beers are the Mountain Sun's forte. Sample the current selections and roll with your preference.

Mountain Sun Pub & Brewery

Opened: October 1993.

Owners: Kevin and Tom Daly.

Head brewer: Jeff Ramirez. Director of brewing operations: John Fiorilli.

Potential annual capacity: 1,200 barrels.

Hours: Daily, 11 a.m. to 1 a.m.

Tours: On request.

Take-out beer: Growlers.

Food: Sandwiches, burgers, and burritos. Good vegetarian options.

Extras: Live music on Sunday (no cover).

Parking: Metered on-street parking and inexpensive nearby lots.

Southern Sun Pub & Brewery

627 South Broadway, Boulder, CO 80305
(303) 543-0886 • www.mountainsunpub.com

The middle sibling of the three-member Mountain Sun family is Southern Sun, which opened in 2002. Southern Sun is located in South Boulder, in the oddly configured, two-level Table Mesa shopping center. With easy access for commuters and mountain travelers, and its close proximity to several research facilities, Southern Sun attracts an interesting cross section of the Boulder population including athletes, outdoor adventurers, and scientists. I lived near the brewpub for ten years and spent many quality hours kicking back with friends over a pint or three.

The brick and glass exterior would be rather inconspicuous if not for the sun- and mountain-themed, multicolored company logo on the building's façade, and a bright white grain silo plunked in the middle of the wide sidewalk. Outside the entrance is a patio with communal picnic table seating and lovely mountain views.

The large dining room has a long bar along one side and a mix of booth and table seating throughout. In a back corner, an arrangement of comfortable couches provides a cushy place to hang out while waiting for a dinner table.

The Southern Sun menu is similar to that of Mountain Sun with one notable exception. The South Boulder brewpub offers chicken wings, and they're some of the best around. They can be ordered with either hot sauce or barbecue. The hot sauce is my preference. The wings are spicy, but not over-the-top, and quite addictive.

The South Boulder brewhouse is used primarily to brew seasonal creations. Of the three brewpubs in the Mountain Sun family, Southern Sun boasts the highest beer consumption.

Year-round beers: Annapurna Amber, Colorado Kind Ale, Illusion Dweller IPA, Isadore Java Porter, FYIPA, XXX Pale Ale, Big Krane Kolsch, Blackberry Wheat (or specialty fruit), and a specialty stout.

The Pick: Isadore Java Porter has a great balance of sweet malt and coffee. It's especially nuanced when served from a nitro tap.

Southern Sun Pub & Brewery

Opened: September 2002.

Owners: Kevin and Tom Daley.

Head brewer: Anthony Lauring. Director of brewing operations: John Fiorilli.

Potential annual capacity: 2,100 barrels.

Hours: Monday, 4 p.m. to 1 a.m.; Tuesday through Sunday, 11:30 a.m. to 1 a.m.

Tours: On request.

Take-out beer: Growlers.

Food: Above-average sandwiches, burgers, and burritos. Excellent buffalo wings. Good vegetarian options.

Extras: Live music on Monday (no cover).

Parking: On-site lot.

New Belgium Brewing Company

500 Linden Street, Fort Collins, CO 80524
(970) 221-0524, (888) NBB-4044 • www.newbelgium.com

In early 1992, when I was a newbie homebrewer, my local homebrew club, Hop Barley & the Alers, had a guest speaker at one of our monthly meetings. His name was Jeff Lebesch, and he gave a slide presentation of the commercial brewery that he and his then-wife, Kim Jordan, were operating in the basement of their home. The name of their small home-based brewery was New Belgium Brewing Company. From these humble beginnings, New Belgium has grown to be the largest craft brewery in Colorado and the third largest in the United States.

Lebesch, a Colorado native, was an electrical engineer and a homebrewer. In 1989, while touring Belgium by bicycle, Lebesch had an epiphany while sampling beers with the owners of Bruges' legendary beer bar, 't Brugs Beertje. Lebesch envisioned opening a brewery back home specializing in Belgian-style beers. Two years later, Lebesch and Jordan launched New Belgium Brewing Company.

The brewery's focus on Belgian-style beers was groundbreaking for an American craft brewery at the time. The first two beers were a Belgian-style dubbel called Abbey, and an amber ale called Fat Tire. The label for Fat Tire depicted a red cruiser bike. From the start, New Belgium has had a close association with bicycles. Each summer, the brewery hosts the Tour de Fat, a traveling festival promoting cycling and raising funds for local nonprofits. Over fourteen years, the event has raised over $3 million.

After operating from the basement for a year, New Belgium relocated to an old train station. Three years after that, the brewery moved into the current facility, which was built from the ground up. Much has changed over the years. New Belgium now employs around three hundred people at the Fort Collins brewery. After employees work for the company for a year, they are given a cruiser bike. After five years, the company takes them to

Year-round beers: Fat Tire Amber Ale, Sunshine Wheat, 1554 Black Ale, Blue Paddle Pilsner, Abbey Belgian-style Ale, Trippel, Ranger IPA, Shift Pale Lager, Rampant Imperial IPA.

The Pick: Take a leap of faith with whatever Lips of Faith series beer catches your attention. These experimental one-offs are nearly always unusual and often exceptional.

Belgium, including a stop at 't Brugs Beertje. Lebesch is no longer involved with the business, which is now employee-owned. Jordan is the CEO. To more efficiently meet the brewery's ever-expanding nationwide audience, New Belgium is building a new brewery in Asheville, North Carolina, that is slated to go online in 2015.

If there's one Colorado brewery tour you shouldn't miss, it's the New Belgium tour. More than just an overview of the brewing process, the tour takes you behind the scenes of the state-of-the-art brewery. There's plentiful sampling along the way and interactive activities including a swirly slide to get you from an upper level to a lower one. You'll have to plan ahead, however. Tours are reserved online up to two months in advance and fill up quickly, especially on weekends.

New Belgium was among the first U.S. breweries to experiment with barrel-aged sour beers. This was largely due to the arrival of head brewer Peter Bouckaert in 1996. Before coming to Fort Collins, the Belgian-born brewer worked at the Rodenbach brewery, which has a long history of producing barrel-aged fermentations. A sampling of straight-from-the-barrel sour ale during a visit to the brewery's "foeder forest," (a foeder is a giant oak barrel) is one of the highlights of the tour.

The New Belgium taproom, called the Liquid Center, keeps a broad selection of standard, seasonal, and specialty beers on tap, including the current Lips of Faith series beers. These two-per-quarter releases feature experimental beers that sometimes require a leap of faith to sample, as they're typically infused with weird combinations of obscure fruits, spices, or other unusual ingredients. The proceeds from all four-ounce tasters sold in the Liquid Center go to local nonprofits.

New Belgium Brewing Company

Opened: June 1991.

Owners: New Belgium became 100 percent employee-owned in 2013.

Head brewer: Peter Bouckaert.

Potential annual capacity: 850,000 barrels.

Hours: Tuesday through Sunday, 11 a.m. to 6 p.m. Closed Mondays.

Tours: Tuesday through Sunday, 11:30 a.m. to 4:30 p.m. Reservations required.

Take-out beer: Growlers, six-packs, twelve-packs, bombers, and kegs.

Food: Food trucks about three days a week.

Extras: Rolle-bolle (Belgian national pastime). AHA member deals program participant.

Parking: On-site lot and free on-street parking.

Area attractions: See chapter intro.

Other area beer sites: See chapter intro.

Odell Brewing Company

800 East Lincoln Avenue, Fort Collins, CO 80524
(970) 498-9070, (888) 887-2797 • www.odellbrewing.com

In the early 1990s, craft beer was a little-known entity in Fort Collins, as well as most of Colorado. Doug Odell was cofounder of the city's first craft brewery, which was producing draught-only beers at the time, and he took a hands-on approach to exposing local beer drinkers to his flavorful, small-batch ales. The owner-brewer would keg beer at the brewery, put it in the back of his pickup truck, drive it to a local bar, tap the keg, and buy a round for everyone in the house.

Apparently, this strategy for bringing beer to the masses worked. Odell Brewing Company has grown to be among the largest craft breweries in Colorado, with a distribution network that currently numbers ten states. Despite its impressive growth, the company remains rooted in the local beer scene and well-respected in the community.

In the late 1980s, Doug Odell was a homebrewer living in Seattle with his wife, Wynne. The couple had aspirations of opening a brewery. They were lured to Colorado by Doug's sister, Corkie, who was living in the state. The husband-wife-sister team launched Odell Brewing Company in Fort Collins in 1989. Over two decades later, the brewery remains a family-owned, family-operated business.

Odell Brewing resides in a handsome modern industrial building on Lincoln Avenue, east of Old Town Fort Collins. The neighborhood is hugely popular with beer travelers due to the close proximity of four well-known craft breweries. During my last visit, the brewery was in the midst of an ambitious expansion project that added a 100-barrel brewhouse to the facility, doubled the size of the taproom, and added an outdoor beer garden.

The Odell taproom is among the most popular stops on the northern Colorado ale trail. The large number of first-time visitors is obvious from the predominance of sampler trays being consumed around the room. Two types of samplers are available. The classic tray includes six of the brewery's year-round beers. The pilot tray includes a few

Year-round beers: 90 Shilling Ale, Cutthroat Porter, Odell IPA, 5 Barrel Pale Ale, Levity Amber Ale, Easy Street Wheat, Myrcenary Double IPA.

The Pick: Purchase a pilot sampler tray, sample some interesting beers, and give a little back to the city that's contributed so much to the Colorado craft beer community. One hundred percent of the proceeds from sampler trays go to local charities.

higher-end, year-round offerings, such as Myrcenary Double IPA, plus an assortment of small-batch offerings from Odell's pilot brewing system. There is sometimes a third choice, the copilot tray, containing beers exclusively from the pilot system.

Over the years, Odell established a broad fan base with a well-rounded lineup of largely British-style ales. As American craft beer palates evolved toward hoppier beers, the brewery released 5 Barrel Pale Ale in 2004. The well-hopped English-style ale was a big hit and remains so, capturing a gold medal at the 2013 GABF. This was followed by an IPA that also was well received and captured a gold medal at the 2007 Great American Beer Festival. The floodgates of experimentation began to open up.

The brewery developed a bourbon barrel imperial stout, which generated a lot of excitement. Soon after, the brewery started its Woodcut Series, an annual release featuring beer aged in virgin oak barrels. From there, it was a short, if nervous, leap to experimentation with barrel-aged sour beers. Odell Friek, a sour blend of kriek (cherry) and framboise (raspberry) ales, was a 2011 GABF gold medal winner.

Today, taproom visitors have the opportunity to choose from a wide array of beers that will typically include classic beer styles, barrel-aged and sour beers, nitro-dispensed beers, and small-batch experimental beers of widely varying character.

The brewery has a long history of giving back to the community that has supported the company for two dozen years. Among its charitable initiatives is the Charites of the Month program, which donates all proceeds from the sale of taster trays to local charities.

Odell Brewing Company

Opened: November 1989.

Owners: Doug, Wynne, and Corkie Odell.

Head brewer: Bill Beymer. Brewmaster: Doug Odell.

Potential annual capacity: 300,000 barrels.

Hours: Monday through Thursday, 11 a.m. to 6 p.m.; Friday and Saturday, 11 a.m. to 7 p.m.; Sunday, 11 a.m. to 6 p.m.

Tours: Monday through Saturday, on the hour from 1 p.m. to 4 p.m.

Take-out beer: Growlers, half-growlers, six-packs, 750 ml bottles, and kegs.

Food: Chips and salsa, crackers and cheese, daily food trucks, or bring your own food.

Extras: Live music on Wednesdays. AHA member deals program participant.

Parking: On-site lot.

Area attractions: See chapter intro.

Other area beer sites: See chapter intro.

Oskar Blues Brewery

Two locations

Oskar Blues Brewery grabbed the attention of beer lovers nationwide when it introduced canned beer to the craft beer world more than a decade ago. In the years since, the ground-breaking Colorado brewing company has maintained its adventurous spirit, exploring new paths while undergoing meteoric growth.

Oskar Blues' humble beginnings date from 1997, when founder Dale Katechis opened Oskar Blues Grill & Brew in the small town of Lyons, fifteen miles north of Boulder. Katechis was a high-energy restaurateur and homebrewer. He had hopes, but no concrete plans, to add an in-house brewery to the casual music-themed restaurant. Reflecting his southern roots, the menu featured Cajun and Creole dishes along with smoked meats. There was a house beer, Oskar Ale, which was brewed by Left Hand Brewing in nearby Longmont.

The following year, Katechis purchased a used 6-barrel brewing system from a defunct California brewery. He loaded it into a U-Haul, drove it to Colorado, and set it up in the basement of Oskar Blues. The first Oskar Blues beer was produced in late 1998.

In 2002, Oskar Blues broke new ground in the craft beer industry with a bold experiment to package its beer in cans. The brewery acquired a tabletop canning machine and set it up in an old barn behind the restaurant. To say the novel concept was a success would be a gross understatement, as the canned-beer concept took the craft beer world by storm. "I've always enjoyed high-risk ventures," explained Katechis, who has shown little hesitation to rock the boat from time to time.

As sales accelerated, the brewery got an additional shot in the arm in 2005 when the *New York Times* named Dale's Pale Ale, the brewery's flagship beer, the best pale ale in the country. When the brewery outgrew its brewpub operation, Oskar Blues opened a large brewing facility in Longmont in 2008. The production brewery has undergone multiple expansions as Oskar Blues has grown to be one of the top thirty craft breweries nationwide. "I never would have dreamed that it was going to be something like this," Katechis admitted.

Oskar Blues has branched out into a variety of peripheral endeavors over the years, which have included the Bone Wagon food truck, a restaurant-taphouse called Liquids & Solids, a burger joint called Chub Burger, a cantina/bike shop called CyclHOPS, a bicycle company called Reeb ("beer" spelled backward), and a fifty-acre farm called Hops & Heifers. The farm raises cattle and other livestock and grows several varieties of hops. To appease the thirst of Oskar Blues fans nationwide, in 2012 the company opened a second production brewery in North Carolina. "I've never been one to let opportunity pass by," said Katechis of his diverse enterprises. "Every time it pops its head up, we grab a hold of it." Oskar Blues seldom passes up an opportunity to help out local brewery startups, too. In my visits to new breweries throughout the Colorado Front Range, I've heard frequent accounts of Oskar Blues staff helping work out technical glitches, donate ingredients, and offer expertise to new breweries working out the kinks of their fledgling businesses.

Oskar Blues' Lyons brewpub and the large Longmont brewery offer different experiences for the beer traveler.

Oskar Blues Grill & Brew

303 Main Street, Lyons, CO 80540
(303) 823-6685 • www.oskarblues.com/restaurant/grill-brew

Oskar Blues Grill & Brew, the original brewpub, sits in the middle of Lyons, a small town of two thousand located between Boulder and Estes Park. Bluegrass and folk music fans know Lyons as the home of two popular summer music festivals, RockyGrass and the Folks Festival. "It's got great music. It's got great beer. It's got great mountain biking," said Chad Melis, a Lyons resident, former bike racer, and current marketing director for Oskar Blues. The brewpub has long helped foster Lyons's thriving music scene by hosting live music four or five days a week, often featuring local musicians.

Year-round beers: Dale's Pale Ale, Old Chub Scotch Ale, G'Knight Imperial Red, Mama's Little Yella Pils, Deviant Dale's IPA, One Nut Brown, Priscilla Wheat.

The top level of the two-level brewpub has a casual dining room, a small bar, and an outdoor patio. The lower level has a larger bar, a music stage, an arcade, and a second outdoor patio. The brewery is located in a detached structure behind the restaurant. The menu has retained its southern theme with po' boys, catfish, jambalaya, and

The Pick: G'Knight is a big, burly, yet balanced brew with a mountainous malt foundation supporting an equally impressive presence of tangy hops.

house-smoked meats. Pub standards, such as burgers and pizza, are also on the menu.

The brewpub is a mostly-locals scene throughout much of the year. During the summer months, out-of-town traffic increases, as Lyons is a convenient stop on the way to Estes Park, the tourist-intensive base camp for visits to Rocky Mountain National Park.

Oskar Blues Grill & Brew

Opened: 1997. Brewery added in 1998.

Owner: Dale Katechis.

Head brewer: Jason Buehler.

Potential annual capacity: 2,000 barrels.

Hours: Daily, 11 a.m. to closing

Tours: On request.

Take-out beer: Growlers.

Food: Southern cuisine, smoked meats, pub standards, and pizza.

Extras: Live music four or five days a week. AHA pub discount program participant.

Parking: On-site lot and nearby street parking.

Area attractions: Planet Bluegrass (outdoor concert venue). Rocky Mountain National Park.

Other area beer sites: Smokin' Dave's BBQ & Taphouse (228 Main St., 303-823-7427). Lyons Fork (450 Main St., 303-823-5014).

Oskar Blues Brewery and Tasty Weasel Taproom

1800 Pike Road, Unit B, Longmont, CO 80501
(303) 776-1914 • www.oskarblues.com

Oskar Blues's large production brewery is located in Longmont, twelve miles east of Lyons. Tucked into a corner of the large facility is the Tasty Weasel Taproom, a lively scene for the after-work crowd and for beer travelers exploring the numerous nearby breweries. Half-walls of corrugated metal separate the taproom from the expansive production area and blend with the industrial environs. A row of tall stainless steel tanks towers over the bar. The taproom is the scene of Tasty Tuesday and Firkin Friday firkin tappings and live music on weekends. An adjacent space contains a trio of Skee-Ball games, steps away from the canning line. A huge deck accommodates sun worshipers. The brewery's Bone Wagon food truck visits the taproom regularly.

Oskar Blues beers feature big, but balanced, flavors. Dale's Pale Ale, Deviant Dale's IPA, G'Knight Imperial Red, and Gubna Imperial IPA all pack a wallop of hops stacked atop a solid malt foundation. Old Chub Scotch Ale and Ten FIDY Imperial Stout come from the opposite direction, bringing mountains of malt to the forefront.

Oskar Blues's runaway popularity has been accompanied by critical acclaim from beer judges in recent years. The brewery captured three medals at the 2011 Great American Beer Festival for its pilsner, Scotch ale, and IPA. This was followed by a gold medal at the 2012 World Beer Cup for the G'Knight Imperial Red Ale.

As Oskar Blues continues its rapid ascent in the craft beer world, I asked Katechis, who is known for his easy rapport with his employees, how big is big enough? "Too big is when I can't walk around the brewery and know something about every employee and know their name and know what their interests are," he replied. "When I can't communicate at that level, it's too big."

Year-round beers: Dale's Pale Ale, Old Chub Scotch Ale, G'Knight Imperial Red, Mama's Little Yella Pils, Deviant Dale's IPA.

The Pick: G'Knight is a big, burly, yet balanced brew with a mountainous malt foundation supporting an equally impressive presence of tangy hops.

Oskar Blues Brewery and Tasty Weasel Taproom

Opened: March 2008.

Owner: Dale Katechis.

Head brewer: Tim Matthews.

Potential annual capacity: 90,000 barrels.

Hours: Daily, noon to 8 p.m. daily.

Tours: Monday through Thursday at 4 p.m. Friday through Sunday, on the hour from 2 p.m. to 5 p.m.

Take-out beer: Growlers, cans, and kegs.

Food: The Bone Wagon food truck is often on-site.

Extras: Tasty Tuesday and Firkin Friday. Live music on Saturday and every other Monday. Skee-Ball league on Sunday and Wednesday. AHA member deals program participant.

Parking: On-site lot.

Pateros Creek Brewing Company

242 North College Avenue,
Fort Collins, CO 80524
(970) 484-PCBC (7222)
www.pateroscreekbrewing.com

During the process of launching a new brewing business, unexpected obstacles can surface midstream. That's what the father-and-son partnership of Bob and Steve Jones discovered as they prepared to cast their new enterprise into the fast-moving waters of the northern Colorado craft beer scene. The business was originally slated to be named Horsetooth Brewing Company after Horsetooth Mountain, a prominent landform near Fort Collins. When the Joneses were informed that the name Horsetooth had been trademarked as a beer name by another local brewery, they decided to avoid a potentially litigious situation by holding a contest to select a new name for the fledgling brewery. With more than seven hundred submissions to consider, they settled on Pateros Creek, an early name for the nearby Cache La Poudre River, which emerges from sinuous Poudre Canyon and flows through Fort Collins.

In June 2011, the Pateros Creek Brewing Company opened its doors to the public. The brewery is located a short distance north of Fort Collins's Old Town Square on College Avenue, the city's major north-south artery. It's a convenient location within easy access, but just beyond, the city's bustling center of activity.

A small patio occupies part of the parking lot that Pateros Creek shares with a neighboring business. The tasting room has a rustic feel from the use of recycled wood collected from an old barn. The tables and bar are constructed of beetle kill pine. The bar sits atop an unusual and attractive base of river rock. A larger room, named the Outpost Room, sits adjacent to the tasting room and contains additional table seating, a flatscreen TV, a pair of dartboards, and a Ping-Pong table.

The family members bring a variety of skills to the business. Steve Jones was a prolific homebrewer and is in charge of the brewing operations. Steve's father, Bob, brings business experience to the enterprise and holds the dual title of business

Year-round beers: Old Town Kolsch Ale, Stimulator Pale Ale, Cache La Porter, Car 21 Best Bitter, Rustic Irish Red, Punk Rock American IPA Gluten Free, and a rotating gluten-free tap.

The Pick: Like the nearby Cache La Poudre River, Cache La Porter meanders gently across your palate with a subtle sweetness followed by a mellow roastiness.

manager and sales director. Steve's wife, Cathy, is the brewery's "creative genius."

The day-to-day brewing operations are overseen by Nick Chase. Chase graduated from the prestigious Culinary Institute of America in upstate New York and worked as a chef in New York City for seven years. "Cooking is extremely stressful," he recounted. "I was working eighty- or ninety-hour weeks." He began homebrewing, which provided some distraction from his hectic work schedule.

When Chase's wife was preparing to start a master's program in food science at Colorado State University in Fort Collins, Chase contacted every brewery in town, hoping to find employment. When he didn't find a job, he volunteered to help out at Pateros Creek at night, when Steve Jones would be brewing after working his regular daytime job. Eventually, Chase was offered a paying position. He is thrilled with his career change. "It's a lot less stressful than cooking. It's a lot more fun. It's a lot more social," said the former big-city chef.

With ten breweries in town, it's necessary that each business establish a unique niche. Pateros Creek produces mainly session beers, eschewing highly hopped creations in favor of more malt-forward brews. One exception is the gluten-free Punk Rock American IPA, which occupies one of two taps dedicated to house-brewed, gluten-free beers. The second gluten-free selection rotates between a variety of styles. The brewery is known locally for its laid-back, welcoming vibe, and friendly, accommodating waitstaff that loves to talk beer.

Pateros Creek Brewing Company

Opened: June 2011.

Owners: Steve and Bob Jones.

Head brewer: Steve Jones. Lead brewer: Nick Chase.

Potential annual capacity: 3,000 barrels.

Hours: Monday, 3 p.m. to 9 p.m.; Tuesday and Wednesday, noon to 9 p.m.; Thursday and Friday, noon to 10 p.m.; Saturday, 11 a.m. to 10 p.m.; Sunday, noon to 7 p.m.

Tours: On request.

Take-out beer: Growlers, cans, and kegs.

Food: Food trucks on Wednesday, Thursday, and Saturday (sometimes Friday and Sunday).

Extras: Trivia on Thursday. Comedy Night on Friday. Live music on Saturday. AHA member deals program participant.

Parking: Small on-site lot. Street parking and nearby lots.

Area attractions: See chapter intro.

Other area beer sites: See chapter intro.

Pumphouse Brewery

540 Main Street, Longmont, CO 80501
(303) 702-0881 • www.pumphousebrewery.com

The planets were apparently in alignment when a team of aerospace engineers launched the Pumphouse Brewery in 1996. Lacking experience but fueled by a spirit of entrepreneurship, they succeeded in their mission to establish a hometown brewpub in downtown Longmont. More than fifteen years later, the Pumphouse is still flying high.

In the mid-1990s, Craig Taylor suggested to a colleague at the Boulder-based aerospace company where they worked, "We ought to just screw the aerospace thing and do something fun." "Like what?" coworker Dennis Coombs inquired. Taylor, who had started homebrewing several years earlier, suggested a brewery. He had Coombs's attention. While discussing the business concept in the lunchroom one day, their conversation was overheard by Dave D'Epagnier, who had also dabbled in homebrewing. When he expressed an interest in the venture, a third partner was added to the team. The idea gained momentum with the addition of engineer and triathlete Tom Charles. Though the group had no restaurant experience, and had only made beer on a homebrew scale, there was no turning back. "We just jumped into it," said Taylor.

They found a location in a dilapidated building in a favorable location on Longmont's Main Street. Realizing they needed someone with expertise to steer the ship in the right direction, they recruited Ross Hagen, who had spent some time with a corporate brewpub chain. The Pumphouse opened for business in the spring of 1996. Each of the five partners still plays an active role in the business.

The Pumphouse anchors a spot on the corner of Main Street and 6th Avenue in downtown Longmont. The huge space is divided into two sections. The quieter family-friendly pub side has table seating and a long full-service bar. The open brewhouse resides behind the bar; a collection of shiny fermentation tanks is lined up above it on

Year-round beers: Wildfire Wheat, Flashpoint IPA, Red Alert Amber Ale, Shockwave Scottish Ale, Spotted Dog Stout, and a rotating fruit beer.

The Pick: Shockwave Strong Scotch Ale is all about malt with a rich sweet character, slight smokiness, and a belly-warming finish.

the second level. On display around the room are various firehouse-themed items such as firemen's jackets, helmets, a fire hose, and a statuette of a dalmatian. The names of some of the house beers—Wildfire Wheat, Flashpoint IPA, Spotted Dog Stout, and others—play on the firehouse theme. Despite the recurring theme, the location was never a firehouse.

The adjacent space is a sports bar called the Red Zone and contains additional booth, bar, and table seating. Within the Red Zone is a video arcade, several pool tables, and an air hockey game. About two dozen flatscreens are distributed around the room. Compared to the pub side, the Red Zone is louder, livelier, and more high-energy. A large, partially shaded patio occupies a space out front overlooking the activity on Main Street. With its various components, the Pumphouse can seat up to 450 people, making it the largest restaurant in Boulder County. A largely local crowd keeps the brewpub buzzing year round.

Targeting a wide demographic, the brewpub offers an extensive menu of American-style pub fare. A separate gluten-free menu is available. Head brewer Stephen Streeter keeps a minimum of ten house beers flowing. There are five full-time beers and up to eight seasonals that will often include adventurous fermentations such as fruit beers, Belgians, smoked beers, and barrel-aged sours. Additionally, there's a selection of three dozen bottled and canned beers from local, national, and international breweries.

Pumphouse Brewery

Opened: May 1996.

Owners: Craig Taylor, Dennis Coombs, Ross Hagen, Tom Charles, and Dave D'Epagnier.

Head brewer: Steve Streeter.

Potential annual capacity: 1,300 barrels.

Hours: Sunday through Wednesday, 11 a.m. to 10 p.m.; Thursday through Saturday, 11 a.m. to 11 p.m. The adjoining Red Zone sports bar is open Sunday through Wednesday until midnight and Thursday through Saturday until 1:30 a.m.

Tours: On request.

Take-out beer: Growlers.

Food: Burgers, sandwiches, Mexican dishes, and miscellaneous entrées. Gluten-free menu available.

Extras: AHA pub discount program participant.

Parking: On-street and nearby lot.

Rock Bottom—Centerra

6025 Sky Pond Drive, Loveland,
CO 80538
(970) 622-2077
www.rockbottom.com/locations/
loveland-centerra-promenade

The Rock Bottom Restaurant and Brewery in Loveland is the northernmost of the chain's six Colorado locations. The restaurant is located within the Centerra shopping complex, or, more precisely, The Promenade Shops at Centerra. The sprawling outdoor shopping mall sits just east of Interstate 25, about seven miles from downtown Loveland. Fort Collins is a fifteen-minute drive north.

The brewpub is recognizable by the large grain silo sitting beside the modern brick structure. There's an outdoor patio for al fresco dining. The layout is typical of most Rock Bottoms. The interior is spacious with a polished, upscale feel, but it is not stuffy. There are separate dining and bar areas. A large island-style bar dominates the bar area, with flatscreens suspended above. The brewhouse sits beyond the bar, visible behind glass. A row of shiny serving tanks resides behind big windows. Directly above, on the second level, stands a row of fermentation vessels.

If you've visited Rock Bottoms in other locations, you won't find any big surprises at the Centerra location. The food menu and beer lineup are designed to appeal to a wide demographic. The company, which has operated under the Craftworks parent corporation since 2010, has a well-defined model that it executes with consistency.

Having visited all of the Rock Bottoms in Colorado, I've been impressed with the skill and professionalism of the brewers. There are four core beers produced at all Rock Bottom facilities—a Kolsch, a white ale, a red ale, and an IPA. Each location also keeps a dark beer of varying style available full-time. Beyond that, each brewer can create beers of his or her own choosing. It's not uncommon for the specialty offerings to equal or exceed the number of core offerings at the restaurant.

Year-round beers: Kolsch, White Ale, Red Ale, India Pale Ale, and a specialty dark beer.

Dave Peacock heads the brewing operations at Centerra. Peacock came from a culinary background and studied at the prestigious Culinary Institute of America in upstate New York. He has

The Pick: To get a taste of the brewer's individuality and creativity, select a specialty beer that sounds appealing.

broad experience in different specializations of food prep, especially baking. Making the transition from the kitchen to the brewhouse was an easy one for the former homebrew hobbyist.

"It really comes down to making things with grain. The more bread I made and the more beer I made, the more I found they really aren't that different," said Peacock. "You've got your yeast cultures. You've got your grain. It's really all the same ingredients. You're just doing different things with it. People joke around that beer is liquid bread. It really is."

Peacock's first jobs with Rock Bottom were in Maryland and in Washington, DC. He later transferred to Arizona. He arrived in Loveland when the facility opened in 2007 and has been there ever since. While some Rock Bottom brewers have certain styles they prefer to concoct, Peacock is more of a generalist when it comes to brewing: "I'm open to anything, really. I don't have a particular style that I love brewing more than another. I just love beer." You'll find up to six specialty beers at Centerra.

Peacock has a collection of used spirits barrels he's acquired from the nearby Dancing Pines craft distillery. The beers that fill the barrels are aged at least six months in order to develop their character. After patient aging, these distinctive fermentations tend to disappear within hours of being tapped. "Labor of love," said the former chef.

Rock Bottom—Centerra

Opened: May 2007.
Owners: CraftWorks Restaurants and Breweries.
Head brewer: Dave Peacock.
Potential annual capacity: 2,000 barrels.
Hours: Sunday through Thursday, 11 a.m. to 11 p.m.; Friday and Saturday, 11 p.m. to midnight.
Tours: On request.
Take-out beer: Growlers and kegs.
Food: Broad selection of pub favorites and diverse entrées.
Extras: AHA member deals program participant.
Parking: On-site lot.

Shine Restaurant & Gathering Place

2027 13th Street, Boulder, CO 80302
(303) 449-0120 • www.shineboulder.com

Before you visit Shine Restaurant & Gathering Place, suspend your notion of what a brewpub is all about. The Boulder restaurant was conceived with a unique vision that attracts not only beer enthusiasts, but also individuals with a diversity of tastes and interests.

Shine is owned and operated by an atypical three-person partnership of triplets Jill, Jessica, and Jennifer Emich. With a goal of creating a community-focused restaurant, gathering place, and event space, the sisters found a suitable location in downtown Boulder that had been the site of three previous brewpub operations beginning in the mid-1990s.

Originally, they were going to remove the brewhouse, as they were unfamiliar with operating a brewery. They reconsidered, however, due partly to the urgings of Mike Kasian, who had brewed at the location while the previous two short-lived brewpub businesses came and went. Kasian was hired to run the brewery at Shine, and has the distinction of having had three different brewing jobs without changing work addresses.

The restaurant is on 13th Street, one-half block from Boulder's animated Pearl Street walking mall. Next door is a European-style beer hall that had once been a wine bar. Coincidently, the wine bar had been owned and operated by the triplets. Above the entrance to Shine is a sign that reads "Welcome Home." The interior is divided into three distinct spaces. In the front is the open and contemporary dining room and bar. Beyond that is the lounge. The latter is an intimate space with an Asian feel and is often used for small parties and networking groups.

Toward the back is "the gathering place," a multipurpose room used for live music, yoga workshops, and other public and private affairs. This is where the monthly "hoopy hour" Hula-Hoop instruction class is held. "It's a happy hour too, so people are having drinks and hula hooping," said Jill, whose tasks include coordinating Shine's daily events. "It's stuff like that that gets

Year-round beers: Shine Pale Ale, Pohoda Pilz, Trilogy IPA, Down Dog Imperial Red, Sanitas Imperial Stout, Liberation Gluten-Free Ale.

The Pick: Tangy hops grab the spotlight in the Trilogy IPA. Its malty costar also plays a prominent role.

me excited because everyone is having a good time."A good portion of Shine's regulars are locals involved in Boulder's thriving arts, music, dance, and yoga communities.

Both Jill and Jessica are graduates of the California Culinary Academy in San Francisco. Jessica, Shine's executive chef, also has a master's degree in holistic nutrition. "[Her] food is holistic in that she considers digestibility and food combinations and that kind of thing," Jill informs me. "We don't really put that in people's faces when they come in. When you eat the food, you just feel really good afterwards."

The kitchen is 100 percent gluten-free. Regular bread is brought in from a local bakery, but stored in a separate room. The kitchen isn't meatless, though there are plenty of vegetarian options and many items can be prepared with meat or without. There's a variety of interesting soups and salads on the menu. You can also get a burger, tacos, or pasta. "The thing about the food is that it's basically comfort food," Jill explained. "It doesn't taste like you're eating really healthy food."

Healthful non-alcoholic potions are made in-house from flower essences and herbs. Cocktails are all organic. Low-alcohol elixirs are produced locally and served at Shine.

The brewhouse might be the most conventional aspect of the brewpub. Kasian keeps a broad range of beers on tap, from a quaffable Czech pils to a crowd-pleasing IPA to more hearty high-gravity beers including an imperial red and an imperial stout. A gluten-free beer is a necessity, of course. Kasian's version is brewed with sorghum, millet, local honey, molasses, elderberries, and lemon balm, and has an interesting fruity and slightly tart character.

Shine Restaurant & Gathering Place

Opened: December 2011.

Owners: Jessica, Jill, and Jennifer Emich.

Head brewer: Mike Kasian.

Potential annual capacity: 800 barrels.

Hours: Monday through Thursday, 11:30 a.m. to close; Friday, 11:30 a.m. to 1 a.m.; Saturday, 10:00 a.m. to 1 a.m.; Sunday, 10:00 a.m. to close.

Tours: On request.

Take-out beer: Growlers and kegs.

Food: Nontraditional brewpub menu with emphasis on nourishing, organic dishes prepared with locally sourced ingredients. Weekend brunch.

Extras: Frequent live music and numerous other events.

Parking: Metered street parking and nearby pay lots.

Twisted Pine Brewing Company

3201 Walnut Street, Suite A, Boulder, CO 80301
(303) 786-9270 • www.twistedpinebrewing.com

Twisted Pine Brewing Company has deep roots in the Boulder craft beer scene. As it approaches its twentieth birthday, the well-establish brewery continues to branch out in new directions.

The business was founded in 1995 by the late Gordon Knight, a well-known figure in the local craft beer scene who launched several craft-brewing businesses in the 1990s. Knight is likely the only brewer ever to win three Great American Beer Festival medals at three different breweries for three different beers. In 1996, Knight sold Twisted Pine to Bob Baile, a former research chemist who was operating the Peak to Peak Brewing Company, a small brewery located in tiny Rollinsville, in the mountains west of Boulder. Baile merged his two companies, retaining the Twisted Pine moniker. The company operated out of a 2,500-square foot Boulder garage.

Twisted Pine grew slowly over the years, eventually outgrowing its cramped headquarters. In 2003, the business moved to its current location in a facility formerly occupied by the Oasis Brewery, which had closed the previous year. Today, the East Boulder brewery and taproom room attracts a lively after-work crowd and an onslaught of weekend beer warriors.

Twisted Pine sits just east of the Twenty-Ninth Street shopping mall on the border of a retail district and industrial area a few miles from downtown Boulder. A wooden bar (pine, of course) occupies a corner of the taproom. Pine-topped tables fill the remaining space. A mural depicting the brewing process runs the length of one wall. There's outdoor seating within a long, shaded patio that runs along the front of the building.

Twisted Pine has steadily broadened its operations over the years, including the addition of an in-house kitchen offering pizza and sandwiches. In 2012, the brewery took over an adjacent space, increasing the size of the brewhouse as well as the taproom. Distribution has undergone a slow,

Year-round beers: Blonde Ale, American Amber Ale, Hoppy Boy IPA, Honey Brown, Cream-Style Stout, Rocky Mountain Wheat, Raspberry Wheat, Billy's Chilies, Big Shot Espresso Stout, Hoppy Knight India Black Ale, Ghost Face Killah Chili Beer.

The Pick: If coffee-flavored beers are your cup of tea, the Big Shot Espresso Stout is smooth and drinkable with a nice balance of malt and coffee flavors.

steady expansion. Twisted Pine beers can now be found in the South, Southwest, and Midwest. The brewery has also become increasingly involved in community affairs and is active in numerous fundraising initiatives and events throughout the year.

An adventurous spirit permeates the brewhouse, with a slew of esoteric creations included in the core lineup of eleven beers. Among them is Big Shot Espresso Stout, a coffee-flavored dark ale and three-time Great American Beer Festival medal winner. West Bound Braggot, a honey beer, was a 2013 GABF bronze medal winner. A longtime seasonal favorite is the Northstar Imperial Porter, a complex yet smooth high-gravity beer. Other more standard beers include blonde, amber, dark, hoppy, and fruity libations.

Billy's Chilies is a chili-infused ale with a devout following. It was first brewed from a homebrew recipe of a former employee. It has a fresh peppery flavor and a warm kiss in the finish. A few years ago, the brewers decided to turn up the heat. They created a specialty beer named Ghost Face Killah, a chili beer brewed with incendiary *Bhut jolokia*, also known as ghost peppers. On the Scoville scale of heat intensity, ghost peppers are rated at 1.1 million units, about three times hotter than palate-erasing habaneros. To everyone's surprise, the world's hottest beer flew off the shelves each time it was brewed. "It's become this whole cult thing," Baile explained of the decision to make the beer a full-time offering. On brew days, gloves, goggles, and a respirator are standard gear for the brew crew.

Twisted Pine Brewing Company

Opened: Founded in 1995. In current location since 2003.

Owners: Bob Baile and Dr. Bill Marshall; CEO Jean Lund.

Head brewer: Bob Baile.

Potential annual capacity: 6,000 barrels.

Hours: Monday through Thursday, 11 a.m. to 9 p.m.; Friday, 11 a.m. to 10 p.m.; Saturday, noon to 10 p.m.; Sunday, noon to 8 p.m.

Tours: Sunday at 2 p.m.

Take-out beer: Growlers, six-packs, bombers, and kegs.

Food: Salads, sandwiches, and pizzas.

Extras: Trivia on Monday. Live music on Wednesday and Saturday. Bluegrass pick on Sunday. AHA member deals program participant.

Parking: On-site lot.

Upslope Brewing Company

Two locations

It was a long uphill slog from conception to production for Upslope Brewing Company. The journey has led to a mountain of success for the Boulder brewery.

In 1996, a year after becoming a homebrew hobbyist, Matt Cutter put together a business plan for a microbrewery. Lacking funds to put the plan into motion, the proposal collected dust for more than a decade. Cutter revisited the plan in 2007, but it wasn't until the following year, when he met a brewer named Dany Pages, that the brewery concept gained real momentum. Pages was visiting Colorado from Ushuaia, Argentina, where he had started Beagle Brewery, the world's southernmost brewery. Cutter and Pages shared a common vision, and a partnership was formed.

Cutter took out a second mortgage on his home to help finance the venture. A third partner, Henry Wood, came aboard to spearhead sales. Upslope brewed its first batch in the fall of 2008. From the start, the Upslope brand has been synonymous with the Colorado outdoor lifestyle. Henry and Dany are avid rock climbers. Matt is a cyclist, backpacker, and skier. To be compatible with that type of active lifestyle, and to reduce environmental impacts, all Upslope beers are packaged in cans.

The partners had anticipated producing 400 barrels their first year. The actual tally was 1,100. The next year they produced 2,400 barrels. The following year, it increased to 3,800. With the brewery unable to keep up with demand, Upslope opened a second, much larger production brewery and taproom in East Boulder in 2013. The original brewery is now used to produce experimental beers.

Pages oversees Upslope's two brewhouses, while Alex Violette holds the title of head brewer. After receiving a biochemistry degree, Violette got hooked on homebrewing. "I think I was brewing my yearly legal limit every weekend," he said of his prolific homebrew habit. He worked for several years at a brewery in Tennessee, then moved to Colorado for the beer culture. "I had never set foot in the state of Colorado before. I had no idea where I was going to live. No idea where I was

Year-round beers: Pale Ale, IPA, Brown Ale, Craft Lager, Imperial IPA.

The Pick: The Upslope Brown Ale starts sweet and finishes dry. In between are notes of toffee, cocoa, and bittersweet chocolate.

going to work," said Violette of his relocation. Apparently, he had a mountain of good karma. He got a job at Upslope and worked his way up to head brewer.

Violette enjoys the challenge of brewing lagers. In fact, the Upslope Craft Lager is the brewery's best seller and one of five year-round beers. Others include a pale ale, an IPA, a brown ale, and an imperial IPA. Upslope also packages seasonal releases including a Belgian pale ale, a stout, a Christmas ale, and a pumpkin beer. The pumpkin beer was a 2011 Great American Beer Festival gold medal winner. At the 2013 GABF, Upslope captured a bronze medal in the Pro-Am Competition with an oatmeal stout.

Flatirons

1898 South Flatiron Court, Boulder, CO 80304
(303) 396-1898 • www.upslopebrewing.com

Upslope's new facility is located in a sprawling East Boulder business park. Not surprisingly, the taproom attracts an after-work crowd of people from nearby businesses. A shiny silver silo stands guard near the entrance. The tasting room is more spacious than its older sibling. The metal tables and concrete bar are design elements borrowed from the original facility. The contemporary industrial feel is accented with a modernistic array of two dozen tap handles suspended from overhead piping. The atmosphere is typically loud and lively.

Upslope Brewing Company—Flatirons location

Opened: April 2013.

Owners: Matt Cutter, Dany Pages, and Henry Wood.

Head brewer: Alex Violette. Director of Brewing Operations: Dany Pages.

Potential annual capacity: 50,000 barrels.

Hours: Daily, 11 a.m. to 10 p.m.

Tours: Monday through Saturday at 5 p.m., or by appointment.

Take-out beer: Growlers, cans, and kegs.

Food: Food truck on Thursday. A restaurant is planned.

Extras: Live music on Thursday. Open mic on Sunday.

Parking: On-site lot.

Lee Hill

1501 Lee Hill Road, No. 20, Boulder, CO 80304
(303) 449-2911 • www.upslopebrewing.com

Upslope's original brewery is in an easily accessed light industrial complex in North Boulder, across the street from a miniature golf course and go-kart track. It has a contemporary look with blond-wood fixtures, steel tables, and a black concrete bar. "I wanted it to retain what our branding is," said Cutter of the taproom's look and feel. "Simple, contemporary, outdoorsy." During the week, people from the nearby neighborhood frequent the brewery, including many families.

Upslope Brewing Company—Lee Hill location

Opened: November 2008.

Owners: Matt Cutter, Dany Pages, and Henry Wood.

Head brewer: Alex Violette. Director of Brewing Operations: Dany Pages.

Potential annual capacity: 7,000 barrels.

Hours: Sunday through Thursday, 2 p.m. to 9 p.m.; Friday and Saturday, 2 p.m. to 10 p.m.

Tours: On request.

Take-out beer: Growlers, cans, and kegs.

Food: Cheese plates. Food trucks on weekends and some Thursdays.

Extras: Live music on Friday. AHA member discount program participant.

Parking: On-site lot.

Verboten Brewing

1550 Taurus Court, Loveland, CO 80537
(970) 988-6333 • www.verbotenbrewing.com

According to the Reinheitsgebot, the German beer purity law enacted in 1516 and still in use today, beer can only be brewed from barley, hops, water, and yeast. All other ingredients are forbidden, or *verboten* in German.

The slogan for Verboten Brewing is "Beer for All." It could just as easily be "rules are meant to be broken," based on the brewery's prodigious use of *verboten* ingredients including fruits, spices, and sugars in many of the house beers. While German purists might consider this breach of protocol less than *wunderbar*, it's a non-issue for the patrons of the Loveland brewery.

Verboten opened its doors in early 2013 in a modern-looking business park east of downtown. With the brewery located along a bike path and in close proximity to several housing developments, many customers arrive on foot or by bike. The brewery occupies a long, narrow space in a building it shares with a Pilates studio and a signage company.

The small tasting room is populated with a half-dozen wooden tables and a compact bar that seats eight. The high ceiling promotes a feeling of openness while the gray walls and interesting clear globular light fixtures add a touch of sophistication. A few paintings by a local artist adorn the walls. There's a small patio in front of the building.

Verboten is owned and operated by two couples, Josh and Angie Grenz and Joe and Keri Akers. Josh and Joe were friends and homebrewing partners who decided to take their passion for brewing to the next level and open a commercial brewery. Along the way, they befriended the proprietor of Dancing Pines Distillery, a Loveland-based spirits producer. When a space opened up across the street from the distillery, the two beverage businesses became neighbors.

At the time of my visit, Josh was the only full-time brewery employee. The numerous other tasks involved in operating the business—bookkeeping, marketing, social networking, sales, and

Year-round beers: Killer Boots Caramel Porter.

The Pick: It's generally a good bet to drink what the brewer is drinking. Brewer Josh Grenz will often be drinking a barrel-aged offering and you should be, too.

anything else—are divided among the other partners. Everyone takes shifts behind the bar.

With Loveland's growing list of breweries, it's important to have a unique niche to create an identity. For Verboten, that niche is a constantly rotating selection of small-batch beers with non-traditional brewing ingredients appearing frequently in their recipes. "Forbidden ingredients are kind of our specialty," according to Grenz. "We're rotating a lot of fun stuff." There was only one full-time beer when I stopped by for a spring visit and sampling session. Killer Boots is a porter infused with caramel made in-house. In the future, other beers may be added to the full-time lineup based on demand. Several recipes, including a lemongrass wit and orange blossom honey wheat, have developed fan bases and reappear from time to time.

Not all beers contain verboten ingredients. I sampled an American golden ale that was based on a recipe from a local homebrewing couple who happened to be sitting next to me at the bar. A Cascadian dark ale was on tap, as was a nicely balanced red ale dispensed from a nitro tap. Verboten's relationship with the nearby distillery provides an ample supply of spirits barrels used to age a variety of beers. It's a fortuitous situation for Grenz, who described his favorite beer style as "anything aged in a barrel." My favorite of the Verboten beers was a bourbon barrel-aged porter. "Nothing stays around very long," said Grenz of the brewery's ever-changing offerings. "There's something unique every time you come in."

Verboten Brewing

Opened: January 2013.

Owners: Joe and Keri Akers and Josh and Angie Grenz.

Head brewer: Josh Grenz.

Potential annual capacity: 250 barrels.

Hours: Tuesday through Friday, 3 p.m. to 9 p.m.; Saturday, 1 p.m. to 9 p.m.; Sunday, 1 p.m. to 7 p.m. Closed Monday.

Tours: On request.

Take-out beer: Growlers and kegs.

Food: Food trucks most weekends and occasional weekdays.

Extras: Live music on Thursday and Sunday. Women's beer appreciation group on Wednesday. AHA member discount program participant.

Parking: On-site lot.

Very Nice Brewing Company

20 Lakeview Drive, No. 112, Nederland, CO 80466
(303) 258-3770 • www.verynicebrewing.com

In the classic film *Monty Python and the Holy Grail*, the French character played by John Cleese describes to King Arthur the Holy Grail that Cleese's master allegedly possesses: "It's very nice." This obscure movie reference was adopted for the name of Very Nice Brewing Company, a small, laid-back brewery in the mountain town of Nederland, a short drive from Boulder.

Nederland has another, less obscure, tie to the entertainment industry. A ranch located a few miles from town once housed a state-of-the-art recording studio. Among the artists who recorded at the Caribou Ranch were John Lennon, Elton John, Michael Jackson, U2, Chicago, The Beach Boys, Stephen Stills, Billy Joel, Tom Petty, Rod Stewart, and Frank Zappa.

The brewery was the inspiration of Jeffrey Green and his wife, Susan. The roots for Very Nice were planted at the 2008 Great American Beer Festival, an eye-opener for Jeffrey: "I loved beer, but I didn't understand it could be so many things." The Ohio transplant had dabbled in homebrewing, but after GABF, it suddenly became an obsession. "I kept getting more and more into beer. All I could think about was brewing beer whenever I was at work," Green recalled of his increasing difficulty in concentrating on his engineering job.

The couple decided to open a brewery. They found a space on the ground floor of a two-story Nederland retail complex. The space is adjacent to the largest grocery store for miles, so many locals pass by the brewery several times a week on shopping runs, giving the upstart business great visibility. A garage-style door was installed in the front wall to open up the modest-sized space and bring in more light. The green walls display an assemblage of interesting paintings from local artists. Picnic tables and a few high-tops provide seating, while a pair of pinball machines provides a diversion. The bar is constructed of thick slabs of beetle kill pine and seats a dozen guests. If the bar seems unusually

Year-round beers: Monk's Phunk Belgian Ale, The Logical Fallacy Stout, Royal We IPA, Steffie's Heffe, Very Nice Pale Ale.

The Pick: Logical Fallacy entices you with the chocolatey smoothness of a stout before a punch of hops adds another layer of flavor to this dark ale.

high, that's because it was designed to accommodate the tall barstools that were acquired from a former restaurant.

Although beer enthusiasts from Denver, Boulder, Longmont, and other nearby Front Range communities make the short trek to Nederland to visit the town's second brewery, Very Nice caters primarily to a local clientele. The taproom's relaxed vibe attracts a lot of young couples with kids. "They can bring in food and sodas for the kids, and they can just hang out and have a beer and not feel like they're in a party bar," Green said of the family-friendly gathering spot.

Very Nice plays host to a variety of events. These have included Pints & Poses, a brewery-hosted yoga session, and Bellies & Beers, a belly dancing class. In the winter, the brewery is a popular après ski stop for visitors to nearby Eldora Mountain Resort.

Green has an adventurous spirit when it comes to concocting new recipes. "Brewing to me is like jazz. You pick a theme and then you expand on it," he explained of his brewing philosophy. "I want to do weird beers for the beer nerds who want to taste something really different. I'm not necessarily brewing a beer that everyone is going to like. I want to push the limits." For the holidays, he concocted a richly flavored spruce beer. While it wasn't universally adored, many people thought it was, well, very nice.

Very Nice Brewing Company

Opened: October 2012.

Owners: Jeffrey and Susan Green.

Head brewer: Jeffrey Green.

Potential annual capacity: 300 barrels.

Hours: Wednesday and Thursday, 2 p.m. to 8 p.m.; Friday, 2 p.m. to 9 p.m.; Saturday, noon to 9 p.m.; Sunday, noon to 7 p.m.

Tours: On request.

Take-out beer: Growlers.

Food: Pizza pickup available at Backcountry Pizza (upstairs). You can also bring your own food.

Extras: Open Mic Night on second and fourth Thursday of the month. AHA member deals program participant.

Parking: On-site lot in retail complex.

Area attractions: Eldora Mountain Resort (2861 Eldora Ski Road, 303-440-8700). The Carousel of Happiness (20 Lakeview Dr.). Nederland Mining Museum (200 N. Bridge St., open June through Oct.)

Other area beer sites: Backcountry Pizza (20 E. Lakeview Dr., No. 212, 303-258-0176). Salto Coffee Works (112 E. 2nd Street, 303-258-3537).

Walnut Brewery

1123 Walnut Street, Boulder, CO 80302
(303) 447-1345 • www.walnutbrewery.com

As Boulder's first brewpub, the Walnut Brewery holds a prominent place in the city's ascendance as a craft beer mecca. Many Boulderites and visitors alike were introduced to the concept of a restaurant-brewery at the venerable Walnut. The pub is also noteworthy for being the model upon which the Rock Bottom brewpub chain was launched. There are currently more than three dozen Rock Bottoms nationwide.

The brewpub came to life in 1990 through the combined efforts of Frank Day and Mark Youngquist (see Dolores River Brewing on page 276). Day was a local restaurateur whose achievements included launching the Old Chicago chain of taphouses in Boulder in 1976. In fact, the original Old Chicago is just around the corner from Walnut. Youngquist was a brewer who had worked at the Bridgeport Brewery in Oregon before relocating to Colorado.

Given the positive reception the Walnut received from the local populace, Day opened the first Rock Bottom in downtown Denver in 1991 using the Walnut as a prototype. Many of the Rock Bottom design elements, especially the upscale-casual ambience, were borrowed from the Boulder pub. Today, the Walnut operates as part of the Craftworks family of restaurants, which includes the Gordon Biersch, Rock Bottom, Chophouse, and Old Chicago chains.

The Walnut resides in a prime downtown Boulder location, close to the Boulder Creek Path and numerous other beer stops. It's a block from the Pearl Street walking mall, which is a dining, shopping, and people-watching paradise.

The brewpub's interior is spacious, with high ceilings and exposed beams. Brick walls, upholstered booths, and dark wood fixtures create a character more classic than cool, but without any stuffiness. A few TVs are mounted in view of the long wooden bar. A row of fermenters sits behind glass on the second level.

Year-round beers: St. James Irish Red Ale, Buffalo Gold, Indian Peaks Pale Ale, Old Elk Brown Ale, Big Horn Bitter, plus a rotating dark beer and a seasonal wheat beer.

The Pick: Old Elk Brown Ale has a malty-chocolatey character without being overly sweet.

A mixed crowd keeps the pub bustling. With Boulder's popularity as a tourist destination, the restaurant attracts a lot of travelers, especially in the summer months. Crowds also pack the pub when the University of Colorado, just a mile away, hosts sporting events or other activities that bring out-of-towners into the city. In the winter months, it's more of a local's scene.

The large and eclectic menu features burgers, pizza, and other pub classics alongside steaks, seafood, and assorted entrées, including some southwestern dishes. A pub favorite is the smoked salmon fish-and-chips, a unique take on the pub classic.

The brewing operation is headed by Rodney Taylor, whose tenure started in 1999. Prior to arriving in Boulder, Taylor had worked at several Rock Bottoms around the country, including the original downtown Denver facility. He offers six standard house beers—a golden ale, a red ale, a brown ale, a pale ale, a specialty dark, and a seasonal wheat. The Old Elk Brown Ale and St. James Red Ale have garnered a combined five Great American Beer Festival medals.

Walnut beers are brewed to be more approachable than adventurous. Taylor leaves more challenging creations to his brewing colleagues around town. "We don't have a beer that will clean your teeth with hops, but we do have hoppy beers," Taylor said of the Walnut's fermentations. "There are breweries (in Boulder) that do really big and over-the-top beers, and I think it's great. I love to go and enjoy them. We're not trying to be that place and they're not trying to be this place. We all kind of fit together like a puzzle."

Walnut Brewery

Opened: May 1990.

Owner: CraftWorks Restaurants and Breweries.

Head brewer: Rodney Taylor.

Potential annual capacity: 2,000 barrels.

Hours: Daily, 11 a.m. to midnight.

Tours: On request.

Take-out beer: Growlers and kegs.

Food: Extensive menu of sandwiches, burgers, pizza, steak, seafood, and other entrées.

Extras: AHA member deals program participant.

Parking: On-street metered parking and nearby lots.

West Flanders Brewing Company

1125 Pearl Street, Boulder, CO 80302
(303) 447-BREW (2739) • www.wfbrews.com

Boulder is about 4,800 miles west of the Belgian province of Flanders, but the Flemish passion for frequenting the local café for interesting beers paired with good food lives on at West Flanders Brewing Company, a downtown Boulder brewpub.

When West Flanders opened in the fall of 2012, it was the rekindling of an old partnership with a long history in the Boulder craft beer scene. Brothers Mark and Chris Heinritz were part-owners of the Redfish Brewhouse, a now-defunct brewpub that opened in 1996. The brothers are also longtime owners of the venerable Sink, Boulder's oldest bar and restaurant, which celebrated its ninetieth anniversary in 2013.

The original Redfish brewer was Brian Lutz, who gained a solid reputation among local craft beer fans by creating distinctive Belgian-style ales long before they had gained widespread popularity in the United States. Eventually, the Heinritz brothers sold their interest in the Redfish, and Lutz moved on to other ventures.

In 2012, BJ's Restaurant & Brewhouse vacated its downtown Boulder location, leaving the brewing setup behind. The landlord, a longtime homebrewer with close ties to the craft beer community, contacted Lutz, who in turn contacted the Heinritz brothers. The trio decided to team up on a new brewpub venture. They added a fourth partner, Barry Wolfman, who has forty years of restaurant experience and works as West Flanders's general manager. You'll recognize him as the guy in constant motion, welcoming new guests while chatting with regulars at the bar and simultaneously carrying on conversations at several different tables.

West Flanders has an enviable location in the heart of Boulder's pulsating Pearl Street mall. A study found that up to 30,000 pedestrians may pass the spot in a single day. Despite its downtown location, the brewpub has the laid-back vibe of a neighborhood café thanks to its casual décor

Year-round beers: Third Kingdom IPA, Daisy Cutter Belgian Strong Ale, Trippel Lutz, Hoffmeister Pilsner, St. Mark's Dubbel, Es Bueno ESB, Angry Monk Belgian-Style Ale, Canniption Pale Ale.

The Pick: Angry Monk is created in the Belgian tradition of making beer that pleases the brewer without regard to style guidelines. The aroma hints of banana, the flavor has notes of caramel, and it finishes with a tummy-warming glow.

and genuinely friendly waitstaff. "We appreciate everyone who walks through the door," said Wolfman, the consummate host.

The main dining area, in the front of the building, is a relaxed and informal space with about ten tables. A wall of picture windows looks out to the small patio, one of Boulder's preeminent people-watching spots. The bar area is in the back. Behind the long bar is a row of shiny serving tanks beyond which a pair of copper-clad brewing vessels sits in full view. Across from the bar, a series of large photographs of veteran local homebrewers are on display. Among them is Charlie Papazian, often referred to as "the father of American homebrewing." I'm honored that my photo is part of that collection.

When you're located in the heart of Boulder's highly competitive restaurant scene, mediocrity is not an option. West Flanders has built a solid customer base by offering food that transcends standard pub fare, and well-crafted beers with an emphasis on Belgian-style ales. The kitchen puts out some pub favorites such as above-average burgers and flatbreads, along with some less pedestrian plates such as wild salmon and coffee-brined chicken. And when "Flanders" is in your name, having mussels on the menu is a no-brainer.

Although West Flanders's beer offerings include an assortment of well-made English, German, and American-style beers, the brewpub is unique in that its best seller is a Belgian-style ale. Angry Monk is an abbey ale that doesn't fit into a well-defined category. Lutz's brewing style was borrowed from Belgian brewers, who don't brew to satisfy judges, but to create unique beers. Belgian ales are his passion. "They're challenging. They're unique. They really satisfy me in a lot of different ways," Lutz said of his favorite beers. "There's really no category to place them in many times. Anything goes."

West Flanders Brewing Company

Opened: September 2012.

Owners: Barry Wolfman, Mark and Chris Heinritz, Brian Lutz.

Head brewer: Brian Lutz.

Potential annual capacity: 1,000 barrels.

Hours: Daily, 11 a.m. to closing in summer. Daily, 11:30 a.m. to closing in winter.

Tours: On request.

Take-out beer: Growlers and kegs.

Food: Small plates, sandwiches, burgers, pizza, and assorted entrées.

Extras: Live music on Friday. Bluegrass pick on Monday. AHA member deals program participant.

Parking: On-street metered parking and nearby lots.

Wild Mountain Smokehouse & Brewery

70 East First Street, Nederland, CO 80466
(303) 258-WILD (9453) • www.wildmountainsb.com

Nederland, the home of Wild Mountain Smoke-house & Brewery, is a small mountain community approximately 16 miles distant, and 2,800 feet above, the city of Boulder at the end of scenic, twisting Boulder Canyon. Ned, as the town is often called, has a penchant for the offbeat, such as the popular winter festival known as Frozen Dead Guy Days. The gathering commemorates Ned's most famous citizen, a Norwegian man known as "Grandpa" Bredo Morstel, whose cryogenically frozen remains were discovered on dry ice in a shed behind the Nederland home of his daughter and grandson.

Among the festival events is the frozen turkey bowling competition, which takes place in front of Wild Mountain, a very normal and attractive brewpub located not far from the town's baffling traffic circle. Before the pub opened in 2007, the community had been without a hometown brewery for almost six years. Now it has two.

Wild Mountain's cofounder and brewer, Tom Boogaard, began his brewing career in the early 1990s at the Otto Brothers Brewery in Wyoming (now Grand Teton Brewing). He then moved on to the highly regarded Snake River Brewing in Jackson Hole, where he was an assistant brewer. "That's when I realized for the first time in my life how satisfying it is to make something with your hands and sit back and watch people enjoy it," Boogaard recalled. After a stint at the Tremont Brewery near Boston, he worked at Boulder's Avery Brewing where he held several positions including head brewer. Boogaard has a lasting legacy at Avery. That brewery's The Reverend, a Belgian quadruple ale, was brewed as a tribute to Boogaard's late grandfather, an ordained Episcopal reverend.

Boogaard, along with his wife Cori, built Wild Mountain from the ground up. Tom was meticulous about details, especially when the brewery's concrete floor was being poured. "I went every couple feet along the wall and I rolled a marble. If it didn't go to the drain, I had them re-pour," he remembered about the construction process.

Year-round beers: Otis Pale Ale, Hop Diggity IPA.

The Pick: Hop Diggity IPA is packed with hoppy goodness supported by a solid foundation of malt. The beer's hop bitterness is neither overaggressive nor understated.

The building's rustic yet contemporary style contrasts with the weathered appearance of many local structures. From the outside, the standalone building looks like an oversized modern cabin with a long front porch and steeply sloping roof, good for shedding snow. The interior is not large, but the cathedral ceilings and numerous windows create a spacious, airy feeling. Green, red, and purple walls are adorned with posters, artwork, and photos of musicians including Jimi Hendrix and Jerry Garcia. A large sunny deck in the back overlooks the forested hillsides behind town.

Aside from the many locals who stop by Wild Mountain regularly, visitors frequently include recreationists—mountain bikers, hikers, skiers—who pass through Nederland on their mountain outings. Trailheads into the Indian Peaks Wilderness are nearby. The ski resort of Eldora is just a few miles away.

Wild Mountain's menu features house-smoked barbecue, including some nontraditional items. The smoked chicken wings are perennial crowd-pleasers, as is the smoked prime rib. The smoked tofu caters to non-carnivores. The small selection of house beers includes Wild Mountain's hugely popular IPA, which emphasizes hop flavor and aroma over bitterness. A pale ale is frequently on tap along with a few seasonal and specialty beers. You'll also find an assortment of guest beers from other Boulder County breweries and a modest but well-conceived selection of bottled beers, including some interesting European imports.

Wild Mountain Smokehouse & Brewery

Opened: March 2007.

Owners: Tom and Cori Boogaard.

Head brewer: Tom Boogaard.

Potential annual capacity: 400 barrels.

Hours: Daily, 11 a.m. to 10 p.m.

Tours: Call or by request.

Take-out beer: Growlers.

Food: American smokehouse with a variety of smoked meats and sauces and smoked tofu.

Extras: AHA pub discount program participant.

Parking: On-street parking.

Area attractions: See Very Nice Brewing Company on page 188.

Other area beer sites: See Very Nice Brewing Company on page 188.

Wild Woods Brewery

5460 Conestoga Court, Boulder, CO 80301
(303) 484-1465 • www.wildwoodsbrewery.com

When I taste the subtle smokiness of Wild Woods' Campfire Red Ale, it brings back sweet memories of carefree camping trips in the Colorado high country. That's exactly the intent of Jake and Erin Evans, proprietors of the East Boulder brewery specializing in "handcrafted beers inspired by the outdoors."

The couple developed an appreciation for great beer in the taphouses of Pittsburgh, where the Wisconsin natives were living after college. With a passion for hiking and camping, they were hoping to relocate to Colorado. Their desire was fulfilled when Jake, an electrical engineer, landed a job in Boulder in 2007.

It didn't take them long to become immersed in the local beer scene. "We ended up living right by Boulder Beer," Jake recalled. "We went there even before we got the keys to our first place." They easily adopted the Colorado lifestyle, spending their free time hiking, camping, and homebrewing. Each backcountry outing included stops at nearby breweries.

In their early homebrewing efforts, they used published recipes for their beers, but soon began concocting their own liquid creations. "We found our best inspiration for recipes came when we were hiking and camping. We had clear minds. We drew inspiration from the tastes and sounds and smells of nature," Jake explained.

Year-round beers: Wildflower Pale Ale, Treeline IPA, Campfire Red Ale, Ponderosa Porter, Smores Stout, Berry Patch Wheat.

The idea of opening a commercial brewery evolved slowly but steadily. As the Evanses grew more serious about the idea, they attended Tom Hennessey's brewery immersion class at the Colorado Boy brewpub across the state in Ridgway. "We knew going into it that we were going to come away either overwhelmed or [thinking] we can do this. We left so inspired, so confident," Jake recalled. Following the class, their efforts accelerated. They found a space for their business in an

The Pick: Ponderosa Porter is a smooth, complex, and delicious dark elixir flavored with oak and vanilla. It all comes together in a harmony of tastes that is equally pleasing to both craft beer novices and more experienced palates.

East Boulder office park and purchased a two-barrel brewing system. Wild Woods Brewery made its debut in September 2012.

The brewery is tucked into a complex of mixed businesses, big and small. The Wild Woods tasting room is not large, but high ceilings give it a comfortably open feel. Liberal use of beetle kill pine for the bar, tabletops, and interior walls softens the industrial nature of the space. A garage-style door opens to a small patio with a pair of picnic tables.

To create beers suggestive of their outdoor experiences, Jake, who runs the brewing operation, often incorporates a variety of non-standard brewing ingredients in the recipes. The Wildflower Pale Ale is flavored with jasmine flowers. The Treeline IPA has an infusion of juniper berries. Wild Woods' crowd-pleasing Ponderosa Porter is brewed with vanilla beans and aged on wood, evoking aromas of ponderosa pine bark. The flavors imparted by these ingredients tend to express themselves with a subtle background presence rather than an in-your-face assault. Wild Woods' choice of flavorings nicely complements the base styles, resulting in satisfying, interesting, and very approachable beers.

One or more rotating specialty beers appear alongside the standard half-dozen ales. The Honey Nut Blonde Ale is brewed with Colorado honey and aged on toasted almonds. The hearty Tropical Paradise Imperial IPA is instilled with fresh ginger and aged on fresh mangoes. The River Rock Brown Ale employs a traditional brewing method of adding hot stones to the brew kettle to impart notes of caramel.

Getting the new brewery established was a time-consuming endeavor, but now that things are on track, the couple is once again trekking to the Colorado backcountry that provided the inspiration for their endeavor.

Wild Woods Brewery

Opened: September 2012.

Owners: Jake and Erin Evans and Charlie and Kristen Rilling.

Head brewer: Jake Evans.

Potential annual capacity: 1300 barrels.

Hours: Tuesday through Friday, 4 p.m. to 9 p.m.; Saturday, 2 p.m. to 9 p.m. Closed Sunday and Monday.

Tours: On request.

Take-out beer: Growlers.

Food: Free delivery from Snarfs sandwich shop. Food trucks on occasion. Restaurant delivery menus on hand or bring your own food.

Extras: AHA member deals program participant.

Parking: On-site lot.

The Southern Front Range

The term "Front Range" generally refers to the part of Colorado east of the Rocky Mountain foothills. More than 80 percent of the state's population resides in the communities located along the eastern base of the Rockies.

This chapter covers the southern portion of the Colorado Front Range. For our purposes, the region is bordered on the north by the town of Castle Rock, and extends south to the city of Pueblo. I've included the mountain community of Woodland Park because of its close proximity to Colorado Springs. I've also included Cañon City in this section because of its proximity to Pueblo.

The majority of the breweries covered in this section are located in Colorado Springs, the second-most populous city in the state behind Denver. "The Springs," as it's often called, has a different feel than the state capital to the north. As the home of a variety of military installations, as well as several high-profile evangelical Christian organizations, The Springs has gained a reputation as Colorado's most conservative city.

Pikes Peak is the most prominent geographic feature in the area, towering over Colorado Springs at an elevation of 14,115 feet. It's said to be the second-most visited mountain in the world behind Mount Fuji in Japan. The summit can be reached by vehicle, by the *Pikes Peak Cog Railway* (515 Ruxton Ave., 719-685-5401), or, for the fit and adventurous, on foot. From the trailhead in Manitou Springs, it's a 13-mile slog with a vertical gain of 7,400 feet.

Garden of the Gods Park (1805 N. 30th St., 719-634-6666), in the western part of the city, is a fantastic destination for an easy hike among the striking red sandstone rock formations. The **United States Air Force Academy** (719-333-2025) is a popular visitor attraction, especially its architecturally unique chapel.

The Colorado Springs beer scene has evolved more slowly than that in Colorado cities to the north, but it's come a long way in recent years. Innovative new breweries such as Trinity Brewing Company and Great Storm Brewing have joined long-established brewing businesses such as Bristol Brewing Company and Phantom Canyon Brewing Company. In addition to the city's hometown breweries, there are a growing number of non-brewing destinations that provide rewarding stops for beer enthusiasts. I've listed some below.

BJ's Restaurant & Brewhouse (5150 N. Nevada Ave., 719-268-0505)

Blue Star (1645 S. Tejon St., 719-632-1086)

Brewer's Republic (112 N. Nevada Ave., 719-633-2105)

Front Range Barbeque (2330 W. Colorado Ave., 719-632-2596)

Il Vicino—Downtown (11 S. Tejon St., 719-475-9224)

Il Vicino—University Village (5214 N. Nevada Ave., 719-590-8633)

Old Chicago (118 N Tejon St., 719-634-8812)

Old Chicago (3190 New Center Point, 719-591-8994)

Old Chicago (7115 Commerce Center Dr., 719-593-7678)

Rabbit Hole (101 N. Tejon St., 719-203-5072)

Other brewery towns on the Southern Front Range are quite diverse. Castle Rock and Monument are bedroom communities located north of Colorado Springs. Woodland Park is in the mountains just west of the city; the bedroom community is also a gateway to the Colorado high country to the west.

Pueblo is a major steel-producing center and the southernmost city on the Colorado Front Range. The main attraction for visitors is the Historic Arkansas Riverwalk, featuring boat rides, restaurants, and entertainment. Cañon City is a seasonal tourist destination west of Pueblo. The major attraction is the deep, narrow canyon called Royal Gorge. The Royal Gorge Route Railroad (888-724-5748) takes visitors on a two-hour excursion into the canyon. The Royal Gorge Bridge and Park (4218 County Rd., 3A, 888-333-5597) was badly damaged by a forest fire in 2013 but is expected to reopen in the spring of 2014. The Arkansas River near Cañon City is a hugely popular destination for white-water rafting.

BierWerks

121 East Midland Avenue, Woodland Park, CO 80863
(719) 686-8100 • www.bierwerks.com

If you don't like crowds, perhaps Pikes Peak is best enjoyed from a distance: a half-million people venture to the summit of the country's most visited mountain each year. Fortunately, the town of Woodland Park, home of the BierWerks Brewery, offers outstanding views of the iconic mountain.

The German-themed BierWerks brewery and taproom resides on bustling Midland Avenue, Woodland Park's main drag and a gateway to the mountains of central Colorado. The bedroom community is located 18 miles distant and 2,400 feet above Colorado Springs.

The brewery came into being in 2010 when Arden Weatherford, along with two partners who have since departed to open Paradox Brewing Company, purchased a former Big O tire shop and transformed it into a brewery and taproom. Weatherford, who had been living in Woodland Park for more than a decade, considered the community "a good place to live but a crummy place to hang out." He created Bier-Werks to provide a quality destination in the community.

From the parking lot, there are awesome views of Pikes Peak. The front of the building, facing the street, is set up for outdoor socializing. There's plentiful seating on picnic tables, patio tables, and benches. A fire pit sits in the middle of the space. The two bay doors of the former tire shop open to the brewhouse. When I visited, there were food vendors at either end of the building. One was cooking pizza in a portable wood-fired oven. The other was pedaling smoky barbecue from a trailer.

The modestly sized interior has a large communal table in the middle of the room. A few smaller tables sit along a wall. There's no seating at the bar. The brewery has a very popular mug club, as evidenced by the dozens of beer mugs hanging from the ceiling. A large map of Germany hangs on a wall, but the German theme is understated. The friendly female servers are not clad in dirndls and there is no oompah music piped into the taproom, which was mostly populated with families during my afternoon visit. The kid-friendly

Year-round beers: Helles, Altbier, Dunkel, Weissbier, Manitou Spring Water Pale Ale, Hop Monster IPA, March of the Fuggles Porter.

The Pick: The easy-drinking Helles is light and delicate with clean, uncomplicated flavors.

Rocky Mountain Dinosaur Resource Center is located across the street from the brewery.

A few food items are available including meat and cheese platters and soft pretzels made by the wife of brewer James McGraw. McGraw began his brewing career at age twenty-two, cleaning draught lines and serving tanks at a BJ's brewpub in California, his home state. After a stint at another Southern California brewery, he moved to Munich to be with his then fiancée. While in Munich, he completed the one-year brewmaster program at the Doemens Academy. His job search for a brewery specializing in German beers brought him to BierWerks in 2012.

There were nine beers available when I visited, plus a cider that's not produced at the brewery. The best seller is the clean, crisp, easy-drinking helles. Several other German-style beers were available including a dunkel, a weissbier, an alt, and a seasonal maibock. All displayed the easy-drinking character that German beers are noted for.

Bierwerks doesn't produce German beers exclusively. The brewery's regular beers include a pale ale, a porter, and an IPA, which is outsold only by the helles. The water used to produce BierWerks' Manitou Spring Water Pale Ale is collected from a natural spring in the nearby town of Manitou Springs, well-known for its mineral springs. BierWerks donates a portion of revenue from keg sales of the pale ale to the Mineral Springs Foundation, an organization dedicated to restoring and protecting the ten natural mineral springs located in Manitou Springs.

BierWerks

Opened: August 2010.

Owner: Arden Weatherford.

Head brewer: James McGraw.

Potential annual capacity: 1,000 barrels.

Hours: Monday through Thursday, 2 p.m. to 10 p.m.; Friday and Saturday, noon to 10 p.m.; Sunday, noon to 8 p.m.

Tours: On request.

Take-out beer: Growlers and kegs.

Food: Cheese plates and Bavarian pretzels. Brick-oven pizza and barbecue food trucks often on-site.

Extras: Live music on Friday and Saturday and sometimes Sunday.

Parking: Small on-site lot, on-street parking, and nearby public lots.

Area attractions: Rocky Mountain Dinosaur Resource Center (201 S. Fairview St., 719-686-1820).

Bristol Brewing Company

1604 South Cascade Avenue, Colorado Springs, CO 80905
(719) 633-2555 • www.bristolbrewing.com

Many southern Colorado beer drinkers learned to appreciate full-flavored craft beer from Bristol Brewing, Colorado Springs's long-established community-focused brewery. The city's thirsty populace can continue its libation education at Bristol's new digs at the historic Ivywild School.

Brewery cofounder and native Coloradan Mike Bristol was a home-brewer when he met his wife, Amanda, while living in Florida. The couple returned to Mike's home state to launch a brewing enterprise. Bristol Brewing opened in an industrial park in 1994. Three years later, the brewery moved to a more central location south of downtown Colorado Springs, where it resided for many years.

In 2009 the local school district closed an old elementary school, built in 1916, that was located a few blocks from the brewery. Bristol saw the vacant schoolhouse as an opportunity too good to pass up. He formed a partnership with a local restaurateur and an architect, and transformed the historic school into a community marketplace and a home for the expanding brewery. The Ivywild School opened in 2013 with a bakery, deli, espresso and cocktail bar, charcuterie, and of course, the new brewery and pub.

The Ivywild School is a large yellow-brick structure with a stately Greek-style façade. The old school building sits above street level, adding to its imposing and impressive character. The renovation has preserved the schoolhouse look of the interior, enhanced by modern artwork on display throughout.

Just off the main corridor is the Bristol Pub. While the drinking space has a mostly modern appearance, several wall sections of red brick, revealed when plaster was removed during the renovation, are reminders of the building's longevity. In the center of the room is a stylish asymmetrical island-style wooden bar. Curvilinear high-tops add to the room's contemporary look. Large art pieces hang on the earth-tone walls. A shuffleboard table

Year-round beers: Laughing Lab Scottish Ale, Beehive Honey Wheat, Mass Transit Amber Ale, Red Rocket Pale Ale, Compass IPA.

The Pick: Bristol's flagship beer, Laughing Lab Scottish Ale, is an approachable and easy-drinking ale with an accent on malt and a subtle sweetness.

runs the length of one wall. The brewhouse sits at a lower level and can be viewed through tall windows in the pub. A huge sun-splashed patio is adjacent to the taproom. Light pub fare, prepared just down the hall, can be delivered to your table.

The first beer Bristol produced was Red Rocket Pale Ale, which is still in the regular lineup. It was another early beer, however, that put Bristol on the Colorado beer map. Laughing Lab Scottish Ale—an approachable, easy-drinking ale with an accent on malt—was an immediate crowd-pleaser, appealing to knowledgeable beer drinkers without intimidating those just stepping out of their light lager comfort zones. The beer captured a bronze medal at the 1994 Great American Beer Festival, the first year it was released. Nine GABF medals later, it has distinguished itself as Colorado's most awarded beer. Interest in Laughing Lab has hardly waned, as the beer represents half of Bristol's sales and production.

Bristol produces five full-time beers including the Scottish ale, a honey wheat, an amber ale, a pale ale, and an IPA. While the standard beers are brewed to be sessionable and true-to-style, the brewery has upped the ante with more adventurous creations. The Brewhouse Series is a collection of small-batch specialty beers sold in bombers. Styles vary widely and have included an imperial IPA, a wit, a RyePA, an imperial stout, and others. Bristol has also embarked on a Belgian series. The first two releases were a dubbel and a tripel packaged in corked and caged champagne bottles. A barrel-aged series was in the works when I visited. Bristol has maintained a local focus, keeping its distribution within Colorado.

Bristol Brewing Company

Opened: June 1994.

Owners: Mike and Amanda Bristol.

Head brewer: Chris Hastings.

Potential annual capacity: 25,000 barrels.

Hours: Monday through Thursday, 11 a.m. to 10 p.m.; Friday and Saturday, 11 a.m. to 11 p.m.; Sunday, 11 a.m. to 8 p.m.

Tours: Check website.

Take-out beer: Growlers, six-packs, and kegs.

Food: Light pub fare is prepared and delivered by a deli down the hall.

Extras: Live music within the complex. Farmers market in parking lot on Wednesday in season.

Parking: On-site lot and on-street, both free.

Colorado Mountain Brewery

Two locations

In the diverse world of Colorado breweries, the two Colorado Springs–based Colorado Mountain Brewery locations stand out as the "lookers" in the group. The sibling brewpubs are housed in elegant buildings of different yet equally impressive character. While there's more to a brewpub than looks alone, the businesses present an attractive first impression.

The original brewpub came to life in 2010 when entrepreneurial-minded Air Force Academy graduate Scott Koons assembled a team of investors to launch the InterQuest facility, located not far from the academy. The second location, west of downtown, opened two years later. Andy Bradley was hired to run the beer-producing portion of the business. Bradley came to CMB after a seven-year stint in the brewhouse at Phantom Canyon.

Identical house beers are served at the two CMB brewpubs. There are five full-time beers of mainstream styles including an amber ale, a blonde ale, an IPA, a hefeweizen, and a stout. More adventurous seasonal and specialty beers, such as barrel-aged lagers, appear throughout the year.

The menu of American grill fare includes pub standards such as wings, fish-and-chips, burgers, and ribs. Upscale dishes, including steaks, smoked prime rib, and seafood entrées share the menu with more exotic items such as bison meatloaf, stuffed quail, and wild boar sliders. Both locations serve pizza.

Year-round beers: Ole 59er Amber Ale, 7258 Blonde Ale, Panther IPA, UniBräu Hefeweissen, Monumental Stout.

The Pick: Monumental Stout is a go-to winter beer with a sweet malt character and dry finish.

Colorado Mountain Brewery at InterQuest Marketplace

1110 Interquest Parkway, Colorado Springs, CO 80921
(719) 434-5750 • www.cmbrew.com/locations/interquest

Interquest is the older of the two CMB brewpubs. It's located on the north end of Colorado Springs about twelve miles from downtown. It sits just east of Interstate 25 across the highway from the Air Force Academy.

The large standalone building has an airy, contemporary mountain lodge style. There are four outdoor patios, one on either end of the building and one on either side of the entrance. The interior features generous use of wood and glass with high ceilings and exposed beams. In the bar area, plush chairs are lined up along the bar. Tables and upholstered booths are in view of the half-dozen flatscreens hanging from the beams. In addition to the house beers, six guest taps dispense beers from other Colorado breweries. The brewhouse sits behind a wall of glass along the far wall. A collection of western and abstract art is on display.

The main dining area features oversized upholstered booths and table seating. Two glassed-in dining areas off the main dining room offer gorgeous mountain views. The building is oriented so there are outstanding views in two directions. The open kitchen sits between the bar and dining areas.

Colorado Mountain Brewery at InterQuest Marketplace

Opened: July 2010.

Owners: Dick and Scott Koons.

Head brewer: Andy Bradley.

Potential annual capacity: 1,000 barrels.

Hours: Sunday through Thursday, 11 a.m. to 10 p.m.; Friday and Saturday, 11 a.m. to 11 p.m.

Tours: Saturday between 1 p.m. and 3 p.m.

Take-out beer: Growlers and kegs.

Food: American grill fare, steaks, wild game, and pizza.

Extras: Summer concert series on Wednesday. Trivia on Tuesday.

Parking: On-site lot.

Colorado Mountain Brewery at the Roundhouse

600 South 21st Street, Colorado Springs, CO 80904
(719) 466-8240 • www.cmbrew.com/locations/roundhouse

Colorado Mountain Brewery at the Roundhouse resides on the west side of Colorado Springs about two miles from the city center. The impressive historic structure dates from 1887 and was originally the roundhouse and maintenance facility for the Colorado Midland Railway. In the 1940s, it became a showroom and workplace for Van Briggle Pottery. Colorado Mountain Brewery is only the third tenant in the expansive cut-stone structure's history.

The two-level interior has a modern upscale appearance. There are mountain views through tall arched windows that were originally the track door openings. The long, gently curving bar sits on a base of stone that matches the walls. Windows look out onto an outdoor patio enclosed by a stucco wall, into which a huge fireplace is embedded. Fifteen guest taps supplement the house beers.

The two-story brewery sits behind glass opposite the bar. A small kitchen bar faces a wood-fired pizza oven covered in handsome blue tiles. A curved staircase leads to a second dining area on the upper level. A collection of historic railroad photos, donated by the local historical society, hangs on the walls.

Colorado Mountain Brewery at the Roundhouse

Opened: September 2012.

Owners: Dick and Scott Koons.

Head brewer: Andy Bradley.

Potential annual capacity: 500 barrels.

Hours: Sunday through Thursday, 11 a.m. to 10 p.m.; Friday and Saturday, 11 a.m. to 11 p.m.

Tours: Not offered.

Take-out beer: Growlers and kegs.

Food: American grill fare, steaks, wild game, and pizza.

Extras: Summer concert series on Wednesday. Trivia on Tuesday.

Parking: On-site lot.

Great Storm Brewing

204 Mount View Lane, No. 3,
  Colorado Springs, CO 80907
(719) 266-4200
www.greatstormbrewing.com

The only thing keeping me from calling Great Storm Brewing a great little neighborhood brewery is its lack of a neighborhood. Calling it a great little strip mall brewery may not sound as appealing, but it shouldn't keep you away from this enjoyable Colorado Springs beer stop. The brewery is small, but there's an ample supply of friendly banter and interesting, creative brews.

Great Storm is tucked inconspicuously into a small generic strip mall in a mixed-use area just east of Interstate 25, about five miles north of downtown Colorado Springs. Among the neighboring businesses is a national pizza chain outlet, providing a convenient food option for brewery visitors.

The brewery was the creation of Jeff and Lynn Jacobs. The couple had been living in the area for almost a decade when they decided to open a brewery. "Jeff was an avid homebrewer, and it just took over his life," said Lynn. "He made great beer and we were interested in starting a business of some kind. We did our homework and it sounded like a good idea on all different levels."

Great Storm opened in early 2012 with Jeff operating the small brewhouse and Lynn running the front of the house and attending to business affairs. For its nondescript location, the proprietors have done well to instill character and a welcoming vibe into the taproom. "You have to work with the space you have," Lynn explained. "You can't come into a strip mall and try to make it an English pub. It doesn't make sense."

A sidewalk patio offers an outdoor sipping spot in front of the generic storefront. Inside, gray walls, black furniture, and surfaces of shiny corrugated metal create an industrial feel. The walls display a collection of photos and art pieces, mostly of a canine theme and including photos of Storm, the Jacobses' dog. A large blackboard lists the current beers with relevant stats including style, SRM (color), IBU (bitterness), and ABV (alcohol content). A few cushy upholstered chairs are arranged

Year-round beers: Seven Wolves IPA (regular and nitro taps), Rum Raisin Stout, Black Bear Zwartbier.

The Pick: The Black Bear Zwartbier, a Belgian black lager, is an intriguing yet easy-drinking brew with a subtle sweetness, some notes of licorice, and a bit of spice.

near the front wall of windows. A bookcase filled with board games sits nearby.

The six-seat bar is at the far end of the room. The unusual bar top is built of frosted glass and sits atop blue holiday lights. The bottom-lit bar top functions as a canvas for aspiring artists to express their inner Van Gogh using erasable markers, which are provided. Behind the bar is a row of eight tap handles. The lightning bolt shape of the handles aligns with the brewery's "storm" theme.

The 1-barrel brewing system is set up along one side of the taproom, separated from nearby tables by a few sections of chain-link fencing. Since my visit, the taproom has expanded into an adjacent space and now offers additional seating and a foosball game.

Jeff's general approach to brewing is to start with classic styles, then add a twist, creating something unique without detracting from the overall drinkability. The four full-time beers include Rum Raisin Stout, a Belgian black lager, and an IPA served as a standard kegged offering or, if you prefer, from a nitro tap.

The specialty list changes frequently and displays a creative and playful approach to beermaking. When I paid a visit, the specialties included a honey amber ale, a braggot, a tangerine-chocolate brown ale, and a witbier. Although the beers tend toward big flavors and above-average alcohol content, I found them to be quite drinkable, unique, and agreeable.

Great Storm Brewing

Opened: March 2012.

Owners: Jeff and Lynn Jacobs.

Head brewer: Jeff Jacobs.

Potential annual capacity: 200 barrels.

Hours: Wednesday and Thursday, 11 a.m. to 9 p.m.; Friday and Saturday, 11 a.m. to 10 p.m.

Tours: On request.

Take-out beer: Growlers.

Food: Domino's Pizza is next door or bring your own food.

Extras: AHA member deals program participant.

Parking: On-site lot.

Paradox Beer Company

106 East Village Terrace, Suite 100, Woodland Park, CO 80866

(719) 686-8081 • www.paradoxbeer.com

As fifteen-year veterans of the Colorado craft beer scene, Jeff Aragon and Brian Horton have had their share of ups and downs. Today, the longtime partners and brothers-in-law are having barrels of fun with their latest venture, Paradox Beer Company. The Woodland Park beer business produces barrel-aged beers exclusively.

In 1999, Aragon and Horton founded a brewpub in southern Colorado near the New Mexico border. After a decade, the business closed, a victim of the stagnant economy. The partners regrouped and, with another partner, opened the German-themed BierWerks in downtown Woodland Park. A year and a half later, they sold their interest in the brewpub to start Paradox.

Paradox Beer Company occupies a warehouse-type space in the bottom floor of a modern multilevel office building a few miles south of central Woodland Park. Downtown Colorado Springs is about fifteen miles away. Beers are not brewed on-site. Rather, several times a week the partners travel to another craft brewery, brew their beers, and then transport the unfermented wort to the Woodland Park location for fermentation and aging.

While the tasting room was intended primarily as a place to sample beers and purchase bottles, it's evolved into more of a hangout. A dartboard and a donated pool table are available for visitors. A pair of sofas imbues a homey touch to the space. The tasting room is open for visitors Thursday through Sunday.

Year-round beers: All beers are seasonal; however, the Belgian Golden is often available.

Barrels play an important role at Paradox beyond aging beer. Once the oak vessels outlive their usefulness as beer-aging containers, they're turned over to an acquaintance who skillfully crafts a variety of barrel stave art pieces for the tasting room. These range from the bar base to wainscoting to striking, decorative pieces of unique character.

The Pick: The brewery has no full-time beers, but any of the Skully Barrel Series of wood-aged sour beers will give your palate plenty to ponder.

The idea of a barrel-centric brewery was born years ago. "We aged a couple of different beers in four barrels fifteen years ago, and it made a lasting impression," said Horton. "Since then, we've wanted to do a barrel-only project. To me, these are the best beers we've produced in our lives."

Many of the Paradox beers begin in a style the partners call "Amero-Belgo," which they describe as having Belgian roots with an American twist such as domestic hops. Once the beers have aged in oak, however, they become their own hard-to-classify beasts.

About 90 percent of the brewery's barrel collection is former wine barrels. The remainder is spirits barrels that once contained whiskey, Scotch, or rum. "The barrels are our fifth ingredient in beer," said Aragon. "They round out the flavors." Some, but not all, of the barrel-aged beers are sour or fermented with wild *Brettanomyces* yeast.

Paradox beers appeal to an audience beyond beer enthusiasts looking for one-of-a-kind fermentations. The barrel-aged creations have found an audience with wine drinkers. "Wine and beer diverged so far. Now we're at a point where they're crossing back over. To me, it's a really exciting place to be," Horton relates.

Unlike the partners' previous experience in the high-turnover world of brewpubs, planning new beers takes a long-range vision due to the extended aging time required for barrel-aged beers to reach their peak. "Whatever we're brewing now is six months, nine months, a year away," Horton explained. On occasion, a barrel produces beer of substandard quality. The partners have a way to deal with that occurrence. "See the barrel art?" said Horton, pointing to a nearby barrel-stave art piece. "That's what they become."

Paradox Beer Company

Opened: February 2012.

Owners: Jeff Aragon, Brian Horton, and Dave Hudson.

Head brewers: Jeff Aragon and Brian Horton.

Potential annual capacity: 1,200 barrels.

Hours: Thursday, 4 p.m. to 9 p.m.; Friday, 4 p.m. to 10 p.m.; Saturday and Sunday, 2 p.m. to 10 p.m.

Tours: On request.

Take-out beer: 750-ml bottles.

Food: Bring your own.

Extras: Live music on occasion.

Parking: On-site lot.

Area attractions: Rocky Mountain Dinosaur Resource Center (201 S. Fairview St., 719-686-1820).

Phantom Canyon Brewing Company

2 East Pikes Peak Avenue, Colorado Springs, CO 80903
(719) 635-2800 • www.phantomcanyon.com

The Cheyenne Building—the home of Phantom Canyon Brewing Company—was built in downtown Colorado Springs in 1901. At that time, gold mining had made the city the wealthiest per capita in the country. By 1904, thirty-five of the country's one hundred millionaires lived in The Springs. While the city no longer claims elite status among the country's well-to-do, Phantom Canyon ensures that The Springs maintains a wealth of liquid assets.

The city's oldest operating brewery sits at the intersection of Cascade and Pikes Peak Avenues in the heart of downtown Colorado Springs. The handsome brick Cheyenne Building originally housed offices at the terminus of the Chicago, Rock Island and Pacific Railroad. The upper floors had sleeping rooms used by railroad agents. It 1909, it became the Cheyenne Hotel, which operated into the 1960s. The historic structure was slated for demolition in 1990 to be replaced by a parking lot, but was saved by the timely enactment of a historic preservation law. The building was purchased by Wynkoop Brewing Company in 1991, restored, and opened as Phantom Canyon Brewing Company in 1993.

If you've ever visited Denver's Wynkoop Brewing, you'll find much that seems familiar at Phantom Canyon. Both are housed in historic downtown buildings. Both have expansive dining and drinking spaces, and both have an in-house pool hall.

Outdoor seating is available on a sidewalk patio at Phantom Canyon. Inside, the bustling pub has the buzz of an urban meeting place while maintaining the demeanor of a casual inner-city retreat. The main dining room is a big, open, airy space. Large windows look out onto the busy downtown intersection. Potted plants sit on shelves attached to thick columns rising to the high pressed-tin ceiling, adding a cheery touch. Colorful artwork and large panes of stained glass brighten the surroundings. There's a long wooden

Year-round beers:
Queen's Blonde Lager, Railyard Ale, Streamliner IPA, Two Moons Pale Ale, Alpenglow Hefeweizen, Zebulon's Peated Porter.

The Pick: The cask-conditioned Zebulon's Peated Porter has layers of flavor that reveal coffee, bittersweet chocolate, and a touch of smoke suggestive of a campfire.

bar and a finely detailed, mirrored backbar that originated in a Pueblo train depot.

Upstairs, there's a second bar and an impressive collection of a dozen regulation-size billiards tables. When I visited, the finishing touches were being applied to a large expansion project that included a brand-new brewhouse, a barrel-aging cellar, and a rooftop patio.

The menu's pub-style comfort food is a notch above typical brewpub fare both in selection and quality. Pub favorites share the menu with more upscale offerings such as smoked pork chops, Colorado lamb, and seafood dishes. The servers are friendly and efficient.

Craft beer veteran Alan Stiles is Phantom Canyon's head brewer. Stiles has brewed professionally in southern Colorado breweries since 1996. He came to Phantom Canyon in 2009. The six standard house beers include a blonde lager, an amber ale, an IPA, a pale ale, a hefeweizen, and peated porter. The porter is one of two cask ales served from a traditional hand pump. Since Stiles arrived at Phantom Canyon, the breadth of beer offerings has increased, a development that has been well-received by the city's increasingly adventurous beer enthusiasts. Up to eleven specialty and seasonal selections are on tap. While these often include English and American-style ales, more audacious creations are also produced. The veteran brewer has instituted a sour beer program producing limited releases of bottled sour ales and occasional sours on tap. "We really think we're on the cusp of making Phantom Canyon, which has been an institution, into more of a cutting-edge brewery," said Stiles.

Phantom Canyon Brewing Company

Opened: December 1993.

Owners: Breckenridge/Wynkoop LLC.

Head brewer: Alan Stiles.

Potential annual capacity: 4,500 barrels.

Hours: Daily, 11 a.m. to last call.

Tours: On request.

Take-out beer: Growlers, bombers, 750 ml bottles, and kegs.

Food: Pub favorites and assorted entrées such as smoked pork chops, Colorado lamb, and seafood dishes

Extras: Pool tables. AHA member deals program participant.

Parking: Metered on-street and nearby pay lots.

Pikes Peak Brewing Company

1756 Lake Woodmoor Drive, Monument, CO 80132
(719) 208-4098 • www.pikespeakbrewing.com

Iconic Pikes Peak rises to an elevation of more than 14,000 feet above Colorado Springs. A trip to the mountain's summit was the inspiration for the song "America the Beautiful." If Pikes Peak Brewing Company had been around during the lifetime of the song's lyricist, Katharine Lee Bates, perhaps she would have waxed poetic about amber pints of ale rather than waves of grain.

The brewery is located in the town of Monument, which sits between Denver and Colorado Springs along busy Interstate 25. Most people know the town as a fuel stop between Colorado's two largest cities, but beyond the bustling frontage road resides a small, tight-knit community.

Pikes Peak Brewing Company sits just east of the highway in a nondescript retail complex. The brewery would attract little notice if not for the tall, attention-grabbing silo beside the brewery that sports the company's distinctive logo.

The taproom has a homey feeling with a collection of upholstered chairs arranged in front of a fireplace opposite the bar. Simple tables fill the remainder of the modest-sized space. There's a second room in the back called the Barrel Room. It contains an attractive bar constructed of barrel staves. A sunny beer garden with mountain views sits outside the taproom.

Brewery founder Chris Wright was introduced to brewing at a brew-on-premises business in Colorado Springs, and was bitten hard by the beer bug. Plans to open his own brewery came to fruition with the opening of Pikes Peak Brewing Company in 2011.

The brewery has developed a strong local following since its inception, and that's just the way Wright intended it. "I wanted to create a place where the community could get together," said Wright, who has called Monument home for more than a decade.

As he fine-tuned his recipes in advance of opening the brewery, Wright became a student of

Year-round beers: The Brits are Back Mild, Ascent Pale Ale, Elephant Rock IPA, Pikes Peak Gold Rush Belgian Golden Ale, Devils Head Red, Summit House Stout.

The Pick: Named for the house atop nearby Pikes Peak, Summit House Oatmeal Stout is a full-bodied dark ale with a big, chewy chocolate character and lofty 7.5 percent ABV.

water chemistry. "The water here in Monument is actually great to drink because it's very, very pure, but crappy to brew with because there's not a whole lot of minerals," said Wright. He found that once he began adjusting water salts to match the beer styles he was creating, his beers improved and became more consistent.

Wright takes a traditional approach to brewing. "There are brewers who are very artistic. I am not one of those. I'm more stylistic," he explained. "To me, styles are important. They frame your expectations." In 2012, the brewery's The Brits are Back English Brown Ale—a traditional English mild ale—was awarded Best of Show at the Colorado State Fair. It was a noteworthy honor, as sessionable British ales don't generally garner much interest among beer judges.

Other house standards include a pale ale, an IPA, a Belgian golden ale, a red ale, and a stout. The Pikes Peak beers are nicely executed, highly drinkable, and brewed true to style. Pikes Peak has begun bottling barrel-aged beers under the Penrose Private Reserve label. The name honors Spencer Penrose, founder of the Broadmoor Hotel in Colorado Springs. During Prohibition, Penrose stockpiled fine wines and whiskeys underneath the pool at the elegant Broadmoor.

In addition to the house beers, Pikes Peak keeps two guest beers on tap from other Colorado breweries. There's also an interesting bottle list of about twenty beers weighted toward barrel-aged and Belgian-style beers.

Pikes Peak has partnered with local vendors to provide an abbreviated selection of food options. Though the menu changes regularly, you're likely to find German pretzels, meat and cheese platters, soups, and sandwiches available during a visit. German chocolate stout cake appears frequently, and pairs nicely with the house stout.

Pikes Peak Brewing Company

Opened: May 2011.

Owner and head brewer: Chris Wright.

Potential annual capacity: 3,000 barrels.

Hours: Monday through Thursday, 11 a.m. to 9 p.m.; Friday and Saturday, 11 a.m. to 11 p.m.; Sunday, noon to 9 p.m.

Tours: On request.

Take-out beer: Growlers and kegs.

Food: Soups, sandwiches, meat and cheese platters, and desserts.

Extras: Live music on Saturday (year round) and once a month on Sunday (summer only). AHA member discount program participant.

Parking: On-site lot.

Rock Bottom—Colorado Springs

3316 Cinema Point Drive,
Colorado Springs, CO 80922
(719) 550-3586
www.rockbottom.com/locations/
colorado-springs

Rock Bottom's Colorado Springs brewpub is the southernmost of the chain's half-dozen Colorado facilities. The restaurant is located on the east side of Colorado Springs along Powers Boulevard, a major north-south artery. Like all the Colorado-based Rock Bottoms except the original downtown Denver location, the Springs-based brewpub resides within a large shopping complex. If you can't find the Rock Bottom restaurant you're looking for within a shopping center, look for the movie theater. The Rock Bottom will generally be nearby. The Colorado Springs Rock Bottom is located in the First & Main Town Center shopping center near the Cinemark theater, the busiest movie theater in Colorado.

Beyond the retail-intensive Powers Corridor is a largely residential part of the city with a suburban feel and a strong military presence. Two Air Force bases reside five and fifteen miles, respectively, from the brewpub. If corporate-owned restaurants are your bread and butter, you'll be quite happy in this part of town.

This location's layout is fairly typical of the standard Rock Bottom model. Patio seating is available along the front and side of the modern standalone cut-stone structure. A tall red grain silo sits along the side of the building next to the tall glassed-in brewhouse.

The large interior space is divided between the dining and drinking areas. A large island-style bar dominates the bar area and has adjacent table and booth seating. A line of serving tanks sits behind tall windows along the back wall. A row of fermenters and a collection of wooden barrels are visible on the second level. The dining area has ample booth and table seating.

Year-round beers: Kolsch, White Ale, Red Ale, India Pale Ale, and a specialty dark beer.

The extensive menu covers all the bases with salads, sandwiches, pizza, burgers, steaks, and a variety of ethnic-inspired dishes. When I stopped by the Colorado Springs facility, there had been some recent shuffling of Rock Bottom brewers on the Colorado Front Range. Michael Dee had

The Pick: Go with a specialty beer, as it shows off the brewer's skill and individuality. Dee has a fondness for brewing English pale ales.

arrived as the new head brewer just a month before my visit. For Dee, this was a homecoming of sorts. Following an Air Force career in which he had been stationed in Colorado Springs, the longtime homebrewer served a three-month internship at the Colorado Springs Rock Bottom as part of a veterans retraining program.

A part-time stint at Bristol Brewing across town was followed by a job as lead brewer at Phantom Canyon Brewing Company, the Springs' longstanding downtown brewpub. When former Rock Bottom brewer Jason Leeman left to take over the recently vacated brewing job at the company's South Denver location, Dee was hired as the new Colorado Springs brewer.

Rock Bottom is all about consistency, and the four standard house beers—Kolsch, white ale, red ale, and IPA—display the clean, approachable character that you can expect at any of the chain's locations. When I visited, Dee had recently released a creditable hefeweizen, his first specialty beer since taking over the brewing position. An American-style IPA was in the works.

Dee's brewing plans also included a malt liquor, a summertime tradition that was initiated by his predecessor. He also intended to continue the barrel-aging program that the former brewer had begun. Dee also has a few twists he'll introduce to his new audience. A schwarzbier (a dark lager) was scheduled for a fall release. In a more experimental project, Dee was planning to formulate an oatmeal cookie beer based on an English brown ale recipe, with toasted oats, raisins, vanilla beans, and cinnamon added to create a cookie-like character.

Rock Bottom—Colorado Springs

Opened: Fall 2005.

Owners: CraftWorks Restaurants and Breweries.

Head brewer: Michael Dee.

Potential annual capacity: 2,000 barrels.

Hours: Sunday through Thursday, 11 a.m. to 11 p.m.; Friday and Saturday, 11 a.m. to midnight.

Tours: On request.

Take-out beer: Growlers and kegs.

Food: Broad selection of pub favorites and diverse entrées.

Extras: Bingo on Tuesday. Running Club on Wednesday.

Parking: On-site lot.

Rocky Mountain Brewery

625 Paonia Street, Colorado Springs, CO 80915
(719) 528-1651 • www.rockymountainbrews.com

The naked truth is you won't stumble across the Rocky Mountain Brewery unless you've stumbled out of the neighboring strip club. The out-of-the-way brewery resides on the eastern fringe of Colorado Springs in an obscure location just north of Peterson Air Force Base. Schriever Air Force Base is farther east. The brewery is a popular stop for the area's numerous military personnel. The city center is seven miles away.

Brewery owner Duane Lujan has operated a homebrew shop since 1996. In 2006, he took over a space that had previously housed a brewery that had gone out of business. The brewing operation was revamped and went online in 2008. The homebrew shop still operates and also functions as an all-grain brew-on-premises business, with brewing instruction provided.

The brewery is located in the end unit of an industrial-looking metal structure that houses a few other businesses. B'z BBQ Company operates out of a bright yellow trailer set up alongside the patio outside the brewery. A few metal patio tables are set up in the outdoor space along with a space heater.

The interior emphasizes function over fashion, with little embellishment to soften the industrial feel of the space. The taproom contains a small collection of simple tables with upholstered seating. The L-shaped wooden bar seats nine and faces a half-wall that separates the drinking space from the brewing operation. A flatscreen TV is mounted above the beer taps. A large American flag is suspended from the ceiling. Next to it hangs another flag honoring POWs and MIAs.

Nick Hilborn is Rocky Mountain Brewery's head brewer. Hilborn arrived at the brewery after studying culinary arts and working at several restaurants. He had no brewing experience, but was interested in learning. Though he wasn't officially employed as a brewer, he showed up at the brewery regularly to help out wherever needed. He began teaching classes for the brew-on-premises operation and gained experience creating a wide

Year-round beers: Blonde Lager, Spirit Hill Amber, Brunette-Nut Brown, Redhead, and Mountain IPA.

The Pick: There's generally a fruit beer or a cider on tap. If you like your fermentations juicy, give it a try.

variety of beer styles. When the brewing position opened up two years after his arrival, he was offered the job.

The brewery produces five full-time beers including a blonde lager, an amber ale, a brown ale, a red ale, and an IPA. Among the other beers available during my visit was a sweet, chocolatey stout dispensed from a nitro tap; a house-brewed, peach-flavored cider was also on the tap list. The brewery produces numerous specialty and experimental beers, with oaked, smoked, and chili-flavored beers often accompanying the lineup of more mainstream styles. Rocky Mountain is best known for its intensely flavored fruit beers, especially the pie-like Da Yoopers cherry beer. The brewery's cherry and peach beers have both been awarded World Beer Cup medals.

Rocky Mountain Brewery

Opened: June 2008.

Owners: Duane Lujan and a small ownership group.

Head brewer: Nick Hilborn.

Potential annual capacity: 700 barrels.

Hours: Monday through Saturday, 11 a.m. to closing. Closed Sunday.

Tours: On request.

Take-out beer: Growlers.

Food: A barbecue truck serves food Tuesday through Saturday.

Extras: Thursday trivia.

Parking: On-site lot.

Rockyard American Grill & Brewing Company

880 Castleton Road, Castle Rock, CO 80109
(303) 814-9273 • www.rockyard.com

The town of Castle Rock, home of Rockyard American Grill & Brewing Company, is named after a prominent rock outcropping on the north end of town. If you find that the geologic feature resembles a castle in any way, therapy might help, and a meal with a good brew or two at the Rockyard certainly wouldn't hurt.

Castle Rock sits about thirty miles south of downtown Denver and forty-five miles north of Colorado Springs along Interstate 25. The town is a bedroom community for commuters to Colorado's two largest cities. It's also a shopper's destination, with a large complex of outlet stores residing on the east side of the interstate, across the highway from downtown. The brewpub sits just south of the shops. The business is easily identified by the two grain silos that sit outside the modern standalone building.

The Rockyard is a family-owned business. Members of the Drabing family developed the site where the Rockyard resides, hoping to sell it to a national restaurant chain. When they were unable to find an interested buyer, they took it upon themselves to build the brewpub. The Rockyard opened in 1999.

You enter into a huge dining area. The room's high, vaulted ceilings accentuate the spaciousness of the interior. A four-sided stone fireplace sits in the middle of the room. A line of windows along one wall provides views of the big rock across the highway. The U-shaped bar is on the opposite side of the long room. The copper-trimmed dark wood bar and upholstered chairs and booths imbue a somewhat upscale ambience. Outdoor seating is available on a spacious covered deck. There are views to the west over the expansive rolling grasslands, with the Rocky Mountains rising far in the distance.

The Rockyard's long and extensive menu and cocktail list are intended to attract an audience far beyond beer enthusiasts. The menu is far-reaching, including salads, sandwiches, burgers, Mexican dishes, pasta, seafood, steaks, and other

Year-round beers: Double Eagle Wheat Ale, Redhawk Amber Ale, Lightning Strike Stout, Hopyard IPA, Lynx Light Lager.

The Pick: The Redhawk Amber Ale, a Scottish-style ale, has a clean malt flavor and a palate-cleansing kiss of hops in the finish.

entrées. A separate gluten-free menu is available. "You'd be surprised how many people come in and don't realize that we're a brewpub," said Jim Stinson, the Rockyard's longtime head brewer.

Stinson's brewing indoctrination began with a homebrew kit he received as a Christmas present. Although his early beers were, in his words, "really nasty," he persevered and upgraded his equipment with positive results. "A couple of homebrew contests later and I thought, 'this is what I want to do,'" Stinson recalled.

His brewing career began in the Chicago area following brewpub operations studies at the Siebel Institute. After relocating to Colorado, he was hired as the Rockyard's assistant brewer while the brewpub was under construction. He later accepted the head brewer position at a now-defunct nearby brewpub, and then returned to the Rockyard as head brewer, a position he has held for more than a decade.

There are five full-time beers and two rotating taps. The house standards include a light lager, an American-style wheat ale, an amber ale, a stout, and an IPA. The biggest seller is not an IPA, as it is in the majority of Colorado breweries, but the Redhawk Amber Ale, a Scottish-style ale. The malty brew was a 2012 World Beer Cup silver medal winner and a bronze medalist at the 2013 Great American Beer Festival.

The two rotating taps dispense a diverse collection of seasonal and specialty beers. "We have a broad range from Kolsch to imperial stout to 10 percent reds. We've had a lot of fun with those," said Stinson. The seasonal Oktoberfest is especially popular, outselling everything else in the limited time that it's available.

Rockyard American Grill & Brewing Company

Opened: April 1999.

Owners: The Drabing family.

Head brewer: Jim Stinson.

Potential annual capacity: 1,800 barrels.

Hours: Open daily at 11 a.m. Dining room closes at 10 p.m. Lounge and bar may stay open later.

Tours: On request.

Take-out beer: Growlers, 12-ounce bottles, bombers, and kegs.

Food: Extensive menu of sandwiches, burgers, Mexican dishes, pasta, seafood, steaks, and other entrées. A separate gluten-free menu is available.

Extras: AHA member deals program participant.

Parking: On-site lot.

Area attractions: The Outlets at Castle Rock.

Other area beer sites: Parry's Pizza (5650 Allen Way, 303-814-8686).

Royal Gorge Brewing Company & Restaurant

413 Main Street, Cañon City, CO 81212
(719) 345-4141 • www.royalgorgebrewing.com

Cañon City, the home of Royal Gorge Brewing Company & Restaurant, is located near the Royal Gorge, a narrow ten-mile long, 1,000-foot deep chasm formed by the frothy Arkansas River. Since we are an industrious people who don't like our chasms unspanned, the country's highest suspension bridge was built over the gorge in 1929 for no purpose other than to attract tourists. Today, the bridge is one of Colorado's most popular attractions. After visiting the bridge, a trip to Royal Gorge Brewing Company will certainly be a purposeful endeavor.

The brewpub resides on Main Street in the middle of downtown Cañon City, a southern Colorado community located forty miles west of Pueblo. A former brewpub operating under a different name occupied the building for a half-dozen years before going under. The business was in foreclosure when it was acquired by Beth Katchmar, owner of a nearby pizza restaurant. She reopened the brewpub in the spring of 2011.

You're unlikely to miss the brewpub, which has an attention-grabbing blue, red, yellow, and white color scheme and a mountain-scene mural painted on the exterior. The small brewhouse, pieced together from used dairy tanks, is visible from the sidewalk through a wall of glass.

The interior has a look suggestive of an Old West saloon. The long interior space has a weathered brick wall on one side and a long dark wooden bar opposite with a gorgeous backbar of sculpted wood inlaid with mirrors.

Polished wooden tables fill the space. Old-style light fixtures hang from the high ceiling. A tiny private room, which would be perfect for a high-stakes poker game, sits in the back behind a pair of ornately carved wooden doors and contains additional table seating. Another small dining area sits on the second level overlooking the bar and dining room. The menu features pub standards and affordable steaks with some western specialties including Rocky Mountain oysters, green chili, and country-fried steak.

Year-round beers: Big House Brown, Territorial IPA, Arkansas Stout, Red Canyon Belgian Ale, Colorado Wheat.

The Pick: Big House Brown toes the line between brown ale and porter with a satisfying maltiness that's more roasty than sweet.

Matt Darling runs the brewing operations at Royal Gorge. The Colorado native grew up in the mountains of Summit County. His early experimentations with fermentation came as a teen when he attempted to produce wine and vodka. "It was absolutely horrible," he recalled. After abandoning that ill-conceived venture, he turned his attention to beermaking. While several of his homebrewing buddies went on to land jobs in local breweries, Darling went off to college to study archeology.

When a friend contacted him with the news that he been hired to brew at the Breckenridge brewpub and needed an assistant, Darling departed academia and headed back to his Summit County roots. "These jobs don't come along too often, so I hopped on it as fast as I could," said Darling. He worked at Breckenridge for five years, the last two as head brewer. Meanwhile, his family had moved to Cañon City. When he got word that the brewing position at Royal Gorge was opening up, he relocated to southern Colorado to employ his brewing talents at the new operation.

Darling produces five house beers including an American wheat ale, a brown ale, an oatmeal stout, an IPA, and a Belgian dubbel. The Big House Brown and Territorial IPA reference the local prison industry (there are thirteen penitentiaries in the area). The Royal Gorge beers I sampled were, clean, bright, and on the dry side. The American wheat ale was brewed with wheat from Alamosa, a town south of Cañon City. The IPA had a fruity aroma contributed by Australian hops. My favorite was the hearty 7 percent brown ale, which had a roasty character and subdued sweetness.

Royal Gorge Brewing Company & Restaurant

Opened: May 2011.
Owner: Beth Katchmar.
Head brewer: Matt Darling.
Potential annual capacity: 1,000 barrels.
Hours: Monday through Thursday, 11 a.m. to 10 p.m.; Friday and Saturday, 11 a.m. to 11 p.m.; Sunday, 11 a.m. to 10 p.m.
Tours: On request.
Take-out beer: Growlers and kegs.
Food: Pub fare, steaks, Rocky Mountain oysters.
Parking: On-street.
Area attractions: Royal Gorge Railroad (1-888-RAILS-4U). Royal Gorge Bridge & Park. Museum of Colorado Prisons (201 N. 1st St., 719-269-3015).

Shamrock Brewing Company

108 West 3rd Street, Pueblo, CO 81003
(719) 542-9974 • www.shamrockbrewing.com

In 1912, an Excelsior brand motorcycle was the first to break the 100-mile-per-hour speed barrier. The first Excelsior motorcycle dealership west of Mississippi was located in Pueblo, Colorado, in a building that now houses the Shamrock Brewing Company.

Pueblo is a southern Colorado city located about a two-hour drive from Denver. The city is unique in Colorado in that it developed largely as a steel-producing industrial center. The Shamrock brewpub resides in a downtown Pueblo building dating from 1908. Originally built as a mercantile building, it was home to a bicycle shop before becoming the aforementioned motorcycle dealership.

In the 1940s, the Shamrock opened for business under the name Shamrock Cafe. The Shamrock is one of Colorado's oldest Irish pubs. The brewery was added in the early 1990s. The same family owned and operated the pub from its origins until 2005, when it was purchased by its current owner, Shawn Sanborn. "I knew that a good quality craft brewery with good quality food was something that Pueblo was lacking," said Sanborn. The Shamrock is Pueblo's lone brewery.

From the street, the old building looks like an Irish pub, with the façade done in black with green trim. The interior also has a Brit flavor, but not to the point where it feels contrived. The pressed-tin ceiling hints of the building's age, while dark wood wainscoting along the cream-colored walls imbues the classic pub ambience. The long mahogany bar is the original from the 1940s. The attractive backbar is inlaid with mirrors. The black-and-white parquet floor tiles are likely of World War II vintage. TVs are distributed throughout the bar area, and were broadcasting English soccer matches during my visit. A row of upholstered wooden booths sits opposite the bar, separated from one another by panes of glass embossed with clover leaves.

Adjacent to the bar area is a large dining room with a fireplace at the far end and original hardwood floors. The brewhouse faces the street in

Year-round beers: Steel City Gold, Arch City Pale Ale, Irish Red Ale, Irish Porter.

The Pick: The Irish Red is more robust than others of the style, with a clean malt character, dry finish, and great balance that keeps you coming back.

front of the dining room. A covered outdoor patio area is located in the back of the building.

The kitchen prepares American and British pub fare including pot roast, shepherd's pie, boxty, and corned beef. I refrained from ordering the Wednesday special, "All You Care to Eat Fish and Chips," in favor of corned beef. It was fork tender, and served with peppery soft cabbage and boiled potatoes. It paired well with the subtly sweet and roasty house porter.

Keith Hefley is in charge of Shamrock's beer production. Hefley was raised on a southeast Colorado farm. "I like to say I've been working with grain my whole life, whether moving it through a combine, a cow, or a brew system," Hefley quipped. His brewing career includes a six-year stint at western Colorado's Gunnison Brewery, followed by two years at Fitger's Brewhouse in Minnesota. He arrived at Shamrock Brewing in early 2013.

The brewpub's four standard beers include a golden beer, an Irish porter, an Irish red, and an American pale ale. "This is a very blue-collar town, and we're proud of it," Hefley said of his clientele. "That's why we think the Irish porter and Irish red are good staples. Kind of blue-collar beers." Several seasonal and specialty beers round out the lineup. They range from Belgian styles to chili beers to spiced beers such as a ginger and orange zest-flavored wheat beer. The beers I sampled were quite approachable. I especially enjoyed the well-balanced Irish Red, which has more character than is often found in the style.

Shamrock Brewing Company

Opened: Opened in 1940s. Under current ownership since 2005.
Owner: Shawn Sanborn.
Head brewer: Keith Hefley.
Potential annual capacity: 600 barrels.
Hours: Monday through Thursday, 11 a.m. to midnight; Friday, 11 a.m. to 1 a.m.; Saturday, 10 a.m. to 1 a.m.; Sunday, 10 a.m. to 11 p.m.
Tours: On request.
Take-out beer: Growlers and kegs.
Food: British and American pub fare including corned beef, pot roast, boxty, and shepherd's pie.
Parking: On-street.
Extras: Trivia on Thursday.
Area attractions: Pueblo Riverwalk with boat rides, paddleboats, and gondolas.
Other area beer sites: Bingo Burger (101 Central Plaza, 719-225-8363).

Trinity Brewing Company

1466 Garden of the Gods Road, Colorado Springs, CO 80907
(719) 634-0029 • www.trinitybrew.com

Colorado Springs may have a reputation as Colorado's most conservative city, but it is also home to one of the state's most progressive and unconventional brewpubs. Trinity Brewing Company combines creatively inspired house beers, atypical beer-friendly food, and a broad selection of high-end guest beers and serves it all up in a distinctive environment that attracts a surprisingly eclectic mix of visitors.

Trinity anchors a corner spot in a modern strip mall about a mile west of Interstate 25, six miles north of downtown Colorado Springs. The awesome Garden of the Gods Park, with its magical red sandstone formations, is a five-minute drive away. "One of the reasons I picked this location is I get to drive through Garden of the Gods on my commute to work every day," explained Trinity founder and head brewer Jason Yester. "It's a pretty damn good way to start a day."

Yester was a homebrewer and microbiology student who found his calling early on. He got a job at Bristol Brewing in Colorado Springs when he was eighteen. The idea of having his own brewery in which to create "fancy, artisanal beers" also came early. "I said to a number of friends in college that I was going to own a brewery by the time I was thirty. I missed it by about six months," said Yester. Trinity opened in the summer of 2008.

A sunny sidewalk patio with views of Pikes Peak provides an inviting welcome to Trinity, but it's not until you step into the taproom that the brewpub begins to reveal its personality. Creative use of repurposed materials is employed throughout the interior. Wood collected from two dismantled barns appears around the room. The bar top is a conversation piece that is constructed of recycled glass from about fifteen trash cans full of beer bottles that were consumed while the brewpub was being built. The bar is lit from the bottom, creating an interesting effect. A collection of fanciful beer-label artwork hangs above a long line of taps dispensing well-selected guest brews.

Year-round beers: Soul Horkey Ale, Sunna Wit Beer, Flo India Pale Ale, Awaken Chicory Coffee Stout, Farmhouse Saison, Slap Yer Mammy, Chi Belgian Pilsener, Saison Man.

The Pick: Sunna Wit Beer is an intriguing low-alcohol refresher. A blend of wit and saison yeast, with fresh lemon and lime zest and coriander, creates a complex and spicy yet approachable brew.

The brewhouse sits opposite the bar behind a wall built to look like the exterior of a rustic structure. A space adjacent to the taproom is used for barrel-aging beers. The room's entrance is framed by an arch constructed of old books that were collected from Trinity patrons in exchange for beer.

Trinity's distinctive yet all-inclusive ambience appeals to a broad audience of beer enthusiasts. "We get everything from twenty-one-year-old college kids who just want to taste good beer all the way to military officers," said Yester.

The beer and food menu arrives in a notebook format. Belgian fries share the menu with unique items such as vegetarian buffalo wings and bacon with maple syrup. Burger selections include Kobe beef, lamb, portobello, and quinoa.

Yester takes a culinary approach to brewing. Many Trinity beers are brewed with unusual combinations of fruits, vegetables, herbs, spices, and flowers. The owner-brewer is especially fond of saisons. A broad selection of unique flavorings has been used in making the more than fifty saison recipes that have been brewed at Trinity. Despite their uniqueness, the saisons share several common traits including a spicy character, dry finish, and light body.

The eight full-time house beers range from a citrusy and session-able wit to a muscular 10 percent ABV double IPA. The brewery produces a series of wild brett beers called Cases of the Mondays, a name inspired by the movie *Office Space*. The first release in the series, named TPS Report, is a two-time medal winner at the Great American Beer Festival. At the 2013 GABF, Trinity captured a gold medal for its Elektrick Cukumbahh, a cucumber-flavored saison.

Trinity Brewing Company

Opened: August 2008.

Owner and head brewer: Jason Yester.

Potential annual capacity: 2,400 barrels.

Hours: Monday through Thursday, noon to 9 p.m.; Friday, noon to 11 p.m.; Saturday, 11 a.m. to 11 p.m.; Sunday 11 a.m. to 8 p.m.

Tours: On request.

Take-out beer: Growlers, 750 ml bottles, and kegs.

Food: Salads, small plates, burgers, and entreés. Good selection of vegetarian and vegan options.

Extras: Monday Soul Runners running club. Wednesday charity fundraiser. First Saturday of the month firkin tapping.

Parking: On-site lot.

Central Rockies

More than any other part of the state, the Central Rockies region is the heart and soul of Colorado. People from outside the state envision Colorado as a land of snowcapped mountain peaks, ski slopes blanketed in knee-deep powder, and icy mountain trout streams. Those who live here, or have traveled around the state, know that these images are the real deal throughout the vast mountainous terrain that dominates the central portion of the state. Sure, the eastern third of the state is flat plains, and large sections in the west are high desert, but that's generally not what brings people to Colorado, either to visit or to live. No matter that more than 80 percent of the state's population resides east of the mountains along the Front Range. The Colorado high country is the state's playground and its source of psychic renewal. Where Coloradans go to play, you'll find great beer, and the region's eighteen breweries are a testament to that.

For the purposes of this book, the boundaries for the Central Rockies region are the Rocky Mountain foothills on the east, the Wyoming border on the north, towns east of Glenwood Springs on the west, and Highway 50 through Gunnison and Salida on the south. The mountains of southwest Colorado are covered separately in this book. I've taken the liberty of placing the mountain towns of Nederland, Central City, and Woodland Park in other sections because of their close proximity to the Colorado Front Range.

The vast majority of Colorado's roughly two dozen ski resorts lie within the Central Rockies. Well-known ski towns including Aspen, Breckenridge, Crested Butte, Steamboat Springs, and Winter Park all have hometown breweries. In fact, all of the breweries covered in this section are within easy reach of an alpine resort.

Many residents of Colorado mountain towns, including many brewers, arrived from other parts of the country to become ski bums and never left. While great snow and abundant sunshine were the original attractions, in many cases it was the spectacular high country summers that convinced them to stay. "People come for the winter and stay for the summer," is a phrase you hear over and over again in the mountain towns of Colorado's Central Rockies.

The communities of Colorado's high country each have their own character, as do the hometown breweries. Although mountain towns are often separated by long distances, they share some common traits. These include fantastic year-round outdoor recreational opportunities, inspiring mountain scenery, abundant sunshine, and a laid-back, low stress, live-and-let-live lifestyle.

Those who want a high country experience without traveling far from the Front Range should head to Summit County, a mere seventy miles from Denver. In and around the towns of Dillon, Frisco, and Breckenridge are four ski resorts; great hiking, biking, fishing, and camping; and four busy brewpubs (with a fifth rumored to be in the works).

Myriad festivals keep the mountain towns hopping throughout the summer. Winter events—such as the Breckenridge Snow Sculpture Championships and the winter carnivals in Steamboat Springs and Crested Butte—are big draws for locals and visitors alike.

The Colorado high country is not just for adrenaline-charged adventure-seekers. Aspen is well-known for being steeped in arts and culture. Salida has a thriving arts scene in addition to world-class fly fishing, white-water rafting, and kayaking.

I've long maintained that beer tastes better at high elevations. Maybe it's the crisp mountain air that piques one's senses, or maybe it's merely that mountain travel often includes outdoor activity, which always heightens one's appreciation of fine fermented beverages. Visit any of the Central Rockies' hometown breweries and I think you'll agree.

Amícas Pizza & Microbrewery

136 East 2nd Street, Salida, CO 81201
(719) 539-5219 • www.amicassalida.com

You won't find bananas on the menu of Amícas Pizza & Microbrewery, although the brewpub resides in what is referred to as Colorado's "banana belt." If your timing is right, however, you might get to enjoy a Colorado Peach Pale Ale, brewed with fresh Colorado peaches and Colorado-grown hops. The downtown Salida brewpub is very big on all things local. In return, locals are very big on Amícas, and for good reason. The wood-fired pizzas are awesome. The beers are flavorful and satisfying. The brewpub has a cheerful, slightly quirky vibe, much like Salida itself.

Amícas is located in Salida's historic downtown district—among the largest historic districts in Colorado—in a weathered standalone brick building that sits amid the town's numerous cafes, art galleries, outdoor stores, and specialty shops. A few blocks away is Riverside Park, the site of the annual Colorado Brewers Rendezvous, a popular all-Colorado beer fest that takes place in July.

Amícas came into being in 2002 when a former brewpub operating in the historic building changed ownership and was rebranded as Amícas. The business quickly became a locals' favorite and a popular stop for Salida's seasonal onslaught of river runners, mountain bikers, art enthusiasts, and skiers.

A pair of rustic log benches sits in front of the building. Flower boxes under the front windows create an inviting first impression. When you enter the long, narrow interior, the enticing aroma of garlic permeates the air.

You order food at the counter, take a number, and find a table in the main dining room or in a smaller dining area in the back. The thin-crust pizza is made from scratch, as are most of the brewpub's food items. Many dishes can be ordered gluten-free. The kitchen is committed to using high-quality, locally sourced meat, produce, and other products.

While your food is being prepared, there are lots of interesting art pieces and curios to peruse.

Year-round beers: Bomber Blonde Ale, Headwaters IPA, Rex's Amber Ale, Big S Brown.

The Pick: Those who appreciate a well-made IPA will find Headwaters IPA a great example of the style. Hop essence runs throughout, with just enough malt poking through to keep this satisfying brew in balance.

A bicycle hangs from the ceiling and a holiday wreath made entirely of wine corks is on display. A collection of medals from the Great American Beer Festival and the Colorado State Fair hangs behind the bar.

Amícas' two dining areas are separated by the tiny brewhouse where brewer Mike LaCroix fashions his tasty fermentations. LaCroix started homebrewing in 1992. The next year, while attending cooking school in Portland, Oregon, he volunteered to work at the Full Sail brewery in Hood River. In 1994, he got his first brewing job at the now-defunct Silver Plume brewery in the small Colorado mountain community of the same name. After a stint at Tommyknocker Brewery in Idaho Springs, LaCroix spent a few years working at several out-of-state breweries. He returned to Colorado to run the brewhouse at Golden City before coming to Amícas, where he's been concocting first-rate brews for more than a decade.

The four full-time beers include a blonde ale, an amber ale, a brown ale, and the locals-favorite Headwaters IPA. These are supplemented by an ever-changing selection of seasonal and specialty offerings. The brewpub's commitment to local sourcing extends to the brewhouse. Amícas' beers are brewed with barley malt from Colorado Malting Company, located about eighty miles away in Alamosa. The house root beer is flavored with local honey rather than high-fructose corn syrup.

Amícas Pizza & Microbrewery

Opened: June 2002.

Owner: Kathie Younghans.

Head brewer: Mike LaCroix.

Potential annual capacity: 560 barrels.

Hours: Daily, 11:30 a.m. to 9ish.

Tours: On request.

Take-out beer: Growlers, bombers, and sometimes six-packs.

Food: Excellent thin-crust pizzas, panini sandwiches, calzones, pasta, and salads. Many dishes can be ordered gluten-free.

Extras: Occasional live music.

Parking: Small lot and on-street.

Area attractions: Salida Hot Springs Pool (410 West US Hwy 50, 719-539-6738). Mt. Princeton Hot Springs Resort (15870 CR 162, Nathrop, 888-395-7799). Monarch Ski Resort is eighteen miles from Salida.

Other area beer sites: Currents Restaurant (122 N. F St., 719-539-9514). The Fritz (113 E. Sackett Ave., 719-539-0364). Benson's Tavern & Beer Garden (128 N. F St., 719-539-9391). The Boathouse Cantina (228 N. F St., 719-539-5004). The Sidewinder Saloon at Monarch Ski Resort (winter only).

Aspen Brewing Company

304 East Hopkins Avenue, Aspen, CO 81611
(970) 920-BREW (2739)
www.aspenbrewingcompany.com

Most people know Aspen as a mountain getaway for movie stars and other high-profile movers and shakers. What fewer people know is that the former mining town barely survived the silver bust of the early 1900s. During that time, the population declined from more than ten thousand residents to fewer than one thousand. The town's salvation came in 1946 when the Aspen Skiing Corporation was founded. The rest, as the saying goes, is history.

Aspen's first brewery dates from the late 1800s. Wild hops can still be found along the Rio Grande Trail, which uses the former railroad corridor through town. The town's first craft brewery, the Flying Dog brewpub, opened for business in 1990. Four years later, Flying Dog relocated to Denver (and later to Maryland), leaving Aspen without a hometown brewery for more than a decade. Then, in 2008, an entrepreneurial graduate from the University of Colorado established the Aspen Brewing Company and put the fabled Rocky Mountain resort back on the Colorado beer map.

During his college days in Boulder, Duncan Clauss immersed himself in the vibrant local beer scene and eventually took up homebrewing. When he discovered that Aspen was without a brewery, he moved forward with plans to bring craft beer back to the resort town shortly after graduating,

The original brewery was a small space on the edge of town. Among its first keg accounts was the iconic J-Bar in the vintage Hotel Jerome, a favorite watering hole of many luminaries including the late Hunter S. Thompson, the gonzo journalist who lived in nearby Woody Creek and whose antics are legendary in the Aspen area. Aspen Brewing's Brown Bear Ale is still served at the J-Bar.

The brewery soon outgrew the space. While relocating within town was desirable, the astronomical cost of Aspen real estate made it impractical. The problem was averted when the company

Year-round beers: This Season's Blonde, Independence Pass Ale IPA, Conundrum Red Ale, Brown Bear Ale, Pyramid Peak Porter.

The Pick: Conundrum Red Ale introduces itself with a sweet caramelly character. The hops soon kick in, providing a finish as crisp as the high country air.

moved its production facility to a business park just outside of town while opening a separate tasting room in a high-visibility area in the downtown district.

While Aspen is known for its high-end restaurants, hotels, and shops, there's an affordable, down-to-earth component that surprises many first-time visitors. The casual, come-as-you-are taproom of the Aspen Brewing Company certainly falls into that camp. It's a compact space with a small bar, a few tables, and an upholstered bench that wraps partly around the room. During my visit, two wall-mounted TVs were showing videos of skiers performing daredevil maneuvers on near-vertical inclines. The front wall is glass and offers a great view of the ski slopes of Aspen Mountain rising above town. There's an outdoor deck with counter seating and an equally stellar view. Aspen Brewing has adopted the fitting motto, "Drink in the view."

The brewing operations are headed by Pj Goudreault, who arrived at Aspen Brewing in 2013 after stints at Odell Brewing, Oskar Blues, and Crazy Mountain. There are ten taps, including a nitro tap, that dispense nine house beers and the house root beer. The six full-time beers include a pilsner, a blonde ale, the locals-favorite IPA, a red ale, and a brown ale. Rotating seasonal and specialty beers round out the lineup.

A tradition has arisen in Aspen in which a rookie ski patroller, or a ski patroller who has received a promotion, is required to buy a keg of Aspen Brewing Company beer for the rest of his or her colleagues.

Aspen Brewing Company

Opened: March 2008.

Owner: Duncan Clauss.

Head brewer: Pj Goudreault.

Potential annual capacity: 2,000 barrels.

Hours: Daily, noon to late.

Tours: Scheduled occasionally at the production facility. Check social media for details.

Take-out beer: Growlers, cans, and bombers.

Food: Bring your own food.

Extras: Live music on Friday and Saturday. Tappin' Tuesday pilot brew releases. AHA member discount program participant.

Parking: On-street metered parking. Free bike parking.

Area attractions: The ski resorts of Aspen, Snowmass, Aspen Highlands, and Buttermilk Basin.

Other area beer sites: Finbarr's Irish Pub and Kitchen (415 East Hyman Ave., 970-925-2719); New Belgium Ranger Station (100 Elbert Ln., Unit M-115, Snowmass Village, 970-236-6277).

Backcountry Brewery

720 Main Street, Frisco, CO 80443
(970) 485-3989 • www.backcountrybrewery.com

Finding a job in the American craft beer industry often requires patience and perseverance. Or just luck. "I was sitting at the bar one night and met the right person," recalled Alan Simons, who fell into a job in sales and distribution at Backcountry Brewery before eventually assuming the head brewing position. The large brewpub has anchored the east end of Main Street in the mountain town of Frisco since the mid-1990s.

For skiers and snowboarders, Frisco is in an enviable location about fifteen minutes from Copper Mountain Resort and within easy access of Keystone and Breckenridge. The Arapahoe Basin and Loveland ski areas are also close by, and Vail is about thirty miles away. Frisco also sits on the shores of Lake Dillon, one of the few bodies of water in Colorado that can honestly be called a sailing destination. Because Frisco has no hometown ski mountain, it tends to be more relaxed, and more affordable, than resort communities with slopeside condos and gondola stations steps from downtown.

Backcountry's motto is "Create your own path," and the path to the long-established brewpub is well-worn by a steady influx of travelers and a core of local beer enthusiasts. The brewpub resides on the second floor of a modern retail building. You enter into a sprawling interior space with an "upscale rustic" feel. The high ceilings and rows of tall windows create an open, airy atmosphere. You can choose from a variety of dining and drinking areas. There are great mountain views, especially from the outdoor tables on the covered deck. Legs weary from a day on the slopes can find solace in a cushy upholstered chair or sofa warmed by a stone-framed fireplace.

Backcountry attracts a lot of families seeking a casual, comfortable dining experience. An enclosed game room, popular with younger folks, contains an assortment of video diversions. There's a viewing area where you can look down into the first-floor brewhouse.

Year-round beers:
Wheat, Pilsner, Amber, Pale Ale, Porter.

The Pick: The Pale Ale (formerly Telemark IPA) has been a locals' favorite from way back. An infusion of American hops is kept in check by an underlying malt foundation. At a reasonable 5.6 percent, you needn't shy away from going there twice.

In the brewery's early days, before hoppy beers were all the rage, Backcountry produced a well-hopped beer called Telemark IPA. It was hugely popular, especially with local ski bums. The beer was a gold medal winner at the 2000 Great American Beer Festival. The beer is still made, but is now classified as a pale ale in light of the evolution of beers styles over the years.

The kitchen puts out a well-rounded selection of American pub standards. Burgers and sandwiches share the menu with pizza, pasta, and a few smoked meats. Buffalo chili and Rocky Mountain oysters are available if you have a hankering for cowboy cuisine.

Simons brews five full-time beers at Backcountry including an American wheat, a European-style pilsner, an amber ale, the aforementioned pale ale, and a robust porter. Depending on the time of year, you'll find a seasonal such as a Berliner weisse, the Breakfast Stout (a coffee milk stout), an Oktoberfest, or a maibock.

Specialty beers are created in whatever style suits Simons's fancy, be it a black IPA, a weizenbock, or a Belgian-style ale. A saison from Backcountry was awarded a silver medal at the 2011 Great American Beer Festival. Six Backcountry beers garnered awards at the 2012 Colorado State Fair. During my ski-season visit, two smooth-sipping winter warmers hit the spot. A bourbon-barrel-aged barleywine shared tap space with a well-fortified doppelbock.

Backcountry Brewery

Opened: September 1996.

Owners: Charlie and Joe Eazor.

Head brewer: Alan Simons.

Potential annual capacity: 4,000 barrels.

Hours: Daily, 11 a.m. to close.

Tours: On request.

Take-out beer: Six-packs, party pigs, and kegs.

Food: Burgers, pizza (gluten-free available), pasta, sandwiches, barbecue, and Rocky Mountain oysters.

Extras: Live music on Fridays during the busy season. Game room. AHA member deals program participant.

Parking: On-site lot.

Area attractions: Frisco marina. Frisco Historic Park and Museum. The ski resorts of Arapahoe Basin, Breckenridge, Copper Mountain, Keystone, and Loveland are all nearby.

Other area beer sites: Prost (313 Main St., 970-668-3688). Ollie's Pub and Grub (620 Main St., 970-668-0744).

Bonfire Brewing Company

127 Second Street, Eagle, CO 81631
(970) 306-7113 • www.bonfirebrewing.com

Bonfire Brewing is a fun-loving little gathering spot and a sure cure for attitude issues. A friendly, laid-back vibe permeates the premises. It's a place where you leave your problems at the door and join in the ongoing party.

The brewery is located in the community of Eagle, which sits adjacent to Interstate 70, thirty miles west of Vail. Culturally, it feels a world apart from that upscale mountain resort. The location provides easy access to a wealth of outdoor activities for which the local residents, at least the beer-drinking ones I befriended during an all-too-brief springtime visit, have a passion.

Prior to becoming business partners, Bonfire cofounders Andy Jessen and Matt Wirtz were roommates in a house owned by Jessen. For his birthday one year, Wirtz received a homebrew kit from his girlfriend, who also lived in the house. "He made one batch on that," Jessen recalled. "It was absolutely horrible." Undeterred, Wirtz, a mechanical wizard, pieced together an all-grain brewing system using some old kegs, casters, and a bed frame. He was soon regularly producing 10-gallon batches of satisfactory homebrew.

When Wirtz and his girlfriend split up and she moved out, the two bachelors were in need of an additional source of income to make the monthly mortgage payment. Selling beer seemed a viable solution. A business plan was drawn up, a space in a former liquor store was leased, and a larger brewing system was pieced together from 55-gallon stainless steel drums. The partners served their first beer in November 2010.

Demand quickly surpassed their production capabilities. Four months after opening, they acquired a used 7-barrel system. With their increased capacity, they began selling kegs to a growing list of local bars and restaurants. In late 2012, they opened a separate production facility, though they continue to brew in the original location where the taproom resides. Jessen keeps the

Year-round beers: Demshitz Brown, Firestarter IPA, Brush Creek Blonde, Seven Bachelors Brew Pale Ale, Tent Pole Vanilla Porter, Awry Rye Pale Ale.

The Pick: With its long bitter finish, Firestarter IPA is the locals' favorite. Grab a pint, head to the fire pit, and make some friends.

business running smoothly while Wirtz keeps a huge selection of house beers flowing.

The brewery sits inconspicuously on a side street near Eagle's compact downtown. The featureless exterior provides little clue as to the nature of this animated gathering spot. The taproom is not large, but it's packed with character.

Dispersed around the room is a playful and quirky collection of random objects including kayaks, skis, snowboards, a surfboard with masking tape on the tip (shark attack?), a life ring, a bowling pin, a topless mermaid, and other assorted knickknacks of unknown derivation. Amusements include a dartboard, a foosball game, and a shuffleboard table. The original homespun homebrew system sits on a shelf above the beer taps.

The preferred gathering spot is on the patio, which has the ambience of a backyard party with a constantly changing group of guests. A random collection of chairs and benches surrounds a gas fire pit, the focal point of the outdoor space. During my visit, patio patrons included several dogs who, judging by their nonchalant demeanors, seemed well acquainted with their surroundings.

A something-for-everyone selection of nineteen house beers was on tap during my abbreviated stay. A few lagers and fruit beers shared the long beer list with numerous ales of British and American derivation. If there was no particular theme, there was certainly no shortage of choices. According to cofounder Jessen, "What defines us more than anything else is our flexibility and our willingness to experiment and not be tied to any specific style."

Bonfire Brewing Company

Opened: November 2010.

Owners: Andy Jessen and Matt Wirtz.

Head brewer: Matt Wirtz.

Potential annual capacity: 6,000 barrels including nearby production facility.

Hours: Monday through Thursday, 4 p.m. to 10 p.m. or later; Friday and Saturday, 4 p.m. to around midnight; Sunday, 4 p.m. to 8 p.m.

Tours: On request.

Take-out beer: Growlers, six-packs, and kegs.

Food: Popcorn, pizza delivery, or bring your own food.

Extras: Live music on Friday. AHA member discount program participant.

Parking: Free on-street parking.

Other area beer sites: The Dusty Boot Steakhouse & Saloon (1099 Capitol St., 970-328-7002).

Breckenridge Brewery & Pub

600 South Main Street, Breckenridge, CO 80424
(970) 453-1550 • www.breckenridgebrewery.com/
food/breckenridge-brewery-pub

The original Breckenridge Brewery, located in the popular mountain resort community and former gold-mining boomtown, was the first mountain-town craft brewery in Colorado. When the brewpub opened in 1990, only a few other breweries were operating in the state.

The brewpub was opened by a ski bum and homebrewer named Richard Squire. The first brewmaster had been a senior brewing engineer for Coors. When the brewpub first opened, there was one beer available, an oatmeal stout. That beer is still brewed today using the original recipe.

Other beers were added to the lineup and were bottled using a two-head filler. Twice a week, a fellow named Todd Usry would drive up to the brewery, pick up beer, and deliver it to liquor stores along the Colorado Front Range. In 1992, Breckenridge opened a second brewing operation in Denver that grew into the city's largest craft brewery. Today, Usry holds the title of Brewmaster and Director of Brewing Operations for the company.

Needless to say, the brewpub was a hit both with thirsty locals and Breck's seasonal influx of visitors, few of whom had ever experienced fresh craft beer. The brewpub remains a bustling downtown destination, especially on summer and winter weekends when outdoor enthusiasts descend on the mountain town to ski, hike, fish, camp, mountain bike, and partake in the myriad other outdoor activities for which the area is well known.

The brewpub is housed in a modern two-story brick structure at the southern end of the town's busy, tourist-intensive Main Street. The interior has a casual contemporary feel without any fancy embellishments. The slopes of the Breckenridge Ski Resort are visible through the wall of windows along the front of the building.

There are several dining areas on different levels. At one end of the building is a pleasant deck screened by several quaking aspen trees. A smaller

Year-round beers: Avalanche Ale, Vanilla Porter, Agave Wheat, Oatmeal Stout, and an IPA.

The Pick: The black, opaque Oatmeal Stout has a hint of chocolate and a roasty character that cuts through the chill of the mountain air.

outdoor dining area resides on the second floor. The most striking interior feature by far is the brewhouse, or more accurately, the lack of a brewhouse. The mash tun and brew kettle sit at floor level, just behind the granite-topped bar and literally a few feet from beer-sipping customers. During brew sessions, the brew crew has to work around busy bartenders. A line of five tall, gleaming, stainless steel fermenters rise impressively behind the brewing vessels.

Brewing operations are headed by Jimmy Walker, who has worked at the brewpub for more than eighteen years. Walker worked his way up the ranks from busboy to waiter to bartender to assistant brewer, and finally head brewer. Along with five full-time beers, Walker creates a variety of specialty and experimental brews. A seasonal spruce beer, brewed for the past several summers, has developed a local following. Walker collects the spruce tips himself from trees growing high up on the Continental Divide. The mountain brewery also acts as a recipe incubator for the big Denver brewery. For example, 72 Imperial Chocolate Stout, now brewed and packaged in Denver, was first developed in Breckenridge.

I get a bit nostalgic when I travel to the mountains and visit the brewery. My first visit was in 1990, the year it opened. I recall the excitement of drinking a fresh pint of oatmeal stout—a novel style at the time—in the new mountain brewery. The Colorado beer scene has evolved immensely since those days, and Breckenridge Brewery was one of the early players that helped lay the foundation for that evolution.

Breckenridge Brewery & Pub

Opened: February 1990.

Owners: Breckenridge/Wynkoop LLC.

Head brewer: Jimmy Walker.

Potential annual capacity: 1,500 barrels.

Hours: Daily, 11 a.m. to closing.

Tours: By reservation.

Take-out beer: Six-packs, growlers, and kegs.

Food: American pub fare.

Extras: AHA member deals program participant.

Parking: On-site lot, on-street parking, and nearby lots.

Area attractions: The Breckenridge Ski Resort and the resorts of Arapahoe Basin, Copper Mountain, Keystone, and Loveland.

Other area beer sites: Relish (137 South Main St., 970-453-0989). Ollie's Pub & Grub (401 S. Main St., 970-453-9148). Après Handcrafted Libations (130 South Main St., 303-868-7990).

Carbondale Beer Works

647 Main Street, Carbondale, CO 81623
(970) 704-1216 • www.carbondalebeerworks.com

Carbondale Beer Works founder, owner, and head brewer Jeff Dahl remembers his first homebrew. It was made from a kit he received as a college graduation present from his mother. "It turned out horrible," recalled the New Orleans native. Undeterred, Dahl continued his homebrewing explorations and received a boost of positive reinforcement when, in the mid-1990s, an early batch of his weizenbock was awarded a first-place medal at the Dixie Cup, a long-running and prestigious homebrew competition held in Houston.

An architecture job brought Dahl to Colorado's Roaring Fork Valley in 1999. Architects generally do poorly in an economic downturn, and when the economy went south, he decided it was time to turn his long-time homebrewing hobby into a business.

To hone his brewing skills, he enrolled in a professional brewing course in England. Of equal importance to the technical information he gained during the program were his visits to local pubs, where he discovered the importance of the pub as a community gathering place. "The idea for this in Carbondale just made perfect sense," Dahl related.

The town of Carbondale sits thirty miles downstream (or "down valley" in the local vernacular) from upscale Aspen. With Aspen's astronomical real estate prices, more affordable Carbondale has evolved into a bedroom community for people who work in the famous resort town. In recent years, gushing write-ups in publications such as *Outside* magazine and *National Geographic Adventure* have focused attention on the excellent fly fishing, biking, kayaking, and cross-country skiing found nearby the tight-knit community of 6,500.

Dahl found an available space for his brewery in the former Carbondale post office, a small brick structure of no particular distinction, in the heart of the town's compact downtown district. After an extensive refurbishing, Carbondale Beer Works opened for business in December 2010.

The sign displayed on the front window of the brewery contains the description, "Ale House &

Year-round beers: Dirty Blonde, Langer Irish Stout, Coal Creek Oatmeal Stout, Avalanche Creek IPA, English IPA, Bone Dog Amber.

The Pick: With its creamy mouthfeel, a hint of cocoa, and a dry finish, the Coal Creek Oatmeal Stout is the brew to savor on the patio as the sun gets low.

Wienery," that is, a purveyor of hot dogs. While you certainly can get a hot dog (or a smaller "puppy dog" for the kids) or a more exotic sausage (Elk Jalapeno Cheddar anyone?) as well as other pub fare, the best reason to visit this folksy small-town brewery is its welcoming ambience and well-rounded selection of house and guest beers.

The interior contains about a dozen wooden tables and a wooden bar sitting atop corrugated metal facing. The red- and gray-painted brick walls display an eclectic mix of paintings by a local artist, and chalkboards list upcoming events and descriptions of the hot dogs. The tiny brewhouse sits beyond the bar, behind a wall of glass. If the décor needed a label, I'd call it rustic-funky-industrial post-post office. A sizeable outdoor patio contains a fire pit and several heaters.

In the early going, Dahl brewed only English-style ales, but soon realized he needed to accommodate the locals' preference for hoppier beers. Today, the full-time lineup includes both an American and English IPA (the latter is served cask-conditioned and dispensed from a traditional British beer engine), an oatmeal stout and a drier Irish stout, an amber, and a blonde ale, in addition to seasonal and specialty offerings.

An interesting assortment of rotating guest taps adds variety and keeps beer flowing when the house beers run low. Some beers are aged in barrels including a Stranahan's Colorado Whiskey barrel. Coincidently, George Stranahan, cofounder of the Denver-based whiskey distillery as well as the Flying Dog Brewery, which originated in Aspen, lives in the community and stops by the brewpub from time to time.

Carbondale Beer Works

Opened: December 2010.

Owner and head brewer: Jeff Dahl.

Potential annual capacity: 250 barrels.

Hours: Winter: Monday through Friday, 4 p.m. to midnight; Saturday and Sunday, 2 p.m. to midnight. Summer: Monday through Friday, 3:30 p.m. to midnight; Saturday and Sunday, 11:30 a.m. to midnight.

Tours: On request.

Take-out beer: Growlers.

Food: A variety of hot dogs, burgers, fried munchies, and salads.

Extras: Live music on Friday and sometimes other days. Trivia every third Thursday of the month.

Parking: On-street parking.

Area attractions: The great outdoors.

Other area beer sites: The Town Restaurant (348 Main St., 970-963-6328).

Crazy Mountain Brewing Company

439 Edwards Access Road, Suite B-102, Edwards, CO 81632

(970) 926-3009 • www.crazymountainbrewery.com

For some crazy reason, the Vail Valley has been slow to embrace the craft beer culture that has permeated much of Colorado. Things are on the upswing, however, and Crazy Mountain Brewing Company has been a major contributor to the area's growing interest in fresh, locally made beer.

Crazy Mountain is the Vail Valley's only production brewery, meaning its primary focus is on packaging and distributing beer. It's also one of the fastest-growing breweries in Colorado, with distribution in a dozen states. As of this writing, the brewery is considering expanding its brewing operations to Denver, possibly in the space that Breckenridge Brewing will be vacating once its new complex south of the city is complete. Beer travelers need not worry, however. Whatever the future brings, Crazy Mountain intends to keep its headquarters at its original location in Edwards.

The brewery came to life in 2010 when cofounders Kevin and Marissa Selvy relocated from California to launch their fledgling business. Kevin is originally from Denver and had spent considerable time in the Vail area over the years, so for him, the move back to Colorado was a return to his roots. While on the West Coast, he had worked in several breweries including the venerable Anchor Brewing Company in San Francisco. Crazy Mountain was named after Loco Mountain, a landform on the Selvy family's ranch about three hours south of Edwards. The mountain is pictured on the brewery logo.

The brewery is located about fourteen miles west of Vail, on the lower level of a retail plaza just off Interstate 70. Its close proximity to the highway ensures a steady stream of travelers visiting the brewery. The tasting room is actually a large garage space that has undergone only minimal embellishment to soften its industrial look and feel.

Seating consists of several large picnic tables and a few high-tops dispersed around the room. The impressive picnic tables are constructed of

Year-round beers: Crazy Mountain Amber Ale, Lava Lake Wit, Horseshoes & Hand Grenades ESB, Mountain Livin' Pale Ale, Hookiebobb IPA, Boohai Red Ale, Cara De Luna Black Ale, Old Soul Strong Belgian Ale.

The Pick: Lava Lake Wit is flavored with chamomile, orange peel, coriander, and grains of paradise, resulting in a bright, spicy, and refreshing quencher that hits the spot after a day of frolicking on the mountain.

large timbers of beetle kill pine. There's no bar, but rather a counter opposite the entry where you order beverages. Behind it, the open brewhouse is visible in the back of the building.

A large mountain-scene mural covers most of one wall, while in front of it stands a half-dozen old-style coin-operated vending machines dispensing a variety of salty snacks. A pinball machine is available for amusement, and an old ski-lift chair is suspended from the high ceiling. There's nothing fancy about the interior, but it's a pleasant enough no-frills drinking and socializing space. When I visited, four well-mannered pooches circulated around the room. To enhance the tasting room experience, food trucks are frequently on-site and live music is scheduled from time to time. A beer garden was in the planning stage.

Crazy Mountain cans and bottles a variety of its beers. Tasting room visitors, however, have a broader selection to choose from. The brewery keeps eight full-time ales on tap in a something-for-everyone range of American and Belgian styles. Seasonal releases include a refreshing Kolsch, a coffee-laced stout, and a burly 10 percent barley-wine with the amusing moniker Lawyers, Guns & Money.

As a means of contributing to the welfare of the community, Crazy Mountain pairs each of its beers with a local nonprofit organization. One percent of revenues from the sales of each beer go to the organization with which it is paired. The nonprofits support environmental, youth-oriented, and health-oriented causes and artistic endeavors.

Crazy Mountain Brewing Company

Opened: January 2010.

Owners: Kevin and Marissa Selvy.

Head brewer: Ethan Osborne.

Potential annual capacity: 20,000 barrels.

Hours: Monday through Saturday, 11 a.m. to 8 p.m. Sunday, 11 a.m. to 5 p.m.

Tours: By appointment only. Call 970-926-3009.

Take-out beer: Growlers, cans, bombers, and kegs.

Food: Pizza delivery or bring your own food.

Extras: Firkin Fridays (summer only). Occasional live music (check website or social media). AHA member discount program participant.

Parking: On-site lot.

Area attractions: The Vail Ski Resort is fourteen miles east of Edwards.

Other area beer sites: Vail Ale House (2161 N. Frontage Rd., West Vail, 970-476-4314). The Atwater at Vail Cascade Resort & Spa (1300 Westhaven Dr., Vail, 800-282-4183).

Dillon Dam Brewery

100 Little Dam Road, Dillon, CO 80435
(970) 262-7777 • www.dambrewery.com

"Get Your Own Dam Beer" is the catchy slogan of Dillon Dam Brewery, a bustling brewpub located in the mountain town of Dillon, about seventy miles west of Denver. Dillon Dam is one of four brewpubs in Summit County, a favorite seasonal destination for outdoor enthusiasts from Colorado's Front Range communities and more distant locales.

The brewery sits just off Interstate 70, and close by Lake Dillon, which is actually a reservoir that was created with the construction of—you guessed it—Dillon Dam. A big green silo displaying the brewery name sits prominently next to the modern-looking structure that has housed the brewpub since 1997.

You enter into an open and airy two-story space. A U-shaped bar, which always seems to be full, sits in the middle of the room, separating a collection of high-tops from a sizable dining area. Additional seating, along with several pool tables, is located on the second level, which looks down into the bar area. There's also an observation space overlooking the brewhouse with signage detailing the brewing process. Long expanses of glass flood the interior with natural light and offer stunning views of the nearby mountains. Outdoor patio seating is available during the spectacular summer season that starts late and ends early at Dillon's 9,000-foot elevation.

A loyal contingent of regular customers shows up for the daily happy hour, when appetizers are half-price. The brewpub also hosts weekly live music performances. The locals tend to lay low, however, during the peak tourist seasons when visitors line up outside the door awaiting a table.

From early on, Dillon Dam built a solid reputation of producing high-quality, approachable ales and lagers in mostly British and German styles. The brewpub has amassed an impressive collection of medals from the Great American Beer Festival, the World Beer Cup, and other competitions.

Year-round beers: Dam Lyte, Wildernest Wheat, Paradise Pilsner, Dam Straight Lager, Extra Pale Ale, Sweet George's Brown, McLuhr's Irish Stout.

The Pick: Dam Straight Lager, brewed in the Vienna style, has a clean malt flavor balanced with just enough hops to cut through the sweetness. It's a beer that will appeal to both drinkers with seasoned palates and those in transition from the macro beer world.

Sweet George's Brown, an English brown ale, and McLuhr's Irish Stout are both multiple award winners. The standard lineup also includes a pilsner, a light lager, an amber lager, an American wheat ale, and a pale ale.

The brewhouse is run by Cory Forster, who became a professional brewer in an unconventional way. In 2001, Dillon Dam's assistant brewer had just departed. Forster, who had no brewing experience, was working as a bartender and was on his way into work when he was approached by the head brewer in the parking lot. "Did you ever think about being a brewer?" he asked Forster. Forster seized the opportunity and got intensive on-the-job training. After five years of working as an assistant brewer, he was offered the head brewing position at another, now-defunct area brewpub. Two years later, the head brewer job opened up at Dillon Dam and Forster returned to run the 15-barrel brewhouse.

Under Forster's direction, the number of specialty offerings has expanded. "We try to have some sort of a whiskey barrel-aged beer at all times," explained Forster, who is not shy about experimenting with different flavor combinations. One well-received experimental beer was called Dreamsicle Stout. "It's our Belgian stout aged in a whiskey barrel with vanilla beans and sweet orange zest." Forster has succumbed to the ongoing obsession with hoppy beers among craft beer enthusiasts. An IPA now appears with some regularity. It was originally named Here's Your Dam IPA.

Dillon Dam Brewery

Opened: February 1997.

Owners: General Manager George Blincoe is part of a seven-person ownership group.

Head brewer: Cory Forster.

Potential annual capacity: 2,500 barrels.

Hours: Daily, 11:30 a.m. to midnight (later on weekends).

Tours: Self-guided or by reservation or request.

Take-out beer: Growlers, six-packs, party pigs, and kegs.

Food: American pub fare and assorted dinner entrées including steaks, seafood, and pasta.

Extras: Tap-It-Tuesday the second Tuesday of the month. Live music on Thursday. AHA member discount program participant.

Parking: On-site lot.

Area attractions: Lake Dillon Amphitheater (176 Lake Dillon Dr., 970-513-9386). The ski resorts of Arapahoe Basin, Copper Mountain, Keystone, Breckenridge, and Loveland are all nearby.

Other area beer sites: Tiki Bar (151 Marina Dr., 970-262-6309). Old Chicago (560 Silverthorne Ln., Silverthorne, 970-468-2882). 6th Alley Bar at Arapahoe Basin.

Eddyline Brewery & Taproom

102 Linderman Avenue, Buena Vista, CO 81211
(719) 966-6018 • www.eddylinebrewing.com

If you've studied Spanish at some time in your life, you'll need to forget everything you've learned regarding pronunciation before speaking the names of Colorado towns of Spanish derivation. A perfect example is Buena Vista, the home of Eddyline Brewery and Taproom. While the "correct" Spanish pronunciation is BWAY-na Vista, the local pronunciation is BEW-na Vista, and apparently has been since the community was founded in 1879.

However you pronounce it, there can be little argument as to the appropriateness of the name, which translates to "beautiful view." The town sits at the base of the strikingly gorgeous Collegiate Range in Chaffee County, which boasts more fourteeners (mountain peaks exceeding 14,000 feet) than any other county in the country. Additionally, the community sits along the Arkansas River, one of the country's most popular white-water rafting destinations.

The name Eddyline is derived from river jargon. An eddy is a pocket of water where there's an interruption in the normal flow of the river. The break point between the normal flow and the eddy is called the eddyline. People who frequent Buena Vista—rafters, kayakers, fishermen—care about eddies and eddylines because these are favorable locations to launch river craft, hook lunker trout, and chill out with some cans of Eddyline beer.

Eddyline Brewing has its roots in New Mexico, where the original owners, Mic and Molley Heynekamp, opened the Socorro Springs Brewery in 1999. They had long wanted to open a brewery in Colorado, and the pieces of the puzzle eventually fell into place. The Eddyline Restaurant & Brewery opened in Buena Vista, close to the river, in 2009. The Heynekamps installed a small, 3-barrel brewing system, but soon discovered they couldn't keep up with demand, especially in the summer months when river runners and mountain recreationalists descend on the area en masse.

In 2011, the Heynekamps, along with cofounders Brian England and Ryan McFadden, opened a new

Year-round beers: Boater Beer Lager, Crank Yanker IPA, River Runner Pale Ale, Kickin' Back Amber.

The Pick: The aptly named Kickin' Back Amber has a toasty maltiness nicely balanced with a crisp hop finish. Neither too sweet nor too dry, it holds your interest without assaulting your senses.

brewery a mile from the original brewpub. The facility has a greatly expanded brewing capacity, a packaging line, a laid-back tasting room, and a kitchen featuring wood-fired pizzas. The original brewpub still operates as a restaurant.

The brewery sits on a corner lot just off Highway 24, in a building with a false Western façade. On one side of the structure is an eye-catching mural depicting a bicycle, a rushing river, and a snowcapped mountain range. The brewery slogan reads, "Whether You're Peakin' or Creekin'."

The interior is a cheerful space with rust-colored walls adorned with brightly colored paintings that continue the outdoor adventure theme. A single-speed fat-tire bicycle sits above the entrance. Wooden benches and tables add a rustic touch. The brewhouse is located in the back of the building and out of sight of the tasting room.

The brewery produces a variety of satisfying ales and lagers with clean, distinct flavors, lacking any cloying sweetness or excessive hoppiness to throw off their balance and drinkability. The something-for-everyone lineup ranges from an unintimidating light lager to a more aggressively flavored IPA. Rotating specialty beers include a raspberry wheat beer, a chile porter, a black lager, and other creations. The River Runner Pale Ale was a gold medal winner at the 2012 Great American Beer Festival.

The brewery's visibility has increased substantially since it began packaging four of its products in 16-ounce cans. England explained why Eddyline opted for the tall cans as opposed to the more standard 12-ounce variety: "Chaffee County has fourteen 14,000-foot peaks. We only felt it right to put our beer in big cans."

Eddyline Taproom & Brewery

Opened: September 2011.
Owners: Mic and Molley Heynekamp, Brian England, Ryan McFadden.
Head brewer: Dave Chichura.
Potential annual capacity: 5,000 barrels.
Hours: Daily, 11 a.m. to 10 p.m.
Tours: On request.
Take-out beer: Growlers, cans, and kegs.
Food: Wood-fired pizza, wings, nachos, soups, and salads.
Extras: Ask about homebrewer discounts.
Parking: On-site lot.
Area attractions: Cottonwood Hot Springs (18999 County Rd. 306, 719-395-6434).
Other area beer sites: Eddyline Restaurant (926 S. Main St., 719-966-6000).

The Eldo Brewery & Taproom

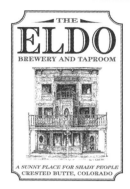

215 Elk Avenue, Crested Butte, CO 81224
(970) 349-6125 • www.eldobrewpub.com

What I like most about the Eldo, located in the high mountain playground of Crested Butte, is that it's exactly what it intends to be: an unpretentious, no-frills, come-as-you-are watering hole where locals and visitors can kick back and relate their recent adrenaline-charged adventures over a good beer and maybe a bite to eat.

In 1996, Ted Bosler rented the space that had formerly been the Eldorado, a local dive bar, with the intent of converting it into a brewpub. Bosler had been the head brewer at a now-defunct brewpub across the street. The new business was renamed the Eldo, and the brewery was added a year-and-a-half later.

Crested Butte's high-energy populace quickly adopted the new brewery and gave it a variety of nicknames including "the living room," "the office," and "the yacht club." Meanwhile, Bosler found that the responsibility of operating the brewhouse while also running the bar and raising a family was too much to handle. In 1998, he sold the business and cut ties with the Eldo. When his replacement in the brewhouse left less than two years later to follow a love interest, Bosler returned as head brewer.

The Eldo is located on Elk Street, the center of activity in the former mining town. The lively street sports a restored late-1800s Old West façade and boasts several buildings dating from that era. The brewpub resides on the second floor of an unpainted wooden structure that appears much older than it really is. The year posted on the building is 1976, but it's often mistaken for 1876.

Year-round beers: Ullr Pale Ale, Hooligan IPA, Wildfire ESB, King's Kolsch, Double IPA.

There's nothing fancy about the Eldo. As you enter the long, narrow space, the bar runs along the wall opposite the entrance. There's a grill at the far end, with the menu posted on a chalkboard above it. You order food at the bar, as there's no table service. In fact, there are few tables. Several booths sit opposite the bar and a double booth near the front can accommodate a large group. A

The Pick: The well-balanced Last Chance ESB, a traditional English ale served from a nitro tap, has a creamy head and silky texture that stays satisfying through several pints.

few small tables reside in the backroom, beyond the bar, along with a pool table, foosball table, dartboard, and a music stage. The caliber of bands that have performed within the modest confines of the Eldo is a bit mind-boggling and includes Phish, Widespread Panic, and The Wailers. According to Bosler, national touring bands frequently comment on the great audiences that attend shows at the brewery.

The Eldo's most inviting feature is the roomy deck overlooking Elk Street. "On Friday afternoon, it's standing-room only," Bosler told me as we sipped a beer on the sun-splashed outdoor space and watched the passersby on foot, bicycle, and skateboard.

The Eldo attracts young, active regulars, "doing whatever they can in order to pay rent and pay for equipment in order to fulfill their outdoor dreams," the brewer told me. As if to underscore his point, he introduced me to the personable young woman tending bar. Her name is Mary Boddington, and she's a world-class snowboarder who calls Crested Butte home.

"I have a very well-educated clientele as far as beer goes," Bosler told me during a tour of the 7-barrel brewhouse that sits out of sight in the back of the building. While the brewer has a preference for drinkable session beers, he also enjoys the freedom to regularly create new beers in whatever style strikes his fancy. "Eighty percent of the beers in the past year are brand new," said Bosler. The Eldo's diverse full-time beer list ranges from a light Kolsch to an imperial smoked porter. While the house IPA has a devout following, the pale ale, named after the snow god Ullr, is the best seller. Somehow, that seems appropriate.

The Eldo Brewery & Taproom

Opened: November 1996. Brewery added in 1998.

Owner: Mike Knoll.

Head brewer: Ted Bosler.

Potential annual capacity: 1,000 barrels.

Hours: Daily, 3 p.m. to 2 a.m.

Tours: On request.

Take-out beer: Growlers and kegs.

Food: Salads, sandwiches, burgers, and finger foods.

Extras: Live music regularly.

Parking: On-street.

Area attractions: Crested Butte Ski Resort. Crested Butte Mountain Heritage Museum and Mountain Bike Hall of Fame (331 Elk Ave., 970-349-6817).

Other area beer sites: Brick Oven Pizzeria & Pub (223 Elk Ave., 970-349-5044).

Elevation Beer Company

ELEVATION
BEER CO

115 Pahlone Parkway, Poncha Springs, CO 81242
(719) 539-5258 • www.elevationbeerco.com

When Elevation Beer Company opened in the spring of 2012, it received more attention than is typical for a new brewery in a small town. Among the guests who showed up in Poncha Springs for the grand opening bash was Colorado's brew-loving governor, John Hickenlooper. Since then, the brewery has continued to receive widespread attention for its delicious, well-crafted beers.

Poncha Springs, population 700, sits in Chaffee County, an area well known for its rafting, fly fishing, mountain biking, and hiking. The tiny enclave is hardly a destination in itself, but it does sit at the crossroads of highways 50 and 285, travel routes to some of the state's most popular tourist destinations and spectacular high country getaways.

The brewery was conceived when four friends with a variety of brewing and business expertise tossed the idea around while tossing back a few beers at a backyard barbecue. The idea stuck, and two years later, Elevation Beer Company opened for business.

From the start, the ownership team plotted a different course than the slew of other new breweries that were springing up around the state. "We looked at a lot of different models and we felt our passion was really in adventurous, barrel-aged, and seasonal beers," explained co-owner and sales and distribution manager Xandy Bustamante.

Since the brewery's focus would be on packaging and distribution rather than on attracting visitors to the taproom, the partners had few restrictions as to where to locate the fledgling business. Two of the partners had attended high school together in Buena Vista, just thirty miles up the road from Poncha Springs. All four were enamored with the plethora of outdoor activities in the area. Locating the brewery in Chaffee County was a no-brainer.

The brewery sits in an industrial park amid an expanse of scrub brush. There are mountain views in all directions. In fact, ten fourteeners—mountains that exceed 14,000 feet in elevation—can be seen from the brewery. The tasting room is spacious with a contrast of contemporary furnishings

Year-round beers: First Cast IPA, Little Mo' Porter, 8 Second Kolsch.

The Pick: The 8 Second Kolsch is a clean, refreshing, drinkable brew that will hold your interest yet won't intimidate timid palates.

and well-weathered, repurposed materials. Art pieces from local artists rotate monthly. Light wood wainscoting exhibits the characteristic blue stain of beetle kill pine. In a unique use of obsolete objects, the bar stools are constructed of old metal tractor seats. The weighty timbers behind the bar somehow arrived in Poncha Springs, and Elevation Beer Company, from an old Morton salt mine near Chicago.

While many breweries that dabble in barrel-aged beers do so as a side project to their everyday beers, it's a major focus at Elevation, although the brewery also produces a variety of more mainstream beer styles. When I visited just a few months after its opening, Elevation had amassed a collection of forty wine and spirits barrels and was expecting to acquire another fifty in upcoming months.

Elevation classifies its beers using a scheme borrowed from the ski industry's system of rating ski trails according to level of difficulty. The blue square series includes everyday beers such as an IPA and porter. These are flavorful beers but moderate in their intensity and alcoholic strength. The black diamond series includes beers with more complexity and bolder flavors such as a Belgian dark strong ale and double IPA. The double black diamond series includes all of the barrel-aged beers.

In its short existence, Elevation Beer Company has been well-received both by Colorado's craft beer community and by its tiny hometown. "I think we're the first brewery in Poncha Springs," Bustamante stated. "I think we're the first anything in Poncha Springs."

Elevation Beer Company

Opened: May 2012.

Owners: Xandy Bustamate, Sheila Bustamate, Carlin Walsh, Christian Koch.

Head brewer: Christian Koch.

Potential annual capacity: 3,000 barrels.

Hours: Summer hours: Monday through Friday, 2 p.m. to 8 p.m.; Saturday and Sunday, noon to 8 p.m. Winter hours may vary.

Tours: Saturday at 1 p.m., 3 p.m., and 5 p.m. or by appointment.

Take-out beer: 40-ounce and 64-ounce growlers, 16-ounce bottles, 750 ml bottles and kegs.

Food: Chips and salsa, pizza delivery, or bring your own food.

Extras: Monthly art shows with local artists. First Firkin Friday every month. Trivia night every last Thursday of the month. Occasional live music. AHA member deals participant.

Parking: On-site lot.

Area attractions: See Amícas on page 229.

Other area beer sites: See Amícas on page 229.

Gore Range Brewery

0105 Edwards Village Boulevard,
Building H, Edwards, CO 81632
(970) 926-BREW (2739)
www.gorerangebrewery.com

The Gore Range Mountains were named for Sir St. George Gore, an Irish aristocrat who led a hunting party through central Colorado in the mid-1800s. His wilderness supplies included a brass bed, a bathtub, and a commode with a fur-lined seat. Each night, he sipped French wine and dined on an iron table topped with a lace tablecloth and set with fine silver and crystal.

Things are a bit more casual at the Gore Range Brewery. The brewpub has been a fixture in Edwards, fourteen miles from Vail, since 1997. In contrast to the largely upscale local dining scene catering to well-heeled visitors to the nearby resorts of Vail and Beaver Creek, Gore Range offers a casual and affordable dining experience appealing to a local clientele and families.

The brewpub resides in a modern-looking structure of brick and glass. The interior has a contemporary western feel. The rectangular bar sits in the middle of the space with dining areas on either side. There's a spacious patio behind the building enclosed by a wall of boulders, mimicking the nearby mountains. The brewhouse sits in a glass enclosure flooded with natural light.

In 2011, the business was purchased by chef Pascal Coudouy, whose culinary journey has included stints at fine restaurants in Paris and New York City. Before assuming ownership of the Gore Range Brewery, the mustachioed Frenchman was executive chef at the luxe Park Hyatt in nearby Beaver Creek.

The food at Gore Range is described as "brewpub fare with a twist." Wood-fired pizzas and other brewpub favorites have been upgraded with gourmet touches. The daily specials often include European-inspired dishes such as house-made country pate, charcuterie with cheeses, and homemade sausages.

When I first entered the building for a weekday visit, I was hit with the appetizing aroma of smoky barbecue. I arrived during happy hour to find the

Year-round beers: GRB Lager, Powder Day Pale Ale, Fly Fisher Red Ale.

The Pick: The Powder Day Pale Ale has a nice progression of up-front malt with hops soon to follow. If finishes crisp and dry.

place bustling with a mostly local clientele. Gore Range regulars have been very receptive to the menu changes as well as to the expanded beer offerings that now include more rotating specialty beers in addition to a few time-tested selections.

The brewing operations are headed by longtime employee Jeremy Pluck. Like many professional craft brewers, Pluck started out as a homebrewer while attending college. Unlike many brewers, he earned a degree in aerospace engineering. Upon graduating, he found the aerospace industry in decline and job prospects grim. In 1994, he read an article about the brewing program at UC Davis. When he discovered that the employment rate among graduates was 100 percent, he enrolled.

He worked at a small California brewpub for a few years. While attending the Craft Brewers Conference in 1997, a job listing for a planned brewpub caught his eye. "Brew beer in Vail, Colorado," it read. He followed up, landed the job, and is the only brewer the sixteen-plus-year-old Gore Range Brewery has ever had.

Pluck has reduced the brewpub's core offerings to three beers—a light lager, a pale ale, and a red ale—freeing up tap handles for a greater variety of rotating styles. "We're going to play around with all kinds of things," he told me, rattling of a half-dozen beers he was planning to brew. True to his word, a selection of adventurous beers has been appearing at Gore Range including a Belgian brown ale, a chocolate stout, and a wine barrel-aged saison.

Gore Range Brewery

Opened: December 1997.
Owners: Pascal Coudouy.
Head brewer: Jeremy Pluck.
Potential annual capacity: 500 barrels.
Hours: Daily, 11:30 a.m. to 11 p.m. or later.
Tours: On request.
Take-out beer: Growlers and cans.
Food: Bar bites, wood-fired pizza, seafood, sandwiches, and a variety of entrées.
Extras: Music on the patio on Friday in the summer.
Parking: On-site lot.
Area attractions: See Crazy Mountain on page 241.
Other area beer sites: See Crazy Mountain on page 241.

Gunnison Brewery

138 North Main Street, Gunnison, CO 81230
(970) 641-BREW (2739) • www.gunnisonbrewery.com

Gunnison, the home of Gunnison Brewery, sits in a broad valley at an elevation of 7,700 feet. Unlike many high-elevation Colorado towns, Gunnison has the feel of a ranching community rather than a mountain town. Highway 50 runs through Gunnison, bringing in scores of tourists en route to and from the high peaks of the central Rockies to the east, and the San Juan Mountains and red rock desert to the west. The ski town of Crested Butte is thirty miles north of Gunnison.

The Gunnison Brewery sits on Main Street, just off the highway. From the street, the weathered wood exterior of the downtown brewpub would look right at home in a western gunslinger movie, if not for the heavily used bike rack on the sidewalk and neon sign in the front window. The interior has a much more contemporary look and feel. The walls are constructed of attractive blond wood, as are the tables and bar in the compact taproom. A display of colorful artwork by a local artist adds a cheery touch to the space. A long row of tap handles, mounted on a shelf above the bar, serves as additional ornamentation. In a back corner, the 2.5-barrel brewhouse is enclosed in a tiny room visible through several large windows.

Behind the building is a private patio. A brightly colored mural is painted on the outer wall of the neighboring building, which defines one side of the relaxed outdoor space. Patio tables with shade umbrellas attract summertime visitors. Outdoor heaters keep things comfortable on cool evenings.

The brewpub is owned and operated by Kevin and Lori Alexander, who opened the business in the summer of 2003. Kevin is the head brewer and a biology professor at Western State Colorado University, located in Gunnison. He's assisted in the brewhouse by Kevin Doherty, a chemistry major at the college. Lori, the "boss lady," handles the brewpub's business affairs.

The food menu offers a modest selection of finger foods, wraps, burgers, sandwiches, and tacos. There are three or four house beers available, but the only full-time beer is the Gunnison Pub Ale, an English-style

Year-round beers: Gunny Pub Ale.

amber ale. When I visited, there were two other selections, a ginger beer and a black IPA. The brewpub keeps a variety of guest beers available including two draught offerings and a half-dozen bottles. When I stopped by, the draught beers included the ubiquitous New Belgium Fat Tire, as well as an IPA from Ouray Brewing in southwest Colorado. The bottled offerings were an odd mix of several Colorado craft beers, an imported English stout, and several beers of no distinction from large corporate breweries.

Note: Gunnison Brewery has been for sale for quite some time. It's possible that when you visit, the brewpub may be under new ownership with a different focus on its food and beverage operations.

Gunnison Brewery

Opened: July 2003.

Owners: Lori and Kevin Alexander.

Head brewer: Kevin Alexander.

Hours: Summer: Monday through Saturday, 11 a.m. to close; Sunday, 4 p.m. to close; Winter: daily, 4 p.m. to close.

Tours: On request.

Take-out beer: Growlers and kegs.

Food: Snacks, wraps, sandwiches, and burgers.

Parking: On-street.

Area attractions: Blue Mesa Reservoir is eighteen miles away. Crested Butte Mountain Resort is thirty miles away.

Other area beer sites: The Last Chance (620 S. 9th St., 970-641-3335).

Library Sports Grille and Brewery

78491 U.S. Highway 40, Winter Park, CO 80482
(970) 726-7951

It shouldn't be surprising to find a college professor, even a retired professor, in the library. In the case of Mitch Kunce, the Library became a second career: he is the head brewer at Winter Park's Library Sports Grille and Brewery.

After teaching economics at the University of Wyoming for twenty years, Kunce retired from academia. Crunching numbers wasn't his only forte. "I was an avid homebrewer," he relates. "Almost an OCD homebrewer."

Following retirement, Kunce had planned to move back to Golden, Colorado, his former home. He got waylaid, however, when he was approached by the new owners of Laramie's Library Brewery. They asked him if he'd consider taking over the brewing position. "I was very reluctant. They drug me kicking and screaming," he joked. Eventually, he agreed. In 2011, an offshoot of the Laramie brewpub opened in a former steakhouse and brewery in Winter Park, Colorado. Kunce relocated to the resort community to run the new brewing operation.

The Winter Park Resort is Colorado's longest continually operating ski area, hosting skiers since 1939. With Denver only sixty-seven miles away, it's the closest major ski area to the state's Front Range population centers. Many native Coloradans learned to carve turns on the slopes of Winter Park.

The Library Sports Grille and Brewery has become a go-to spot for a casual meal and a quality pint or two. The brewpub is located in the town's commercial district, which is dispersed along Highway 40, the main thoroughfare through town. The brewery resides in a large modern structure with a steep-pitched roof designed to shed the 350-plus inches of snow that falls annually at Winter Park's 9,000-foot elevation.

The brewpub's interior is spacious and open, with a rectangular bar sitting in the middle. True to its sports bar designation, a cluster of flat-screens is suspended over the bar, broadcasting a variety of sporting events. The sports theme isn't

Year-round beers: Rattle-snake Rye Pale Ale, Big Nose Bitter, Hideaway Helles Bock, Hummer Honey Wheat, Winter Park Ale, Oats & Cream Stout, Pomegranate Blueberry.

The Pick: Oats & Cream is a sweet, chewy, full-bodied oatmeal milk stout. Think of it as comfort food in a glass.

overdone, however. There's plenty of opportunity to enjoy a meal without the distraction of an overhead video screen. During the day, the expansive dining area is bright and airy, filled with natural light from tall windows along several walls. Gamers head upstairs where a pair of billiard tables shares the space with a foosball table, a Skee-Ball machine, and a video game. There's a peaceful patio enclosed by plantings of spruce and aspen on one end of the building. There's a second outdoor seating area near the entrance with a few tables and benches.

Beyond the bar and down a few steps is the open brewhouse, its collection of stainless steel vessels kept spotless by the meticulous brewer. "I call it the pit," said Kunce of the inverted stage where he creates a lineup of quality American, English, and German-style ales and lagers in view of anyone who cares to peer down into his workspace.

One such spectator was an English visitor named Chris Bingham, who was on a ski vacation in Winter Park when he ventured into the Library for a drink. Bingham, the head brewer at a small brewery outside London, introduced himself to Kunce. After talking shop, the two decided to swap recipes. Bingham's Brickworks Bitter was brewed at the Library while a batch of the Library's Rattlesnake Rye Pale Ale was concocted at the Bingham's Brewery in England. Bingham reported that his version of the Rattlesnake Rye had a "distinctive bite."

Library Sports Grille and Brewery

Opened: July 2011.
Owners: Nate Jorgenson, Bryan Gay, Tonya Gay.
Head brewer: Mitch Kunce.
Potential annual capacity: 1,200 barrels.
Hours: Tuesday through Saturday, 11 a.m. to 2 a.m.; Sunday and Monday, 11 a.m. to midnight. Hours may be shorter in offseasons.
Tours: On request.
Take-out beer: Growlers.
Food: Burgers, sandwiches, pizza, steaks.
Extras: Occasional live music in summer months. Ask about homebrewer discounts.
Parking: On-site lot.
Area attractions: Winter Park Ski Resort, Devil's Thumb Ranch Resort & Spa (cross-country skiing, hiking), Granby Ranch (skiing, biking, golf), Rocky Mountain National Park.
Other area beer sites: Cheeky Monk Belgian Beer Cafe (130 Parry Peak Way at the base of Winter Park Resort, 970-726-6871), Heck's (at Devil's Thumb Ranch, 3530 County Road 83, Tabernash, 970-726-7013).

Mahogany Ridge Brewery & Grill

435 Lincoln Avenue, Steamboat Springs, CO 80487
(970) 879-3773
www.mahoganyridgesteamboat.com

Mahogany Ridge is a split-level restaurant with a split personality. On one level, it's a lively happy hour destination where locals and the après-ski crowd flock for one-dollar tapas and half-price drinks. On another level, literally, it's an upscale restaurant geared to vacationers seeking a fine-dining experience.

"We're more geared toward [being] a nice restaurant that happens to make its own beer versus a brewpub," explained Charlie Noble, who owns and operates Mahogany Ridge along with his wife, Nancy. The restaurant occupies the site of the former Steamboat Brewery & Tavern, which opened in 1992 and closed a decade later. In 2003, it reopened as Mahogany Ridge. Noble had been a brewer at the original brepub. Prior to his professional brewing career, he had extensive experience in the restaurant business.

The restaurant is located in downtown Steamboat Springs, near the intersection of Lincoln Avenue, Steamboat's main thoroughfare, and 5th Street. The Yampa River, popular for tubing and fly fishing, is two blocks away. The Steamboat ski resort, where the term "champagne powder" was coined, sits a few miles south of town. Trivia buffs might be interested to learn that Steamboat Springs has produced more Olympians than any other town in North America. While many Colorado mountain towns were born during the mining boom of the late 1800s, Steamboat's roots are in ranching. The community proudly retains its cowboy-town persona.

The interior of Mahogany Ridge is stylish and attractive, with an upscale contemporary feel. The bar area is on the lower level. The long wood-trimmed bar runs the length of the room. A half-dozen shiny serving tanks are framed by a row of windows behind the bar. A collection of brightly colored paintings stands out against the dark walls. A long communal table runs down the center of the room. High-tops provide additional seating.

Year-round beers: Alpenglow Amber Ale.

The Pick: Alpenglow Amber Ale is an easy-drinking, unassuming anytime beer with enough character to keep your interest without demanding your undivided attention.

The dining room is on the second level, a few steps up from the bar area. Cushioned wooden booths are arranged along the walls, while tables of varying configurations fill the interior space. The pale yellow walls create a warm, soothing ambience. An outdoor patio off the dining room is a comfortable place to enjoy a meal on a mild summer evening.

Expect an animated scene during happy hour. In addition to half-price drinks, you can select from a list of ten tapas-style plates for a dollar each. If you're craving chicken wings, the house version is dry-rubbed with Jamaican jerk spice. Other finger-food options include curry samosas, brie and mango phyllo cups, and house-smoked salmon tostadas.

The dual-personality dinner menu is divided between pub-style sandwiches and brewery plates on one side, and more adventurous "dipping entrées" on the other. The brewery plates include familiar brewpub fare such as ribs and fish-and-chips, along with unique offerings such as noodle bowls and southwestern duck confit pot pie. The dipping menu lists a variety of meats and seafood that can be accompanied by a long list of dipping sauces. Exotic meats, including elk and buffalo, are popular with visitors from distant regions seeking some Colorado flavor.

Mahogany Ridge keeps seven beers on tap, but only one full-time beer. The easy-drinking Alpenglow Amber Ale has been the house favorite for years. The remaining half-dozen taps rotate regularly among twenty or so house recipes. During my visit, the tap list included a cream ale, a Scottish ale, a brown ale, two pale ales (English and American), and a stout dispensed from a nitro tap.

Mahogany Ridge Brewery & Grill

Opened: March 2003.

Owners: Charlie and Nancy Noble.

Head brewer: Wolf Levenshtein.

Potential annual capacity: 1,000 barrels.

Hours: Opens daily at 4 p.m.

Tours: On request.

Take-out beer: Growlers.

Food: The brewery plates include pub standards such as burgers, sandwiches and fish-and-chips, plus noodle bowls and pasta. The dipping menu features a variety of meats, seafood, and tofu served with a choice of dipping sauce.

Extras: Live music on occasion.

Parking: On-street.

Area attractions: Steamboat Ski Resort. Strawberry Hot Springs (44200 County Rd. 36, 970-879-0342).

Moonlight Pizza & Brewpub

242 F Street, Salida, CO 81201
(719) 539-4277 • www.moonlightpizza.biz

The late beat poet Alan Ginsberg once said, "Follow your inner moonlight; don't hide the madness." Salida's Moonlight Pizza & Brewpub certainly follows its inner moonlight. The laid-back, folksy pizza joint has been serving up tasty pies, with just a touch of madness, since 2002. A brewery was added in late 2011. The Ginsberg quote is lettered on an eye-catching, multicolored art piece hanging prominently in the front window.

The restaurant sits on a corner lot in downtown Salida. The small one-story beige stucco building provides an odd contrast to the weathered two-story brick structures in Salida's downtown historic district. Two bike racks are located out front, providing parking for the locals' preferred mode of transport. A trio of decommissioned kayaks sits outside the entrance, their cockpits containing large flowerpots. There's a tiny bar toward the back. Beyond the bar, stuffed into a back corner, the 5-barrel brewhouse resides behind a wall of rusty corrugated metal. The ultra-casual, modestly sized dining room fits a half-dozen tables. You can dine al fresco in either of two outdoor patios. One is enclosed by a stucco wall while the larger one overlooks the street scene on F Street. Spontaneous acoustical music jams have been known to break out on the patio.

The food menu offers a few starters and salads, hot sandwiches, moonzones ("a lot like a calzone, only much huger") and, of course, pizza, which the adrenaline-charged local population and recreation-minded visitors have been swooning about for years. The dough used for the pizza, calzones, and sandwich bread is made fresh in-house daily.

The pizza is of the thick-crust variety in a style described by the menu as "fancy schmancy pizza." While you can get a pie with standard toppings at Moonlight, the more exotic combinations have garnered legions of devout fans. The Mirkwood (from Middle Oven), for example, is topped with chicken, onion, green chili, and cream cheese. While the

Year-round beers: Moon-Lite Cream Ale plus five rotating taps that usually include an IPA and a porter.

The Pick: MoonLite Cream Ale won't scare away those who drink mass-produced light lagers. A subtly sweet aroma leads to a mild grainy flavor finishing with the slightest whisper of hops.

trio of meats on the carnivore-friendly Caveman may not be exotic, according to the menu, "this pie has turned local yoga instructors into snarling savages (in capri pants)." Pizza from Moonlight also possesses "super power," according to the business sign out front.

Drinks are dispensed from a row of ten taps. The tap handles are playfully hand-labeled in chalk with the name of their assigned beverages. One is devoted to the ultra-light Moonlite Cream Ale. An IPA and a porter are usually available. There are three other house beers. Their style is determined by "whatever we feel like brewing that day," according to head brewer and co-owner Scott Bouldin. The remaining four handles are reserved for homemade sodas including vanilla creme, root beer, limeade, and a spicy ginger ale. The bar also serves mixed drinks using spirits produced in Colorado distilleries. The brewery also keeps things local, using malt from Colorado Malting Company, located eighty miles away in Alamosa.

Though plenty of tourists find their way to the brewpub in the summer months, Moonlight, at its core, is a locals' place. The business is deeply entrenched in the local community and shows its commitment by donating 10 percent of its sales each Monday "to programs in Salida we believe make this town amazing," according to the website. In an effort to reduce waste, the restaurant doesn't supply either straws or coasters. I'm sure Alan Ginsberg would have approved.

Moonlight Pizza & Brewpub

Opened: Pizzeria opened in 1992. In current location since 2002. Brewery added November 2011.

Owners: Scott and Kim Bouldin, Bryan Ward, Kyle Buskist, and Brenna Eaker.

Head brewer: Scott Bouldin.

Potential annual capacity: 500 barrels.

Hours: Summer hours: Sunday through Thursday, 11 a.m. to 9 p.m.; Friday and Saturday, 11 a.m. to 10 p.m. Closes one hour earlier in winter.

Tours: On request.

Take-out beer: Growlers and kegs.

Food: "Fancy Schmancy Pizza," "Moonzones," "Hot Sammies," and a variety of homemade sodas.

Extras: Occasional live music including impromptu jams on the patio.

Parking: Small lot and street parking.

Area attractions: See Amícas on page 229.

Other area beer sites: See Amícas on page 229.

Pug Ryan's Steakhouse & Brewery

104 Village Place, Dillon, CO 80435
(970) 468-2145 • www.pugryans.com

The motto of Pug Ryan's Steakhouse & Brewery is "Brewed for the outlaw in you." I suspect that when you visit this enjoyable mountain brewpub, you'll fare better than the outlaw for which it is named. In 1898, Pug Ryan and his gang robbed the Denver Hotel in Breckenridge, stealing valuables from prominent citizens who were gambling at the time. He was captured four years later, but escaped confinement through a sewer pipe. He was arrested soon after in the town of Cripple Creek and died in prison years later.

Pug Ryan's Steakhouse opened in 1975, making it one of the oldest continuously operating businesses covered in this book. In 1996, a brewery was added to the well-established eatery. Today, Pug's is equally suited to a casual meal, a dinner of substance, or a pint or two of exceptional beer.

The brewpub resides in the town of Dillon, a few blocks from the shores of Lake Dillon. The ski resort of Keystone is eight miles away, and the Arapahoe Basin ski area is a few miles beyond that. Not surprisingly, Pug's sees its biggest crowds during the peak of ski season and in the summer months when hikers, mountain bikers, campers, boaters, and city dwellers descend on Summit County for some high-elevation recreation.

Despite the seasonal upsurge in visitors, Pug's is first and foremost a locals' place. "Our local crowd is what keeps us going. We have a very loyal local following," said Chris Caldwell, Pug Ryan's amiable sales and marketing guy. He goes on to explain that many pub regulars arrived in the area to be ski bums years ago and never left. "Winters bring you here. Summers keep you here," he said, echoing a sentiment you hear often in Colorado's mountain towns.

Pug's is decked out in a rustic, mountain cabin theme. The walls are covered with a collection of vintage skis, sleds, toboggans, snowshoes, mining paraphernalia, and various other artifacts

Year-round beers: Morning Wood Wheat, Over the Rail Pale Ale, Scottish Ale, Peacemaker Pilsner, Vanilla Stout, Hideout Helles Bock, Dunkel.

The Pick: The Peacemaker Pilsner is a wonderful example of this Bohemian classic. It's pale-colored, clean and crisp, with a pleasantly sweet greeting and a dry farewell that is accented with a generous dose of noble hops.

associated with the mountain lifestyle of an earlier era. The interior's wooden bar, dark wood beams, and antler chandeliers add to the rustic flavor.

Large windows in the dining room feature views of Lake Dillon and the white-capped mountains beyond. A small patio runs the length of the dining room. A larger deck near the entrance adds more outdoor seating options with impressive views of the Tenmile and Gore Range Mountains.

Pug Ryan's menu combines steakhouse staples with more casual pub fare such as burgers, sandwiches, and flatbread pizzas. The brewpub has a well-deserved reputation for producing clean, consistent, and stylistically accurate beers of high quality.

The brewhouse is headed by longtime employee Dave Simmons, who started as an assistant brewer when the steakhouse added the brewery in the mid-nineties. He eventually assumed the head brewer position. In 2012, Ed Canty, a veteran of both the Colorado and Florida craft beer scenes, joined Pug's brew crew.

Simmons's preference for German-style lagers is evident in the brewpub's full-time lineup, which includes a Bohemian pilsner, a helles bock, and a dunkel. Other full-time beers include an American-style wheat ale, a Scottish ale, a vanilla stout, and a pale ale. While there's no house IPA, the Over the Rail Pale Ale is well fortified with spicy hops.

During my visit, I sampled a whiskey barrel-aged version of the vanilla stout, which was a great treat, and a saison that hit all the right notes. The brewery has been awarded six medals at the Great American Beer Festival, with the pilsner a three-time GABF award winner.

Pug Ryan's Steakhouse & Brewery

Opened: Restaurant opened in 1975. Brewery added in 1996.

Owners: Travis and Annie Holton (since 1986).

Head brewer: Dave Simmons.

Potential annual capacity: 5,000 barrels.

Hours: Summer hours (beginning June 1): daily, 11:30 a.m. to 2 a.m. Winter hours: Monday through Friday, 3 p.m. to 2 a.m.; Saturday and Sunday, 11:30 a.m. to 2 a.m.

Tours: On request when brewer is available. Self-guided tours all other times.

Take-out beer: Growlers, cans, and kegs.

Food: A mix of American pub fare and steakhouse entrées.

Extras: Live music on Friday or Saturday in summer.

Parking: On-street and nearby lots, all free.

Area attractions: See Dillon Dam on page 243.

Other area beer sites: See Dillon Dam on page 243.

Tommyknocker Brewery & Pub

1401 Miner Street, Idaho Springs, CO 80452
(303) 567-2688 • www.tommyknocker.com

In January 1859, a gold nugget was found at the confluence of Chicago Creek and Clear Creek in the mountains west of Denver in what is now the town of Idaho Springs. It was Colorado's first significant gold discovery. Scores of prospectors soon descended on the area. For years, Clear Creek County was a frenzy of mining activity.

In the 1860s, miners from Cornwall, England, immigrated to Colorado to work the mines. They brought with them tales of elf-like characters who lived in mines. The mischievous creatures, called Tommyknockers, were seldom seen, but their antics, such as stealing tools, dumping lunch buckets, and snuffing out candles, were well known. Tommyknockers were said to have saved many a miner from impending danger. The miners would sometimes leave food offerings for the Tommyknockers, believing they would be led to rich veins of ore as a reward.

In December 1994, Tommyknocker Brewery & Pub opened in Idaho Springs less than a half mile from the site of the original gold discovery of 1859. Idaho Springs sits alongside Interstate 70, thirty miles west of downtown Denver and only twenty-five miles from the Loveland Ski Resort. The brewpub resides in a historic building dating from the late 1800s. The sprawling restaurant and brewery is a hugely popular meal and beverage stop for motoring tourists, skiers, mountain travelers returning from high country outings, and river rafters concluding a day of white-water adventure on nearby Clear Creek.

The brewpub was the concept of Tim Lenahan and Charlie Sturdavant. Both had been involved in opening other early Colorado breweries. (Sturdavant is the founder of Golden City Brewery.) While most brewpubs primarily produce beer for consumption on-site, Tommyknocker beers are packaged and distributed to more than twenty states from coast to coast. The brewpub is one of the largest in the state, with seating for more than

Year-round beers: Maple Nut Brown, Jack Whacker Wheat Ale, Alpine Glacier Pilsner, Pick Axe IPA, Butt Head Bock, Vienna Amber Lager, Imperial Nut Brown Ale, Hop Strike Black IPA, Rye Porter, Black Powder Stout.

The Pick: Butt Head Bock, a well-fortified 8 percent ABV doppelbock, is malty but not cloyingly sweet, with just enough hops to cleanse your palate for the next sip.

three hundred guests. Even so, there can be a wait for tables during peak times.

The restaurant attracts a steady influx of return visitors with a well-rounded menu of pub-style comfort food. The Friday night all-you-can-eat fish fry sees familiar faces week after week. There are a half-dozen variations of buffalo burgers. In fact, the brewpub is the second-largest seller of buffalo in Colorado.

The bar area resides alongside the open brewhouse, placing pub visitors in the midst of the brewing activities. Beer production is under the direction of longtime employee Steve Indrehus, who has been with the brewery since 1996. Over that span, Tommyknocker beers have accrued an impressive twenty-one combined Great American Beer Festival and World Beer Cup medals. Butt Head Bock, a smooth, malty, and deceptively potent doppelbock, has won gold medals at both the GABF and WBC. The medal collection is prominently displayed in the bar area.

The brewery is not content to rest on its laurels, as new seasonal and specialty beers continue to be introduced into the expansive beer portfolio. Head brewer Eric Rode said he was encouraged to "think outside the patch" to create the Small Patch Pumpkin Ale, a popular fall seasonal brown ale flavored with pumpkin, spices, and molasses.

Tommyknocker is tremendously popular with families. Four sodas—root beer, orange crème, strawberry crème, and almond crème—are made in-house with organic flavors and are available in bottles. For cocktail drinkers, the bar serves Colorado-produced spirits in support of the state's thriving craft spirits industry.

Tommyknocker Brewery & Pub

Opened: December 1994.
Owners: Thirty-member ownership group.
Head brewer: Eric Rode.
Director of Operations: Steve Indrehus.
Potential annual capacity: 20,000 barrels.
Hours: Daily, 11 a.m. to 10 p.m.
Tours: On request.
Take-out beer: Growlers, six-packs, and kegs.
Food: Well-rounded menu of American pub fare.
Extras: AHA member deals program participant.
Parking: Free street parking and free city lots nearby.
Area attractions: Argo Gold Mill and Museum (303-567-2421).
Other area beer sites: The Rathskeller at Loveland Ski Resort (winter only).

Southwest Colorado

Southwest Colorado is a rewarding part of the state to explore if you're a beer traveler seeking awesome scenery, unlimited outdoor recreation, and numerous brewery stops. The region is cut off from points east by the imposing San Juan Mountains, often referred to as the "American Alps." For our beer-intensive purposes, the area is bordered by the small town of Ridgeway to the north, Utah to the west, New Mexico to the south, and Wolf Creek Pass to the east. I've actually stretched my own boundaries a bit to include two towns farther east—Del Norte and Alamosa—in this section, because they don't fit well anywhere else and are frequented by travelers en route to or from the southwest part of the state.

To fully experience the best of southwest Colorado, bring along your outdoor gear of choice, be it a bicycle or a fly rod or just a pair of hiking shoes and a camera. Take your time exploring, stop often, walk around the old mining towns, and get acquainted with the locals at the numerous laid-back beer stops that proliferate in this extraordinarily beautiful part of Colorado.

One thing that makes this part of the state especially desirable for leisurely beer-themed travel is that thirteen of the sixteen breweries included in this section reside on or near the **San Juan Skyway**. The Skyway is a 230-mile scenic loop that traverses high mountain passes and travels through historic Victorian towns born of the mining boom of the late 1800s.

The Skyway is anchored on the south by Durango, the largest town in this corner of the state and one of my favorite Colorado beer towns. The community of 17,000 sports five brewing businesses, each with its own character and appeal. In a cooperative spirit that typifies the Colorado craft beer scene, the Durango breweries have banded together to create the Bootleggers Society, an association that facilitates a team-based approach to raising and distributing funds to charitable causes in the community.

In addition to Durango's hometown breweries, other local beer destinations you may want to check out include:

El Moro Spirits and Tavern (945 Main Ave., 970-259-5555)

El Rancho Tavern (975 Main Ave., 970-259-8111)

Lady Falconburgh's (640 Main Ave., 970 382-9664)

Purgy's (1 Skier Pl. at Durango Mountain Resort, 970-247-9000)

Tourists descend on Durango in the warm-weather months to ride the historic **Durango & Silverton Narrow Gauge Railroad** (888-872-4607). The coal-fired, steam-powered train takes passengers through the mountains on a forty-five-mile journey to the old mining town of Silverton. The rail line was completed in 1882, and the train has been running continuously ever since.

The Durango area is a haven for outdoor recreation including road and mountain biking, hiking, white-water rafting, and fly fishing. For winter sports enthusiasts, Durango is a convenient base camp for visits to **Durango Mountain Resort**, twenty-seven miles north of town. Durango is also the eastern gateway to the incredible cliff dwellings of **Mesa Verde National Park**, about forty-five miles away.

Cortez is the closest town to the west side of Mesa Verde. The area around Cortez is said to have the highest concentration of archeological sites in the country. Dolores is a short distance north of Cortez and a good place for a dinner stop at the friendly Dolores River Brewery. If you can time your visit to include a live music performance at this under-the-radar brewpub, all the better.

The resort town of Telluride is a necessary stop for a few hours, or better yet, a few days. The historic community has a lovingly preserved Victorian downtown and the most jaw-dropping mountain scenery from the center of town of any place you're likely to ever visit. Budget travelers can pitch a tent in **Telluride Town Park**, a short walk from downtown, except during certain festival weekends. The free gondola runs throughout summer and winter and transports you over the slopes of **Telluride Ski Resort** to the ski village high above town. Telluride hosts a near nonstop lineup of festivals throughout the warm-weather months. World-class festivals featuring various musical genres, yoga, mushrooms, and film fill the weekend calendar. My favorite is the stellar ***Blues & Brews Festival***, which provides a great excuse for a September getaway.

The northern apex of the Skyway is in the small, agreeable community of Ridgway, where you'll find top-notch pizza and a proper pint at the Colorado Boy Pub & Brewery. The eighty-mile drive from Ridgway to Durango along the eastern section of the Skyway passes through the old mining outposts of Ouray (pronounced U-ray) and Silverton. The remnants of the area's intensive mining activity are much in evidence along this high-elevation stretch of highway. The climb out of Ouray up 11,000-foot Red Mountain Pass is a true white-knuckle experience. The narrow, twisty road features sheer drop-offs and no guard rails. You can decompress in Silverton with a stop at the locals-favorite Avalanche Brewing Company.

Hopefully, your southwest Colorado visit will take you through Pagosa Springs, an hour east of Durango. The town's popular riverside hot springs pools are among the nicest developed natural hot springs in the state. The lovely beer garden at Pagosa Brewing is not to be missed. A second Pagosa Springs brewery opened too recently to be covered in this book: Riff Raff Brewing was opened by a friend and former member of my Boulder homebrew club, Hop Barley & the Alers. I haven't had a chance to visit, but initial reports are quite favorable.

East of Pagosa is Wolf Creek Pass, which descends into the vast San Luis Valley and the communities of Del Norte and Alamosa, both boasting hometown breweries.

Avalanche Brewing Company

1067 Blair Street, Silverton, CO 81433
(970) 387-5282
www.avalanchebrewing.com

Silverton is nestled high in the San Juan Mountains at an elevation of 9,300 feet. You arrive in the tiny enclave either by driving north from Durango over Coal Bank and Molas Passes (10,640 feet and 10,970 feet, respectively) or by driving south from Ouray over Red Mountain Pass (11,018 feet). The drive over Red Mountain Pass is not for the faint of heart. The windy, narrow, two-lane road has steep drop-offs and an absence of guard rails, leaving little margin for error.

Silverton has six hundred residents and a main street that has maintained an authentic Old West feel, though most of the restored buildings now house tourist-intensive shops and cafes. In the summer months, the historic Durango & Silverton Narrow Gauge Railroad deposits scores of camera-wielding tourists on the town for several hours each afternoon. The Silverton Mountain ski area is nearby and is regarded as one of Colorado's most challenging.

The Avalanche has existed under a variety of owners since 1992. Since 2010, it's been under the guidance of owner-brewer Austin Lashley. Lashley got hooked on homebrewing at an early age while attending high school in Durango. After college, he got his first brewery job in the packaging room of Ska Brewing before relocating to Alaska. While he was away, his family purchased the Avalanche. Lashley returned to Colorado to run the restaurant. Among the major changes he implemented was the addition of a 7-barrel brewing system in a neighboring building.

In a town where nearly every business is tourist-dependent, Avalanche Brewing Company marches to a different beat as the place where locals congregate for morning coffee, lunchtime sandwiches, and fresh beer. The cafe sits on a corner lot, a block from Silverton's main road. It's hard to miss the bright purple building, which has red and yellow trim and a pair of hitching posts out front.

Year-round beers: White-Out Wit, Treasure Mountain Pale Ale, Sultan IPA, Pride of the West Porter.

The Pick: The White-Out Wit is complex, approachable, and refreshing with a spicy, citrusy character.

A few tables sit on the small, partially covered front deck facing 13,700-foot Kendall Mountain. Inside, a unique copper-topped bar sits atop a base of weathered wood and corrugated metal. Five wooden bar stools are supported on legs of small-diameter tree trunks. On a wall in the adjacent dining area is mounted the sawed-off front portion of a red bicycle. A plaque identifies it as "Ole Red, Faithful Companion across two continents," and "Winner, Tour de Franzia, 2007." Apparently, the Tour de Franzia is an event involving both biking and drinking boxed wine in some quantity.

I arrived early for my meeting with the owner-brewer. While I waited, a personable bartender sporting an unexpected Texas drawl offered samples of the café's rich homemade soups and dangerously delicious pecan and lemon bars. When Lashley arrived, he explained that he was currently producing four beers: a pale ale, an IPA, a porter, and a witbier. The most popular is the White-Out Wit, a Belgian-inspired wheat ale flavored with grains of paradise, fresh orange peel, coriander, and chamomile. It's fermented with a saison yeast, adding complexity to the spicy, refreshing brew.

All the food at Avalanche is made from scratch. "The baked goods are mostly my mother's recipes," Lashley explained. "Especially the decadent ones. The healthier ones are usually my recipes." To meet the needs of the many customers who are outdoor adventurers, there is an emphasis on producing portable food that can be taken on a hike, bike ride, or ski outing. "We couldn't sell a slice of pie to save our lives but we can sell a lot of pecan bars," said Lashley.

Avalanche Brewing Company

Opened: Restaurant opened in 1992. Under current ownership since 2010.

Owner and head brewer: Austin Lashley.

Potential annual capacity: 200 barrels.

Hours: Summer: Thursday through Monday, 7 a.m. to 9 p.m.; Tuesday and Wednesday, 7 a.m. to 3 p.m. Winter: Thursday through Monday, 7 a.m. to 11 a.m. and 3 p.m. to 9 p.m.; Tuesday and Wednesday, 7 a.m. to 11 a.m.

Tours: On request.

Take-out beer: Growlers and kegs.

Food: Baked goods, breakfast burritos, sandwiches, and wraps. Pizza after 3 p.m.

Extras: Trivia on Monday. Homestyle family dinners on Friday. Free beer sampler for homebrewers.

Parking: Free on-street parking.

Area attractions: Durango & Silverton Narrow Gauge Railroad (888-872-4607). Silverton Mountain Ski Area.

Brew Pub & Kitchen

117 West College Drive, Durango, CO 81301
(970) 259-5959 • www.brewpubkitchen.com

When I visited Durango's Brew Pub & Kitchen, I greatly enjoyed getting to know Bruno, Betty, Corey, Cid, and Cyril. My five new acquaintances were, of course, the five house beers. The brewpub gives all its beers people names. It's a unique touch, one of many in the stylish restaurant and brewery.

Brew is well-situated in downtown Durango, just off Main Avenue, Durango's main drag. The interior of the single-story brick structure is an attractive space with an open, uncluttered appearance. A glass-paned garage door opens to the sidewalk. The long irregular-shaped bar sits atop a visually stunning base of multihued wooden strips. A collection of landscape photos on the mustard and rust-colored walls adds to the room's tasteful appeal. The brewhouse sits in the back corner, enclosed in glass.

The brewpub is the creation of Erik Maxson and his wife, Lainie. Maxson broke into the brewing biz in 1996 at the Phantom Canyon brewpub in Colorado Springs. A few years later, he moved to Durango with aspirations of becoming a ski bum. He landed a job at Carver Brewing, eventually becoming head brewer. In 2012, he left to begin the process of creating a new brewpub. Brew Pub & Kitchen opened in early 2013.

Maxson takes a unique approach to beer and brewing. "I wanted to remove the rainbow of tap offerings," he explained. "A yellow beer, a red beer, a brown beer, a black beer, are great for people who want to pick a color to drink by. But they don't really talk about what the beer is about. When you say I drink red beers, is it a lager? Is it an ale? Is it hoppy? Is it malty? The color tells you nothing about that. I wanted to bring ingredients forward. What makes a great Märzen is the malt. What makes a great hefeweizen is the yeast. What makes a great pale ale is the hops."

Like many brewers, Maxson brews a wide range of styles. But unlike other brewers, he classifies them by their primary flavor component

Year-round beers: No year-round beers, but always beers in four categories: Malt, Hops, Yeast, and Session.

The Pick: Fine-tune your palate with a sampler tray, then follow up with whatever strikes the right chord.

rather than by color. All beers are created to fit one of four categories: malt, hops, yeast, and session. Styles vary from batch to batch, but each new brew emphasizes one of the primary brewing ingredients (except water), or is a session (low-alcohol) beer. Beer color has no relevance in the classification scheme, as beers of any color can fit in any of the categories. "Hopefully, it allows people to step out of their comfort zone a little bit," said Maxson. "We had a sessionable beer that was a brown ale. I can't believe the positive response that I got from people who swore they don't drink dark beers."

Of course, not all beer styles fit nicely into this scheme. To fill in the gaps, Brew offers an assortment of mostly local guest taps. If you just want to enjoy a beer or two without thinking about it too much, no worries. Maxson's beers are excellent, with clean, distinct tastes that successfully highlight their intended flavors while maintaining a balance that keeps them interesting and drinkable.

The same could be said for the tasty salads, small plates, and entrées coming from the kitchen. "I don't have anything against spinach-artichoke dip, but I don't think the world needs another spinach-artichoke dip," Maxson said of the menu. Among the small-plate selections are fries with gravy, hand-pulled mozzarella, and delicious shishito peppers. Entrées range from sandwiches to fried chicken to whole-roasted cauliflower.

Brew Pub & Kitchen

Opened: March 2013.

Owners: Erik and Lainie Maxson.

Head brewer: Erik Maxson.

Potential annual capacity: 600 barrels.

Hours: Tuesday through Sunday, noon to close.

Tours: Saturday at 3 p.m. or on request.

Take-out beer: Growlers and kegs.

Food: Interesting small plates, salads, sandwiches, and assorted entrées.

Parking: Street parking and nearby lots are free at night.

Carver Brewing Company

1022 Main Avenue, Durango, CO 81301
(970) 259-2545 • www.carverbrewing.com

The first thing you should know about Durango's Carver Brewing Company is that it was the first of the town's five breweries. In fact, Carver was the first brewery to open in the Four Corners region after Prohibition. Carver boasts other firsts as well. The restaurant-turned-brewpub was Durango's first coffee shop, first non-smoking bar, and first green-powered restaurant. For many, it's the first stop of the day. Remaining true to its coffee shop roots, Carver serves breakfast daily. The brewpub's hearty breakfasts are legendary in Durango. "You can get a great beer after seven a.m., too," jokes co-owner and manager Michael Hurst.

The brewpub holds down a prime Main Avenue location in downtown Durango, just as it has since 1986, when brothers Bill and Jim Carver opened Carvers Bakery/Café serving breakfast and lunch. Bill was a homebrewer and had thoughts about opening a brewery, a novel concept in the mid-1980s. At the time, Boulder Beer was the only operating microbrewery in the state. The cafe added a brewery two years later, just a month after John Hickenlooper opened Wynkoop Brewing Company in Denver, the state's first brewpub. With the new brewery in place, the business was renamed Carver Brewing Company. Demand for fresh, locally produced beer was brisk. With a need to expand the brewing operation, the baking operation was eventually phased out and the brewery was relocated to the former bakery.

Carver resides in a building that once housed the local newspaper. Legend has it that the printing press is buried in concrete underneath the floor. Given the building's modest storefront, the interior is deceptively large. The dining room maintains its original coffee shop character. A few high-tops sit along the front wall, with tall windows overlooking the busy street scene on Main Avenue. A cruiser bike is suspended from the ceiling. The bar, with seating for eight, is in the front

Year-round beers: Lightner Creek Lager, Old Oak Amber Ale, Colorado Trail Nut Brown Ale, Jack Rabbit Pale Ale, Iron Horse Oatmeal Stout, and Celebrated Raspberry Wheat.

The Pick: Jack Rabbit Pale Ale introduces itself with a hop theme that stays a short step ahead of a malty undercurrent. It finishes with a bitter kiss—not a punch—that invites you back for another visit.

section of the long dining area, which contains a mix of booth and table seating.

There's a second bar area in the back of the building, with additional bar and table seating. A large window behind the bar looks into the brewery. Adjacent to the backroom is a leafy patio that's among the nicest outdoor dining spots in town.

Jeff Albarella runs Carver's brewing operation. The former home-brewer joined Carver in 2009 as an assistant brewer after completing the Siebel Institute brewing program. When former head brewer Erik Maxson left to open his own Durango brewpub, Albarella stepped into the head brewing position.

While Carver's time-tested portfolio of six full-time beers remains intact, Albarella has instituted some changes to the brewpub's specialty offerings. A rotating selection of Belgian-style beers has been added, and the selection of hoppy beers has increased. Both updates have been well-received by Durango's knowledgeable and adventurous beer enthusiasts. Despite Durango's huge influx of summer visitors, keeping the local population happy is Carver's main priority.

"Our locals are our bread and butter," stated Hurst. "That's what keeps this place running." He described Carver's clientele as "a microcosm of the whole community." "At one table you have some guys who just got out of jail. The next table over is the attorneys who prosecuted them," he joked.

Despite its longevity, western Colorado's oldest brewing company has hardly been resting on its laurels. In 2008, after Carver installed a solar hot-water system that was Durango's largest at the time, the brewpub was named Green Business of the Year by the local chamber of commerce. At the 2013 Great American Beer Festival, Carver captured a gold medal for its Munich Dunkel.

Carver Brewing Company

Opened: Restaurant opened in 1986. Brewery added in 1988.

Owners: Jim and Bill Carver, Michael Hurst, Dave Cuntz.

Head brewer: Jeff Albarella.

Potential annual capacity: 1,000 barrels.

Hours: Daily, 6:30 a.m. to 10:30 p.m.

Tours: Ask on arrival.

Take-out beer: Growlers.

Food: Great breakfasts. Burgers, sandwiches, pasta, and dinner entrées after 5 p.m.

Parking: On-street metered parking.

Colorado Boy Pub & Brewery

602 Clinton Street, Ridgway, CO 81432
(970) 626-5333 • www.coloradoboy.com

If Colorado Boy Pub & Brewery has the intimate, welcoming feel of a small British pub, it's no accident. The inspiration for the brewpub came while Tom Hennessy and his wife, Sandy, were traveling in Scotland. "One night, it was raining outside," Tom recalled. "We went into this little pub. I ordered the steak-and-ale pie and a cask bitter. The combination of the atmosphere, the wet cold climate, that cask ale, and that pie. I almost had tears in my eyes, it was so good." He thought a small, intimate pub could be successful in tiny Ridgway, where he and his wife were living. Colorado Boy came into existence in 2008.

The Hennessys were no strangers to breweries and brewpubs. In 1993, while operating a pizza restaurant in New Mexico called Il Vicino, Hennessy fabricated an inexpensive brewing system composed largely of used dairy equipment. The next year, he moved to Salida, Colorado, and did the same thing for a new branch of Il Vicino. As a lark, he made a how-to video of the process of constructing a small commercial brewery that would cost far less than the purchase of a turnkey system. He called it Frankenbrew.

The concept has been adopted by scores of fledgling breweries throughout Colorado and beyond. In addition, Hennessy offers monthly brewery immersion classes in which prospective brewery entrepreneurs travel to Ridgway for first-hand instruction on the many aspects of operating a brewery. People from around the country, and several foreign countries, have taken the class.

Ridgway sits at the northern apex of the San Juan Skyway, a 230-mile scenic driving loop that passes through old Victorian mining towns and over 10,000-foot mountain passes in the awesome San Juan Mountains of southwestern Colorado. Ridgway is a quiet town of less than 1,000 residents, but there's more to the town than first meets the eye.

The 1969 movie *True Grit*, starring John Wayne, was filmed here. The actor Dennis Weaver, who

Year-round beers: Irish Ale, IPA, and a cask ale. An English pub ale and a blonde or a Dortmunder are often available.

The Pick: Treat yourself to whichever cask-conditioned beer is on hand and enjoy the nuances of a well-made session beer served in a traditional manner.

starred in the TV shows *Gunsmoke* and *McCloud*, chose Ridgway for the site of his off-the-grid "earthship." Ralph Lauren has an expansive ranch just outside of town. Across the street from the brewpub is a highly specialized company that manufactures the statuettes handed out each year at the Grammy awards.

Colorado Boy was named after an old mine in nearby Ouray. (Other mines in the area have names such as Yankee Boy, Tom Boy, Buffalo Boy, and Yankee Girl.) The brewpub resides in a wedge-shaped brick building dating from 1915. The vibe is warm and inviting. The interior is quite small, but high ceilings and tall windows prevent it from feeling cramped. There are many contemporary upgrades with just a few hints of the building's advanced age. The wooden bar, inlaid with granite tiles, seats six. Brewing vessels are tucked into a corner. Tall, skinny fermentation tanks, typical of the Frankenbrew system, maximize the limited floor space.

Foodwise, Colorado Boy does a few things well rather than trying to be all things to all people. There are several salad selections and a choice of ten varieties of pizza, including a Nutella dessert pizza. Gluten-free crust is available. The food is delicious.

The house beers are approachable, flavorsome, and satisfying, without demanding your undivided attention. The full-time beers include an Irish ale and an IPA. The Irish Ale was a 2013 Great American Beer Festival silver medal winner. An English pub ale, and a blonde ale or Dortmunder lager, are often available. There's always a cask-conditioned ale on hand, dispensed from a traditional British beer engine. "We brew traditional session ales that people can sit down and enjoy and not get toasted," Hennessy explained. "It's not putting a pint on a pedestal. It's about friends getting together and having a conversation."

Colorado Boy Pub & Brewery

Opened: December 2008.
Owners: Tom and Sandy Hennessy.
Head brewer: Tom Hennessy.
Potential annual capacity: 750 barrels.
Hours: Tuesday through Sunday, 4 p.m. to 9 p.m.
Tours: On request.
Take-out beer: Growlers and kegs.
Food: Excellent salads and pizza.
Extras: AHA member deals program participant.
Parking: On-street.
Area attractions: Ridgway is on the scenic San Juan Skyway loop drive.

Dolores River Brewery

100 South 4th Street, Dolores, CO 81323
(970) 882-HOPS (4677) • www.doloresriverbrewery.com

What's the next career step once you've become Vice President of Brewing Operations for a nation-wide brewpub conglomerate overseeing installation teams, brewery training centers, and regional brewing managers from coast to coast? For Mark Young-quist, the answer was to leave it all behind, move to a town of nine hundred in a remote corner of Colorado, and open a small brewpub where friends and families could gather in a relaxed setting.

Dolores River Brewing is located in the tiny town of Dolores, in extreme southwest Colorado, about as far from Denver and the Colorado Front Range as you can get and still be in the state. It's a quiet place, with nearby attractions being the river that flows through town, the San Juan Mountains to the east, and the red rock desert to the west. Durango and Telluride are both about an hour away by car, and worlds away in temperament.

Youngquist is a veteran of the country's craft beer scene. He started homebrewing in 1979 with a homebrew kit purchased at a Denver Safeway store. "It was beer only a mother could love," he remembered. His homebrewing exploits continued with a group of friends at Lewis & Clark College in Oregon. Interestingly, many of his homebrewing buddies went on to professional brewing careers. (In an unrelated, though interesting bit of trivia, Lewis & Clark is also the alma mata of Monica Lewinski).

In 1986, Youngquist got a job at the fledgling Bridgeport Brewing Company in Portland, Oregon. A few years later, he moved back to Colorado just after the opening of Wynkoop Brewing in Denver, Colorado's first brewpub. He met local restaurateur Frank Day and, in 1990, they opened the Walnut Brewery in Boulder with Youngquist in charge of brewing. Day had bigger plans. He opened the first Rock Bottom Restaurant in downtown Denver in 1991. The Rock Bottom concept quickly spread nationwide, and Youngquist acquired the position of VP of Brewing Operations. His immersion in the corporate world

Year-round beers: Mild, Pale Ale, ESB, Dry Stout, IPA.

The Pick: The Pale Ale is a well-balanced and quaffable amber-hued ale with just enough bready malt to support the prominent yet nonaggressive hop finish.

came at the expense of actually brewing beer and tinkering with brewhouse equipment, his passions. "In the end, it outgrew me," he said of his decision to leave the company, pack up his family, and change locations and lifestyles in tiny Dolores. In 2002, five years after the move, he opened Dolores River Brewing.

"The vision was to create a community meeting center where people could relax. Not be hurried. Not be harassed by a waitperson," Youngquist explained. He located the brewpub in a nondescript brick building constructed in 1931 as a telegraph office that later became a post office. The original skylights, ceilings, and floors are still in place. The wood-fired pizza oven, framed music posters, disco ball, and brewhouse are more recent additions. In the back is a spacious patio with a music stage that hosts regular live performances. The brewpub brings in top-notch performers, and the locals have no inhibitions about dancing up a storm.

In the comfortable, unpretentious environment, Dolores River could get away with average food and beer. But that's not an option for Youngquist and his staff. The pizzas and calzones that emerge from the wood-fired pizza oven are the equal of any big-city pizzeria. The beers tend toward sessionable English and American-style ales, but Youngquist has no qualms about adding a German lager, a barleywine, a black IPA, or a peach saison into the mix. Dolores River packages a selection of beers in 16-ounce cans for purchase at the brewpub.

I happened to meet a longtime Dolores resident while I was biking in the area. When I asked him about Dolores River Brewery, he told me, "The town was really quiet before the brewery opened. Without it, Dolores would wither up and die."

Dolores River Brewery

Opened: February 2002.
Owner and head brewer: Mark Youngquist.
Potential annual capacity: 350 barrels.
Hours: Tuesday through Sunday, 4 p.m. until closing.
Tours: On request.
Take-out beer: Growlers, 16-ounce cans, and kegs.
Food: Salads, sandwiches, and tasty brick-oven pizzas and calzones.
Extras: Live music up to twice weekly. Check website for upcoming shows.
Parking: On-site lot and street parking.
Area attractions: Mesa Verde National Park is about twenty miles away.

Durango Brewing Company

3000 Main Avenue, Durango, CO 81301
(970) 247-3396 • www.durangobrewing.com

The town of Durango was established in 1880. The railroad arrived the following year, and scores of new businesses opened soon after, providing goods and services to the new southwest Colorado hub. Among the early enterprises was Durango Beer and Ice Company.

In 1990, an electrical engineer launched a new hometown brewery and resurrected the old brewery name, minus the "Ice," of course. Durango Brewing Company was one of Colorado's original microbreweries. The brewery logo—a steam engine locomotive within a horseshoe—commemorates the town's railroad heritage and is prominently displayed on the brewery's exterior. In the early 2000s, the business was purchased by Mark Harvey, the current owner.

Of Durango's five hometown breweries, Durango Brewing Company has found its comfort zone as a small, unpretentious gathering spot with the look and feel of a friendly neighborhood pub. The long-established brewpub anchors the northern end of the brew-loving community.

The brewery is located in a simple one-story structure on the corner of Main Avenue and 30th Street, about two miles from downtown Durango. A few tables sit on a small patio in front of the building, with more set up on a grassy strip along the side.

The informal interior contains a small U-shaped wooden bar sitting atop a base of corrugated metal. Additional seating is available on some high-top tables. One wall is done in a railroad boxcar motif. Other walls display a collection of brewing competition medals, historic photos, framed beer label artwork, and assorted other ornamental accoutrements. A shuffleboard table hugs a wall of the L-shaped room, with a video game nearby.

There's an abbreviated menu of snacks, salads, sandwiches, and burgers. When the brewery first opened, it produced traditional lager styles. "A lot of those beers are now being brewed as ales,"

Year-round beers: Durango Golden Ale, Durango Wheat Beer, Durango Amber Ale, Durango Dark Lager, Derail Ale Double Golden Ale.

The Pick: Inviting and uncomplicated with a pleasantly dry finish, the oft-decorated Durango Dark Lager will hold your interest through an extended sipping session.

explained head brewer Nathan Watkins. "They're brewed at a low temperature. It takes a little longer, but it keeps them pretty clean." Watkins arrived in Durango in early 2013. Prior to that, he had spent a half-dozen years producing beers at Boulder's Mountain Sun and Southern Sun brewpubs.

Since arriving at Durango Brewing, Watkins has been tweaking the brewhouse operations. "We're trying to keep the identity of the place alive and do some more progressive things on the beer end," said Watkins. One change he implemented was to eliminate filtering several of the house beers, such as the IPA. Many brewers believe that filtering strips away some desirable hop character that's important to hop-forward styles such as India pale ales. The changes have been well-received, as IPA sales have skyrocketed since the change was implemented. New seasonal beers, including a pumpkin porter and Oktoberfest, have also been popular.

The brewpub is well-known for its American dark lager, a rarely seen style in the Colorado craft beer scene. Durango Dark is a smooth, easy-drinking lager with a clean malt character. The beer is popular locally and can be found in numerous Durango restaurants and watering holes. It was a silver medal winner at the 2010 World Beer Cup and a gold medal winner at the 2011 Great American Beer Festival. On the opposite end of the intensity scale is the category-defying Derail Ale, a strong golden ale that captured gold medals at the 2007 and 2008 GABF in the catchall "Other Strong Beer" category.

Durango Brewing Company

Opened: 1990.

Owners: Mark Harvey.

Head brewer: Nathan Watkins.

Potential annual capacity: 3,000 barrels.

Hours: Sunday and Monday, 3 p.m. to 9 p.m.; Tuesday through Saturday, noon to 10 p.m.

Tours: On request.

Take-out beer: Growlers.

Food: Snacks, burgers, and sandwiches.

Extras: Bluegrass jam on Wednesdays.

Parking: Small on-site lot and on-street parking.

Main Street Brewery and Restaurant

21 East Main Street, Cortez, CO 81321
(970) 564-9112 • www.mainstreetbrewerycortez.com

The town of Cortez, home of Main Street Brewery, sits amid the highest concentration of archeological sites in the country, including the spectacular cliff dwellings of Mesa Verde National Park. The town itself feels like it's from a different era, though more like the 1950s or '60s than Ancestral Puebloan.

The town has agricultural roots, but its close proximity to the national park and other ancient Anasazi sites makes it a convenient stop for tourists who descend on the area in droves during the warm-weather months. "Without the tourism, we're cattle ranchers and farmers," said Main Street brewer Branden Miller, who arrived in Cortez during his high school years.

Main Street Brewery opened in 1995 in the center of Cortez, on the town's broad Main Street. The yellow-brick building that houses the brewpub dates from the nineteenth century. It's had a variety of uses over the years, and supposedly once had a speakeasy operating in the basement.

The interior is a long expansive space divided down the middle by a row of chalkboards listing beers, wines, and Italian sodas. The high, pressed-tin ceiling is evidence of the building's age, and along with the dated wood paneling and wooden booths covered in green vinyl upholstery, gives the impression that you've stepped back in time. There's a long wooden bar along one side of the room with a brass handrail mounted on the front.

The décor is a bit odd. There's a buffalo head mounted on a wall, and several model ships sitting on shelves. On a platform above the kitchen in the back of the room, an assemblage of seemingly random items is on display including an old single-speed bicycle, a pair of wooden snowshoes, two stuffed penguins, a headless mannequin, and a miniature Goodyear blimp.

Above the bar is a long mural of an almost indescribable dreamscape composed of aliens, monkeys, whales, a starship, sea horses, and a hookah-smoking caterpillar. It's a peculiar bit

Year-round beers: Crystal Wheat, Honey Raspberry Wheat, Pale Export, Porter, Maibock, Schnorzenboomer Doppelbock, Uberpils, Slow Pitch Scottish Export, IPA.

The Pick: The Porter is light-bodied and slightly sweet with the character of a brown ale. A hint of roastiness kicks in at the finish.

of ornamentation in the turn-of-the-century building, but amusing nonetheless.

The menu is standard American pub fare and pizza. Steaks and prime rib are offered for dinner. If you want to sample some ranch cuisine, Rocky Mountain oysters are available. Miller, who has been brewing at Main Street for more than a decade, is largely self-taught. In 2002, he was operating a commercial janitorial business. The brewpub was one of his accounts. The brewer at the time was preparing to depart, and the former owner asked Miller if he was interested in learning to brew. "I'd never brewed beer, never drank beer. I said okay, fine," Miller explained. "I had a porter and fell in love. The original brewer showed me how to brew a couple times. After that I read books, magazines, went online. Engulfed myself in the process."

There are nine full-time beers, including three German-style lagers created by Main Street's original brewer, who was from Bavaria. Some of the house beers are available in bombers. Compared with other parts of the state, local tastes are conservative, but Miller is doing his best to introduce his clientele to a variety of styles, with mixed success. "I did a framboise (Belgian raspberry beer). I only did a little five-gallon batch. It didn't go well. It stayed on for about a month," he recalled. He was undeterred, however. "I have an Oktoberfest coming out. I do a foreign extra stout in the wintertime. I do an extra blonde during the summer. An Irish red in the spring. A little curveball here and there."

Main Street Brewery and Restaurant

Opened: 1995.

Owners: Bob and Janet Woods.

Head brewer: Branden Miller.

Potential annual capacity: 2,000 barrels.

Hours: Daily, 11 a.m. to midnight or so.

Tours: On request.

Take-out beer: Growlers, bombers, and kegs.

Food: American-style pub food, steaks, pizzas, and Rocky Mountain oysters.

Parking: Free on-street parking.

Area attractions: Mesa Verde National Park is about an hour away from Cortez. There are many other ancient Anasazi sites in the area.

Ouray Brewery

607 Main Street, Ouray, CO 81427
(970) 318-1376 • www.ouraybrewery.com

The oft-mispronounced town of Ouray (the correct pronunciation is U-ray) is one of several high-elevation towns along the San Juan Skyway of southwest Colorado with a mining-intensive history, jaw-dropping mountain scenery, wide streets, and turn-of-the-century Victorian architecture dripping with Old West character. The community of less than one thousand residents is also the scene of the annual Ouray Ice Festival, considered the world's premier gathering of ice-climbing enthusiasts. Thousands show up each January to watch events such as the speed-climbing competition and to attend seminars with names like "Yoga for Climbers."

The Ouray Brewery is a popular stop for a burger and a brew for the scores of travelers and outdoor adventurers who pass through the town. Brewery cofounder Erin Eddy had been working in the real estate business in Ouray during a decline in the market. Eddy sold the building in which Ouray Brewery now resides to a businessman from outside the area. When business plans for the building fell through, Eddy partnered with the buyer to create the brewpub. Though Eddy's only experience in the beer business was through his father, who worked at Coors for thirty years, he took on the challenge of building and operating the brewpub. His partner isn't active in the business, so Eddy runs the show. "I run and operate the brewery and restaurant full-time year round. I refer to myself as 'The Cleaner,' like Harvey Keitel in *Pulp Fiction*. I fix problems," Eddy said of his multiple job responsibilities.

Ouray Brewery sits in a three-level brick building on the corner of Main Street and 6th Avenue in downtown Ouray. Unlike many of its elegant Victorian neighbors, the brewpub is a modern structure. The ground-floor level contains a bar and some table seating. The unique bar seats are actually metal-backed swings suspended from the

Year-round beers: Camp Bird Blonde, Revenue Red Ale, Box Canyon Brown, San Juan IPA.

The Pick: Give your parched palate a reprieve with an easy-drinking Camp Bird Blonde. The pale golden pilsner features a delicate sweetness and restrained hoppiness that won't offend your light beer–drinking buddies.

ceiling by thick steel cables wrapped in strings of red holiday lights. The second level has another small bar and some booth and table seating.

Most visitors head to the shaded rooftop patio on the top level. Counter seating is available along the perimeter of the space, offering gorgeous views of downtown Ouray and the surrounding mountains. Picnic tables fill the interior. Tourist traffic accounts for most of the brewpub's business in the warm-weather months. The winter brings skiers and ice climbers into the restaurant.

Food choices include a modest selection of appetizers, burgers, and sandwiches. The brewing operation was once located in the restaurant, but outgrew the confines of the downtown location and was moved to a separate site about one mile north. It resides within a warehouse-looking structure that sits along the Uncompahgre River, not far from Ouray's popular hot springs pool. Though the brewery has a taproom and beer garden, there were no set hours when I visited, so it was hit or miss as to whether someone would be available to show visitors around and pour beers. The situation may be different now.

The brewery produces four full-time beers including a blonde lager, a red ale, a brown ale, and an IPA. The blonde, the biggest seller, is a light-flavored pilsner that appeals to the tastes of travelers unaccustomed to the more assertive beers generally favored by local beer enthusiasts. Other styles rotate seasonally and include a spring saison, a summer hefeweizen, a fall dunkelweizen, and a winter stout.

Ouray Brewery

Opened: August 2010.

Owners: Dennis McKee and Erin Eddy.

Head brewer: James Walton.

Potential annual capacity: 1,200 barrels.

Hours: Daily, 11 a.m. to 9 p.m.

Tours: On request at off-site brewery (1900 Main Street).

Take-out beer: Growlers and kegs.

Food: Salads, burgers, and sandwiches.

Parking: Free on-street parking.

Area attractions: Ouray Hot Springs Pool (1200 Main Street, 970-325-7073). Silverton Mountain Ski Resort is close by.

Ourayle House Brewery

703 Main Street, Ouray, CO 81427
(970) 903-1824 • www.ourayehouse.com

The beauty of operating a small business such as a nanobrewery is that, with few limitations, you can run it any way you want. You can conform to what are considered standard business practices, or ignore them altogether and write your own rules. You can welcome all comers, or target a narrower clientele in your establishment. You don't even have to be nice. Maybe that's why it's called *free* enterprise.

Being nice is not the modus operandi of Jim "Hutch" Hutchison, the founder-brewer of the Ourayle (pronounced UR-ale) House. In fact, Hutchison can be a bit ornery. Normally, I would hesitate to share this information; however, Hutchison has themed his business around that fact. The official name of the brewery is Ourayle House Brewery, doing business as the Mr. Grumpy Pants Brewing Company. Hutchison made sure I was aware of this information during a short conversation we had when I stopped by for a springtime visit. This was the only bit of information about the business he seemed interested in sharing.

Hutchison failed to show for our planned late-afternoon meeting, but he did wander in thirty minutes later. In the interim, I busied myself sampling the house beers and extracting whatever information I could from the bartender, a very amiable fellow. When Hutchison arrived and agreed to have a chat, it lasted all of two minutes. My inquiries as to his background, the brewery's history, and the details of a planned relocation of the business resulted in short, vague answers.

I won't get into details about the configuration of the Ourayle House, as the business was scheduled to move to a nearby location on Ouray's Main Street a month or so after my visit. I assume certain policies will be carried over to the new location.

The Ourayle House is not family friendly. A hand-lettered note on the wall reads, "We're begging you people . . . cash + adults only." Above it, a second note reads, "It's not that we don't like kids, but we don't drink beer at your child's daycare either." The brewery has no set hours. A rambling explanation on a whiteboard in the front window concludes with, "Tap room hours can vary due to brewing schedules, cleaning times, snow depths,

Year-round beers: No full-time beers, but there is usually a light, a dark, and a hoppy offering among the four or five beers on tap.

The Pick: The pale ale I sampled had a nice malt-hop balance.

river flows, trail and avalanche conditions, puppy outings, what we did the night before, what we're doing right now, and the fact that sometimes we like to hang out @ someone else's bar." The bartender I spoke with told me he opens the place at 3 p.m. on his work days. He only works a few days a week, however.

There are no full-time beers at the brewery. A light, a dark, and a hoppy offering are generally among the four or five beers on tap. Despite the quirky nature of the brewery, the five beers I sampled—stout, blonde, IPA, smoked ale, pale ale—were actually pretty decent. The best of the bunch was a well-balanced and drinkable pale ale. The blonde ale was light and quaffable, but not uninteresting. When I asked Hutchison about his preference in beer styles, his answer was direct and to the point: "Beer is beer."

Ourayle House Brewery

Opened: November 2007.
Owner and head brewer: Jim "Hutch" Hutchison.
Potential annual capacity: 200 barrels.
Hours: Whenever. Sometimes opens around 3 p.m. Often open in evenings.
Tours: Depends on owner's mood.
Take-out beer: Growlers.
Food: Bring your own.
Parking: On-street.
Area attractions: See Ouray Brewery on page 282.

Pagosa Brewing & Grill

118 North Pagosa Boulevard, Pagosa Springs, CO 81147
(970) 731-2739 • www.pagosabrewing.com

The career paths of craft brewers tend to be meandering routes, as many arrive in the brewhouse after testing the waters of other professions. Tony Simmons, founder of Pagosa Brewing & Grill, is a prime example. Simmons came from the world of corporate marketing as the London-based worldwide account manager for Nestlé Brands. London was fertile ground for a beer enthusiast. "I had a wager with my boss as to who could have more beer. I'd try a new beer every time I went to a different pub," Simmons recalled of his London experience.

But something was lacking in the urban lifestyle. "I was looking for a sense of community," Simmons said of his decision to leave city life behind and settle in the small southwest Colorado town of Pagosa Springs. Though he had long-range plans to open a brewery, the idea fermented for many years before coming to fruition.

After moving to Pagosa, Simmons became a "voracious homebrewer." When the nearest homebrew shop, located an hour away in Durango, closed its doors, he opened his own homebrew shop in his garage. His brewery plans got a big boost when he won scholarships to attend brewing schools in both the United States and Germany. Pagosa Brewing opened in 2006, ten years after Simmons arrived in Pagosa Springs.

The town of Pagosa Springs is well situated for recreation-minded travelers. Wolf Creek Ski Area is just east of town and is known for its reliable deep powder. Hiking, camping, and fishing in the surrounding national forests are popular summer activities. In the center of town is Pagosa Hot Springs, a series of mineral pools of various configurations where you can soak and decompress alongside the San Juan River.

At first glance, the taproom of Pagosa Brewing is somewhat reminiscent of an English pub, thanks to dark wood furnishings throughout the modest-sized interior. A major expansion, which will triple both indoor seating and brewing capacity, is scheduled for completion in late 2014. A

Year-round beers: Wolf Creek Wheat, Peachy Peach, Kayaker Cream, Chili Verde Cerveza, Pagosa Pale Ale, Powder Day IPA, Rodeo Rider Red, Poor Richard's Ale, Coconut Porter, and a rotating stout.

The Pick: Poor Richard's Ale brings forward a sweet aroma, clean malt flavors, and a whisper of molasses leading to a pleasantly dry finish.

huge draw for the brewpub is the large, appealing beer garden. Shaded by aspen and pine, the outdoor space has a music stage, seating for nearly two hundred, and a kids' play area.

Simmons is a perfectionist by nature, and it shows in what emerges from both the kitchen and the brewhouse. "We strive for delicious and we strive for over-delivering expectations both in the beer and in the food," he said of Pagosa Brewing's in-house creations. "Every single one of our main dishes is either handmade, locally sourced, or wild-harvested. Everything is totally sustainable." Beer is incorporated into many dishes. The best-selling entrée is the salmon fish-and-chips made with wild-caught Alaskan salmon.

Beers are well crafted across the board. True-to-style English, German, Belgian, and American beers share the taps with specialty offerings such as peach beer, chili beer, or honey beer. Pagosa Brewing has acquired dozens of medals in regional and national competitions, including a 2013 Great American Beer Festival gold medal for its Peachy Peach fruit wheat beer.

Another beer that received national attention is Poor Richard's Ale, which was the winning entry in a recipe competition commemorating Benjamin Franklin's 300th birthday in 2006. The competition required brewers to create a beer that Franklin might have consumed in his lifetime. Submissions had to be easily replicable. Simmons's research revealed a shortage of malt and hops during the colonial days, so his recipe included malted corn and molasses, ingredients that would have been available to brewers of that era. His winning recipe was re-created by more than one hundred breweries nationwide. The tasty brown ale is now a year-round offering at Pagosa Brewing.

Pagosa Brewing & Grill

Opened: November 2006.

Owner and head brewer: Tony Simmons.

Potential annual capacity: 850 barrels.

Hours: Daily, 11 a.m. to 10 p.m.

Tours: Mondays at 4 p.m. Other times by reservation or request.

Take-out beer: Growlers.

Food: Sandwiches, burgers, pizza, and seafood, including salmon fish-and-chips.

Extras: Open mic night on Tuesday (summer only). Kids' play area. AHA member discount program participant.

Parking: On-site lot.

Area attractions: Pagosa Hot Springs Resort (165 Hot Springs Blvd., 970-264-2284). Chimney Rock National Monument. Navajo Lake State Park. Wolf Creek Ski Area.

San Luis Valley Brewing Company

631 Main Street, Alamosa, CO 81101
(719) 587-2337 • www.slvbrewco.com

If you were to ask my advice on opening a brewpub in an out-of-the-way community in the middle of a vast agricultural valley two hours from the nearest city, I would tell you it's a bad idea. After all, the location is wrong. The demographics are wrong. There's no way it should work. Fortunately, Scott and Angie Graber didn't ask my advice before opening the San Luis Valley Brewing Company. The entrepreneurial couple with a strong sense of community opened the Alamosa brewpub in 2006 and has never looked back.

Alamosa sits in the San Luis Valley of south-central Colorado. Within the valley, 40,000 acres of barley is grown for MillerCoors. The Great Sand Dunes National Park, containing the tallest dunes in North America, is thirty-five miles away.

In 2000, Scott Graber arrived in Alamosa after completing graduate work in theology at Notre Dame. "I was trying to figure out all the god questions," he said. His plan was to do volunteer work with local youth for a year, then return to school for a doctorate. He couldn't afford good beer, so he took up homebrewing. While working in Alamosa he met his future wife, who was also working with youth in the community. She was a microbiologist with plans to go to pharmacy school. They never left Alamosa.

The couple saw that breweries were on the upswing in Colorado, but hadn't yet reached their sparsely populated part of the state. They decided to create a hometown brewpub that would function as a gathering place. "We wanted to build it as a place of community. We both had come out of Judeo-Christian backgrounds and felt there was a lot of community that could happen around a table and around a quality beverage," Graber explained.

They restored a former downtown bank building dating from 1897 into a brewpub. The stately brick structure sits on a corner lot on Alamosa's

Year-round beers: Valle Especial Mexican-style Lager, Valle Caliente Green Chili Lager, Hefe Suave American Wheat Ale, Alamosa Amber Ale, Grande River IPA, Ol' 169 Oatmeal Stout, Royal Gorge Route Rogue, Scenic Rail Pale Ale.

The Pick: The Valle Caliente Green Chili Lager is based on the crisp, quaffable Valle Especial Mexican-style Lager. An infusion of Hatch chilies creates an interesting flavor profile without adding much heat.

Main Street. The interior has a comfortable old-time feel with high ceilings, brick and stucco walls, and arched windows. Two interesting multipanel murals—one with an agricultural theme, the other with a railroad theme—are displayed on one of the walls. Each panel was painted by an art student from nearby Adams State University. The small brewhouse is tucked into a back corner. The cold room, where finished beer is stored, is located in the former bank vault. The massive vault door now sits behind the bar.

When the brewpub first opened, it was a challenge to get the locals to drink the house beers. "Our area is not Denver, and people were scared to try anything other than Budweiser or Miller or Coors," Graber recalled. "We did a hefeweizen to try to get their feet wet."

The local palates have evolved considerably since then. "It's been a learning process," said Graber. "The first two or three years, if I brewed a strong Scotch [ale], it was hard to get people to try it. Now, folks are to the point where they're chomping at the bit and emailing and calling saying, 'when's your next seasonal?'" In response, the brewery has gotten increasingly adventurous. Belgian beers, smoked beers, barrel-aged beers, and other seasonal and specialty brews now appear alongside the eight standard house beers.

The brewpub has partnered with the Alamosa's Rio Grande Scenic Railroad in a unique annual event. The Rails & Ales Brewfest takes beer fans high into the mountains for an afternoon of music, barbecue, and beer from more than two dozen breweries. In recent years, the event has attracted close to one thousand people.

San Luis Valley Brewing Company

Opened: March 2006.

Owners: Scott and Angie Graber.

Head brewer: Andrew Clair.

Potential annual capacity: 1,400 barrels.

Hours: Daily, 11 a.m. to closing.

Tours: On request.

Take-out beer: Six-packs, bombers, growlers, and kegs.

Food: Burgers, sandwiches, pasta, assorted entrées, and locally made sausages.

Extras: Live music on summer Fridays (occasionally in winter). AHA member deals participant.

Parking: On-street and nearby lots, all free.

Area attractions: Rio Grande Scenic Railroad (877-726-7245). Great Sand Dunes National Park. Colorado Gators Reptile Park (9162 CR 9 North, Mosca, 719-378-2612).

Ska Brewing Company

225 Girard Street, Durango, CO 81303
(970) 247-5792 • www.skabrewing.com

It was the mid-1980s. Dave Thibodeau and Bill Graham were Denver-area high school buddies who liked to party. One day, they discovered an old homebrewing logbook that belonged to Thibodeau's father. They were intrigued. With ingredients purchased at the local supermarket, they concocted their first batch of beer. Thus began a brewing partnership that lasted through college and beyond.

The partners adopted a ritual for their brewing sessions. "When we homebrewed, we had two rules," recalled Thibodeau. "The first being that we had to drink our last batch of homebrew. The other rule was we had to listen to ska music when we brewed; otherwise, the beer wouldn't turn out any good."

Following college and without jobs, both Graham and Thibodeau relocated to Durango for a lifestyle change. They continued to homebrew. "We started talking about trying to open a brewery somehow. We didn't have any money. We didn't have any means of getting any money. We had jobs that barely paid anything," Thibodeau remembered. Undeterred, they put together a business plan.

Potential financers wanted nothing to do with them. They eventually found an investor in Graham's father, who loaned them just enough money to pay for a used brewing system from a Spokane, Washington, brewery.

The duo leased a space in the corner of a warehouse a few miles from Durango and brewed their first commercial beer in 1993. In the cooperative spirit that has been integral to the Durango brewing scene since its early days, Ska's first keg account was at Carver Brewing, the community's original downtown brewpub.

After a year in business, Ska added a third partner, Matt Vincent, who had been working at Durango Brewing Company. The company grew by leaps and bounds, and in 2008, Ska relocated a few blocks away to a new brewery built from the ground up.

Year-round beers: True Blonde Ale, Steel Toe Stout, Pinstripe Red Ale, Buster Nut Brown Ale, Modus Hoperandi, Special E.S.B., Decadent Imperial IPA, True Blonde Dubbel, Nefarious Ten Pin Imperial Porter.

The Pick: Modus Hoperandi is an IPA drinker's IPA. The piney, citrusy qualities that define an American IPA sit atop a substantial malty base in this bold and satisfying brew.

Ska Brewing World Headquarters, as the proprietors prefer to call it, occupies a lot in an area of mixed businesses and open fields about three miles from downtown Durango. Brushy hills rise behind the brewery.

The taproom has a contemporary, industrial feel with gray walls, a ceiling of corrugated metal, and a wooden bar and tables constructed of former bowling alley flooring. An interior window provides a view of the canning line. There's a beer garden behind the building. In 2013, the brewery added a restaurant to the complex. The Container, constructed of repurposed shipping containers, features brick-oven pizzas, sandwiches, snacks, and sweets.

The first batch of beer the brewery produced was a blonde ale. Thibodeau remembers well the brewery's second attempt to brew the blonde: "We got about halfway through mashing in and realized we didn't have the right ingredients. On the fly, we had to come up with a recipe, and that's where Pinstripe (Red Ale) came from. It just took off right out of the gates and kind of became our flagship." In 2009, Ska released Modus Hoperandi, an assertively flavored, hoppy, and highly satisfying American IPA. It quickly became the brewery's best seller and is one of my go-to beers when I'm craving a hop fix.

Ska's head brewer is Thomas Larsen, who arrived in Durango after a decade at Denver's Wynkoop Brewing Company. Under Larsen's direction, Ska has amassed an impressive collection of brewing awards. Steel Toe Stout, a sweet stout, was a gold medal winner at both the 2011 Great American Beer Festival and 2012 World Beer Cup. True Blonde Ale captured a gold medal at the 2013 GABF. Ska now distributes to nine states and several foreign countries.

Ska Brewing Company

Opened: September 1995.

Owners: Matt Vincent, Bill Graham, and Dave Thibodeau.

Head brewer: Thomas Larsen.

Potential annual capacity: 45,000 barrels.

Hours: Monday through Friday, 9 a.m. to 8 p.m.; Saturday, 11 a.m. to 7 p.m. Closed Sunday.

Tours: Monday through Saturday at 4 p.m.

Take-out beer: Growlers, cans, six-packs, bombers, and kegs.

Food: Salads, sandwiches, burgers, pizza.

Extras: Trivia on Tuesday (except summer). Ska-B-Q on Thursday (summer only). AHA member deals program participant.

Parking: On-site lot.

Smugglers Brewpub

225 South Pine Street, Telluride, CO 81435
(970) 728-5620 • www.smugglersbrewpub.com

Embarking on a new career takes dedication and courage. On June 24, 1889, a ranch hand named Robert Leroy Parker, better known as Butch Cassidy, launched a new career in crime by robbing the San Miguel National Bank in downtown Telluride. A few blocks away from the site of that bank heist, and 123 years later, Nancy and Warren Daniel launched new careers as restaurateurs by taking ownership of Telluride's Smugglers Brewpub and infusing fresh energy into a business in need of some TLC.

Telluride sits in a Shangri-la setting at the end of a box canyon at 8,750 feet elevation. From its Victorian downtown, you can see Bridal Veil Falls cascade down the steep canyon walls at the end of the valley. Smugglers occupies a corner lot a few blocks south of Colorado Avenue, Telluride's main drag. From the brewpub, it's a short stroll to Telluride Town Park, home to several festivals of national stature including the Telluride Bluegrass Festival in June and Telluride Blues & Brews in September.

Smugglers occupies the site of a former weigh station where minerals extracted from the surrounding mountains would be weighed before being loaded onto the railroad that once came into town. The old weigh station was deconstructed, then reconstructed as a brewpub in 1996. The exterior of the one-story structure consists of well-weathered panels of corrugated metal. The interior is a long, narrow space with lots of wood, old and new, creating a rustic character. Booths run along the front wall. The long bar faces the back wall and a row of TVs. Tables fill the middle of the space. A pleasant shaded patio sits off the end of the building. The brewhouse is in the basement.

In the tourist-intensive ski town where pricy high-end eateries proliferate, Smugglers provided a casual and affordable alternative for the tight-knit local community as well as for Telluride's seasonal onslaught of visitors. In recent years, several ill-timed expansion attempts and some ownership

Year-round beers: Rocky Mountain Rye, San Juan Skyhop, Smuggler's Strong Scottish Ale, Wildcat Wheat, Two Planker Porter, No Name Blonde, The Reckoning Pale Ale, Debauchery Belgian Tripel, Palmyra Pils, Road Rash Red, Ingram's IPA, Shred Betty Raspberry Wheat.

The Pick: Two Planker Porter keeps things interesting with a nicely balanced interplay of sweet malt, dry roastiness, and hints of chocolate.

indifference put the brewpub in a downward spiral. In late 2012, Nancy and Warren Daniel made a decision to abandon plans of a relaxed retirement and take on the task of resurrecting the hometown brewpub.

"We were getting a little too lazy," stated Nancy Daniel, who first arrived in the storied resort town in 1992 and has established deep roots in the community. With no restaurant experience, but a surplus of enthusiasm, Nancy and Warren have enjoyed the challenge of bringing respectability back to this longstanding Telluride gathering spot. "If it was a house, you would say this pub has good bones," said Nancy.

One part of the business that didn't need an overhaul was the brewing operation headed by T. J. Daly. Daly came to Telluride from Vermont, where he was the head of the grounds crew at Stowe Mountain Resort. The long days that started at 4:30 a.m. were taking their toll on the former homebrewer. Through a mutual friend, he hooked up with Smugglers' former brewer, Chris Fish, who hired him as an assistant. When Fish departed in 2011 to launch Telluride Brewing Company, Daly took the reins in Smugglers' brewhouse.

Daly has an ambitious brewing schedule, keeping a dozen full-time beers on tap including British, American, German, and Belgian styles. There are five rotating seasonal beers including a pale ale infused with local juniper berries. Daly is an admirer of Belgian-style ales and usually has two on tap.

Smugglers has formed a partnership with the Telluride Mushroom Festival. For the past few years, Daly has created a unique mushroom-infused beer for the annual fest. The beer has no psychoactive properties, but it's packed with antioxidants. "You can't really say it's medicinal, but you're getting those beneficial qualities from the mushroom," said Daly.

Smugglers Brewpub

Opened: 1996. Under new ownership since November 2012.

Owners: Nancy and Warren Daniel.

Head brewer: T. J. Daly.

Potential annual capacity: 1,500 barrels.

Hours: Daily, 11 a.m. to 10 p.m.

Tours: On request.

Take-out beer: Growlers and kegs.

Food: American pub fare.

Extras: Live music on occasion.

Parking: On-street, metered.

Area attractions: The historic town of Telluride. Telluride Ski Resort.

Steamworks Brewing Company

801 East Second Avenue, Durango, CO 81301
(970) 259-9200 • www.steamworksbrewing.com

The fun-loving folks of Durango have a zealous devotion to beer and bicycles. While these two passions are generally enjoyed separately, Steamworks Brewing Company has brought them together in a most unique way. On two occasions, mountain bike races have been routed through the brewpub. Glass panes were removed from the front window and a ramp constructed to bring riders into the building. The race course took cyclists through the bar, out the side door, and down a second ramp. Patrons at the bar had front-row seats for the multilap criteriums.

Steamworks sits on a corner lot on Second Avenue, a short block from Durango's Main Avenue. The brewpub is large and very casual. The long bar includes footrests made from former train rails. Several dining areas fill the expansive interior. A large covered patio resides in back of the building. During the summer, when outdoor seating is available, the brewpub can accommodate four hundred guests. The brewhouse sits behind walls of glass in the middle of the pub. "The brewers like to call it 'The Fishbowl,'" according to Steamworks cofounder Kris Oyler.

Oyler grew up on the Colorado Front Range and acquired an appreciation for good beer through homebrewing and by visiting the handful of Denver-area breweries that were open in the early 1990s. He had plans to open a brewery, but hadn't pinpointed a location when he visited Durango in 1994 to have a look around. He never left. "I love to hike and I love to ski. Both of those things are abundant here," Oyler said of his decision to plant roots in the adrenaline-charged southwestern Colorado community.

Plans for the brewpub gained momentum when a space was found in a former car dealership dating from the 1920s. Oyler and managing partner Brian McEachron opened Steamworks in 1996, making it the fourth of Durango's five hometown breweries. Oyler now holds the title of CEO, while McEachron is the director of marketing.

Year-round beers: Colorado Kolsch, Steam Engine Lager, Third Eye Pale Ale, Lizard Head Red, Conductor Imperial IPA, Backside Stout, Prescribed Burn Chili Ale.

The Pick: Colorado Kolsch proves that a light, quaffable ale can also be interesting. A pleasant sweetness up front is perfectly balanced with a kiss of hops and a crisp effervescence.

The name Steamworks has dual meanings. First, it refers to the famous Durango & Silverton Narrow Gauge Railroad, which has been operating steam locomotives through the San Juan Mountains since 1882. The train is Durango's most popular tourist draw. Second, it relates to the brewpub's steam-jacketed brewing vessels.

The kitchen and brewery both strive to accommodate a wide range of tastes. "In Durango, you have to be a little bit of all things to all people. I think we've done that pretty successfully," Oyler explained. Food options are numerous and diverse. Pub favorites and pizza share the menu with southwestern dishes, steaks, seafood, and pasta. The signature dish is the Cajun Boil, a spicy medley of crab, shrimp, andouille sausage, potatoes, and corn.

From the start, Steamworks has placed an emphasis on creating balanced, sessionable beers. Drinkability is the keyword in the crisp, quaffable Colorado Kolsch and in the amber-hued Steam Engine Lager, brewed in the California Common style. Other full-time selections cover a spectrum of pale, hoppy, and dark fermentations. Rotating specialty beers, including some barrel-aged creations, add interest and uniqueness to the lineup.

All Steamworks servers, whether food server or bartender, are required to pass the cicerone certification first-level exam, the beer equivalent to wine's sommelier certification. More than fifty Steamworks employees have passed the exam.

Over the years, Steamworks beers have been awarded a combined fifteen Great American Beer Festival and World Beer Cup medals. In 2012, Steamworks' Berliner Weiss was a WBC gold medal winner, while the brewery's Slam Dunkel took home gold at the 2013 GABF.

Steamworks Brewing Company

Opened: September 1996.

Owners: Cofounders Kris Oyler and Brian McEachron, plus seventeen employees with ownership shares; there are seventy-five investors in all.

Head brewer: Ken Martin.

Potential annual capacity: 1,800 barrels.

Hours: Daily, 11 a.m. to 11 p.m. or beyond.

Tours: On request.

Take-out beer: Cans, bottles, and growlers.

Food: Diverse selection of American pub fare, pizza, and southwestern cuisine. The signature dish, the Cajun Boil, is available after 4:30.

Extras: Patio dining with a view.

Parking: On-street parking. Nearby city lots are available after 5 p.m.

Telluride Brewing Company

156 Society Drive, Telluride, CO 81435
(970) 728-5094 • www.telluridebrewingco.com

To say that Telluride Brewing Company arrived on the Colorado craft beer scene with a bang is an understatement. The brewery was open only a few months when its Face Down Brown, an American-style brown ale, was awarded a gold medal at the prestigious 2012 World Beer Cup. The upstart brewery proved it was no one-shot wonder when the same beer captured a gold medal at the Great American Beer Festival that same year. For co-owners and business partners Chris Fish and Tommy Thacher, it was an exciting kickoff to a business concept that had been fermenting for years before coming to fruition.

The two met at Smugglers Brewpub in downtown Telluride where Fish was the head brewer and Thacher was a bartender. They spoke of someday opening their own brewery, even after Thacher left Smugglers to become a middle school teacher. Over the years, the brewery concept began to take shape. They gathered a group of investors, but there was a major roadblock to overcome: Telluride's Aspen-esque real estate market made locating an affordable site a daunting task. Eventually, a space was located in a business complex about four miles outside of town. Telluride Brewing Company opened in October 2011.

The brewery shares the mixed-use office and retail development with a deli, a bakery, a coffee roaster, and other assorted businesses. You enter directly into the two-story brewhouse. The whitewashed walls and thick wood timbers soften the industrial look of the space. There's no separate tasting room. A small bar is set up in a corner of the brewhouse. Fish and his crew work their brewing magic steps away.

Like many professional craft brewers, making beer was not Fish's original career objective. After finishing college, he decided to take a break before beginning graduate studies in hydrology. In 1997, he got a job washing kegs at Boulder's Mountain Sun brewpub. He never made it to grad school.

Year-round beers: Bridal Veil Rye Pale Ale, Smoke Shack Porter, Local's Lager, Ski-in-Ski-Stout, Redfish Ale, Face Down Brown, Whacked Out Wheat, Tempter IPA, FISHwater Double IPA, Beaver Pond Blonde.

The Pick: Like the surrounding mountains, the FISHwater Double IPA is big and bold and not to be taken lightly. A blast of tangy hop flavor is supported by a sturdy base of chewy malt. It finishes warm and bracing.

He worked his way into a brewing position that lasted four years. Wanting to spend more time on the ski slopes, he relocated to Steamboat Springs and landed a position at the now-defunct Steamboat Brewery. In 2002, he was offered the brewmaster position at Smugglers, and he's been in Telluride ever since.

Fish and Thacher have been surprised from the start at the number of visitors that arrived at the brewery. Perhaps they shouldn't have been. Telluride is a small town and the partners had made many acquaintances over their years of living there. Furthermore, Fish had acquired a reputation as a skilled brewer from his tenure at the downtown brewpub. So the brewery immediately had a built-in fan base.

Combined with the attention the brewery received from its WBC and GABF medals, the Telluride Brewing Company has become a popular destination for beer enthusiasts. "The numbers are blowing our mind," Fish confessed about the unexpectedly brisk tasting room business a year after the brewery had opened its doors.

Fish described his beers as being an "American twist on classic styles." Among the biggest sellers is Tempter IPA, featuring a liberal dose of citrusy American hops. The Face Down Brown Ale is a hopped-up version of a traditional British-style ale. The batch that won the World Beer Cup medal was only the second batch of that beer that had been produced since the brewery opened.

TBC's flagship is Bridal Veil Rye Pale Ale, an American-style pale ale brewed with rye malt, which adds a tangy flavor. Fish is especially proud of his Fishwater Double IPA, an assertively flavored and potent 8.5 percent ABV ale. "I'm really happy with that beer. I think it's one of the best things I've ever made," relates the brewer.

Telluride Brewing Company

Opened: October 2011.

Owners: Chris Fish, Tommy Thacher.

Head brewer: Chris Fish.

Potential annual capacity: 4,000 barrels.

Hours: Monday through Saturday, noon to 7 p.m.; Sunday, noon to 5 p.m.

Tours: On request.

Take-out beer: Growlers, cans, and kegs.

Food: The Aemono Restaurant, next to the brewery, has excellent sandwiches and pizza that you can order to go.

Extras: AHA member deals program participant.

Parking: On-site lot.

Area attractions: The historic town of Telluride. Telluride Ski Resort.

Three Barrel Brewing Company

586 Columbia Avenue, Del Norte, CO 81132
(719) 657-0681 • www.threebarrelbrew.com

To most travelers, the little south-central Colorado town of Del Norte (the local pronunciation is del NORT) is not a destination in itself, but a place you pass through en route to better-known locales. For beer travelers in the know, however, Del Norte is a rewarding destination. The community is home to Three Barrel Brewing, an unexpected and amiable little nanobrewery producing a lineup of intriguing sour ales along with more standard offerings.

Del Norte is a quiet town of around 1,700 in the agricultural San Luis Valley. An hour east on Highway 160 brings you to the Great Sand Dunes National Park. Drive west for an hour and you arrive in Pagosa Springs, where you can chill out in the hot springs pools. Beyond that is Durango and the San Juan Mountains.

Three Barrel's founder and brewer is John Brinker, an insurance agent by trade. Bricker's early attempts at producing fermented beverages were winemaking ventures meant to please his wife of Italian heritage. When the results were less than stellar, he turned his attention to homebrewing, which proved much more gratifying. After purchasing a building in Del Norte, he set up his insurance office in the front and a small commercially licensed brewery in the back. There was no formal taproom. When visitors stopped by, he'd conduct tastings in the insurance office. Eventually, he moved his insurance business next door, making room for a visitor-friendly tasting space.

Three Barrel resides in a small building with a nondescript brick and glass storefront in Del Norte's compact commercial district. The taproom is a small, inviting space that looks nothing like an insurance office. A few shiny metal tables are assembled around the room. There's space for six at the granite-topped bar. A wood-fired pizza oven is nestled in a corner behind the bar, surrounded by attractive cut stone. Beyond the tasting room and down a few steps is the three-barrel brewery in a space that had been a garage at some point.

Year-round beers: Bad Phil Pale Ale, Hop Trash IPA, Burnt Toast Brown Ale, Trashy Blonde Ale, Pemba Sherpa Saison Ale, Black Copter Stout.

The Pick: You should definitely sample whatever sour beers are available during your visit.

Bricker's early commercial beers included a blonde ale, a pale ale, and an IPA. There were no bottling capabilities. Beer was sold from the brewery in party pigs. Bricker's interest in sour ales began when he attended Vail's annual Big Beers, Belgians & Barleywines Festival, where he was exposed to sour beers from some well-known breweries from around the country.

Bricker was encouraged to try his hand at quirky ales by Peter Bouckaert, brewmaster at New Belgium Brewing Company. Bricker's sour ales attracted immediate attention at beer festivals among beer enthusiasts who had never heard of the obscure, small-town brewery. While Bricker has little local demand for his unusual ales, there's a huge demand for them elsewhere in the state. Since they require aging for as much as two years, it's been impossible to keep up with demand. When I last visited the brewery, the taproom supply of sours was unfortunately depleted.

With help from Bricker's son-in-law, Will Kreutzer, the business is growing. The opening of the taproom in 2012 has attracted a growing audience of beer explorers. While the party pigs are still available, Three Barrel beer can now be purchased in growlers and bombers. Distribution is slowly increasing. "We want to grow, but we want to grow at an enjoyable pace," said Kreutzer.

In addition to embracing sour beers, Bricker has also developed a passion for saisons. "Every saison can be a little bit different," he explained. "You develop your own style with spices or different things you put into it. It gives you a lot of latitude. The whole idea is go outside the lines rather than stay in the lines. It's a lot of fun to do that."

Three Barrel Brewing Company

Opened: November 2005.
Owner and head brewer: John Bricker.
Potential annual capacity: 750 barrels.
Hours: Daily, 10:30 a.m. to 8 or 9 p.m. or later.
Tours: On request.
Take-out beer: Growlers, bombers, and party pigs.
Food: Wood-fired pizzas, strombolis, and calzones.
Parking: Free street parking.
Area attractions: Penitente Canyon (climbing, hiking, mountain biking). Great Sand Dunes National Park. Wolf Creek Ski Area.

The Western Slope

Some sources will tell you that Colorado's Western Slope includes everything west of the Continental Divide. This designation encompasses a huge area of vastly contrasting character and is of little help to those on a quest of fermentation exploration. If we take some beerographic liberties and narrow the definition to include only those areas with an elevation below 6,000 feet, then we're onto something. This beer-centric definition includes a manageable region beginning at Glenwood Springs to the east and extending west along the Interstate 70 corridor to the Utah border. It also includes the area south of Grand Junction to Montrose as well as the town of Paonia, southeast of Grand Junction.

This is largely an area of farmland, ranchland, and orchards. Unlike the mountainous terrain to the east and south, this is high desert country, with dramatic mesas and plateaus emerging from the lower elevations. The Colorado River flows through the area, providing many miles of recreational opportunities for river runners and fisherfolk. Hiking the rugged canyons and mountain biking on well-established trail systems are popular activities both for visitors and for the local populace, many of whom are escapees from the population centers of the Colorado Front Range.

Beerwise, the sparsely populated region has the fewest number of breweries of the six regions covered in this book. Though not numerous, the nine breweries discussed in this section are easily accessible from busy Interstate 70 or other well-traveled highways. In addition,

Colorado has a fledgling hop-growing industry, and the Western Slope is the largest hop-producing area in the state.

While most Western Slope communities have a rural disposition, Glenwood Springs has a different character. Glenwood is a hugely popular tourist destination, especially for family getaways. The town is situated at the western terminus of Glenwood Canyon, a steep-walled, eighteen-mile-long canyon cut by the Colorado River. A paved, mostly flat bike path extends the length of the canyon. The town's major draw is *Glenwood Hot Springs*, the world's largest hot springs pool. People from around the world travel to Glenwood Springs to soak in the therapeutic waters. The *Glenwood Caverns Amusement Park* offers guided cave tours, a roller coaster, and other family-oriented amusements. White-water rafting trips on the Colorado River are very popular. The Glenwood Canyon Brewing Company resides in the Hotel Denver near downtown Glenwood Springs.

The *Sunlight Mountain Resort* is a small ski mountain—at least by Colorado standards—located twelve miles south of Glenwood. It's known for being family friendly and affordable. Glenwood is a crossroads town of sorts. Highway 82, which heads south from Glenwood, provides the easiest access to the storied ski town of Aspen, forty miles away.

Continuing west along I-70, you arrive at Palisade, a riverside fruit-growing community best known for its wine vineyards and delicious peaches. A stone's throw from Palisade Brewing Company is a highly acclaimed distillery, *Peach Street Distillers*, with ownership ties to southwest Colorado's Ska Brewing Company. Palisade is also home to numerous wineries and a meadery.

Grand Junction, just west of Palisade, is western Colorado's largest city, although the city of 58,000 is hardly a pulsating metropolis. With its mild banana belt climate, and easy access to the San Juan Mountains to the south and the awesome red rock desert country to the west, Grand Junction is increasingly attracting an outdoor-oriented populace seeking a more laid-back lifestyle than is found in Denver and other Front Range communities.

Just west of the city is *Colorado National Monument*, an area of colorful rock formations and deep canyons. The monument can be explored by car, on foot, or, for very fit cyclists only, by bicycle. The *Powderhorn Mountain Ski Resort*, forty-five minutes east of Grand Junction, is on Grand Mesa, the world's largest flattop mountain.

Grand Junction is home to two brewpubs: the Rockslide and Kannah Creek Brewing Company. A third brewery, called the Edgewater Brewery, is an offshoot of Kannah Creek. It opened too recently to be covered in this book.

Fruita is the westernmost town along the Interstate 70 corridor to be of interest to beer explorers. There are two hometown breweries, the Copper Club Brewing Company and Suds Brothers brewpub. The small farming and bedroom community is well known among mountain bike enthusiasts for the *18 Road Trail System*. The network of singletrack trails runs along the dry, brushy hills at the base of the Book Cliffs. Just west of Fruita is the trailhead to the legendary *Kokopelli's Trail*, a challenging 142-mile mountain bike trail that ends in Moab, Utah.

About sixty miles south of Grand Junction is Montrose, home to the Horsefly brewpub and Two Rascals brewery. Montrose is near the farming community of Olathe, famous for its sweet corn. The Misty Mountain Hop Farm is also located in Olathe. Just east of Montrose is the entrance to *Black Canyon of the Gunnison National Park*. The spectacular canyon is a deep, dark, narrow, and nearly impenetrable chasm. A roadway runs along the rim, with numerous overlooks and hiking opportunities of varying lengths and difficulties. Montrose is at the junction of two highways frequented by recreation-minded travelers: Highway 50 east leads to the West Elk Mountains, while Highway 550 south leads to the San Juan Mountains. The *Tabeguache Trail* (pronounced TAB-a-watch) is a 140-mile mountain bike route that connects Montrose with Grand Junction.

The town of Paonia, home of Revolution Brewing Company, is a bit more remote than the other Western Slope communities with hometown breweries, but it is still well worth a visit. The town sits in the North Fork Valley southeast of Grand Junction. There are numerous organic farms and orchards nearby and several hop farms have sprung up in the area in recent years. Wine grapes are grown in the area and there is a cluster of small, family-owned wineries. The eclectic population includes farmers and ranchers, but also environmental activists. The progressive publication *High Country News* is based in Paonia. East of Paonia is McClure Pass. With large stands of aspen trees, it's an excellent destination for fall leaf-peeping.

Copper Club Brewing Company

223 East Aspen Avenue, Fruita, CO 81521
(970) 858-8318 • www.copperclubbrew.com

Copper Club Brewing Company is located in Fruita, a small town in extreme western Colorado that sits along Interstate 70, twelve miles west of Grand Junction and seventeen miles from the Utah border. For years, Fruita functioned as a farming town, a bedroom community for Grand Junction, and a fuel stop for long-distance travelers. In recent years, the town has gained a newfound identity as one of the planet's premier mountain bike destinations. The extensive, well-maintained 18 Road Trail System is located just a short distance from town. A few miles down the highway is the trailhead to the legendary 142-mile Kokopelli's Trail.

After an outing on bike or on foot, the beers at Copper Club Brewing Company go down especially well. The brewery sits on a corner lot on Aspen Avenue, Fruita's main drag, in a building constructed in 1901. Copper Club serves well-crafted beers to an audience of appreciative locals as well as travelers, mountain bikers, and explorers of western Colorado's fascinating high desert landscape.

Before arriving in Fruita, Copper Club proprietors Daniel Collins and his wife Michelle had been living near Flagstaff, Arizona. He was a traveling salesman selling heavy equipment to the construction industry. She was a surveyor. With the downturn in the construction industry, it was time for Daniel to make a career change. A long-time homebrewer, he enrolled in the brewing program offered by the American Brewers Guild.

While searching for a location for a planned homebrew shop and brewery, the Collinses arrived in Fruita, where the couple had lived for a short time fifteen years prior. "We came back to Fruita during a fall festival. We had such a great time we started looking at some spaces to lease. It just snowballed from there," Daniel recalled.

The homebrew shop opened first. The brewery went online in December 2012. The taproom has a homey, inviting ambience. The cheery yellow-and-red walls display photos dating back

Year-round beers: Hoocheweizen, Moonlight Rye, 18 Road IPA, F-Town Amber, Aspen Street Coffee Porter.

The Pick: Moonlight Rye walks a tightrope between an amber ale and a pale ale. A big malty introduction leads to an assertive hoppy bitterness that keeps it all working in balance.

to 1910, historical displays of legendary cowboys, and artwork that rotates monthly. A dozen or so tables of varying sizes occupy the modest space. A small bar with a few chairs sits at the far end of the room. The unusual bar top is inlaid with roughly 8,500 pennies donated by the Grand Junction Senior Center. A unique collection of tap handles is mounted on the wall below a chalkboard listing the current beer offerings. The distinctive handles were created from bike parts at the bicycle shop across the street.

The local tastes seem divided between two beers. The 18 Road IPA, brewed with Colorado hops from nearby Olathe, emphasizes balance over hop intensity. The other crowd pleaser is the Hoocheweizen, a refreshing and easy-drinking German hefeweizen. I enjoyed the half-dozen approachable and distinctly flavored beers I sampled during my visit, especially the tangy Moonlight Rye. The experience was enhanced by the friendly and outgoing crowd of regulars who seemed to all know each other, and were quite welcoming to newcomers.

After a rewarding visit to Copper Club, take a stroll down Aspen Avenue in search of the statue of Fruita's most famous local celebrity, the late Mike the Headless Chicken. In 1945, a Fruita farmer named Lloyd Olsen cut off Mike's head in preparation for a tasty chicken dinner. Mike, however, had other ideas. Despite his decapitation, the plucky bird refused to cash in his chips and carried on as if still intact. His life spared, "The Headless Wonder Chicken" toured the country from coast to coast until he died in an Arizona motel room eighteen months later. It's a true story. I kid you not.

Copper Club Brewing Company

Opened: December 2012.

Owner and head brewer: Daniel Collins.

Potential annual capacity: 5,000 barrels.

Hours: Monday, Wednesday, and Thursday, 4 p.m. to 9 p.m.; Friday and Saturday, 2 p.m. to 11 p.m.; Sunday, 2 p.m. to 8 p.m. Closed Tuesday.

Tours: On request.

Take-out beer: Growlers.

Food: Restaurant delivery menus available or bring your own food.

Extras: Monday night potluck dinners. Acoustic jam on Thursday.

Parking: On-street and nearby lots, all free.

Area attractions: Colorado National Monument. 18 Road and Kokopelli's mountain bike trails.

Other area beer sites: Hot Tomato Café (124 N. Mulberry St., 970-858-1117).

Glenwood Canyon Brewing Company

402 7th Street, Glenwood Springs, CO 81601
(970) 945-1276 • www.glenwoodcanyonbrewpub.com

More than anywhere else in Colorado, the town of Glenwood Springs, home of Glenwood Canyon Brewing Company, is synonymous with "family getaway." This is, of course, due to the town's feature attraction, the Glenwood Hot Springs Pool and Spa, the world's largest hot springs pool. People have been soaking in the therapeutic waters since the native Utes inhabited the area and named the springs Yampah, or Big Medicine.

Glenwood Springs straddles Interstate 70 at the western end of a long, steep-walled canyon containing the rushing waters of the Colorado River, 160 miles from Denver. The town has been visited by numerous famous and infamous characters through the years. In 1887, the notorious gunfighter Doc Holliday came to Glenwood hoping the hot springs would relieve his tuberculosis. He died a few months later in the town's Hotel Glenwood. Theodore Roosevelt visited frequently in the early 1900s on bear-hunting expeditions. In the 1920s and early 1930s, the Chicago gangster Diamond Jack visited often; during one visit he shot a man in the Hotel Denver. When offered a choice of a five-year prison sentence or leaving the state, he departed Colorado and was soon killed by rival gangsters.

Today, the town is a bustling tourist destination, especially in the summer months and during school holidays. In addition to soaking in the hot springs, other popular attractions include rafting on the Colorado River, cave touring at the Glenwood Caverns Adventure Park, biking on the eighteen-mile Glenwood Canyon bike trail, and skiing at the nearby Sunlight Mountain Resort.

Glenwood Canyon Brewing Company offers therapeutic waters of a different sort. The expansive brewpub is uniquely situated on the ground floor of the historic Hotel Denver across the street from the train depot that dates from 1903.

Prior to the brewpub, other restaurants had existed in the space adjacent to the hotel lobby, but had never generated much excitement. In the mid-1990s, the hotel's owners, Steve and April

Year-round beers: Hanging Lake Honey Ale, Grizzly Creek Raspberry Wheat, Vapor Cave IPA, St. James Irish Red, No Name Nut Brown Ale.

The Pick: The St. James Irish Red, a 2012 GABF gold medal winner, has a clean malty character that stays drinkable through several pints without demanding a lot of attention.

Carver, were visiting Durango and met Jim and Bill Carver (no relation), owners of Durango's Carver Brewing Company, one of Colorado's oldest brewpubs. They formed an alliance and opened Glenwood Canyon Brewing Company in 1996.

You can enter the brewpub from the street or directly from the hotel lobby. In fact, it's perfectly acceptable to grab a pint or a pitcher from the pub and enjoy it in the hotel atrium or in your hotel room. Two large dining areas, one with a long bar, sit at different levels. The busy pub area, with table and bar seating, is in a separate space adjacent to the dining room.

Ken Jones oversees Glenwood's brewing operations. He had been an assistant brewer at Carver Brewing Company and was offered the head brewer job in Glenwood when the brewpub opened. He typically offers eight beers on tap, half of which are full-time brews. The unassuming Hanging Lake Honey Ale tends to be popular with out-of-state tourists while the Vapor Cave IPA and heartier seasonal offerings appeal to the more beer-savvy palates of locals and visitors from the Colorado Front Range.

Over the years, the brewery has amassed an impressive collection of twelve medals from the Great American Beer Festival and seven medals from the World Beer Cup. The Honey Ale was a 2013 GABF silver medal winner. The prestigious medals are prominently displayed in the bar area. Glenwood Canyon is generous with its award-winning brews: after an active day of outdoor adventure, parched pub patrons are rewarded with 20-ounce imperial pint pours rather than the standard 16-ounce U.S. pints.

Glenwood Canyon Brewing Company

Opened: March 1996.

Owners: Steve and April Carver, Jim and Bill Carver, Ken Jones, Tim Mason.

Head brewer: Chip Holland. Brewery Manager: Ken Jones.

Potential annual capacity: 1,200 barrels.

Hours: Sunday through Thursday, 11 a.m. to 11 p.m.; Friday and Saturday, 11 a.m. to midnight.

Tours: On request.

Take-out beer: Growlers and kegs.

Food: American pub fare.

Extras: AHA pub discount program participant.

Parking: On-street and nearby lots.

Area attractions: Glenwood Hot Springs Pool (401 N. River St., 970-947-2955). Glenwood Caverns Adventure Park (51000 Two Rivers Plaza Rd., 800-530-1635).

Horsefly Brewing Company

846 East Main Street, Montrose, CO 81401
(970) 249-6889 • www.horseflybrewing.com

Within the first week of opening a new hotel business in Montrose, a western Colorado community sixty miles south of Grand Junction, homebrewer Nigel Askew was visited by a local police officer. He wasn't in any trouble. The policeman, Phil Freismuth, was a fellow homebrewer and wanted to check out Askew's brewing system.

Some time later, the two visited Revolution Brewing in nearby Paonia. Impressed with the simplicity of the small, family-run brewing operation, the two decided to become partners in their own commercial brewing venture. In September 2009, Horsefly Brewing opened in a miniscule 1,000-square-foot space with a 1.5-barrel brewing system and fourteen-seat tasting room.

Horsefly is the name of a 10,000-foot peak rising from the nearby Uncompahgre Plateau. According to local lore, when the snow disappears from Horsefly, the area's persistent spring winds stop blowing. Wanting the business name to have a local reference, Askew and Freismuth settled on Horsefly. Also, according to the brewery website, "they couldn't spell Uncompahgre."

It wasn't long before Horsefly outgrew its small space and moved into its current location, a former KFC located on the eastern end of Main Street. The fun and quirky brewpub is barely recognizable as a one-time fast food franchise. There's abundant outdoor seating on two sides of the building. Hop plants grow along a picket fence in the open front patio. A collection of kitschy items is scattered among the tables.

The expansive side patio is shaded by trees and colorful sails and is partially enclosed by a tall fence on which a collection of license plates is mounted. An outdoor bar that wouldn't look out of place on a beach in the Caribbean was constructed where the drive-through window was once located. When I stopped by for dinner on a warm spring evening, the outdoor space was bustling with a mostly local crowd.

Year-round beers: Bug-Eyed Blonde, Tabano Red, Six Shooter American Pale Ale, Highland Scottish Ale, Porter, Jazzy Razzy Raspberry Blonde.

The Pick: If you have fond memories of drinking ale in a British pub, the seasonal Cascade Pale Ale, a British bitter, is the beer for you. With a dry, hoppy character and 4.2 percent ABV, it will keep you interested, and functional, after several pints.

The interior décor is a playful collection of beer and brewery paraphernalia. Several unusual light fixtures are constructed from glass growlers. The laminated wooden bar is inlaid with a collection of bottle caps. Beers are dispensed from several tap towers constructed of metal kegs. A pair of dartboards—used for weekly dart tournaments—are mounted on the front wall. Chess/checkerboards are inlaid on some of the tables. Engraved on the counter opposite the bar is the saying, "Time's Fun When You're Having Flies." The quote, according to co-owner Askew, is from Kermit the Frog.

The kitchen outputs American pub favorites. A popular menu item is the "Wing-Nuts," a choice of nine different sauces to be tossed on either chicken wings or, for the more adventurous, Rocky Mountain oysters.

Askew runs Horsefly's brewery. The British expat, who was born in Northern Rhodesia (now Zambia) and educated in England, developed a beer palate at an early age. "My father would give me a bottle of lager on Sunday when I was seven or eight as a treat," he explained. Around age fifteen, he began homebrewing.

Askew's fondness for British and German-style beers was evident in the specialty and seasonal beers that supplemented the half-dozen full-time offerings during my visit. The English Pub Ale had an authentic British character, while the Old Ale was a creditable Old Peculiar copy. German-style selections included a hefeweizen and a helles bock. The full-time offerings cover the range of light, dark, malty, hoppy, and fruity. Beer can be purchased to go, packaged in two-pint milk cartons in addition to the familiar glass growlers.

Horsefly Brewing Company

Opened: September 2009.

Owners: Nigel Askew and Phil Freismuth.

Head brewer: Nigel Askew.

Potential annual capacity: 1,500 barrels.

Hours: Sunday through Thursday, 11 a.m. to 9 p.m.; Friday and Saturday, 11 a.m. to 11 p.m.

Tours: On request.

Take-out beer: Growlers, two-pint milk cartons, and kegs.

Food: American pub fare.

Extras: Weekly darts (check website for day and time). Discounts for AHA members.

Parking: On-site lot.

Area attractions: Black Canyon of the Gunnison National Park.

Other area beer sites: Colorado Boy Pizzeria (320 E. Main St., 970-240-2790). RnR Sports Bar (35 N. Uncompahgre Ave., 970-765-2029).

Kannah Creek Brewing Company

1960 North 12th Street, Grand Junction, CO 81501
(970) 263-0111 • www.kannahcreekbrewingco.com

They say good things happen to those who wait. Kannah Creek Brewing Company, in Grand Junction, would seem a perfect example of those words of wisdom. The lively brewpub was a long time in the making. In 1998, Jim and Bernadette Jeffryes purchased riverfront property along the Colorado River, which flows through Grand Junction, with the intent of building a brewery. Ongoing funding issues delayed progress on the project for years. Finally, in 2005, things were falling into place when the city announced plans to construct a parkway that would put the brewery site in the middle of a construction zone for several years. Once again, the project was put on hold.

About that time, Jim Jeffryes noticed a "for lease" sign on a former steakhouse that had been vacant for a year. "It just dawned on me that might be a perfect building to put a brewpub into," he recalled. This time, it all came together and Kannah Creek Brewing Company opened in October 2005.

Grand Junction is the largest city in western Colorado. The Grand Valley, as the area in and around the city is called, is well known for its fruit orchards and grape vineyards that thrive in the valley's hot summer days and cool evenings. If you visit during the harvest season, roadside fruit stands offer the sweetest peaches on the planet. Just west of the city is the Colorado National Monument, which is not, as some believe, a statue of some sort, but rather a large plateau with unearthly rock formations and towering red-walled canyons. It's well worth a visit.

Kannah Creek is located a few miles from downtown near Colorado Mesa University. The brewpub's long, open interior hints of its steakhouse origins. The front section is divided by a half-wall with the dining area on one side and the bar on the opposite side. There's additional dining space at the far end of the building. A wood-fired pizza oven is the centerpiece of the open kitchen, which sits just beyond the bar. A collection of

Year-round beers: Island Mesa Blonde, Highside Hefeweizen, Lands End Amber, Standing Wave Pale Ale, Broken Oar IPA, Pigasus Porter, Blacks Bridge Stout.

The Pick: Lands End Amber Ale, a German-style altbier, features an enticing clean malty character that is delicately balanced with a smooth, hoppy finish that keeps inviting you back. A great anytime beer.

stunning river photographs documenting canyon country float trips is on display. (In one photo, the silhouette of a person standing in a narrow canyon donning a cowboy hat looks a lot like ET.) In mild weather, visitors congregate on the large patio for al fresco dining and drinking.

While the kitchen offers a few pub standards, the menu has a mostly Italian theme. Tasty wood-fired pizzas, calzones, and toasted panini sandwiches are house specialties. Pizza dough and focaccia bread are made fresh daily. Sauces and soups are made from scratch.

The brewing operation is run by Jim Jeffryes, whose brewing resume includes stints at C.B. & Potts on the Colorado Front Range and at nearby Palisade Brewing. Jeffryes and assistant brewers Emma Faulkner and Matt Simpson produce seven standard beers that are augmented with one or two specialty offerings. Lagers appear with frequency in the summer months, a welcome refresher in the hot, dry, high desert climate. The pub's top seller is Lands End Amber, an altbier. In recent years, the beer has garnered medals at the Great American Beer Festival and World Beer Cup. I found the entire lineup, from the well-balanced IPA to the silky nitro-dispensed stout, to be well-crafted and enjoyable.

The original plans for the riverfront brewery were not abandoned. With the city's parkway project completed, Kannah Creek commenced construction of a second production brewery on the property purchased long ago. The Edgewater Brewery opened in the spring of 2013.

Kannah Creek Brewing Company

Opened: October 2005.

Owners: Jim and Bernadette Jeffryes and Eric and Tina Ross.

Head brewer: Jim Jeffryes.

Potential annual capacity: 1,000 barrels.

Hours: Sunday through Thursday, 11 a.m. to 10 p.m.; Friday and Saturday, 11 a.m. to 11 p.m.

Tours: Not offered.

Take-out beer: Growlers and kegs.

Food: Soups, salads, sandwiches, brick-oven pizzas, and calzones.

Extras: Firkin tapping on Monday. Occasional Beer 101 classes offered on Sunday.

Parking: On-site lot.

Area attractions: Colorado National Monument. The Powderhorn Ski Resort is forty miles away.

Other area beer sites: The Ale House (2531 N. 12th St., 970-242-7253). Old Chicago (120 North Ave., 970-244-8383).

Palisade Brewing Company

200 Peach Avenue, Palisade, CO 81526
(970) 464-1462 • www.palisadebrewingcompany.com

There's a saying you hear from time to time in Colorado's wine-producing areas such as Palisade. "It takes a lot of beer to make good wine," the saying goes, referring to the fact that winemaking is a labor-intensive occupation, and a just reward after a hard day in the vineyards or winery is a refreshing beer or two. It's not unusual to find winery workers among the eclectic crowd of peach farmers, ranchers, outdoor enthusiasts, artists, and travelers kicking back over fresh beers at the Palisade Brewing Company.

The town of Palisade sits along the Colorado River at the base of Grand Mesa, considered the world's largest flat-top mountain. The city of Grand Junction is a few miles west. The small, agricultural community is known for its numerous wineries and fruit orchards, especially peaches. I get a kick out of the odd numerical street names in the area, such as 37³⁄₁₀ Road.

Palisade Brewing Company is located in a tall metal structure that was once used as a fruit-packing shed. It resides in an industrial-looking complex a few blocks from the town's pleasantly walkable downtown district. Railroad tracks run alongside the brewery. When a train passes by, you know it. Neighbors in the complex include the DeBeque Canyon Winery and Peach Street Distillers. Fans of distilled beverages will be interested to learn that Peach Street, whose owners include two founders of Ska Brewing Company, was named the 2012 Distiller of the Year by the American Distilling Institute.

The original brewery on the site opened in 2005 but closed its doors in 2010. A new owner stepped in and the business reopened as Palisade Brewing Company in June of that year. Outside the entrance is an expansive patio containing an assortment of tables, a portable fireplace, and a big white silo. The tasting area is in the front section of the big open interior. There's a small bar that seats six, a few booths, and some table seating. The brewing operations take place in the back

Year-round beers: Laid Back Blond, Dirty Hippie Dark Wheat, High Desert Red, Off Belay IPA, Paw Print Porter.

The Pick: When you're thirsting for a hop fix, but without the intensity of an IPA, High Desert Red is your liquid meal ticket. This amber ale features a floral hop aroma and flavor with medium bitterness and a dry finish.

half of the building. The 20-barrel brewhouse and fermentation tanks are in full view. A collection of framed photographs mounted on the brightly colored walls around the tasting area softens the industrial nature of the space just a bit. It's a relaxed, come-as-you-are kind of place and that's just the way people like it.

Danny Wilson worked at the original brewery. He started out cleaning brewery equipment and working on the bottling line. Eventually, he worked his way up to a brewing position. When the new business opened in 2010, Wilson took the reigns as head brewer. Wilson has one rule he adheres to as a brewer: "I don't brew beers that I don't drink," he explained. Fortunately, the beer palates of the local clientele have evolved considerably in recent years. The big, aggressively hopped beers for which Wilson has a fondness no longer sit around with few takers.

In response to ongoing requests for a wheat beer, Wilson formulated a unique brew. Dirty Hippie Dark American Wheat, a malty yet quaffable concoction, quickly became the brewery's best seller. It's one of three Palisade beers packaged on a new canning line. The can's cartoonish label depicts the sometimes contentious nature of Palisade's many contrasting lifestyles. It shows a long-haired male sporting a peace symbol and electric guitar being shot at by a rifle-wielding farmer.

The brewery offers an abbreviated food menu featuring house-smoked meats and a few snacks. There are also regular weekly events including live music and poker nights to keep the devout crowd of local patrons entertained.

Palisade Brewing Company

Opened: 2010 under current ownership. Original brewery opened in 2005.

Owner: Sean O'Brian.

Head brewer: Danny Wilson.

Potential annual capacity: 4,800 barrels.

Hours: Monday through Thursday, noon to 10 p.m.; Friday, noon to 11 p.m.; Saturday, 11 a.m. to 11 p.m.; Sunday, 11 a.m. to 9 p.m.

Tours: Fridays at 5:30 (summer only) or by reservation or on request.

Take-out beer: Growlers, cans, and kegs.

Food: House-smoked meats.

Extras: Live music on Wednesday, Friday, and Saturday. Poker on Monday and Thursday. AHA member discount program participant.

Parking: On-site lot.

Area attractions: Palisade is home to more than a dozen wineries, a meadery, and a distillery. The Powderhorn Ski Resort is forty miles away.

Other area beer sites: See Kannah Creek.

Revolution Brewing

325 Grand Avenue, Paonia, CO 81428
(970) 209-9265
www.revolution-brewing.com

Revolution Brewing was one of the first Colorado breweries I visited while writing this book. In many ways, this agreeable little brewery set the tone for the numerous wonderful small-town brewery visits that would follow.

When Revolution Brewing opened in Paonia in the spring of 2008, it quickly established itself as a much-needed community gathering spot. The west-central Colorado town of 1,500 is located in a rural area populated by an eclectic mix of ranchers, fruit growers, coal miners, organic farmers, environmental activists, and artists. Colorado's fledgling hop-growing industry is taking root on nearby farms. The area is also known for its wines, which are produced at numerous small family-run wineries.

A stroll through Paonia's old-style downtown brings back the charms of an earlier era. A collection of New Agey enterprises are evidence that Paonia is by no means stuck in the past. It's the kind of place where a vintage VW microbus painted with peace signs looks equally at home as a pickup truck with a gun rack mounted in the cab.

Revolution Brewing sits just beyond Paonia's downtown district. The proprietors are the husband-and-wife team of Mike and Gretchen King, Colorado natives who were living in Alaska when they decided to return to their home state to transform Mike's homebrewing hobby into a business. They were in search of a small, family-oriented community to raise their young son when, in 2007, they rolled into Paonia to have a look around.

"We drove into town, and we just had that feeling," Gretchen relates. "We saw tricycles on the sidewalks, people walking around. No brewery." Within a year, they had relocated to Paonia and opened Revolution Brewing in a desanctified former church. The brewery name is painted on a snowboard hanging over the entry to the tasting room. If you don't see the sign, you could easily mistake the business for a private residence.

Year-round beers: Miner's Gold Golden Ale, Jessie's Garage Pale Ale, OAO Amber Ale, Colorado Red Ale, Rye Porter, Stout Ol' Friend Irish Stout, SEIPA India Pale Ale.

The Pick: The Colorado Red Ale is a go-to beer any time of year. With an up-front maltiness and liberal infusion of hops, it maintains its interest beyond a single pint. At 6.2 percent ABV, it's an approachable brew but by no means wimpy.

Originally, the brewery and tasting room shared the same space. During business hours, the brewing equipment would be moved out to make room for patrons. At first, the tasting room was scheduled to be open three days a week, but it often had to close early because the Kings would run out of beer. Eventually, the brewhouse was moved to a nearby location and has undergone several expansions.

The modest-sized taproom has the ambience of a country home with a few contemporary touches. Seating is available at a few small tables and at the L-shaped wooden bar, which seats ten. A collection of abstract paintings by a local artist adorned the walls during my visit.

The area's mild climate invites outdoor lounging, and the front porch and backyard beer garden provide plenty of room to kick back and socialize. The beer garden is a cheerful and inviting space enclosed by thick hop vines and flowering plants. Sections of fencing are composed of old skis. A visit feels like a backyard party at your neighbor's house.

Revolution's half-dozen full-time beers include light, amber, dark, malty, and hoppy offerings. Two of the house beers, Miner's Gold and Jessie's Garage Pale Ale, have a distinctive quality imparted by rare Polish hops. Being located in a prolific fruit-growing region, King concocts fruit beers from time to time that incorporate the seasonal harvest, especially local organic cherries. King also makes a delicious cherry soda for children and non-imbibers.

Revolution Brewing

Opened: May 2008.

Owners: Mike and Gretchen King.

Head brewer: Mike King.

Potential annual capacity: 600 barrels.

Hours: Tuesday through Friday, 4 p.m. to closing (last call is usually 8:30–9 p.m.); Saturday and Sunday, 1 p.m. to closing. Closed Monday.

Tours: On request.

Take-out beer: Growlers and cans.

Food: Beer-boiled brats made from locally raised Welsh Black Mountain sheep are served daily. Skewers are available on Wednesday. You can bring your own food.

Extras: Live music on Wednesday.

Parking: On-street.

Area attractions: About a dozen small family-run wineries are located in and around Paonia. Black Canyon of the Gunnison National Park is close by.

Other area beer sites: No beer sites, however the tasting room at Delicious Orchards Organic Farm Market (39126 Hwy. 133, Hotchkiss, 970-527-1110) is a great place to sample local wines.

Rockslide Brewery and Restaurant

401 Main Street, Grand Junction, CO 80501
(970) 245-2111 • www.rockslidebrewpub.com

Grand Junction, the home of Rockslide Brewery and Restaurant, is western Colorado's largest city. With easy access to the mountains, desert, numerous wineries, and other attractions, the city is a popular stop for vacationers. In the warm-weather months, Main Street bustles with foot traffic as visitors and families check out local shops and stop to admire the numerous folksy sculptures placed along the sidewalks. A life-size bronze sculpture of a man in a bathtub, writing and smoking, honors Dalton Trumbo, a famous playwright from Grand Junction who did most of his writing in the bathtub while soaking and smoking up to six packs of cigarettes a day. I suspect he would've sipped good local beer also, had it been available a few decades earlier.

Amid the sights of downtown Grand Junction, Rockslide provides a convenient destination for a casual meal and a fresh brew. The brewpub has been packing them in since 1994. Rockslide is located in a historic building that was constructed in 1890 as a bank. Five years later, it became a men's fine-clothing store, and eventually a second-hand store. In the mid-1990s, the building underwent a year-long renovation. Aluminum siding was removed, exposing the handsome brick façade.

Next to the entrance, large windows allow passersby to see into the brewhouse from the sidewalk. Al fresco dining is available on an enclosed sidewalk patio in front of the building. A more secluded outdoor dining area is located in the back. The dining room sits on two levels, breaking up the long space. High ceilings keep the room from feeling claustrophobic. A collection of landscape photographs is mounted on the brick walls that run the length of the room.

The bar area is separated from the dining room by a brick wall. There's a U-shaped bar of polished metal and plenty of table seating. TVs are in ample supply around the room. Along the front wall, tall windows look into the brewhouse. On the back wall, an oddly placed door sits high off the floor without access, making for an interesting conversation piece.

Year-round beers: Kokopelli Cream Ale, Raspberry Wheat, Big Bear Stout, Cold Shivers Pale Ale, Rabbit Ears Amber Ale, Widow Maker Wheat, Horsethief IPA.

The Pick: Big Bear Stout weaves a tapestry of sweet malt and dry roastiness into a deceptively potent package of 7 percent ABV.

Like many urban brewpubs, Rockslide understands the diverse nature of its clientele, and offers a varied selection of food and beer without straying from the tried and true. The food menu covers a lot of territory from burgers and sandwiches to seared ahi, tempura shrimp, and a variety of southwestern dishes. The menu lists suggested food pairings with the seven full-time beers.

Zorba Proteau is in charge of Rockslide's beer production. Proteau's brewing career began when he was a homebrewer working as a cook at Kannah Creek Brewing Company, another Grand Junction brewpub. Eventually, he moved from the kitchen to the brewhouse. In addition to his on-the-job training, he received his Intensive Brewing & Science program certification from the American Brewers Guild and an associate degree in biology from Colorado Mesa University in Grand Junction. When the head brewer position opened up at Rockslide in early 2012, he landed the job.

Rockslide's full-time beers include a standard yet well-rounded lineup, including a blonde, a wheat, a raspberry wheat, a pale ale, an amber ale, an IPA, and a stout. The top-selling beer is the Widowmaker Wheat, an American-style wheat ale. I've observed that Colorado breweries that are frequented by out-of-state visitors seem to pour a lot of lighter-flavored pale beers. Local palates gravitate to more aggressively flavored, hoppier ales. Since Proteau added the Horsethief IPA to the full-time lineup, it's become one of Rockslide's better-selling beers. To keep things interesting for the growing number of local beer enthusiasts, Proteau keeps two tap handles dedicated to seasonal and specialty brews in a diversity of styles.

Rockslide Brewery and Restaurant

Opened: November 1994.

Owners: Mike Bell and Scott Howard.

Head brewer: Zorba Proteau.

Potential annual capacity: 1,000 barrels.

Hours: Monday through Saturday, 11 a.m. to closing; Sunday breakfast buffet starting at 9 a.m.

Tours: On request.

Take-out beer: Growlers.

Food: American pub fare served all day. Steaks and other entrées available for dinner.

Extras: Occasional live music.

Parking: Metered on-street parking and nearby lot.

Area attractions: See Kannah Creek on page 309.

Other area beer sites: See Kannah Creek on page 309.

Suds Brothers Brewery

127 East Aspen Avenue, Fruita, CO 81521
(970) 858-9400 • www.sudsbrothersbrewery.com

When you visit a place infrequently, changes become more apparent. I hadn't visited Fruita for quite some time when I ventured to the small western Colorado community for a spring visit. The town had undergone some interesting changes. The big dinosaur statue still stood in the grassy traffic circle as it has for decades. Fruita's main street was still home to a collection of typical small-town businesses: an auto parts store, an insurance agency, a flower shop. But there were several new businesses that hadn't been around when I last visited. These included a new yoga studio, an acupuncture clinic, and two new breweries.

The older of the two is Suds Brothers Brewery, which opened in March 2012. I wasn't sure what to expect when I entered the beige stucco building at the corner of Aspen Avenue and Mulberry Street. What I didn't expect was a polished, spacious, and surprisingly urbane brewpub that would look perfectly at home in downtown Denver.

Suds Brothers Brewery was opened by two local couples, Fred and Terri Martinez and Jerry and Rochelle Tufly. The husbands, who work for the same energy company, discovered they had been eyeing the same vacant building in Fruita with the same business plan in mind. The couples decided to team up. Together, they purchased the downtown building that had been the site of two failed breweries.

The Martinezes were no strangers to the brewpub business. In 2007, they had opened a Suds Brothers Brewery in Evanston, Wyoming. They put their experience to good use in Fruita. It took fourteen months to retrofit the building to their specifications.

You enter the brewpub through a covered patio with ceiling fans mounted overhead. It's a pleasant space for outdoor dining protected from the intense western Colorado sunshine. Inside, cool blue and black surfaces, wood tables, and black seating add a touch of sophistication, though not in a stuffy way. The bar area, which is adjacent to the dining room, has a curvy wooden

Year-round beers: Bizzy Bee Hefe, Orange Blossom Wit, Herdin' Kats American Pale Ale, Red Monkey Butt Amber Ale, Keeper Kummin Nut Brown Ale.

The Pick: Herdin' Kats American Pale Ale rocks to a hoppy beat with a quick, dry finale.

bar and a classy look and feel. Big-screen TVs are mounted on either end of the bar and from the ceiling, in view of the room's ample table seating. At the far end of the bar, a row of tap handles extends from a striking polished metal surface inlaid with the brewpub's name. Big glass doors beyond the bar lead into the brewhouse.

On display throughout the restaurant is an interesting collection of rock-and-roll memorabilia including framed vintage posters, photographs, and LPs. Some items are signed. There are great photos of Bob Dylan and Jimi Hendrix, and one of Kurt Cobain sucking on a cigarette while holding a guitar. A wall devoted to the Beatles includes an original *Meet the Beatles* LP and a drum head signed by Paul McCartney, George Harrison, and Ringo Starr. An assortment of guitars and other instruments is on display in various locations around the restaurant.

The food menu features standard pub favorites. The owners decided not to include pizza on the menu in deference to a popular pizza spot just up the street. The house beers are the efforts of Nate Sitterud, who had been working at the Evanston facility before moving to Fruita. After brewing in the isolated southwest corner of Wyoming, Sitterud is smitten with Colorado's vibrant beer culture. He had eight beers on tap during my visit, covering a diversity of styles from a clean and delicate Munich Helles to an American IPA well-infused with Colorado hops from the nearby Misty Mountain hop farm in Olathe.

Suds Brothers Brewery

Opened: February 2012.

Owners: Terri and Fred Martinez and Rochelle and Jerry Tufly.

Head brewer: Nate Sitterud.

Potential annual capacity: 2,500 barrels.

Hours: Monday through Thursday, 11 a.m. to 10 p.m.; Friday and Saturday, 11 a.m. to 11 p.m.; Sunday, 10 a.m. to 8 p.m.

Tours: On request.

Take-out beer: Growlers and kegs.

Food: Burgers, sandwiches, and some American pub standards. Friday night is prime rib night. Saturday night the brewery does a seafood boil.

Extras: Open mic night on Thursday. Live entertainment on Saturday.

Parking: On-street and nearby lots, all free.

Area attractions: See Copper Club on page 303.

Other area beer sites: See Copper Club on page 303.

Two Rascals Brewing Company

147 North 1st Street, Montrose, CO 81401
(970) 249-8689 • www.tworascalsbrewing.com

Fighting wildland fires is no laughing matter. So when Brandon Frey started laughing as he dug a hand line while battling a fire, his coworker and homebrewing partner, Daniel Leonardi, wondered what was up. "I was like, what are you laughing at?" Leonardi asked. "This isn't funny. It's a hundred degrees out here. Are you having heat stroke or something?" "No," Frey explained. "I went to see my grandpa, and he's called me a rascal since I was like five. It cracks me up. I don't know why." "I can see that," replied Leonardi. "You're kind of a rascal." "You're a rascal," Frey retorted. Thus a brewery name was born.

After a combined fourteen years of firefighting, the two decided to pursue the idea of taking their homebrewing hobby to the next level and go commercial. They took a brewery immersion course from Tom Hennessy in nearby Ridgway (see Colorado Boy on page 274), procured the necessary capital, and opened the doors to Two Rascals Brewing Company in September 2012. Frey runs the business end of things while Leonardi is in charge of beer production.

Once you turn off Main Street in downtown Montrose onto First, and proceed a short block west, you can't miss Two Rascals. The word BREWERY is painted in oversized letters on the old two-story, box-shaped yellow-brick building where the brewery resides. The building was constructed between 1910 and 1920 and was originally used as a packing house for the railroad. The Montrose area is historically agricultural. Produce from local farms would be collected in the building and loaded onto trains. On the brick façade, in fading paint, is the name of the former business, J. F. Warren Shipper. Under that are the words Onions, Apples, and Potatoes.

Year-round beers: IPA, Amber, Wheat, and a stout or porter.

You enter into the tasting room, a space that's not too small to have a private conversation nor so large that one feels disconnected from other visitors. Brick walls, hefty exposed posts and beams, and the well-worn original wooden flooring contribute to the room's vintage charm. The U-shaped bar is constructed of a slab of shiny black

The Pick: The Wheat Beer, brewed with American yeast and German hops, is a beat-the-heat refresher. It's light on the palate with a surprisingly bright appearance and slightly sweet wheaty taste.

concrete sitting atop a brick foundation. There are some contemporary touches, such as the wood-and-steel seats and bar stools and polished steel tables that provide a contrasting modern industrial look.

Behind the bar, two brass beer towers emerge from a dark wood cabinet that was salvaged when Two Rascals moved into the building. The towers were purchased on eBay, and were black when they arrived. Considerable elbow grease was required to restore their classic brassy luster.

The simple open brewhouse is tucked into a back corner of the tasting room. I visited on a Monday, when $1 tacos were being prepared from a table set up next to the mash tun, a converted dairy tank. Out back, a long communal picnic table sits on a narrow patio, along which a row of hop vines was emerging during my early spring stopover. A deck adjacent to the patio was under construction.

According to Leonardi, local beer fans have somewhat different tastes than those on the Colorado Front Range: "They [Front Range drinkers] want more hops and more malt and just bigger, darker, crazier beers. Over here, a lot of people are just starting to get into it. They'll start with the lighter stuff and then work their way up." Two Rascals keeps four full-time beers on hand: the brewery's popular IPA, an amber ale, a wheat ale, and a dark ale that rotates between a stout and a porter. The brewery also offers a variety of seasonal and specialty beers. Two Rascals frequently hosts live music, a popular draw for their core of regular customers.

Two Rascals Brewing Company

Opened: September 2012.

Owners: Daniel K. Leonardi and Brandon Frey.

Head brewer: Daniel K. Leonardi.

Potential annual capacity: 1,100 barrels.

Hours: Monday through Thursday, 4 p.m. to 9 p.m.; Friday and Saturday, 1 p.m. to 10 p.m.; Sunday, 1 p.m. to 8 p.m.

Tours: On request.

Take-out beer: Growlers and kegs.

Food: $1 tacos on Monday. Delivery menus on-hand or bring your own food. Outdoor grill available.

Extras: Live music most Fridays. Acoustic jam on Tuesday. Occasional live music on Thursday and Saturday.

Parking: On site lot.

Area attractions: See Horsefly on page 307.

Other area beer sites: See Horsefly on page 307.

Index